PROGRESSIVE COUNTRY

★

PUBLISHED IN COOPERATION WITH
THE WILLIAM P. CLEMENTS CENTER FOR SOUTHWEST STUDIES,
SOUTHERN METHODIST UNIVERSITY

★ ★ ★ ★ ★ ★ ★ ★ ★ ★

PROGRESSIVE COUNTRY

HOW THE 1970S TRANSFORMED THE TEXAN IN POPULAR CULTURE

★ ★ ★ JASON MELLARD ★ ★ ★

UNIVERSITY OF TEXAS PRESS, AUSTIN

Copyright © 2013 by University of Texas Press
All rights reserved
Printed in the United States of America
First edition, 2013

Requests for permission to reproduce material
from this work should be sent to:
Permissions
University of Texas Press
P.O. Box 7819
Austin, TX 78713–7819
http://utpress.utexas.edu/index.php/rp-form

The paper used in this book meets the minimum requirements of
ANSI/NISO Z39.48–1992 (R1997) (Permanence of Paper). ∞

Design by Lindsay Starr

Library of Congress Cataloging-in-Publication Data

Mellard, Jason.
Progressive country : how the 1970s transformed the Texan in popular culture /
by Jason Mellard. — First edition.
p. cm
"Published in Cooperation with the William P. Clements Center for
Southwest Studies, Southern Methodist University."
Includes bibliographical references and index.
ISBN 978-0-292-77193-2
1. Country music—Texas—History and criticism. 2. Country music—Social aspects—
Texas—History. 3. Country music—Texas—Austin—1971–1980—History and criticism.
4. Texas—In popular culture—History. I. Title.
ML3524.M45 2013
781.64209764'09047—dc23
2013007455
First paperback edition, 2014

doi: 10.7560/753006

Contents

Acknowledgments
vii

Introduction
"Too Much Ain't Enough," or, The Texan in the Late Twentieth Century
1

1
The Empire of Texas
Lone Star Regionalism Sets the Stage, 1936–1968
19

2
Home with the Armadillo
Austin's Progressive Country Music Scene
55

3
This New Cross Between Baba Ram Dass and Sam Bass
Cosmic Cowboydom and the 1970s
89

4
The Vanishing Texan
The Party of the Fathers Realigns
125

5
You a Real Cowboy?
Texas Chic in the Late Seventies
171

Conclusion
199

Notes
209

Bibliography
241

Index
263

Acknowledgments

Writing this book has left me with a sense of gratitude as big as Texas. As any scholar knows, a book's composition involves many hours alone, but its conception, research, and revision always rely on a supportive community. I have been lucky with this project to find such support in the Department of American Studies at the University of Texas at Austin, in the Clements Center for Southwest Studies at Southern Methodist University, and among the rich cultural resources of the city of Austin.

I owe my first thanks to my mentors at the University of Texas at Austin who nurtured this project in its initial stages and have guided me throughout its development. Jeffrey Meikle, Karl Hagstrom Miller, Neil Foley, and John Hartigan Jr. brought careful questions, discerning eyes, and the toolkits of their respective disciplines to bear on the work. Above all, Janet Davis's advice, insight, and direction helped shape me as a cultural historian in the interdisciplinary American Studies mold. Davis also led a productive writing group that commented on many early drafts. Heartfelt thanks are due to the members of that group, as well as to others who provided peer support, including Andrew Busch, Greg Carter, John Cline, Daniel Gerling, Benjamin Gregg, John Gronbeck-Tedesco, Anna Thompson Hajdik, Victoria Hill, Jennifer Jefferson, Sebastian Langdell, Ben Lisle, Allison Perlman, Phil Tiemeyer, John Troutman, Amy Ware, Amy Nathan Wright, and Tracy Wuster. In my years at the University of Texas, Joel Dinerstein, Elizabeth Engelhardt, Steve

Hoelscher, Randolph Lewis, Julia Mickenberg, Neil Nehring, Mark Smith, and the late William Goetzmann all supported my efforts or otherwise influenced my thinking along the way. Cynthia Frese, Lisa Jaskolka, Valeri Nichols-Keller, and Ella Schwartz provided indispensable administrative support. I would also be remiss should I neglect my time in Aggieland, where David Vaught and the late Bob Calvert of Texas A&M University initially sparked my historical imagination.

A year as the Summerlee Fellow in Texas History at the Clements Center for Southwest Studies of Southern Methodist University made possible the completion of this manuscript. I feel lucky to have enjoyed the Center's generous support during the period in which the indefatigable Benjamin Johnson stood at the helm. Executive Director Andrea Boardman and Assistant to the Director Ruth Ann Elmore deftly facilitated my time in Dallas. In the study of the Southwest, few programs provide such an atmosphere of scholarly exchange as the Clements Center does, and the gathering they hosted to discuss this work allowed for the incisive contributions of outside readers Joseph Crespino and Diane Pecknold. SMU's faculty and staff, Clements Fellows, and the meeting's other participants offered a sense of intellectual community and interdisciplinary support: Daniel Arreola, Tim Bowman, Gregg Cantrell, Sami Lakomaki, Matthew Liebmann, Alexis McCrossen, Sam Ratliffe, Jennifer Seman, Michael Seman, Sherry Smith, Clint Starr, Elizabeth Hayes Turner, and Steven Weisenberger.

In the archival field, I drew on the rich resources of the Briscoe Center for American History at the University of Texas at Austin, and I extend my thanks to John Wheat, Aryn Glazier, Kathryn Kenefick, and the Briscoe's other archivists and staff. Steve Davis of the Wittliff Collections at Texas State University at San Marcos directed me to sources there and shared his knowledge of Bud Shrake's career.

This book found a fortuitous home in the University of Texas Press, as did so many of the authors I study in the following pages. Editors Allison Faust, Casey Kittrell, Victoria Davis, and Leslie Tingle have shepherded the book attentively and with a level of engagement that left this first-time author impressed. The readers the University of Texas Press selected for the manuscript, Aaron Fox and Travis Stimeling, both provocative scholars of American music, helped to refine my thinking on the relationship between country and the broader field of American culture.

A number of universities have provided an institutional home as I prepared the manuscript for publication. I originally came to know Gary Hartman and the Center for Texas Music History at Texas State University through my

ACKNOWLEDGMENTS

research on the Armadillo World Headquarters. The meeting blossomed into a series of opportunities to contribute to the Center's work preserving the state's musical past and advancing the scholarly conversation on the region's cultural heritage. Similarly, Bill Bush and Amy Porter at Texas A&M at San Antonio, Todd Onderdonk and Laura Hernández-Ehrisman at St. Edward's University, and Mary Brennan and Diann McCabe at Texas State University kept an otherwise reclusive author engaged in one of his very favorite activities, teaching.

In exploring the cultural history of 1970s Texas, though, I have accrued my greatest debts among those participants in the Austin scene who have taken the time to share stories, resources, points of view, and company over the last several years. First and foremost, I have concluded that Austin, Texas, is blessed to have such a cultural visionary, popular historian, promoter, and provocateur as Eddie Wilson. He may not recognize the seeds that he planted that have grown into this book, but the whole endeavor would not have been possible without the many conversations we shared about Austin's cultural past. Further, the entrée he provided into the network of the Austin scene was indispensable. I am not sure that I can ever thank him enough for all that he has done on my behalf.

Leea Mechling at the South Austin Popular Culture Center has never failed to make time to accommodate my research requests, provide access to the Center's extensive holdings, reproduce images, or provide contact information at a number of critical junctures. The artist Bob Wade has been similarly generous with his time and insights and turned me on to narrative threads I might not have otherwise discovered regarding the art world and the Austin–New York axis. Being able to watch him at work, whether talking with an elderly bar owner in Lockhart about her eccentric decorative sense or organizing the airlift of a giant iguana sculpture onto a roof at the Fort Worth Zoo, has been one of the unanticipated thrills attendant to my research. Craig Hillis, musician and fellow historian of the Austin scene, also shared much. In particular, in conjunction with filmmaker Aaron Brown, Hillis conducted, shared, and facilitated a productive series of oral history interviews. Each of these individuals has become more than a research "source" or "informant"; they have become collaborators in our shared attempts to commemorate this rich cultural moment in the recent Texas past. And thanks to the much larger group of those who shared information, time, contacts, images, or stories along the way: Sterling Allen, Hank Alrich, Clifford Antone, Kerry Awn, Gerald Barnett, David Brown and KUT, Cathy Casey and *Texas Monthly*, Sonny Carl Davis, Lisa Dirks, Danny Garrett, Jim Franklin, Oliver Franklin, Denny Freeman, Joel Aaron Gammage, Henry Gonzalez, Ray Hatch, Cleve Hattersley, Ryan

Hennessee, John Inmon, Guy Juke, Emma Little, Bob Livingston, Bill Narum, Gary P. Nunn, Joe Nick Patoski, William Philpott, Alan Pogue, Micael Priest, Jan Reid, Mack Royal, Fabrizio Salmoni, Gilbert Shelton, Bud Shrake, Isabel Stensland, Powell St. John, Mike Tolleson, Minor Wilson, Richard Zelade, and all the others I have met in the process of this project. Some of you offered an anecdote or comment in passing. Others stayed in near constant contact as we worked through a particularly knotty issue regarding Texas culture. I could not have written the first page of this book without you.

It should go without saying that I also could not have created this book without the very first Texans I ever met, the family who has supported me in this endeavor from day one: Mark, Melissa, Doug, and Weston Mellard. Though I began this project at the University of Texas as an adult, my parents likely planted the seeds much earlier during time spent at chili cook-offs and livestock shows in Victoria, or with that Willie Nelson eight-track that rarely seemed to leave the stereo. My in-laws in California, Ginny and Alex Rouch, have also shown patience and good cheer, even as I kept their daughter in the Lone Star State a good deal longer than they might have hoped.

If I owe all those above a debt of gratitude, words fail to express just how thankful I am that Andrea Mellard decided to stick around Austin. The credit for the completion of this book belongs wholeheartedly to her. She had faith in my ability to conquer such a task long before I did, stood by me in stressful and joyful moments, and just generally made life better, day after day, month after month, year after year. That she came up with the idea to have our wedding in Luckenbach was just icing on the cake.

PROGRESSIVE COUNTRY

Introduction

"TOO MUCH AIN'T ENOUGH," OR, THE TEXAN IN THE LATE TWENTIETH CENTURY

In March 1975, *Atlantic Monthly* devoted an entire issue to Texas. The magazine intended it to open a series highlighting American spaces for the coming bicentennial. However, apart from a shorter story on the Pacific Northwest months later, this issue on a single state stood alone. The editors chose Texas for its evocative, even polarizing, qualities, the sense of it as "a place that some who know . . . love to hate, and many who have been shaped by it hate to love." In eighteen articles over one hundred pages, William Broyles, David Broder, T. R. Fehrenbach, John Graves, Molly Ivins, Barbara Jordan, Larry L. King, Larry McMurtry, Katherine Anne Porter, Al Reinert, Jack Valenti, Richard West, and others explored the notion of Texans' perceived difference from the rest of the nation, tacking between its mythologized frontier past and its swaggering Sunbelt modernity. The juxtaposition of the two, in the national imagination and in the lives of Texas residents, made for intriguing moments in the 1970s. The process rendered Texas, and the notion of Texanness, an interpretive key to American culture and politics in the years following the end of the long post–World War II economic boom.[1] This book uses that key to understand better the relationships between region and nation, place and identity, in the late twentieth century. One evening in December 1972, for example, two Texas singer–songwriters stood backstage at the Armadillo World Headquarters nightclub in Austin. They knew each other from their time together in Nashville, until one of them left, frustrated with his uncertain prospects as star material in Music City. The defector had recently moved to Austin. Soon thereafter, he called the Texan still in exile to let him know that he had "found something" down here, which is why they were backstage at the Armadillo. The two had played any number of dubious honky-tonks and dance halls across the country, but preparing to take the stage after a raucous country-rock act named Commander Cody and His Lost Planet Airmen and peering out at a screaming crowd of long-haired cosmic cowboys and peasant-bloused honky-tonk angels, Waylon Jennings just was not sure what to make of it all. He turned to his friend, visibly worried. "What the hell have you got me into, Willie?"[2]

No wonder the currents coursing through that audience surprised Jennings. Texas in the 1970s portended, at various times, the boosterism of an energy-led Sunbelt future in Houston and Dallas, the activist democracy of a post-Anglo majority in San Antonio and Crystal City, the rise of a new creative class born of the counterculture in Austin, and, in a few exemplary moments, a full-blown cultural renaissance that enveloped the state as a whole. These developments dovetailed with an ongoing, statewide fascination with the very quality of Texanness and its purportedly special position within the 1970s United States. As Eddie Wilson, founder of the Armadillo World Headquarters, stated the case in introducing Willie Nelson during the televised *Armadillo Country Music Review* in 1973:

> There's a story going around the United States of America, going around about the same time that the government's crumbling and that economics are falling apart and the prices are going up, and the story . . . is that there's something weird going on in Austin, Texas. And what seems to be weird is the cowboys and the hippies are getting along better, probably, than anywhere in the world. And maybe it's because the cowboys took a look at the hippies a couple of days ago and said, "They look more like my grandfather than I do."[3]

This narrative of the coming together of the hippies and the cowboys (more commonly parsed as the hippies and the rednecks) took quick root and signified an attempted coming-to-terms with the oppositions of urban and rural, modern and traditional, and the politico-cultural valences of left and right in the 1970s. In all, the capital city of Austin provided some of the best illustrations for the decade's substantive fascination with and attempted revision of "the Texan."[4] Artists, writers, and entrepreneurs there often fed the projection of a Texas chic for national audiences in a period of political and economic malaise, re-inventing the discursive possibilities of the bountiful frontier in an era otherwise marked by America's discovery of its distinct limitations.

INTRODUCTION

This study charts the contested iconography of "the Texan" and its relation to Texan identities in the latter half of the twentieth century, and situates that contestation as a defining aspect of the broader social and political contours of the state and nation in the 1970s. This is an exploration of the recent past, then, but its echoes carry strongly into the present. In his 2011 inaugural address, Governor Rick Perry predicted that historians would look on the twenty-first century as the "Texas century," one in which small government, low taxes, minimal regulation, and the privatization of public services would lead the way out of America's latest malaise. In doing so, he participated in a long tradition of deploying Texas as an ideological and symbolic marker, one resonant across the twentieth century as it surely will be across the twenty-first. As a set of symbols, Texas signified richly. It spoke to excessive appetites and boisterous behavior in the service of the pragmatic remnant of a frontier Americanism. In the early 1960s, journalist John Bainbridge focused on these qualities in labeling Texans the "Super-Americans" in a book of the same name. Country singer–songwriter Billy Joe Shaver of Waco updated the equation of American and Texan appetites in a different arena, singing in "Old Five and Dimers (Like Me)" in the 1970s that "too much ain't enough." On the one hand, this book extends Bainbridge's argument and Shaver's phrase concerning consumption, materialism, patriotism, and economic power in the Lone Star State. At the same time, this pursuit of more, of "too much," was itself never quite enough for many Texans, and in the 1970s, a decade of fiscal limits and libidinal excess, "the Texan" overflowed its symbolic borders. Groups that seemed to stand outside the symbol's charged circle—African Americans, Mexican Americans, and women of all races—challenged and expanded the public sense of Texanness, and new generations appropriated the state's classic iconography. The old manner of being Texan took on new meanings. How, then, do we periodize these consistent invocations of "the Texan," and why focus on the 1970s in doing so?

Popular memory lionizes the 1960s as a decade of substantive change. But those years should be more properly framed as vanguard, as it was in the 1970s that the shifts in the nation's understanding and experience of race and gender difference, morality and cultural sensibility, and skeptical attitudes toward established authority and expertise rippled outside the coterie of activists, intellectuals, and politicians who defined the sixties agenda. As David Frum has written, for the "typical" American voter—say, the forty-seven-year-old white machinist's wife from Dayton, Ohio—the 1960s may as well have been the 1940s. It was only in the next decade that she experienced divorce, discovered cappuccino, and cast her first Republican ballot.[5] Similarly, it was the 1970s, not the 1960s, in which Texas experienced its largest antiwar demonstrations,

La Raza Unida defeated the Anglo political machines in the border counties, and long hair and drug references proved popular among the state's country-western artists. And even as the sixties liberation ethos became more accessible and diffuse, new social movements among conservatives achieved increasing levels of organization, visibility, and viability. Taken together, the rise of a liberationist identity politics and the New Right's growing activism, the continued commodification of the counterculture and the rising profile of the evangelicals, make the 1970s particularly compelling in terms of recent American history.

Change often arrived in unexpected forms and unlikely places, from the Armadillo World Headquarters to Michael Levy's *Texas Monthly*, from the electoral victories of the "new politics" in municipal elections to the United Farm Workers organizing drives on the border, from chili cook-offs and festivals in Luckenbach to the progressive country music of Willie Nelson, Michael Murphey, and Jerry Jeff Walker. Revisions of traditional Texan iconography occurred amid tremendous regional change—Sunbelt suburbanization, oil-fueled prosperity in the midst of the energy crises, the ongoing partisan realignment of the solid Democratic South, and the revolutionary social movements for black, Chicano, and women's rights. They also coincided with shifts in the stature of Texas on the national stage, embodied in the political careers of Lyndon Johnson, John Connally, Barbara Jordan, and George H. W. Bush, and crowned by the success in popular culture of outlaw country music, the film *Urban Cowboy*, and the prime-time soap opera *Dallas*.

The confluence of country-western performance, countercultural sensibilities, and an emphatic Anglo-Texan masculinity, in particular, runs against the most common generational and regional narratives of the 1960s. In particular, the locally celebrated subcultural union of the "hippies" and the "rednecks" in a storied space like Austin's Armadillo World Headquarters strikes the casual observer steeped in the Manichean worlds of *Easy Rider* or the New York City hard-hat riots as quite odd.[6] And yet, this oddity, this inability to securely place the Texan 1970s in an easy generational or ideological narrative, makes these seemingly unlikely phenomena fit well with historians' developing sense of a rather contrarian decade. How does Nixon's silent majority square with Carter's Southern centrism on the rapidly shifting political ground of Texas? What does country songwriter Willie Nelson's transformation into a honky-tonk hippie signify as the counterculture became diffuse and omnipresent, as more men wore long hair and loudly colored business suits, and consumption driven by the quest for the authentic self came to dominate the mainstream? What did the raucous celebration of Anglo-Texan identity mean amid American defeat

INTRODUCTION

in Vietnam, stagflation, and Watergate, developments that cast a pall, a malaise, over the national mood? From the death of Lyndon Johnson to Willie Nelson's picnics, from the Brown Berets in San Antonio to the spectacle of Texas chic on the streets of New York City, Texas mattered in these years not simply as a place but as a repository of long-standing American myths and symbols, and at a historical moment when that mythology was being deeply contested.

This book maps the messy ground of the 1970s in Texas along several paths, but it also oversteps that chronology and geography to accomplish a larger goal. Fundamentally, it explores how the idea of Texas operated in the cultural politics of the latter half of the twentieth century and in the frames of local, regional, and national imaginaries. Figures of Anglo-Texan masculinity have traditionally embodied this idea of Texas.[7] Invocations of "the Texan" in popular discourse tend to find representation, in the first instance, in some variant of the white cowboy, wheeler-dealer, or oilman despite the Mexican origins of Texas ranching, the role of women in the settling of the state, and the significance of cotton production, which occupied a larger portion of laborers (men and women, Anglo, African American, Mexican American, and Mexican) through much of the state's history than did either cattle or oil. I focus, then, on tracing the cultural operation of Anglo-Texan masculinity, but I do so not in the interest of re-inscribing the dominance of these representations. In fact, by demonstrating the plasticity and historicity of this body of symbols, I hope to accomplish quite the opposite.

One of my key interests lies in exploring moments in which actors invoked the symbolic weight of Anglo-Texan masculinity for progressive political ends. Anglo-Texan men who attempted to expand on, amplify, or alter these symbols responded to the unfolding identity politics of the 1970s. During that decade, as civil rights and feminist movements challenged dominant notions of the representative Texan, icons of Anglo-Texan masculinity—the cowboy, the oilman, the wheeler-dealer—came in for a dizzying round of both celebration and critique. Participants in the scene around the Armadillo World Headquarters in Austin did so, in part, to fracture the relationship between such symbols and the exercise of reactionary state power, a task in uneasy tension with the scene's obvious affection for these symbols and their bearers. To the extent that such re-inventions succeeded, they did so due to the scene's dialogic relation with the civil rights and feminist movements. To the extent that they failed, they did so due to the tendency to re-inscribe the symbols as insular and exclusive reactions to, rather than dialogues with, the decade's expansive identity politics. These two trends competed vigorously with each other in the tastes and fashions of late twentieth-century Texas.

Three Men in Texas: Shrake, Barnes, and Franklin

Understanding the operation of "the Texan" requires examination of the shifting political economy and partisan alignments of the Lone Star State in the middle and later decades of the twentieth century. I will attend to these matters, but most of the work here will be cultural. Literature, film, journalism, art, and popular music had long traced the contours of the figurative Texan. However, its cultural propagation did not simply involve images on a screen or text in a magazine. Rather, I frame Texanness as, in part, a performance, a set of strategies and gestures, some conscious, some not, by which individuals enacted "the Texan." It is often necessary to draw the line between Texans—individuals who live within the political boundaries of the Lone Star State—and "Texans"—those brash creatures of the imagination who perpetuate the state's mythologies. Such Texans and "Texans" often lead parallel but distinctly separate lives. At other times, though, the two intersect in instructive ways. Anglo-Texan masculinity had signified for the American nation and developed a performative dimension long before Willie and Waylon's 1972 backstage encounter. It dated from the first Anglo American incursions into the territory in the early nineteenth century, but its performance in the 1970s carried specific significances that help to explain the historical period and national mood. Reckoning those requires a glimpse back to the late 1960s, and to the kinds of performances carried out on the stages of everyday life. Illustrative moments from the lives of three young Anglo-Texan men—Bud Shrake, Ben Barnes, and Jim Franklin—help to make the point.

Few knew the resonances of the performative Texan in the 1970s as did Edwin "Bud" Shrake. A friend, associate, or acquaintance of such Lone Star notables as Billy Lee Brammer, Gary Cartwright, Willie Nelson, Ann Richards, and Jack Ruby, Shrake's journalism for *Sports Illustrated*, *Harper's*, and *Texas Monthly* placed him in fitting situations from which to recount the changing cultural politics of his time. In one such instance, in the spring of 1967, Muhammad Ali had flown to Houston to refuse induction into the armed forces, and, as he often did when he came to Texas, requested that Shrake pick him up at the airport. Shrake rented a Cadillac convertible for the occasion, thinking a leisurely open-air drive through the streets of Houston would do Ali good. Instead, Ali immediately urged Shrake to take him "where the trouble was"— that is, to the site of ongoing protests over police brutality racking the traditionally black Texas Southern University in the city's Third Ward. The protestors reacted wildly to Ali, but the nationalist spirit on campus also meant that the Anglo-Texan Shrake came in for verbal abuse as he tried to drive the Cadillac

INTRODUCTION

into the heart of the protest. Finally, Ali got up, stood on the car, and shouted to the assembled, "Leave this honky alone! He's my personal chauffeur!"[8] The rest of the afternoon passed without incident, and Shrake had gained a glimpse of a new racial politics, a reordering of traditional notions of authority, identity, race, and nation that, while perhaps not so total as Ali voiced it, made for a changing cultural and political landscape in Texas in which nonwhite voices spoke back to Anglo power.

The new politics affected Texans far from Houston's Third Ward. To a considerable extent, the meanings "the Texan" carried in the late 1960s derived from the floundering presidency of Texan-in-Chief Lyndon Baines Johnson. Johnson had glad-handed and boy-howdied his way through five years in office following Kennedy's assassination in Dallas, enacted a dizzying array of domestic reforms, and crashed against the debacle of Vietnam. During the last week of August 1968, a frayed Democratic Party gathered for its nominating convention in Chicago. It had been only six months since the Tet Offensive nixed the plausibility of victory in Vietnam, five since Johnson stated he would not run for re-election, four since the assassination of Martin Luther King Jr., two since Robert Kennedy had been murdered in Los Angeles, and mere days since the Soviet crackdown in Czechoslovakia. Tensions ran high as protestors and police battled in the streets, and the ideological differences among the Democrats began to look irreconcilable. Vietnam towered over everything else and intertwined with the issue of how the party should handle its unpopular sitting president and the delegation from his home state of Texas. Party liberals had placed a motion on the floor that the Johnson loyalists from Texas be refused entry outright. Southern conservatives threatened, in turn, to place LBJ acolyte John Connally in nomination for president.[9]

To forestall the Connally revolt, Vice President Hubert Humphrey, LBJ's preferred candidate over the antiwar Eugene McCarthy, unsuccessfully sought to name Ben Barnes, the thirty-year-old Speaker of the Texas House of Representatives and another LBJ protégé, as floor leader for the Texas delegation. Most delegates and activists treated Barnes, like much of the Texas delegation, as an LBJ surrogate personally responsible for the Vietnam War. At one point, protestors swarmed the cars carrying Barnes and the other Texas delegates back to their rooms at the Conrad Hilton. As Barnes remembered the incident, his aide Nick Kralj then "reacted in true, if unexpected, Texas style. He pushed his way out of the car and whipped out a pistol he'd brought with him from home. 'Everybody move back!' he shouted, holding the gun high above his head. 'This car is moving through!' I'll tell you what, those people parted like the Red Sea. From the looks on their faces, I don't believe they'd seen anything like that before."[10] Now, by 1968, we can rest assured that such a crowd had indeed seen on a movie screen, or at least imagined, a Texan with a gun before, and the image would not have been entirely unexpected. Barnes gave a wide-eyed recounting of the 1968 protests in his 2006 memoir, but Texans back home already knew something of the divisive new political and cultural landscape that the Speaker of the Texas House encountered in Chicago.

Austin artist Jim Franklin was one young Texan who had begun to sense and interpret these shifts. In the summer of 1970, Franklin sat in the audience during jury selection for a high-profile trial in Los Angeles. Charles Manson surely looked guilty to those assembled, but Franklin thought this was the frame-up job of a vindictive establishment jealous of countercultural freedoms. Reporting for the Austin underground newspaper *The Rag*, Franklin stared daggers at the district attorney and fantasized how that "DA could run for President on the Ant[i]-acid ticket with all the hippie-killer-freak bullshit." The difference of opinion between Franklin and the herd may have been due in part to his distractions during jury selection, as he sketched the Texas-themed designs for which he would soon become renowned as the creative spirit of the Armadillo World Headquarters. Upon completing the drawings, Franklin passed them to a Manson Family attorney, Paul Fitzgerald, to let Manson know that he had allies on the outside. One drawing of which he was particularly proud pictured two armadillos in a rather indelicate position with the caption, "These armadillos are balling for you, Charlie!"[11] The counterculture had been so maligned in Franklin's home state that he could not quite imagine Manson's guilt. And yet, even as Franklin was writing these words, the venue that would launch the Texas counterculture into a mainstream phenomenon was opening its doors for the first time, testing the waters of Austin's new acceptance of seventies hippiedom. The Armadillo World Headquarters, with Franklin as artist-in-residence and emcee, would soon command attention where the sixties counterculture in Texas had only drawn scorn.

In each of these examples, Anglo-Texan men confronted the transformation of American life in the late 1960s: surrounded by perceived hostiles, besieged as if in a new Alamo. Shrake, a young journalist, learned something of the new terrain of cultural nationalism in identity politics; Barnes, a Johnson protégé, faced off with the spirit of protest against and disregard for the authority of politicians; Franklin, the countercultural artist, exhibited suspicion of the gathering forces of law and order. Each considered himself the repository of the "true Texas style": Shrake and his Cadillac, Barnes and his gunslinger, Franklin and his armadillos. These examples indicate the shifting terrain on which Anglo-Texan masculinity would operate in the coming decade of the 1970s. In triangulating the three moments, one might easily project forward into that backstage scene at the Armadillo World Headquarters in 1972 with Willie and Waylon, two country-western artists performing for a deeply Texas-inflected counterculture.

In just such moments, individuals perform "the Texan." Leigh Clemons has explored the subject well in *Branding Texas: Performing Culture in the Lone Star State*, arguing that "Texan cultural identity is a complex set of performances that creates and maintains the *idea* of the state as a distinct entity and as a site of identity for its inhabitants."[12] Such notions of performance and performativity will play a role here, by which I suggest both the conventional performance of musical artists in concert and on recordings, but also the ways in which individuals perform roles in everyday social interactions.[13] This mythic expression of Anglo-Texan masculinity, then, possessed an experiential dimension, an element of creative performance that Anglo-Texan men tended to internalize. Some individuals, sympathetic to the 1970s currents of cultural and political liberation, worked to refigure, retool, and reform the traditional iconography and identity of "the Texan." The long-haired, antiwar Shrake hardly would have been spending time with Ali had he felt otherwise. Others retreated into the image's swagger, making it a reactive pose of what musicologist Travis Stimeling has termed the "three Texas nationalist ideals: masculinity, colonization and ownership of indigenous peoples, and a rhetoric of Texan exceptionalism."[14] Kralj's confrontation with the Chicago protestors in "true Texas style" leaned toward this second category.

Myth and Symbol in the Malaise Decade

For most Texans, though, the reality proved more complex than such either/or, progressive/reactionary binaries. The changing representations and experiences of Anglo-Texan masculinity go far toward explaining the shifting terrain of race, gender, class, region, and nation at work in the 1970s. The year 1968 saw the collapsed presidency of a mid-century liberal in the guise of a crude Texas wheeler-dealer; the year 1980 witnessed the ascension of another president, born of the Hollywood imagination and frequently pictured on horseback, riding in to right liberalism's troubling malaise. The years between witnessed strange feats of alchemy whereby it seemed that the wounds opened by the social upheavals of the 1960s, the violence of Vietnam and Mississippi and Chicago, partially healed through the American mythos of the cowboy.

This myth signified nationally and internationally, but also locally, as it did much to determine the texture of Anglo-Texan identities. Two books appeared in 1968 that supplement the experiences of young Anglo-Texan men like Barnes, Shrake, and Franklin: Larry McMurtry's *In a Narrow Grave: Essays* on *Texas* and T. R. Fehrenbach's epic *Lone Star: A History of Texas and the Texans*. In the first of these, McMurtry continued grappling with the Texas myth in the modern age as he had in the novels *Horseman, Pass By* (1961) and *The Last Picture Show* (1966). McMurtry crowed over the creative possibilities of the present, seeing in late 1960s Texas a "stage of metamorphosis when [the state] is most fertile with conflict, when rural and soil traditions are competing most desperately with urban traditions—competing for the allegiance of the young." Simultaneously, he evinced nostalgia for that frontier world he feared lost.[15] This notion of a passing agrarian order provides a narrative key not only to the discourse of America and the American West (from James Fenimore Cooper and Frederick Jackson Turner to Henry Nash Smith and Leo Marx), but also to the historic consciousness of Western civilization writ large.[16] For McMurtry, in 1968, this tipping point was at hand for his home state, and he chose as a primary theme for this book of essays the idea that "The God Abandons Texas," by which he meant the rural way of life and, for him, its paragon, the Anglo-Texan man on horseback. As McMurtry stated the problem, "The god who abandoned Antony was Hercules—what is the name of the god who now abandons Texas? Sometimes I see him as Old Man Goodnight, or as Teddy Blue, or as my Uncle Johnny . . . but the one thing that is sure is that he was a horseman, and a god of the country. His home was the frontier, and his mythos celebrates those masculine ideals appropriate to a frontier."[17] For McMurtry, this essence pervaded the state's existence, fused its identities and landscapes in the guise of white men engaged in the conquest and taming of a territory. Modernization, to McMurtry, heralded a disenchantment—the secularization and dispersal of the patriarchal gods who suffused the land.

T. R. Fehrenbach's classic *Lone Star* also appeared in 1968. Historians had long rendered the state's past in hagiographic terms, and Fehrenbach's work, even amid the upheavals of 1968, provided that school's apotheosis. It is a work rigorously researched with a narrative exhaustively told, but nevertheless anchored in an imperial vision of the heroic white man conquering the Texas frontier.[18] Fehrenbach did not step into this thicket unaware of the myths that shadow historical scholarship on the state. After all, he wrote, "all nations have their national myths, and Texas became enough of a nation within a nation to formulate its own. Many of Texas' legends, historically unproven and even historically insupportable, are fondly held and fiercely defended. This is not unique to Texas. The American nation has its own mythology. This book was not written to destroy myths but so far as possible to cut through them to the reality underneath."[19] Ostensibly, historians do just this kind of work, cutting through myths to the material "reality underneath," but even a cursory

INTRODUCTION

knowledge of historiography begs the formulation of surface mythology and substratum reality that Fehrenbach purported.

Other Texans had employed this sense of the American West before Fehrenbach. Indeed, it provided a seminal notion for the Myth and Symbol School, one of the founding movements of the interdisciplinary field of American Studies in the 1940s and 1950s. Dealing with a set of loaded historical signifiers similar to those Fehrenbach noted, Dallas-born Henry Nash Smith defined myth in the introduction to *Virgin Land: The American West as Symbol and Myth* as "an intellectual construction that fuses concept and emotion into an image."[20] Smith's myth, then, invoked rationality limned with affect, seeming to interpret the material world through an emotional lens. Smith clarified his interpretation of the relation between myth and reality, though: "I do not mean to raise the question whether such products of the imagination accurately reflect empirical fact. They exist on a different plane. But as I have tried to show, they sometimes exert a decided influence on practical affairs."[21] Such notions of mythology and mythmaking figure largely in this study. To ask whether "the Texan" is real misses the contextual signification and experiential depth of the notion's countless deployments—from mass-mediated films in the international marketplace to local social relations and performances—and the real effects these cultural products engender. The lives of Texans thus intersect at various points with the myth of Texas, and "the Texan" has indeed often exerted a "decided influence on practical affairs."

Turning to another cultural theorist elaborates Smith's parsing of myth. In his 1957 work *Mythologies*, French critic Roland Barthes in part summed up the meaning of myth by concluding that "wine is objectively good, and at the same time, the goodness of wine is a myth. The mythologist gets out of this as best as he can: he deals with the goodness of wine, not with wine itself."[22] However, what does it mean to deal with the idea of Texas, rather than Texas itself? Though paramount for the semiotician, cultural history might trace this relation between, on the one hand, the material spaces of and social relations that occur within the boundaries of the state of Texas and, on the other, the vast mythologies woven around, and partially motivating, material conditions. Robert Dorman described just such a relation in addressing the mutual constitution of myth and social life in his work on American regionalism: "Myths are not 'fairy tales,' make-believe constructs debunked by 'true' life. They are instead ordered, value-laden symbols and narratives, communally shared and transmitted, that interpret an irrational world and provide guideposts for action within it. Myths have concrete existence *in* history, but only in partially realized, problematized form."[23]

The mythic "Texan" and the inhabitants within the political borders of the state of Texas cannot always be easily separated, and, rather than focus on one or the other, I intend to trace the lived consequences of mythmaking, the ritual performance of mythic types, and the inscription of cultural geographies in identity formation. We are back, then, to Barthes's dilemma—not denying that there is some relationship between the empirical world (wine) and the myths woven around it (wine's goodness), but to say that the relationship is sometimes best left in suspension for the purposes of cultural analysis. Or, at least, we can hew to Smith's fusion of concept and emotion or Dorman's concrete existence of myth in history to get at the consequences of myth in the material world.

It is just this sort of talk that Houston's "king of the wildcatters" Glenn McCarthy sought to defuse while performing for journalists. McCarthy proved an attractive magnet for caricatures of the Texan nouveau riche in the mid-twentieth century. Born to humble circumstances in an East Texas oil town in 1907, McCarthy had won and lost several fortunes in the search for new fields. Famed for his garish tastes, affinity for bourbon, and extravagant footprint on the Houston cityscape, McCarthy so embodied Texas oil wealth that he served as the model for the fictionalized Jett Rink of Edna Ferber's *Giant*, immortalized on screen by James Dean. McCarthy courted this attention and played his part well. While at an oil field, say, with a writer for *Time*, McCarthy would stoop down, "rub his hands in thick crude oil and mutter: 'This is oil.'"[24] For all the mythic representations of the state in film, literature, and music, McCarthy grounded the discussion in the material substratum, but then again, he performed his gesture toward materiality for a national journalistic audience. While McCarthy's empirical, material attention to oil brings us out of the realm of myth, his projection on the screen as Jett Rink/James Dean in *Giant* returns us to it.[25]

McCarthy's gesture reminds us, too, that mythmaking is always implicated in material relations and political economy, in the process often naturalizing structures of inequality. The Anglo-Texan propagation of the state's mythos portrays it as an essentialist category that floats above social relations, but myth is, in fact, relational, dialectical, and affected by constructions and assertions of difference—racial, ethnic, and gendered. Indeed, the Anglo-masculine elite's deployment of a unitary mythic sense of "the Texan" to elide the state's ethnoracial diversity is always enmeshed in the exercise of and resistance to power. The borderlands of Texas, with its peoples of diverse racial, ethnic, and national histories, belies the essentialisms of the United States and Mexico, South and West, nation and region, black and white. Myth's "decided influence

INTRODUCTION

on practical affairs" in this context has typically involved attempts to foreclose alternate visions to the state's Anglo-dominated social relations. For every T. R. Fehrenbach, though, there exists an Américo Paredes, a theorist engaged in the critique of the Anglo-Texan myth and the elaboration of a divergent public memory of the state's history.[26] This study treats the later decades of the twentieth century as a particular opening whereby this contestation over the state's history and identities came to the fore with unprecedented consequence.

In 1968 the looming presence of Lyndon Johnson often outstripped the most garish of oil millionaires or the most radical of social justice activists in national perceptions of "the Texan." Just as "the Texan" operated in the center of the American national myth as late as the 1960s, so did a Texan stand near the center of the decade's political turmoil. Through the presence of LBJ and his adoption of a civil rights agenda that upended the partisan loyalties of the white South, a story of political realignment joins itself to this moment of cultural and social transformation in which African Americans, Mexican Americans, women, and other traditionally disfranchised groups fought for, and gained, greater access to the public sphere. Mythic notions complicated political realities. Feminism not only brought into focus the subjugated status of women but also interrogated the nature of masculinity. Black and Chicano nationalism sparked new interest in white ethnicity and, eventually, the normative construction of whiteness itself. Finally, the regional resurgence of the Sunbelt brought attention to the newest version of the New South in ways that simultaneously ratified national narratives of progress and rattled the political economy of the New Deal and Great Society.

Public discourse has long trumpeted the pivotal nature of 1968 on a global scale, but most accounts tend to focus on the near, rather than the far, side of that divide, reinforcing a slide-show version of the sixties that elevates the decade's significance far above the years that surround it. The year 1968 represents, in this view, the explosive culmination of all-that-came-before, while the following decade involved a long and painful declension in which real, progressive change was somehow evaded. As opposed to the talk of revolution or reckoning in the 1960s, individuals from Christopher Lasch to Tom Wolfe to Jimmy Carter developed a seventies vocabulary around malaise, superficiality, narcissism, and retreat from the grand historical march that ended in the streets of Paris, Prague, and Chicago. The following years provided a stark contrast for some in that, as the title of one of the seventies' first published histories proclaimed, "It seemed like nothing happened."

And yet, even in 1982, historian Peter Carroll intended the emphasis of his title to fall on the "seemed" rather than the "nothing happened." Beneath the headlines, he argued, "a quiet, almost subliminal revolution was altering the cultural landscape." While the Revolution never came to pass as the radicals of 1968 hoped, myriad revolutions nevertheless transpired, and Carroll took as his subject the "dialogue between established values and the emerging alternatives" that he saw as the central narrative of the seventies.[27] Carroll's initial attempts to establish the significance of the decade, however, did not resonate at the time, and the historical revaluation of the decade began in earnest only at the beginning of the twenty-first century. Authors as varied as Beth Bailey, Sam Binkley, Jefferson Cowie, Alice Echols, David Farber, David Frum, Andreas Killen, Bruce Schulman, Natasha Zaretsky, and Julian Zelizer have since re-framed the 1970s as a key turning point in the nation's history. Bruce Schulman has argued that in "race relations, religion, family life, politics, and popular culture, the 1970s marked the most significant watershed of modern history."[28] The year 1973 alone, Andreas Killen has noted, witnessed the end of American combat involvement in Vietnam, the eruption of the Watergate scandal, and the oil embargo. "Any one of these events alone would have challenged America's image of itself; together they shook the national psyche to its very core."[29] This is the historians' new view of the 1970s, and one that has a timely basis for those who see it as an immediately usable past.[30]

If this self-examination involved image or psyche alone, the mythologies would not have been so sorely tested, but the crises that Schulman and Killen indicate reached to the deepest levels of political economy. Cultural geographer David Harvey, like Frum, Schulman, and Killen, regards the 1970s as a turning point in world history. Harvey sees these years as marked by an acceleration in the shift from the regime of Fordist production to that of flexible accumulation, from the New Deal compromise among big business, big labor, and big government to the postmodern ethos of short-term employment, niche production, corporate authority, and the more fluid global migration of laborers and capital.[31] The disconcerting experience of the old order fading led contemporary observers to predict the fall of the American empire. New York City's experience of the seventies, and that experience's projection in cinema and popular music, speaks to this discourse. Fewer spaces offered greater contrast with the petroleum-driven prosperity of the Texan corner of the Sunbelt. In contrast to the nation at large, the oil crisis engineered by the Organization of the Petroleum Exporting Countries had an uneven, but typically positive, effect on the Texas economy.[32]

The material conditions of global production and consumption had a decided influence on the national life of "the Texan." The figure's swagger across the 1970s malaise owed to the divergent Texan and American experiences

INTRODUCTION

of the decade, rooted in the history of the oil industry. In the broadly shared American affluence of the 1960s, Texas oil, for decades a primary symbol of American wealth, first came up against its limits, facing greater foreign competition, on the one hand, and the increased expense derived from extracting oil as domestic reserves shrank, on the other. In the 1970s, these fortunes reversed, with the larger American economy facing the limits of international competition and higher fuel prices and Texas oil rebounding in the same environment.

The popularity of the performative dimension of Texanness at times could seem to close this gap between Rust Belt stagnation and Sunbelt prosperity. Among its other attributes, the postmodern turn in the 1970s introduced throughout the United States a new, flexible orientation toward the self as an ongoing project of improvement and expression. By decade's end, New Yorkers or Pennsylvanians could escape industrial malaise through the blustery representations of Texans in the music of Waylon Jennings, the televised J. R. Ewing of *Dallas*, or John Travolta's mechanical-bull–riding in the film *Urban Cowboy*. Indeed, such representations created a space for these individuals to play, or perhaps become, "Texan" through the consumption and conspicuous display of the proper regalia. This flexible orientation toward and performativity of the self is just one of the arenas in which the conservative valences of "the Texan" collided and melded with the mainstreaming of the counterculture. In *Getting Loose: Lifestyle Consumption in the 1970s*, sociologist Sam Binkley argues that countercultural notions of authenticity drove shifting patterns of consumption and their relation to self-presentation in the 1970s in ways that demand both macroeconomic and microsocial consideration. Economic and structural arguments, in Binkley's words, "while supplying us with overarching explanations of change on a massive scale, tempt us to read historical events as simple deterministic effects of these changing economic currents. The loosening of the self . . . must be grasped on a smaller scale, in the thin cultural slices in which people encountered it in their everyday lives."[33] Lifestyle consumption in the interest of projecting an authentic identity that diverges from the mainstream makes for much in these "thin cultural slices." I aim to dissect such moments, focusing on youth subcultures, Texas-based intellectuals, popular music venues, and local journalism in addition to the mass-mediated images of literature, television, and cinema that dictated Texas iconography on a global scale.

This work treats the subject of Texas within such international, national, regional, and local frames, but it also focuses in particular on the city of Austin, the capital of the Sunbelt South's largest state. Austin is not always the physical locale in which this study takes place, but its primary actors pass through

Austin at notable junctures and consider their time there significant. The social networks generated by their frequent passage make the city particularly illustrative of the social, political, and cultural trends reconstituting "the Texan." Austin's place in popular music history, too, motivates this focus. In the years 1970–1980, various performers, critics, producers, and audiences positioned Austin as an alternate node of music production to New York, Los Angeles, and, especially, Nashville. "Cosmic cowboys" and "hippie–rednecks" studded cultural–political discourse in the city. Such subcultural narratives operated in the transcendence of opposites, the subversion of the "generation gap" that seared the 1960s. The seventies vogue for country music nationally fused populist nostalgia for supposedly simpler times with the countercultural preoccupation with authenticity and the natural, making Austin's progressive country music scene primed for national exposure. This is not to give short shrift to the length and breadth of the expansive Lone Star State. Dallas's ostentatious orientation to the generation of wealth may have had a greater symbolic purchase for Americans during the decade's economic doldrums; Houston was on its way to becoming a Sunbelt megalopolis rivaled only by Los Angeles; and San Antonio and El Paso pointed the way to the democratic politics of a majority–minority America. These other stories come into view in the following pages, but Austin remains the study's anchor.[34] My hope is that a cultural history of the Texan 1970s, though a bit Austincentric, may help to open a space for more specific narratives concerning these other locales.[35]

Looking Ahead with Joe Buck in the Rearview Mirror

With a close reading of the Austin scene as its guiding spirit, this study ranges afield to many other spaces in which Texas signifies. Looming large among these is New York City, a place with a high profile in national narratives of the 1970s. In 1969, the John Schlesinger film *Midnight Cowboy* depicted the city on the brink of the decade. Jon Voight portrayed the lead character, Joe Buck, a Texan who moved to New York to become a gigolo.[36] Mass-mediated cultural product though he is, Joe Buck stands at that same nexus of old and new, provincial and metropolitan, rural and urban, frontier and nation, that snared Bud Shrake, Ben Barnes, and Jim Franklin. In New York, he affects an elaborate cowboy guise that in part deflects from his identity through burlesque as much as it advertises his true Texan origins. When an artist at a Warholite party inquires of Joe whether he's really a cowboy, he answers, "Well, I tell you the truth, now, I ain't a f'real cowboy, but I am one hell of a stud." Thus Joe Buck performs "the Texan," the frontiersman, the rugged individual, the

INTRODUCTION

hypermasculine man alone in the world, all the while denying the alienating effects of that isolation and his desire for union with his male companion Ratso, played as a prototypical New Yorker by Dustin Hoffman. The film ends with Ratso dying as the pair moves south to Florida, the Sunbelt dream wilting the New York hustler. From whence does Joe Buck come, and where does he go in the years that follow? This is yet another of our starting places.

This study contextualizes the representations, performances, and experiences of Anglo-Texan masculinity in the 1970s, tacking between a national setting of malaise and the state's popular celebration of "the Texan." The book does not analyze the Texan 1970s in exhaustive or definitive fashion, but instead proceeds through the analysis of evocative examples to make some sense of the whole. As a way of introduction, chapter 1 analyzes the period between the Texas Centennial Exposition of 1936 and Lyndon Johnson's political demise in 1968, when the symbols associated with Texas in the modern United States received their full articulation: the cowboy, the braggart, the nouveau-riche oilman, the wheeler-dealer. It then documents the social justice movements that African Americans and Mexican Americans waged against this Anglo establishment in Texas during the same period. These movements would largely define the cultural politics of the 1970s, and it is necessary to frame their expansion of who counts in the public sphere as "Texan."

The success of these movements opened a space for some Anglo-Texans to adopt and adapt the state's traditional iconography to create new resonances for the stereotypical Texan. Chapters 2 and 3 address this progressive re-visioning of "the Texan" in the countercultural scene of Austin, with its "cosmic cowboys" who grew their hair long, opposed the Vietnam War, and attended country-western benefits for striking workers. In the process, such figures negotiated between the normative representations of the Anglo-Texan and the challenges to them by professing allegiance to a modern, inclusive polity nevertheless rooted in the agrarian conservatism of the cowboy figure. Next, chapter 4 analyzes texts in which Anglo-Texan men invoked themes of fathers and sons, the agrarian and the industrial, and Texas as nation and empire to make sense of their subject position in the 1970s. Further, it pushes these concerns into a sociocultural interpretation of partisan realignment to understand how the political monopoly of the Democratic "party of the fathers" began to unravel. Chapter 5 concludes the book by looking to the late 1970s and early 1980s phenomenon of "Texas chic," whereby an unreconstructed vision of "the Texan" again found a national audience through such productions as *Urban Cowboy* and *Dallas*, eclipsing the earlier attempted revisions of the cowboy figure.

T. R. Fehrenbach wrote *Lone Star* to fill a perceived absence of "modern general histories" of the state.[37] In like fashion, I write this study to fulfill the continuing need for cultural histories of modern Texas. The recent close of yet another contentious presidential administration in which Anglo-Texan identities continued to signify, used as a cipher by observers to explain the character and actions of George W. Bush, begs such examination.[38] Bush shadows this work nearly as much as its other avatars, Lyndon Johnson and Willie Nelson, but he will not enter again explicitly until the conclusion. Instead, the work begins far from him with the prehistories of Joe Buck, Lyndon Johnson, Ben Barnes, Jim Franklin, Waylon Jennings, Larry McMurtry, Bud Shrake, Willie Nelson, and T. R. Fehrenbach in the Texas centennial year of 1936, in Dallas rather than Austin.

The Empire of Texas

LONE STAR REGIONALISM SETS THE STAGE, 1936-1968

On June 12, 1936, Franklin and Eleanor Roosevelt toured the sprawling Texas Centennial Exposition in Dallas. A tribute to Anglo-Texan civic leaders' sense of the state's history, culture, and industry, fairground displays commemorated the centennial of Texas's independence from Mexico, sought to buoy local spirits amid the Great Depression, and marketed Texas to the nation as a place to do business and spend tourist dollars. Roosevelt spoke to two audiences at the close of that tour, one of Texans and tourists physically gathered in the Exposition's Cotton Bowl, the other of radio listeners tuned to a national broadcast. He acknowledged the Exposition's multiple purposes, selling the fair as an event, not only for Texas, "but for the other forty-seven states" and as a platform for discussing the New Deal in a contentious election year. He ended with words ratifying the Exposition's organizing principle: the state's self-declared grandeur and sense of distinctiveness. As the president's centennial tour of the state drew to a close, he concluded by proclaiming, "I salute the Empire of Texas."[1]

Though imperial pretensions had long coursed through speechifying on the American West (and Roosevelt's "Empire State" of New York was an Eastern counterpart to this rhetoric), few other states fit FDR's peroration so well. A salute to the "Empire of Iowa" or the "Empire of South Carolina" would not have made sense to a national audience. Americans had a history of hearing Texas deployed in this manner, however, and the word evoked a ready stock of images of a distinct, outsize space in the American landscape. As geographer D. W. Meinig has observed, "Texans have long been taught to think of their homeland as an 'empire' and to use that word as something more than a grandiose name for a large area . . . the Texan claim is substantial and their use of the term more than metaphorical."[2] The imperial conceit that Roosevelt read into the Centennial Exposition, as with many expressions of Texan identity, lay somewhere between Meinig's substantial and metaphorical levels.

Political history lent the notion substance. The brief existence of the Republic of Texas served as the Centennial's subtext, a period that generated an entire rhetorical arsenal defining Texas as a country apart. In the nine-year span between Mexican and American sovereignties, the leadership of the threadbare republic engaged in ethnoracial nation-building through warfare and territorial appropriation aimed at Mexico and the Native Americans. For some, however, including President Mirabeau Lamar, nationhood was never enough for Texas, and alongside the construction of Texan nationality they wove an imperial vision of Texas as a Southwestern rival to the United States. Maps of the Republic delineating its far-fetched western boundary of the Rio Grande and northern boundary of the Arkansas River still sell briskly as a testament to these pretensions. Anglo-Texans, then, imagined a community marked by radical difference not only from Mexicans and Native Americans, but also, through their more vigorous conquest and eradication of these groups on the far frontier, as inheritors of a manifest destiny that surpassed the American nation itself.

And yet, modern Texas undeniably remained a political unit of the United States, rendering its national and imperial pretensions metaphorical. Moreover, the Anglo-Texan claim to profound difference, whether in 1836 or 1936, typically cited as evidence qualities that amplified the most basic tenets of American nationalism. If Texas aspired to empire, it merely echoed America's larger project of continental expansion. If Texas prized its status as the largest state in the union in 1936, it was still only a single state in the world's largest democracy. If acquisitive, vulgar, brimming with braggadocio, and quick to violence, well, so had America been branded with this set of qualities by observers on the world stage. "The American" and "the Texan" constituted parallel national ideologies, and the garish projection of the latter through mass cultural forms allows for a close reading of the former's transmission and function.

Arguably, these notions flashed to the minds of FDR's audiences upon the use of the word "Texas," but propagators of the state's mythos cast its long shadow not just through language but also through image, not just in rhetoric but also in performance. The myth spread through its perpetual incarnation in the figure of "the Texan" in dime novels, Western films, journalism, and popular music, to say nothing of those real live Texans in the world who felt compelled to mirror such mass-mediated representations. Though a diverse state, this "Texan" invariably took the form of Anglo-Texan masculinity, due largely to the Anglo, male dominance of the state's political leadership and the nation's cultural producers. The gendered and ethnoracial monopoly of this designation, the elision of "the Texan" with the white cowboy guise, possessed significant consequences for the discursive formation of "the American."

This chapter outlines major historical currents that made "the Texan" a powerful symbol and site of contestation in the cultural politics of the middle decades of the twentieth century. The 1936 centennial celebrations, the Lone Star regionalism of Walter Prescott Webb and J. Frank Dobie, the furor over "un-American" activities in the 1950s, and the political career of Lyndon Baines Johnson all deployed articulations and performances of Anglo-Texan masculinity as authentic, masterful, populist, and born of the labored soil. The oilman, the wheeler-dealer, and the cowboy all signified a triumphalist Americanism rooted in the earth but always striving in pursuit of the big money and the main chance. In the years when the United States achieved superpower status, then, such wheeler-dealer-cowboy-oilmen allowed for a contrarian celebration of stable agrarian identities comfortable with the disintegrative forces of modern capital.

"The Texan" figure fit the dominant discourses of mid-twentieth-century American identity. Though demographically by 1920 the United States had fulfilled Richard Hofstadter's aphorism that America "was born in the country and has moved to the city," the transformation of Texas was ongoing in these years.[3] From the point of view of the U.S. census, it was only in 1950 that the state's demographics tipped from predominantly rural to predominantly urban.[4] Moreover, this urbanization coincided with the imposition of political solutions to the strains of modernity and industrialism that the United States had borne for decades. Geographer David Harvey characterized the period from the 1930s to the 1960s as a new form of reckoning with the crises of mass production, resulting in a compromise among the forces of big business, big labor, and big government.[5] The Roosevelt administration and its immediate successors managed financial meltdown and labor insurgency through the machinery of the New Deal. In effect, this political formation, in tandem with the consumerist industrial strategy dubbed "Fordism" by Antonio Gramsci, took off the table the earth-shattering prospect of revolution as well as the worst ravages of laissez-faire capitalism.[6] It promised stability in a world turned upside down by economic depression and global war. The new regime reconfigured not only America's political economy, but also its ways of life, its sense of self, its articulations of race and class and nation. To this end, Roosevelt's first term mobilized an unwieldy coalition of organized labor, farmers, African Americans, Northern political machines, ethnic immigrant communities, Southern conservatives, and progressive intellectuals. By 1936, the year of FDR's speech at the Exposition, the New Deal had reined in the worst of the Depression, and, with FDR engaged in a new wave of reforms, his coalition began to fracture. The solid Democratic South pushed back at Roosevelt's agenda, couching their critique in states' rights philosophy while wringing their hands over the region's sacrosanct legal strictures regarding white supremacy.

Texas does not typically figure in national histories that treat the forging of these compromises. Yet the Lone Star State played a pivotal role in material, political, and cultural terms, in both the construction of twentieth-century statist liberalism as well as its countercurrents and dissolution. The latter looms large in narratives of postwar American history. The pantheon of archetypal far-right bogeymen, after all, would be much impoverished in the absence of the Texas oilman. As FDR's adviser Tommy Corcoran surmised, "The whole liberal cause went down the drain when oil became gold. . . . The boys from Texas took over."[7] But the state's contributions to the construction of American liberalism from the New Deal to the Great Society remain more obscure. National narratives that render Texas a reactionary monolith ignore substantial struggles over labor, race, and political economy in the state's experience of the twentieth century. In the 1930s, a Texas establishment hostile to organized labor nevertheless bolstered FDR's New Deal coalition to maintain party unity and, perhaps more to the point, to secure massive federal aid for public works projects. McCarthyism's rise and fall also had significant Texan prologues and epilogues, from Representative Martin Dies of Orange, the first chairman of the congressional committee to investigate un-American activities, to humorist John Henry Faulk, who in 1962 won one of the largest libel suits in U.S. history against defendants who charged him with Communist affiliations.[8] In the 1960s, the state tragically lurched to the center of the American political stage. John F. Kennedy's assassination in Dallas marked the city as a den of reactionary zealots, even as Lyndon Johnson used the event as political capital to elaborate one of the most progressive domestic agendas in the country's history.

This political profile did not arise independent of the state's charged mythology. Mass-mediated popular culture, politics, commerce, and folklore all collaborated in these years to create the classic image of the swaggering Anglo-Texan man. Primarily the marker of a supposedly simpler frontier past in the guise of the cowboy, "the Texan" could also act as a towering modern subject, the independent wheeler-dealer oilman as unlikely architect of the industrial order. The iconography of modern industry centered on Northern archetypes of the well-heeled capitalist, brawny factory worker, abstemious clerk, and earnest reformer, but what would the forging of the Fordist order be without Ford's automobile itself, its combustion engine, and, finally, gasoline? The explosive growth of petrochemical industries and technologies in Texas fueled Fordism just as OPEC's restructuring of the resource's distribution augured the Fordist order's later collapse.

When Pattillo Higgins and Anthony Lucas struck oil at Spindletop in East Texas in 1901, they glutted the market for petroleum, a substance not yet an indispensable fuel, but a source of illumination and lubrication. The single well at Spindletop produced as much oil as the thirty-seven thousand oil wells then back east. The scale of the industry, previously centered in Pennsylvania and California, changed overnight and burgeoned with the mass production of gasoline-fueled automobiles. By the 1950s Texas provided much of America's and nearly a quarter of the world's oil.[9] By the middle of the twentieth century, invocations of "the Texan" in popular parlance focused on the perceived gaucheries of the state's nouveau riche, drenched in the geological accident of their oil wealth.[10] The classic articulation of "the Texan" figure in the 1940s and 1950s joined the frontier image of the cowboy to the wheeling-and-dealing new wealth of the capital frontiers of petroleum. As the oil industry modernized Texas through the growth of refining capacity, labor unions, innovative technologies, and the international development of oil fields, "the Texan" gave modern America a figure that straddled the nation's past and present and could be used to articulate a sense of the national character as the country navigated its rising geopolitical profile.

"Opening the Eyes of the People": Lone Star Regionalism's Rise in the 1930s

These representations by no means originated with the Texas Centennial, but the highly orchestrated, yearlong celebration did concentrate and refine them in significant ways.[11] Its originators in the early 1920s conceived the Centennial as a marketing tool for the modern business environment of Texas, even as the event ratified the old cowboy garb to gain greater visibility. It arrived at a propitious moment, not merely as the marker of a century of "independent" Texas, but at the maturation of the political economy that Richard Flores has called the "Texas Modern." In parallel with incipient Fordism, Flores argues that the period between 1880 and 1920 in Texas constituted the "working out of new relationships, habits, and practices, resulting in the establishment of a social order segmented into various ethnic and class divisions."[12] This restructuring proceeded along several interlocking fronts and involved the closing of the open cattle range, drastic shifts in cotton tenancy, railroad consolidation, the political revolt of the Farmers' Alliances and Populists, the Spindletop discovery, and the armed rebellion of the *sediciosos* in South Texas.

These developments rigidified the strident ethnoracial dimensions of labor and politics in the state. Prior to the closing of the open cattle range in the fence wars of the 1890s, that "open" status itself had been finally realized by the military defeat of the Comanche and their exile to Oklahoma.[13] Anglo displacement of Mexican Americans penetrated the remaining *tejano* redoubts of the Lower Rio Grande Valley along with the railroads.[14] The disfranchisement and segregation of African Americans, dating at least to the collapse of Reconstruction, found new fuel in law and custom in the wake of the interracial Populist Revolt. Agrarian activists failed to stanch the collapse of the yeoman farmer class in the face of rising tenancy.[15] By the 1920s, the activist energies of Populists and Debsian Socialists had run their course, and Texas Rangers had defeated the tejano insurgencies against the trans-Nueces penetration of American capital, just as the Mexican Revolution had been contained across the Rio Grande.[16]

Against this backdrop, New York business editor and former cotton broker Theodore Price delivered a speech to the tenth district meeting of the Associated Advertising Clubs of America in Corsicana, Texas, in 1923. His address, "What Texas Has to Advertise and How to Advertise It," focused on the "transcendent value" of the state's "gloriously romantic history," and suggested a centennial exposition to draw attention to the state. The advertising clubs, the Texas Press Association, and Corsicana boosters spread news of the idea and secured the backing of Governor Pat Neff. By January 1925, the Centennial Governing Board of One Hundred had arrived at its strategy to "Texanize Texans" by 1936, or, as folklorist J. Frank Dobie expressed his aims, to "open the eyes of the people to the richness of their own traditions."[17] In order for this marketing gambit to work on the nation at large, the Centennial's organizers required that Texans discipline themselves to the romantic identity they sought to sell. Business leaders, politicians, and the culture industries of the state worked hard to brand a certain image of "the Texan" strongly on the minds of the state's residents and potential visitors and business partners abroad.

Popular culture had primed national audiences to receive such images. The musical articulation of Texas masculinity, as in Gene Autry's *The Big Show* filmed on the grounds of the Centennial Exposition, was of paramount importance in how the nation consumed "the Texan." In addition to the singing cowboy cohort of Autry, Roy Rogers, Tex Ritter, and the Sons of the Pioneers, the 1930s witnessed the regional confluence of big band jazz with Southwestern imagery in the Western swing of Bob Wills, Milton Brown, and Spade Cooley. In the early years of the Great Depression, Wills and Brown pioneered the music as the Light Crust Doughboys on a Fort Worth radio program hosted by W. Lee "Pappy" O'Daniel. After flour-salesman-turned-politician O'Daniel ran Bob Wills out of the Light Crust Doughboys, Fort Worth, and the state, Wills elaborated the Western swing sound from a home base in Tulsa before establishing a broad audience that included Depression and war work migrants in California. In short, Western swing took the forms of big band jazz, mixed and occasionally replaced the horn section with string instruments (including some of the earliest steel and amplified guitar), and dressed the entire package in the elaborate Western wear popularized for performers by the singing cowboy films. The band alternated among straight covers of big band standards, blues numbers, and spirited arrangements of Southwestern fiddle tunes. Western swing thus popularized the Texas image with an aurally inclusive version of Texas culture from the Western swing dance halls of California to the East Coast.[18] The Centennial fit nicely with such commercial images of Texas and the West then on the rise.

In addition, the Centennial's declaration of Texan distinctiveness hewed to contemporaneous currents of intellectual and artistic regionalism. A sense of modernity's homogenizing influences—the collapsing of distance through automobile and radio, the dual alienation from labor and consumption in mass production—led many intellectuals to the project of salvaging the sense of vibrant difference they felt passing from local settings. In the Midwest, painters Thomas Hart Benton, Grant Wood, and John Steuart Curry and writers Meridel Le Sueur, Carl Sandburg, Thomas Craven, and Jack Conroy explored the notion of the Plains states as "Middle America" or the "heartland," giving rise to a notion of the Midwest as a mirror for the American nation.[19] Midwestern regionalism, in this sense, ratified intellectuals' propensity to celebrate American nationality amid the anxiety of the Great Depression. The desert Southwest, too, fired the regionalist imagination, as intellectuals rendered the Native American and Mexican American populations of New Mexico as exotic others defining the outer bounds of this Americanism. Over time, artists Joseph Henry Sharp, E. Irving Couse, Ernest Blumenschein, Victor Higgins, Raymond Johnson, Marsden Hartley, and Georgia O'Keefe, writers D. H. Lawrence and Oliver La Farge, and socialite Mabel Dodge Luhan took up residence in the vicinity of Santa Fe and Taos and deployed their newly donned Southwesternness in critique of urban modernity, but with their experimental aesthetics intact.[20]

In the South, regionalism served different ends. In part, it shared the Midwesterners' critique of urban modernity and spoke to the two regions' shared political past in agrarian Populism. But Southern authors shied from identifying the South as essentially American, as the Midwesterners did for their region, choosing rather to shadow the Southwest's claims of distinction from the American mainstream. Indeed, the South spoke to America's oldest sense of regional division in a way that went beyond local color to the divergent political economies of mercantilism and plantation agriculture that defined the early republic. In North Carolina, sociologist Howard Odum helped define the field, but the Nashville Agrarians set the strident tone for much of Southern regionalism. Their influential essay collection *I'll Take My Stand* appeared in 1930, a scathing critique of the modern industrial order that nostalgically evoked the antebellum South, including its enforcement of racial strata.[21]

Regionalism's various strains demonstrate its multiple instrumentalities. In the Midwestern case, regionalism sought an authentic America framed by its difference from the supposedly alien populations and ideologies of the Eastern cities. Thomas Hart Benton made these ideas explicit in his critical retreat from what he saw as the decadence of New York art circles to the plainspoken Americanism of his home soil.[22] In contrast, Southwestern regionalism recognized ethnic difference within American borders as an alternate critique of the homogenizing forces of modernity. Throughout, then, regionalism bespoke a temporal as well as a spatial dimension. The conservative and progressive valences of the regional shared a sense of the provincial as uncorrupted by modern global capitalism. These regions, "behind" the avant-garde metropolis in grand historical terms, served as sites of salvage for artists and intellectuals to rediscover the possibilities of social relations free from alienation.[23]

For all of its exceptionalist bluster, Texas fit this larger regionalist discourse. The Centennial Exposition provides the most publicized example, but the official commemorations of 1936 built on more organic articulations of the regional turn. Lone Star regionalism revolved around intellectuals based at the University of Texas at Austin but with influence throughout the state's colleges, media, museums, and businesses, including, over time, American Studies scholar Henry Nash Smith, folklorists Mody Boatwright and William Owens, humorist John Henry Faulk, illustrator Tom Lea, painters Jerry Bywaters and Alexandre Hogue, historians Eugene Barker and J. Evetts Haley, authors George Sessions Perry and John Graves, photographer Russell Lee, and folk music collectors John and Alan Lomax, among others. The *Southwest Review*, the Texas State Historical Association, and the Texas Folklore Society helped knit them one to another. The triumvirate of historian Walter Prescott Webb, folklorist J. Frank Dobie, and naturalist Roy Bedichek, however, held this cohort together and largely defined its aims. To this day, Webb, Dobie, and Bedichek stand as a shorthand reference to an entire era of Texas arts and letters. The reference tends to be a condescending one, with several factors placing these authors' reputation in eclipse.[24] Understanding the cultural formations of mid-century Texas remains impossible, however, without examining the triumvirate's often-undervalued work.[25]

Austin served as an intriguing seat for the regionalist endeavor as, geographically, the city's location laid bare the challenge of framing Texas as a single region with a common identity, situated between the more obvious regional units of the cotton South, the ranching West, and the Mexican borderlands. The political and intellectual capital of Texas, Austin could hardly claim itself as representative of the state. Government, academia, and their attendant service sectors occupied more people in the Austin area than did the dominant Texan affairs of cotton, cattle, and oil. Austin as the epicenter of the Lone Star regionalists' vision offered an opportunity to hybridize the understandings of South, West, and Border, to account for difference and culture and race and labor as they played across these diverse landscapes. In practice, though, the equation of Texas with the Anglo-Western cowboy predominated in the cultural productions of the period. Exceptions occurred, of course. Novelist George Sessions Perry strayed from the herd not only in moving physically to the world of New England academia, but also in focusing artistically on the cotton culture that tied Texas so closely to the South in his classic *Hold Autumn in Your Hand* (1941). Katherine Anne Porter did much the same with even greater success, but her national renown made few ripples in the Texas literary community.[26] Scholars of Texas music, too, gravitated to the Southern aspects of the state's culture. John Lomax began his career publishing cowboy songs, but the most enduring aspect of the Lomax legacy lay in the recording of African American blues, first in Texas, and later throughout the South. Like Perry and Porter, John and Alan Lomax left the state to find their fortunes.[27] Back in Texas the cowboy figure, and intellectuals and artists who took the cowboy as their subject, remained dominant in public figurations of state identity.

J. Frank Dobie and Walter Prescott Webb solidified this westering of "the Texan" in their academic works of the 1930s, but they had already sketched the contours of their major theses in the previous decade. As businessmen and politicians prepared for the centennial, Dobie and his allies in the Texas

Folklore Society began to open their eyes to local traditions. As with intellectuals across the country, they hungered for a literature based in the experiences of their own region. As Dobie wrote Webb as both men were beginning their careers, "Think of the hundreds of western novels, poems, and travel books and essays that have been written, and not an American scholar has touched the field. Plenty on Southern literature; too much on New England literature; oceans of rubbish on the prototype of Rosalind in Spencer's Shepherd's Calendar. . . . I have been working into that field and working hard and now damn it, I am exiled from my own birthright."[28]

Not yet a folklorist, Dobie struggled to find his place in the English department at the University of Texas. Suffering the perceived snubs of colleagues who felt he still had "too much of the cowboy in him," Dobie often retreated from Austin. He took time off to work his family's ranch in South Texas and teach in Oklahoma. Through it all, Dobie persistently desired to record and study Texas experiences in literature. The pull of "the Texan" owed something to a provincial inferiority complex (the English department feuding had this cast to it), as well as to Dobie's recognition of a career opportunity in the wide-open field of Western literature. Overall, though, the desire issued from a sense of loss in the moment of the Texas Modern. Dobie continued to recruit Webb in the project of constructing a Southwestern literature. Another letter of 1923 reads as follows:

> As surely as there came to be a literature of New England, of the Old South, of New York, of the Middle West, there is coming to be a literature of the Southwest—a literature at once local and national. Look how Washington Irving used the legends of the Hudson; look how Whittier and Longfellow used the legends of New England. I am collecting the legends of Texas and the Southwest for the Irvings, the Whittiers, the Longfellows of this Texas and the Southwest. And, believe me, those poets of the cattle land pioneers— are on their way.[29]

Here, Dobie contends that America's literary canon derived from regional writers like Irving and Longfellow. And yet, even as Dobie makes this statement he must concede that the corresponding Texan litterateurs are still simply "on their way." Indeed, when Dobie first proposed his signature university course, "Life and Literature of the Southwest," the paucity of Texan literary texts turned his attention to folk culture and lifeways, encouraged by pioneering folklorist Stith Thompson. In the process of their research and publications, Dobie, his colleagues, and his students went far toward rectifying the lack of a literary tradition in the state. At the same time, they reified the notion of a distinct Texas culture in ways that obscured its continuities with America at large as well as its internal diversity. The few significant exceptions to the Anglo-Texan bias of Dobie's Texas Folklore Society, such as Jovita González or the African American folklorist J. Mason Brewer, initially served more to buttress the group's academic hegemony than to complicate it.[30]

The Centennial drew on these developing currents of Lone Star regionalism, but cautiously, often borrowing from the regionalists' celebration of the state while denying their critical elements.[31] When it came to J. Frank Dobie, however, the man's popularity as a Texan public intellectual made the prospect of his exclusion difficult. When Dobie signed on as historical consultant for the state's centennial celebrations in 1935, he was in the middle of his most prolific decade. Following the period in which Dobie wrote the above letters to Webb, he collected folk tales for what he conceived of as a single book of Texas lore. Instead, he began a four-decade career in which he would do little else other than engage in attempts to "open the eyes of the people to the richness of their own traditions." Though he intended to raise awareness of the passing generation of "Texans out of the Old Rock," his own ceaseless self-promotion led to his identification, in the public mind, with "the Texan" he sought to depict and preserve. Dobie's production from the beginning of the Great Depression through America's entry into World War II included *A Vaquero of the Brush Country* with John Young (1929), *Coronado's Children* (1930), *On the Open Range* (1931), *Tongues of the Monte* (1935), *Apache Gold and Yaqui Silver* (1939), and *The Longhorns* (1941). By 1942, George Sessions Perry could say that Dobie was "as unmistakably Texan as a Longhorn steer, as the sight of a lone cowboy laying his fresh fried bacon in neat strips on an absorbent plop of last year's cow dung to drain off the grease."[32] He maintained a busy speaking schedule, wrote a widely syndicated newspaper column ("My Texas"), edited the journal of the Texas Folklore Society, hosted a radio program, and acted as a consultant for Hollywood Westerns.

Steve Davis's compelling recent biography of Dobie has revisited the folklorist's orientation to the times in which he lived, and the historian Walter Prescott Webb invites a similar revisionist view. While Davis and other scholars have remarked on Dobie's ambivalence in political and cultural matters, comparing the conservatism of his books to his feisty, progressive stance as a public intellectual, Webb's caution in his professional life allows for the conservative, ethnoracial strains of his work to predominate. Dobie and Webb participated in a Texas regionalist turn that did not, for the most part, possess an overt or unitary political agenda. At first sight, a preservationist impulse trumped celebration or critique in the work itself. A sense of profound loss motivated them both, a notion that the heroic Texas into which they had been born was on the cusp of passing from rural to urban, from adventurous to urbane, from freedom to constraint. Prior authors utilized this same nostalgic voice of the Dobie/Webb/Bedichek contingent, and it would continue long after they were gone. Indeed, the persistence of this nostalgia, in which typically Anglo observers bemoan the constant vanishing of an old, original Texas every few years, provides one of the major themes of this study. The voice speaks to contemporary anxieties and acknowledges the subjective experience of historicity, but the "real Texas" it invokes seems to have been always receding and never really present.

Audiences and critics relished the authors' nostalgia, and those books most redolent with such themes made the names of Dobie and Webb. Webb established a reputation as a historian of national consequence through two books published in the 1930s, *The Great Plains* (1931) and *The Texas Rangers* (1935). Together, both books overshadowed a third text of the thirties, one that contained Webb's most critical interpretation of the American past. The short *Divided We Stand: The Crisis of a Frontierless Democracy* (1937) constituted a virtual call-to-arms that poet Carl Sandburg labeled "one of the great modern American pamphlets."[33] *The Texas Rangers*, *The Great Plains*, and *Divided We Stand* were Webb's major works prior to World War II. The first was popular in orientation, the second academic, and the third political, but each shared a definition of the West as a specific, bounded geographic space. In an extension of the Anglo-Saxon germ theory that undergirded the origins of American historical scholarship, Webb constructed an ur-narrative of the forest cultures of Anglo American pioneers moving onto the Plains. That movement into the New World required not merely cultural and social, but technical adaptations, in the form of the six-shooter, the windmill, and barbed wire. These adaptations to Western aridity, in turn, fed cultural, social, and legal change. Webb's historical interpretations, then, are of a materialist bent, his regionalism one that privileges the causality of the physical environment. *The Great Plains* of 1931 remains a monumental work of history in its environmental determinism and in its prescience concerning the impending Dust Bowl, but *Divided We Stand* better sketches Webb's orientation to the crises of the 1930s.

Originally published in 1937, *Divided We Stand* is a curious document. On the one hand, the book neatly extends Webb's variant on Frederick Jackson Turner's frontier thesis. In this view, the windfall of the Western frontier had long subsidized American democracy and economic abundance. In the absence of that "free" bounty, the decades between the 1890s and the 1930s challenged the nation to adjust to an Old World notion of limits. The new situation required, in Webb's estimation, an extensive and vital reform of the nation's most basic cultural and political assumptions. Where Webb critiques the notion of the public domain as free bounty, he brings attention to the federal government's role in the exploration and dispersal of those lands while he rarely highlights their appropriation through the conquest of pre-existing indigenous or Mexican sovereignties. In this regard, *Divided We Stand* is Turnerian, reformist, and ethnocentric, a practically oriented distillation of Webb's thought that connects the broader and more academic assessments of *The Great Plains* and his later synthetic work *The Great Frontier* (1951).

On the other hand, the book also speaks in the voice of regionalist screed, echoing the Nashville Agrarians. The root of the nation's problems, for Webb, lay in the imperialistic reach and seemingly inherent greed of Northern capital over and against the agrarian South and West. Unlike the Nashville Agrarians, however, Webb staked his hopes on the development of the federal government as a popular bulwark against the growing power of corporations rather than in a retreat to hidebound communitarian and white supremacist traditions. Webb's elaboration of the South-and-West-as-colony argument, then, did not look backward to the Agrarians' *I'll Take My Stand* (1930) but forward to C. Vann Woodward's *Origins of the New South* (1951). Webb underscored the fundamental difference of the South and West from the North, based in a vision of political economies born at the intersection of geographies and institutions: "These dividing lines so nearly follow the country's social, economic, and political history and its climatic and topographical lines that, when viewed from the future, I believe it will be clear that there have been developed in this country three fairly distinct cultures, ways of life" among the North, the South, and the West.[34] The regionalist shorthand obscures the tremendous diversity beneath these labels, but also speaks to the most basic narratives of American identity that, traditionally, held the North to be normative, the South a deviation, and the West a blank canvas, a "virgin land" in which the American character was either gestated or renewed.[35]

If these ideas seem disparate, their Southwestern jingoism out of step with Webb's New Deal loyalties, it may be because the coherence of these positions owed less to Roosevelt's response to the Great Depression than to the Populist Revolt of the 1890s. Activist government as a tool to restrain corporations lay in Populist theory prior to its adoption by Progressives in the 1910s and New Dealers in the 1930s. The regionalisms of the Midwest, South, and Texas all drew on the language of Populist insurgency that pitted the "interests" against the "people." But few authors built directly on the Populists' economic arguments as did Webb. Populism remained something of a disavowed progenitor of American progressivism in these years, regarded as provincial and unsophisticated. However, the movement born out of the Farmers' Alliances founded in Lampasas, Texas, in 1877 offered a telling critique of the rising power of American capital and crafted a range of responses that found later ratification in the New Deal.

In this vein, Webb concludes *Divided We Stand* with demands for the dispersal of industry across the country, the reform of intellectual property laws that favored Northern monopolies, the revision of judicial opinions that rendered corporations legal persons, and an overhauling of railroad freight rates that favored Northern cities. Among the most relevant insights here, Webb disavowed the rugged individualism that many Westerners marshaled as counterargument against activist government: "[It] is no wonder that democracy was able to succeed. If a man turned farmer, the government gave him a free homestead; if a miner, gold; if cattleman, free grass; if railroader, free right of way and nearly 13,000 acres of land and a loan of a fortune of cash for each mile; if he turned manufacturer, the government gave him patents and high protective tariff, and probably a Civil War pension."[36] In other words, the federal government had always been in the business of dispersing entitlements and had in the process developed the West in a manner that, ironically, gave rise to the cultural vision of the rugged individualist. Patricia Nelson Limerick and Richard White deployed this notion as a key tenet of the New Western History in the 1980s, but Webb suggested the way as early as 1937.[37] The figure of the rugged individualist would survive Limerick and White just as it survived Webb. Indeed, the contradiction of a publicly trumpeted libertarianism yoked to the infusion of federal dollars in state capitalist development largely defined the rise of the Sunbelt in the years following Webb's work. The muscular exercise of free enterprise continues to stand as a key component of the Texas myth. Webb exposed it as such—mere myth—long ago, but his exposé in *Divided We Stand* never gained anywhere near the traction that his celebratory account of the Texas Rangers did. Nevertheless, Webb provides an early example of an Anglo-Texan man deploying the state's Western history and tradition toward economically progressive ends.

With few exceptions, the cohort led by Dobie and Webb supported Franklin Roosevelt, further testament that an orientation toward regional tradition did not preclude advocacy for the modern, activist state.[38] As Webb and others exposed the history of federal government as a tool used by private concerns, they supported the New Deal as a further development of the federal government's instrumentality, only this time in the defense of the citizenry as a whole.

Disagreements did occur, of course, and the cultural conservatism of much of the Texas electorate had its proponents among the state's intelligentsia. Prominent folk music collector John Lomax frequently chided his old Austin friends for their politics.[39] His son Alan fit more neatly the New Deal, and even Popular Front, mold, and John's hand-wringing over what he perceived as his son's Communism served as a source of continual humor for the Austin intellectuals.[40] Ranching historian and future Republican activist J. Evetts Haley provided another exception. In a letter to Webb, Roy Bedichek documents the political ire that could arise between colleagues, in this case folklorist William Owens and Haley. Owens confessed to Bedichek that he and Haley had "quarreled violently" on a recent folklore-collecting trip. Bedichek asked about the source of the quarrel, and Owens responded, "Well, Haley thought I couldn't use our recording machine out in the country because of lack of power. I told him that since we had Rural Electrification, it was easy. When I said 'Rural Electrification' it was just like *touching a match to him*—he exploded about the New Deal, and we had it up and down from then on."[41] For an academic like the folklorist Owens (to say nothing of Hill Country farmers), such things as rural electrification made the benefits of the New Deal manifestly concrete, and one did not even have to venture into the countryside west of town to witness the transformation.[42] For these writers based in Austin, the New Deal order revolutionized the urban landscape, eventually creating a series of dams that brought the perpetually flooding Colorado River that ran through downtown under control and providing a boon to a town centered on the service industry of administration as home to the state capital and its flagship university.[43]

The activist orientation and material dispensations of New Deal governance persisted during World War II, even if the progressive content of its politics did not. With the political climate shifting from reform at home to war abroad, conservative politicians began to wield anti-communist rhetoric to combat the influence of activist intellectuals. At the same time, the war strengthened both the cosmopolitan perspective and the Texas accent of the state's homegrown authors and artists. Their orientation to the past, their preservationist impulse, their absolute devotion to the iconic man on horseback, did not preclude a progressive politics, but neither could Dobie and Webb escape the performance of "the Texan" in their own everyday lives.

The two authors spent a portion of the war years at universities in England, Dobie at Cambridge and Webb at Oxford. Dobie returned to Europe in the immediate postwar period to speak and teach in army camps in England, France, and occupied Germany and Austria. In these capacities, both Dobie and Webb sought to move beyond their status as regional intellectuals while, in reality, cementing their personal association with "the Texan" in the minds of their publics at home and abroad. Webb attempted to use the teaching opportunity at Oxford to expand his horizons and dispel stereotypes. That this was on his mind is suggested by the manuscript of an autobiography that he composed in his spare time at Oxford, in which he emphatically stated:

> I wish to say one word about myself. [The next sentence, crossed out in the manuscript, reads: "So far as I know I am about the only person who has written about the West who does not claim to be a cowboy."] Though I grew up in the edge of the cattle country, I was never a [crossed out: "real"] cowboy. I owned and rode horses and associated with boys who were cowboys. Lynn Landrum of the *Dallas News* once intimated that I had the qualities of a cowboy. It is easy for any one who grew up in the West before 1910 to claim cowboy descent. People rather expect it. I might best be described in these early years as a sort of reluctant dry-farmer.[44]

At the same time, Webb found his English reception as a cowboy stimulating and played the part to good effect. As he wrote to his wife, Jane, from Oxford, "That Stetson hat is a real hit. I had some misgivings about it, and bought in Washington a hat that was more conventional. . . . I wore the Stetson, the first one here perhaps." And to his children, Webb wrote that the "Stetson's fame is spreading. I hear that the undergraduates say, 'This is the real thing.'"[45] Webb delighted in the attribution of authenticity, and, though he did not revel in the performance of "the Texan" as did Dobie, the Stetson nevertheless remained part of Webb's image until his death.

The English experience broadened Dobie's horizons, as well. Of the intellectuals at the core of the Lone Star regionalist cohort, observers frequently noted that Dobie had the greatest claim to the cowboy guise so often equated with "the Texan." He had grown up in a ranching family in Live Oak County and, even alongside his academic career, continued to work cattle. Dobie's maverick reputation had been long in the construction, but its political bent accelerated during World War II. Indeed, his politicization derived in part from his experience of the war against fascism. As he wrote home to Bedichek from Cambridge:

> I have lots of things to put in my books, out of the old innocent days. I suppose that if I withdraw myself from current life, my imagination will take me into them as of yore. However, I can't get into them and remain interested in the rapidly evolving world that right now is the only reality to me. On the other

hand, I am too damned ignorant to be effective in writing about the realities of the present. That is what comes from having spent nearly a quarter of a century of my allotted years in doing nothing but soak in the lore of coyotes and cowboys.[46]

Dobie's subsequent career is mired in this ambivalence. The European sojourn added the term "fascist" to his vocabulary, as well as recognition of continuities between Southern white supremacy and the causes of the devastation he witnessed abroad.[47] His professed ignorance to the contrary, Dobie upon his return became an outspoken liberal, using his weekly syndicated newspaper column to harass the state's Dixiecrat politicians. In his books, however, Dobie never strayed far from the "lore of coyotes and cowboys." For the most part, Dobie's folklore remained at the level of Webb's popular *The Texas Rangers*. His postwar works followed the pattern of his prewar books: *The Voice of the Coyote* (1949), *The Ben Lilly Legend* (1950), *The Mustangs* (1952), *Tales of Old Time Texas* (1955), *Up the Trail from Texas* (1955), *I'll Tell You a Tale* (1960), *Cow People* (1964), and *Rattlesnakes* (1965), never shifting in tone or scope to produce a work like *The Great Plains*, to say nothing of the advocacy of *Divided We Stand*. Nevertheless, the stands that Dobie took publicly cost him dearly in the postwar environment.

More than any other single event, the firing of University of Texas President Homer Rainey sharpened these critical perspectives on Dobie's and Webb's return.[48] With regard to the regionalist intellectuals, the affair played out over three moments: Rainey's firing in 1944, his gubernatorial candidacy in 1946, and Dobie's dismissal from the university in 1947. Though at first glance the incident seems to consist of typical bickering between university administrators and professors, the Rainey affair in fact traced the growing schisms within the state Democratic Party. As the initial successes of the New Deal ameliorated the worst of the Great Depression, conservatives who had participated in Roosevelt's coalition out of necessity began to oppose FDR's attempts to consolidate the newly activist federal state. The 1936 Centennial brought FDR to Dallas not out of romantic attachment to the state's mythology, but because the state had begun to distance itself from the president in an election year in which even FDR's vice president, Texan John Nance "Cactus Jack" Garner, began to grouse.[49] Taking a cue from the shifting political winds, conservative Democratic governors W. Lee O'Daniel (1939–1941) and Coke Stevenson (1941–1947) used appointments to the state university's Board of Regents to ensure tighter control over curriculum in what they considered to be Roosevelt's Trojan horse in Texas.

By the 1940s, the composition of the Board of Regents finally allowed for a purge of New Deal influences in Austin, and they sought to dismiss controversial faculty.[50] University President Homer Rainey publicly denounced the Regents' actions in October 1944, an occasion that led to his dismissal and quickly roused the faculty in his defense. The Regents did not reinstate Rainey, and he used the platform created by his dismissal to run for governor in 1946. Though unsuccessful, Rainey's run against Beauford Jester in the Democratic primaries set the fault lines between the conservative Regulars and the liberals loyal to the national party, a rift that would define political realignment in coming decades.

J. Frank Dobie became a belated casualty of Rainey's dismissal. Returning from Europe in 1946, and having attended the Nuremberg trials of Nazi leaders, Dobie was newly sensitive to issues of authority and civil liberties. University officials reasoned that Dobie's long absence from campus during the war and the fact that he still did not have his PhD constituted valid reasons for his dismissal in 1947, but his growing tendency to refer to the Regents as "homemade fascists" surely did not help matters.[51] As with other professors, Dobie supported Rainey in the 1946 primaries, and came to regard the conservative faction of the state Democratic Party, the Regents included, as akin to Nazis. In a letter to Bedichek, Dobie drew the distinction sharply: "I actually think that if we Liberals get behind a good man like Rainey . . . the Coke Stevenson Texas Regulars will be driven into a hole as deep as Hitler's."[52] Dobie was not alone in sketching these evocative, if overstated, parallels. As Bedichek himself wrote to Webb regarding Webb's attacks on Rainey's replacement as university president, Theophilus Shickel Painter, "You caught the action of this man in clear amber of a purely factual account in which it will be preserved for those students of a later generation who happen to become interested in studying the nazification (or the attempt to Nazify) the University."[53] Such passages equating the university administration with Nazism began to reach levels of near hysteria amongst the Rainey camp in ways that may seem overly dramatic to the modern reader. Historian Doug Rossinow has identified this penchant for paranoia as a defining characteristic of Texas liberalism, but he also points to the fact that such thinking was, often, justified. "Others in less difficult straits might see Texas liberals at times as afflicted by paranoia and delusions of heroism," he argued, "but from the Texas point of view, it was only realism." The Texas establishment, Nazis or no, was, indeed, out to get them.[54]

Bedichek, Blut, und Boden

As tempers cooled through the 1950s, many university officials, in particular Chancellor Harry Ransom, regretted Dobie's dismissal and attempted to convince him to return. Their efforts proved unsuccessful, and Dobie continued his prolific literary career and held seminars for students at his home just blocks north of campus until his death in 1964. The duality of Dobie's folkloric concerns and his progressive beliefs begs further examination, though, as this tension between an Anglo-Texan nationalism based in the received traditions of the state and a desire for progress beyond the state's social and political conservatism later resonated in the 1970s just as it did in the 1940s. The third figure of the mid-century Lone Star regionalist triumvirate, naturalist Roy Bedichek, provides a fitting subject through which to explore these issues.

Though older than Dobie and Webb, Roy Bedichek began his career as an author late in life with *Adventures with a Texas Naturalist* (1947) and *Karankaway Country* (1950). He had known Dobie and Webb for most of their careers at the University of Texas, and predated them in the cohort of Lone Star regionalists, having first worked with John Lomax in the university's registrar office in 1898. Lomax left the University of Texas due to Governor Jim Ferguson's prior purge of the university in 1917, and Bedichek remained in administration as the head of the University Interscholastic League. He used frequent trips traveling across the state on UIL business, monitoring high school sports programs and debate contests, to indulge his hobby as a naturalist. By the late 1940s, Bedichek, exhausted with the political fights over Rainey, gave in to Webb and Dobie's suggestions to set aside time for writing. As Bedichek wrote to John Lomax in 1946, "I took this year's leave because I was nauseated with the University situation and wanted to get as clear of it as I possibly could."[55] The classic *Adventures with a Texas Naturalist* was the result.

Bedichek's life as a bureaucrat and a naturalist would seem to place him outside the mainstream of the rancorous political debates roiling the university. To the contrary, Bedichek's deep connectedness in the social web of Texas letters and his voluminous correspondence meant that he actively shaped the conversation, and often did so in ways that intersected with his studies of nature and humanity's relation to it. For example, the heightened vigilance for "un-American activities" sparked reflection over the meanings of patriotism among these intellectuals so deeply invested not only in the documentation of things American, but also in the parallel nationalism concerning all things Texan. As Bedichek wrote Dobie during World War II, "I have threatened several times to write a philosophic article on the value of such articles as you write in developing patriotism—and I mean *patriotism*, that is a love of country (and by country I mean *country*, rocks, soil, creeks, rivers, hills, and valleys) not flag and a lot of gaseous intangibles. There is no patriotism without love of your physical environment just as there is no romantic love without a love of the physical body of some individual woman."[56] For Bedichek, patriotism did not reside in ideologies, but in a sort of gendered relationship to the material environment. He is responding here to a column that Dobie had written on the subject in which he claimed the following: "If I were some sort of dictator going over the country extracting oaths of loyalty from people and came across a man or woman or child who had manifestly been made happy by the sight of a particular bird belonging to his own homeland, I should mark that person down as more satisfactorily loyal than a thousand oaths would make me feel toward some other people. Like knowledge, patriotism is concrete, particular, not vague and generalized."[57]

Webb, Dobie, and Bedichek all based their regionalist work in a kind of historical materialism. Each cataloged reactions, adaptations, and stories that arose from contact with specific places, in which the supposed character of those places as embodied in landscapes (typically rendered as rural, as it was a rural Texas in which each came of age) remained paramount. World War II shifted the terms of the debate, calling on the intellectuals to think in terms of global events and ideologies while also drawing Texas further into an industrial, urban modernity. Against this backdrop, Webb, Dobie, and Bedichek retrenched the nostalgic voice in their published work. Bedichek claimed that "modern technology has done much to destroy patriotism, as I have described this emotion. Worldwide communications have battered indigenous cultures to pieces; transportation has made globetrotters of us all; the local deities of the ancient communities, haunting streams and woodlands, really the personalized affections of the people for features of the home landscape—these local deities are dead. And with their death, our attachment to the soil is weakened. We tend to become, if not actually proletarians, then proletarians in spirit."[58] Bedichek typically showed more care in describing the effects of technology, but here he offered mass communications as a major cause for the rupture of a true patriotism rooted in physical soil that served as bedrock for his own brand of regionalism. He also compared this to the alienation from labor engendered by mass production, seeing in patriotism based only in "gaseous intangibles" a proletarianization of the spirit.

Debates over "un-American" activities and ruminations over the definitions of patriotism in the work of Webb, Dobie, and Bedichek continued the arguments behind the regionalist vogue of the 1930s. In their insistence on the highly material nature of "love of country," foregrounding the relationship between countrymen and their soil, these authors, perhaps unwittingly, tapped the same veins of nationalist thought as their conservative opponents. At times, they willfully did so, making a move to capture the ground of the authentic, rooted "Texan" from those who would use the state's iconography for ends with which they did not agree.

The relationship between tradition and change remained paramount in these discussions. As historian, folklorist, and naturalist, respectively, Webb, Dobie, and Bedichek thought long and hard on the subject. Interestingly, it was the naturalist, Bedichek, who theorized the most nuanced relationship of people to country. As a forebear to ecological thinkers of the next generation, Bedichek did not reify the dichotomy of civilization and wilderness as did Dobie and Webb, but instead focused his attentions on their mutual constitution, detailing how natural phenomena responded and adapted to the presence of human activity.[59] He occasionally took to chiding tones, as in his long discussion of the relation among brush-clearing, erosion, and the human uses of water in the later chapters of *Karankaway Country* or of the industrialization of poultry-raising in *Adventures with a Texas Naturalist*.[60] However, he frequently highlighted instances where the unintended consequences of human behavior provided opportunities for natural adaptation, as in the expanded northern range of the vermilion flycatcher due to the construction of ranching "tanks"; or seeing in the brush country not the natural state of South Texas but a landscape created by longhorns on the hoof; or the rise and fall of Austin woodpecker populations due first to the erection of telephone poles and their later coating with creosote.[61] Most important, Bedichek understood, and exposed, the dangers of projecting notions from human culture onto the natural order, thereby inviting the reverse metaphors to arise. In a telling passage, the bucolic Bedichek detailed the extension of racial stereotypes into the folk naming of animals and plants, and how that process then naturalized racial stereotyping itself.[62]

Nevertheless, there remains a "blood and soil" quality to many of these midcentury paeans to Texas.[63] One of Dobie's highest compliments was to declare a person a "Texan out of the Old Rock," by which he meant to convey a rugged, masculine authenticity that constituted an identity between the person and the land itself. To the extent that Texas exists as a kind of metaphorical nation, Lone Star regionalists invoked a rhetoric that dates to the origins of nationalist thinking in the German Romanticism of Johann Gottlieb Fichte and Johann Gottfried Herder. The gendered and ethnoracial aspects of these expressions were of paramount significance in establishing the normativity of Anglo-Texan masculinity even as most of these men considered themselves liberal regarding the state's politics.

Such national aspects of Anglo-Texan identity first came to be articulated in the context of the Republic's war against Mexico and the Native Americans. Dobie's and Bedichek's insistence on the relation between men and soil occasionally betrayed their recognition of such prior sovereignties. As Dobie wrote to John Henry Faulk, "My dear old friend Gnardo del Bosque . . . summed up the matter when he said, 'Yo tengo raices aqui' (I have roots here). A powerful element in British civilization that we have only scatteringly, for we are too mobile for it, is the belonging of many generations to the same plot of earth, roots going deeper and deeper."[64] Dobie thirsted for those same roots and worked to construct them through an Anglo-Texan national folklore, collecting tale after tale of "Texans out of the Old Rock" despite the incessant mobility he acknowledged there that precluded such roots in the soil. When lamenting the lack of roots, even when using the example of a Spanish-speaking acquaintance, Dobie fell back on the supposed British experience of ancient, organic community, effacing the fact that Texas had residents with deeper "raices" there than his own. Roy Bedichek, an Illinois transplant, also recognized the history of movement and human adaptation that belied ideas of *patria* as they related to Texas and titled his observations on the Texas coastal region *Karankaway Country*, after the territory's absent native inhabitants. What was "the Texan" in this context, and why did it continually invoke this national frame? A national character literature of Texas arose at mid-century to answer these questions.

The Dobie contingent's critical engagement with patriotism and the notion of the "un-American" ran headlong into a celebratory Americanism deployed to unify and discipline the public in the early years of the Cold War. The celebration–critique dialectic operative in American regionalism gave way by the late 1940s to a unitary definition of the American way of life as the paramount expression of human freedom and prosperity, a "city on a hill," in a world threatened by totalitarianism and want. As a space associated in the national mind with the rugged individualism of the frontier and the freedom of wide-open spaces, Texas served as a useful ideological marker of difference from the perceived collectivisms of Europe and Asia. The American national-character literature of the decade had a curious corollary in a cottage industry of books that investigated the "nation" of Texas. In lockstep, it would seem, with Daniel Boorstin's *The Genius of American Politics* (1953) and David Potter's *People of Plenty* (1954), came George Sessions Perry's *Texas: A World in Itself* (1942), Frank Goodwyn's *Lone Star Land: 20th Century Texas in Perspective*

(1955), George Fuermann's *Reluctant Empire: The Mind of Texas* (1957), Mary Lasswell's *I'll Take Texas* (1958), and John Bainbridge's *The Super-Americans* (1961).

It is worth examining some of these texts to trace their deployment of the Texan national frame. George Sessions Perry's *Texas: A World in Itself* provides a counterpoint in Texas letters by an author who focused on the state's Southern, rather than Western, experience. In *Reluctant Empire: The Mind of Texas*, George Fuermann, columnist for the *Houston Post*, leaped past the national metaphor to extend the state's imperial conceit, but did so with an appreciation for the changes that the past several years had visited on the state. Even as each highlighted aspects of the contemporary state not always visible in the Lone Star regionalist vein, though, both authors dedicated their works to J. Frank Dobie. Seeming to follow Perry's Southern stylings, Mary Lasswell's titular claim *I'll Take Texas* offered a variant of the Nashville Agrarians' *I'll Take My Stand*. And yet, Lasswell follows Fuermann in identifying the present as a welcome transition, and "the Texan" not as a stable, unitary figure on the verge of passing, but as a vessel of adaptation itself: "The more a Texan changes, the more he becomes truly himself. Change and adaptability are among his basic inherited patterns of behavior; resourcefulness is characteristic of him. The country itself is suddenly and violently changeable, often in clashing conflict with itself, elementally, spiritually, and physically, all at the same time, like a Texan's conflict between his pioneer past and his urban present."[65] Rather than strength-in-inflexibility, Lasswell fastens onto the frontier heritage to argue for adaptability as a central characteristic of Texas identity. She even equates these qualities with the land itself, executing an end run around the bucolic jeremiads that peek through so many of the Lone Star regionalists' works. The theme of change and adaptation fits Lasswell's biography. She was an author and humorist raised in the border town of Brownsville who prided herself on Texas roots while spending much of her life in Southern California and the Northeast.

Lasswell also attended to the performative aspects of the Texan, spending the better part of a chapter ("The Land and the Man") on the subject: "In his politeness, the Texan likes to do what is expected of him. He has been known to buy his first cowboy boots and ten-gallon hat for a trip to New York."[66] Like Webb with his Stetson in Oxford or, later, Larry L. King with his accent at Elaine's in Manhattan, Lasswell noted the phenomenon of Texans abroad performing to the cultural expectations of "the Texan" type. The performances of Texans on the national stage, in Lasswell's reading, fed a kind of existentialist need: "The myth of the Typical Texan seems to me to be the result of man's eternal desire to believe that there is in existence, somewhere, the man he would like to be: a man of super vitality, of monumental size, gargantuan appetites, and epic bravery."[67] Lasswell made clear the conflation of "the Texan" with frontier masculinity, even as she attended to the complexity of the figure's historic performativity. This "Typical Texan" did not denote specific men who actually existed, but a persona to be desired, a projection of the cowboy that individuals within and without the state's borders continually found ways to appropriate.

This appropriation fed a national market for all things Texan that produced the most popular of these national-character texts. In 1960, *New Yorker* contributor John Bainbridge spent a year in Texas to write a book on the foibles of the nouveau-riche oilmen then garnering the nation's attention. When *The Super-Americans* came out the following year, it was readily apparent that the book stood in the tradition of 1950s national-character studies, or even perhaps those early Boasian ethnographies of the exotic "other" meant largely to instruct Americans about themselves. In fact, though Bainbridge singled out Texas for a microcosmic study, he employed it consistently as a metonym for American values. Bainbridge contended that, culturally speaking, Texas occupied a symbolic space in relation to the rest of the country, just as the United States has traditionally stood in relation to Europe. He demonstrated the argument by presenting parallel accounts of traveling "foreigners." Alexis de Tocqueville and other European voyeurs of the American shadowed the narrative throughout and entered a conversation with Northerners, Frederick Law Olmsted prominent among them, visiting and commenting on Texas culture and mores: "The faults in Texas, as they are recorded by most visitors, are scarcely unfamiliar, for they are the same ones that Europeans have been taxing us with for some three hundred years: boastfulness, cultural underdevelopment, materialism, and all the rest. In enough ways to make it interesting, Texas is a mirror in which Americans see themselves reflected, not life-size, but, as in a distorting mirror, bigger than life."[68]

Bainbridge's account included discussions of the oil industry, travel, climate, and braggadocio, but he spent the greatest number of pages on Dallas, from architecture and Neiman Marcus to cocktail parties and politics. In retrospect, Bainbridge's playful indictment of the class of Dallas arrivistes gained more sinister tones through the city's association with the Kennedy assassination. His inclusion of George H. W. Bush as an exemplar of the Ivy League colonization of the Permian Basin in the early 1960s may have proven even more prescient.[69] However, Bainbridge's key contribution was in isolating the cultural work of "the Texan" as a means of thinking through "the American."

The Performative Texan in Politics

The performative dimensions of Texanness, amplified through film, music, and journalism, also resonated in the state's politics. Though politicians came primarily from the elite, deeply implicated in oil and urban finance, their efforts to brand themselves as "Texan" carried an investment in the cowboy image. Performing the cowboy for the electorate produced immediate recognition, but also raised questions concerning who "real" cowboys were, anyway. Angus Lauchlan has analyzed this tendency in the media of the period, citing a 1955 piece in the liberal *Texas Observer* that provided a guide to the authenticity of the state's various cowboys. "It all started with the cowhand," the *Observer* journalist begins. "You used to find him from Cuero in the east to Encinal in the south and Uvalde in the southwest to Pecos in the far west and then up north to Dalhart." The simple working cowboy with his "serviceable boots" is no longer the norm in 1950s Texas, however, as a series of senatorial, oilman, and chain-hotel cowboys have adopted and adapted the style. Such preeners, in this view, communicated an inauthentic Westernness through their Cuban cigars, ladylike boot-heels, stitched inlays, and Hollywood tailoring. Such sartorial creep has edged out the original cowhands: "Now we see our original cowhand riding into the west. Equipped with neither Havanas, sample case, nor Cadillac, he has become too conspicuous on the Texas scene, and that reserve which approaches bashfulness has caused him to move on to make room for the typical Texans who have taken his place."[70] Small distinctions in fashion and accessories—boots, shirts, tobacco—signified in the 1950s, just as they would for the cosmic cowboys of the 1970s, and critics in this period, as later, weighed those signs on the scale of authenticity and artifice. Here we see on display the tangle of gender, commerce, and performance that attends discussions of "the Texan" in political and cultural terms.

The debate over the cowboy guise often entered specific campaigns, as in the William Blakely–Ralph Yarborough senatorial race of 1958. By the 1950s, the fault lines originating in Roosevelt's New Deal and solidified by the 1946 Rainey–Jester gubernatorial primary had become a pitched intra-party battle between conservative Allan Shivers and liberal Ralph Yarborough, protégé of former governor James Allred. Shivers defeated Yarborough in gubernatorial primaries twice in the 1950s. Yarborough then filed for the senator's seat in 1958, facing William Blakeley, a conservative West Texas socialite who branded himself a cowboy. As Blakely and Yarborough squared off for the U.S. Senate in 1958, Dobie dissected Blakely's studied cowboy image:

He's a fake cowboy and he's a fake man in his pretenses to qualifications for being a United States Senator. . . . "If the day is come—and it seems it has—when the people of a local community—through sovereign state government—are denied the right to educate their children without interference from outside influence—then no freedom is left in the land." What does this mean? You could gather up all the cowboys who ever rode after Brahman-blooded cows over prairie grass along the Gulf of Mexico, who ever popped brush in the chaparral thickets of South Texas, who ever went up and down the breaks of the Pecos or the Double Mountain fork, who ever listened to northers whistle through their slickers on the Staked Plains, and even all the cowboys who have had the example of William Alvis Blakely on his own ranches. You could gather up all these cowboys and sift their brains and sift their language, you wouldn't find a single deceitful sentence like the one just quoted. It means, "I don't believe in letting Negroes into the schools with white people." Why doesn't he come out like a real cowboy and a real man and say what he means? . . . But he can't buy his way into the Senate of the United States because there are too many real people, including a considerable number of real cowboys, who know the difference between a genuine article and a fake.[71]

In a letter of July 22, Bedichek voiced his approval: "You were never more authentically the 'voice of Texas' than you are in blasting that blatherskite Blakely."[72] These attentions to the demonstrative power of the cowboy figure, and the contestation over its uses, bring into view a range of anxieties concerning Texan masculinities of the era in the context of rapid social change.

What Fuermann, Lasswell, and Blakely's victorious opponent Yarborough recognized, and what political cowboys like Blakely did not belabor, was the ongoing transformation of Texas into an urban state. This recognition would characterize the best of the cultural productions to come out of Texas in the 1960s and 1970s, beginning perhaps with Billy Lee Brammer's exemplary 1961 novel *The Gay Place*. Brammer had been a young aide to both Ralph Yarborough and Lyndon Johnson in Washington, and *The Gay Place* offered a melancholy comedy of manners in which Austin's young liberals, roustabouts, politicians, and bohemians navigated the tricky terrain of the new modern Texas. Brammer placed one of the novel's key arguments in the mouth of Governor Arthur Fenstemaker, a caricature of Brammer's former boss Lyndon Johnson. Fenstemaker exclaims of a political opponent that "he's way ahead of some of his people, but what he doesn't know is that most of us came into town one Saturday a few years ago and stayed. . . . We're urban, by God. All of a sudden the people in the metropolitan areas outnumber the rednecks."[73]

Over and against the striving, frontiering, yet somehow bucolic world of the ranges of South and West Texas, a new cultural formation arose in the cities that came to be seen as a threat to these older ways. Fenstemaker's model LBJ fit well the part of contrarian symbol of Anglo-Texan masculinity.

Indeed, Lyndon Johnson provides the touchstone and apotheosis for the burlesque performance of Anglo-Texan masculinity on the national stage. Picking up his dog by the ears, showing abdominal scars to reporters, speaking to aides from the toilet, reeling off lewd folk sayings, Lyndon Baines Johnson fit the character of "the Texan," deploying braggadocio to mitigate or perhaps subvert feelings of inferiority to Eastern elites. Son of the soil and consummate professional Texan, Johnson served as the complex marker of the state's transformation, a key leader and instrument in forging the Sunbelt Synthesis that brought industry, scientific research, and federal defense and aerospace projects south. Far more than Nixon's supposed "Southern strategy," Johnson set in motion the region's political realignment not just through signing the Civil Rights Act, but also through the momentous shifts in political economy that his administration accelerated.[74]

Though the JFK assassination branded Dallas a hotbed of right-wing reaction, Johnson combined Kennedy's agenda with his own legislative acumen to crown the New Frontier with the even more ambitious Great Society. He did this despite, or perhaps with, the strategic deployment of his performative image as buffoonish Texan. Johnson made frequent and sentimental use of his Hill Country forebears in Texas, establishing the first of the Western White Houses on a sprawling ranch near Stonewall. The president entertained there with barbecues, country music, and elaborate tours of the grounds. Richard "Cactus" Pryor, who worked for the Johnsons' media holdings in Central Texas, served as organizer and emcee for many of the events at the ranch. He described the flavor of one barbecue held for United Nations dignitaries during Johnson's term as vice president: "One could hardly escape the traditions of Texas. They were unavoidable. You had but to turn around and a member of the Travis County Sheriff's Posse would come charging up on a palomino to volunteer his services. . . . There was a real western band playing the old cowboy songs of Texas. I know they were real cowboy songs because I spent half the preceding night teaching them to our 'real western band.'" The event also featured a bullwhip demonstration by a UT co-ed, a sharpshooter who made the Secret Service visibly uncomfortable, an exhibit by a renowned painter of bluebonnet landscapes, and a monkey in cowboy duds herding sheep from the back of a dog.[75] As Anglo-Texan men affiliated with LBJ climbed the political ladder to be the movers and shakers in Washington, "the Texan" was constructed for audiences—local, national, and international—in purposive ways. "The Texan" was performed and performing, articulating a sense of national difference for the Lone Star State, but one still very much limited to a certain segment of Texan society.

Between Two Worlds: Race and the Assimilationist Dilemma, 1936–1968

"In your native homeland a stranger you will be by the law of the rifle and the law of cold steel." Américo Paredes began the poem "Alma pocha" with these words in the centennial year of 1936 before continuing, "And if perhaps you do survive, it will be without pride, with bitter remembrances of what was once yours; your lands, your skies, your birds, your flowers will be the delight of the invaders."[76] With these lines, Paredes offered a very different take on the Texas centennial than that of J. Frank Dobie or Gene Autry or Franklin Roosevelt. A young man in Brownsville when he composed "Alma pocha," Paredes stood at the beginning of a momentous career. As a journalist, musician, activist, folklorist, and cultural studies scholar, he would challenge the celebratory Anglo-Texan nationalism of the Lone Star regionalists at their high tide. In light of Dobie's remark that a love of native birds should be the true mark of patriotic loyalty, Paredes's exhortation that "your lands, your skies, your birds, your flowers will be the delight of the invaders" draws our attention to the blind spots belying the Lone Star regionalists' attempts to bind men and soil— "Texans out of the Old Rock." The "Empire of Texas" Roosevelt saluted in 1936 rested on the historical conquest of Mexican and Native American populations and the enslavement and exploitation of African Americans. Texas politics and public culture had made this hierarchy seem second nature to many Anglo-Texans by the early twentieth century, but the agency of those thus disfranchised would not allow for the persistence of such ruling assumptions.

This section explores the social movements that African Americans and Mexican Americans waged against the Anglo establishment in Texas from the 1940s to the 1960s. In the context of this study's focus on historicizing Anglo-Texan masculinity, the current section sketches a moment in the dialectical development of a culture. In other words, events like the Centennial Exposition elaborated a thesis to which individuals like Américo Paredes antithetically responded.[77] The resulting struggle over the nature of Texan identities enabled the later synthetic endeavors of the Austin counterculture to re-tool the cultural projection of Anglo-Texan masculinity in light of these subaltern critiques.

Disfranchised groups in Texas had always contested power over the cultural field in a manner that ratified E. P. Thompson's definition of culture as "the study of relationships in a whole way of conflict."[78] The hegemonic force of Anglo-Texan masculinity endured long periods of subterranean resistance punctuated by instances of vocal protest or outright revolt. The openings brought by protest and revolt, however, were likely to be temporary ones that provoked a redoubling of oppressive Anglo rule. After the Civil War, freedmen sought redress for slavery through racial equality in Radical Reconstruction, only to be reduced to secondary citizenship after the Redeemers drove Governor Edmund Davis from office and marginalized the Republican Party.[79] In the 1890s, Populist activism promised to reduce the burdens and defuse the racial caste of the exploitive tenancy system, only to spark the near-complete disfranchisement of African American voters at the turn of the twentieth century.[80] In South Texas, from Juan Cortina in 1859 to the sediciosos in 1915, tejanos forcefully reclaimed their lands and their rights again and again, only to face military defeat and brutal suppression by Texas Rangers.[81] Periods of reform and revolt thus alternated with periods of serious repression, and Anglo-Texan men retained their authority over political institutions, economic resources, and, key to this study, the cultural projection of "the Texan" that ideologically bound these spheres together.

In the wake of World War II, however, a number of historical factors converged to create an opening unlike those prior periods of protest and revolt, rendering the full exercise of formal, equal citizenship attainable. First, the experiences of African American and Mexican American soldiers in war and those of women in the home-front workforce gave a sense of participation and hard-won entitlement to previously disfranchised groups. Second, the Cold War context of global ideological conflict made obvious inequalities embarrassing for a United States that had so recently defeated Nazism abroad, strengthening the will of the federal government to bring the Jim Crow South in line with constitutional norms.[82] Third, changes in agriculture that hobbled the semifeudal order of the Southern countryside in the 1930s and 1940s drew people to the freewheeling atmosphere of the cities in which organization and activism proved more feasible.[83] Along with and spurred by all these factors, a generation of committed and able activists contributed to the long rights revolution of the 1940s to the 1970s.

These movements would define the state's cultural politics in the 1970s, and to understand that era's revision of "the Texan," it is first necessary to frame these movements' expansion of who could lay claim to Texanness in the public sphere. In the years following World War II, middle-class movements for racial equality in the African American and Mexican American communities of Texas broadly sought integration into and assimilation with the political and cultural mainstream. In that moment, such assimilation meant dealing with the Lone Star regionalist cohort that typically regarded the whiteness, and often the masculinity, of "the Texan" as the natural spoils of martial victory over the state's prior stewards. Critiques of this notion tended to remain either counternarratives outside the public sphere or, if they erupted into intellectual and political debate, often had a deferential cast. Jim Crow laws largely prevented African Americans from speaking truth to power in the universities or state capital but the porous boundaries of whiteness allowed some Mexican Americans, inflected through class hierarchies, a voice in Texas institutions of learning and politics. As early as the 1920s, J. Frank Dobie trained Jovita González, the first Mexican American woman to receive a master's degree from the University of Texas and the first woman to head Dobie's Texas Folklore Society. She was among the first Mexican Americans to turn the academic folkloric gaze to the borderlands in a wide range of articles and short stories.

Another Dobie associate who brought a borderlands critique into the Lone Star regionalist circle was state representative J. T. Canales of Brownsville. Canales represented well the tensions visited on leaders in the Mexican American community. With a South Texas lineage dating back to the Spanish land grants, Canales had worked in ranching in Texas, Oklahoma, and Kansas, gone to college in Austin and Ann Arbor, and both clashed with and participated in Jim Wells's political machine in Cameron County. During the sedicioso uprising just prior to American involvement in World War I, Canales served as a commander of a Mexican American scouting unit for the U.S. Army, but he was also one of the few Mexican American politicians to criticize the Texas Rangers' overwhelming, violent response to the incident.[84]

Canales underscored the continuous history of Texas Mexicans in the border region that, by the measures of the 1848 Treaty of Guadalupe Hidalgo, gave them an undeniable claim on U.S. citizenship and its attendant rights. To this end, Canales authored much of the founding constitution of the League of United Latin American Citizens and helped establish the organization's early prioritization of Mexican American claims on U.S. citizenship.[85] During the 1950s, Canales penned both the two-volume *Bits of Texas History in the Melting Pot of America* (1950, 1957) and *Juan Cortina: Bandit or Patriot?* (1951). Both works carefully rebutted Anglo-Texan triumphalist history in keeping with the cultural pluralist ideology of early LULAC. Despite this apparent caution, Canales did not shrink from disagreeing with prominent Anglo academics on interpretations of the South Texas past. For example, Canales once wrote Dobie on the subject of Juan Cortina, a prominent rancher who, briefly, took the city of Brownsville by force in 1859 in response to repeated Anglo violations of Mexican American rights:

> My dear friend "don Pancho" Dobie: Several years ago you and I had a conversation about Juan N. Cortina in your office. I called to your attention what I thought were some unfair statements in your book "A Vaquero of the Brush Country" about Cortina and showed you some documents which made you say "I thought I had read everything about Cortina that was ever written but of these I did not know." . . . My relative, Cortina, was not a saint, but neither was he a "bandit" in the real sense of the term; or a thief. . . . He was a disillusioned and, perhaps, a misguided reformer, who was unfortunate in wrongfully taking the law in his own hands to vindicate what he conceived to be his rights.[86]

Canales addressed these concerns at length in *Juan Cortina: Bandit or Patriot?*, reclaiming a forebear delegitimized by the catchall "bandit" slur for Canales's own project of placing Texas Mexicans squarely as defenders of American constitutional rights. Such compatriots as González and Canales offered some critique from within the Dobie version of "the Texan," but their differences could also strengthen Dobie's intellectual hand through their continued public deference to his leadership.

Such deference issued in part from political, financial, and bureaucratic matters relating to the University of Texas, which had made Dobie's cohort gatekeepers in academic publishing and professional development. But affairs in the academy would not always be so. As the post–World War II period progressed, discourses of resistance entered the public sphere in new and meaningful ways. Coming close on the heels of Canales's cautious debates with Dobie, the significance of Américo Paredes's more forceful historical critique cannot be underestimated. In the late 1950s, Paredes moved beyond the cautious tone of gentle nudging to outright confrontation in *With His Pistol in His Hand: A Border Ballad and Its Hero* (1958). The book examined the *corrido* "The Ballad of Gregorio Cortez," a song about a man accused of a crime he did not commit. In June 1901, a stolen horse in Karnes County led Sheriff Brack Morris to the home of Gregorio Cortez, who was rumored to have just such a new horse. He did, in fact, but it was one legitimately acquired. However, the language barrier between Sheriff Morris and Gregorio Cortez led Cortez to answer "no" when asked if he had a new horse. After more mistranslations, a firefight ensued in which Morris drew his gun on the Cortez brothers and was shot and killed by Gregorio in return. Cortez fled, and almost made it to the border before being apprehended. Governor Oscar Colquitt pardoned Cortez in 1913 due to political pressure, and Cortez left for Mexico shortly thereafter.

Paredes's book began by tracing the region's and Cortez's history, but more important, it explicated the song craft, folklore, and legend that developed around Cortez's accusation, stand, and flight. In intellectual terms, Paredes's book revolutionized folkloric work in the state. Early in *With His Pistol in His Hand* he included a chapter very much in the Dobie vein, recounting the Cortez legend just as it was told in the campfire settings with which Dobie was so enamored. "They still sing of him," begins the chapter titled "The Legend," "in the ranches when men gather at night to talk in the cool dark, sitting in a circle, smoking and listening to the old songs and tales of other days. Then the guitarreros sing of the border raids and the skirmishes, of the men who lived by the phrase, 'I will break before I bend.'"[87] So far, Paredes has done a passable impression of Dobie. He quickly moves on from this voice, though, to tell the story as an academic folklorist and ethnomusicologist, listing different variants of the corrido of Gregorio Cortez and speculating on their social evolution, and how that evolution reflected the needs of the communities in which the song traveled.

This social context, and its explicit critique of reigning borderlands historiography, made *With His Pistol in His Hand* a metaphorical call to arms. In the work Paredes also took a stand for his rights, through a withering critique of the dominant Dobie–Webb interpretation of Texas history then at the height of its powers. Walter Prescott Webb came in for the more devastating criticism, brought on by the racism of his celebratory account of the Texas Rangers. It is worth quoting Paredes's sarcastic introduction of the Webb legend early in the book. While outlining the status of mainstream historiography on Texas Mexicans, Paredes quoted from Webb's *The Texas Rangers*:

> Without disparagement, it may be said that there is a cruel streak in the Mexican nature, or so the history of Texas would lead one to believe. This cruelty may be a heritage from the Spanish of the Inquisition; it may, and doubtless should, be attributed partly to the Indian blood . . . the Mexican warrior . . . was, on the whole, inferior to the Comanche and wholly unequal to the Texan. The whine of the leaden slugs stirred in him an irresistible impulse to travel with rather than against the music. . . . For making promises—and for breaking them—he had no peer.

After the quote, Paredes continued, "Professor Webb does not mean to be disparaging. One wonders what his opinion might have been when he was in a less scholarly mood and not looking at the Mexican from the objective point of view of the historian."[88] Though Webb was an economic populist and a self-declared progressive, Paredes easily reveals the hypocrisy of the historian's pretense to racial liberalism. In the late 1950s, a decade when the fight for racial equality still faced an uphill battle in the public eye, Paredes confidently presented Webb's words as obviously false. It was an assertive move, for Webb was still a professor of history and famed public intellectual at Paredes's University of Texas. Indeed, when Webb died in a car crash in 1963, the student newspaper the *Daily Texan* ran it as the cover story, with a doctored photo of an ethereal Webb floating above the campus. Accompanying the picture were gushing testimonials from academic peers as well as Vice President Lyndon Johnson and Senators John Tower and Ralph Yarborough.[89] Such were the dense social networks of the Anglo-Texan hold on cultural production in the capital city of Austin, and the unified field of cultural power that critics such as Paredes confronted.

Paredes also assailed J. Frank Dobie's paternalism, a man he rather magnanimously considered "a very lovable old fraud."[90] As early as the 1930s, Paredes had parodied Dobie as the character K. Hank Harvey in his novel *George Washington Gómez*, though that work was not published until 1990.[91] In private, Paredes mocked Dobie's "expert" status on the borderlands in view of his abysmal Spanish, a situation that might account for Dobie's remark to Canales, "I thought I had read everything about Cortina that was ever written but of these I did not know." On the occasions in which Paredes and Dobie met in person, they did not discuss border folklore. Paredes felt that this was due to Dobie's embarrassment for what he knew he did not know.[92] So, with Webb branded a villain and Dobie a fraud, Paredes forcefully opened the way for new visions of the Texas past that took account of a much greater number of its inhabitants.[93]

Paredes's academic work arrived just as the African American and Mexican American civil rights movements had begun to command national attention. Though Paredes pointed the way forward to the nationalist tones of the later Chicano movement, his immediate intellectual and activist cohort worked toward the more liberal goal of assimilation of Americans of Mexican origin through full access to U.S. citizenship and establishing "Mexican American" as akin to an immigrant ethnicity rather than racialized other.[94] The genesis of this Mexican American Generation, as Mario García has labeled them, lay in the defeat of the sedicioso movement in 1915, the last movement of open, violent resistance seeking to reclaim sovereignty over South Texas. This development led the Mexican American middle class in South Texas to organize first in the League of United Latin American Citizens in 1929, then in the American GI Forum in 1948, to assert U.S. citizenship rights rather than contest the sovereignty of South Texas.[95] These organizations, even in their names, ratified the categories of Anglo-Texan nationality by appealing to masculine, martial tradition and replacing the charged term "Mexican" with "Latin" to defray the deeply ingrained antagonisms in the rhetorical constructions of early Texas history.

African American activism progressed along similar lines in Texas. Just as LULAC and the American GI Forum spoke the language of respectable Cold War Americanism, the NAACP followed existing legal channels to establish full constitutional rights to citizenship. In *Smith v. Allwright* (1944) and *Sweatt v. Painter* (1950), the Supreme Court handed down two Texas-based decisions instrumental in the abolition of the South's Jim Crow legal structure.[96] The level of organization required to put forth defendants in such cases was, to some extent, more readily available in Texas in the 1940s than in the Deep South states of Mississippi or Alabama. Texas was not racially liberal, by any means. However, the issue of segregation was slightly less of a third rail in Texas politics, and a black middle class with a pronounced sense of civic engagement had grown up in the major cities, especially Houston and Dallas.[97]

In the first of these two cases, *Smith v. Allwright*, the Supreme Court struck down the all-white Democratic primary that essentially determined political power in the one-party states of the South. Though local authorities continued to obstruct African American voting through other means prior to the Voting Rights Act of 1965, the tide had turned. Intensive activism and personal sacrifice in the Deep South continued to push against the strongest redoubts of white supremacist reaction, widening the openings that cases such as *Smith v. Allwright* afforded. Shortly after *Smith v. Allwright* augured changes in Southern voting rights, *Sweatt v. Painter* provided a needed wedge in the desegregation of schools by striking down the separate-but-equal doctrine in graduate and professional education. Heman Sweatt applied to the University of Texas Law School in 1946 and was denied admission on account of race. Often portrayed as a "postal worker from Houston," Sweatt was also an educator who had spent some years in Ann Arbor, an occasional writer for the African American *Houston Informer*, and a backer of the NAACP who took an interest in the suits the organization was bringing against the Jim Crow laws. This included *Smith v. Allwright*, which led to Sweatt's desire to study law. He sued for admission in a case argued before the Supreme Court by Thurgood Marshall along the same lines as the later *Brown v. Board of Education* (1954).[98] Not only was there no separate law school for blacks, Marshall argued, but even if such a school were to exist, it could not be considered equal to the prestigious faculty and social contacts afforded by the University of Texas Law School. The Supreme Court found in Sweatt's favor, and the new dean of the Law School, W. Page Keeton, admitted him in 1950.[99] Sweatt endured threats on his life, vandalism of his property, heart attack, ulcers, divorce, and an appendectomy upon entering law school. Under such pressures, he eventually withdrew without completing his degree. Nevertheless, the Rubicon had been crossed, and the integration of the University of Texas proceeded at all levels, unevenly but apace, with the first black undergraduates matriculating in 1956.

In that same year, the governor of Texas resisted the integration of public high schools. Two years after *Brown*, Governor Allan Shivers briefly allied the Texas government with the strategy of massive resistance to integration. In Mansfield, Texas, a standoff arose when a federal court called on the Mansfield School District to allow African American students to attend the public high school in the small town southeast of Fort Worth. Indeed, the Mansfield incident prefigured the events at Central High School in Little Rock, Arkansas, the following year. In this instance, however, the federal government did not intervene. The Justice Department did not act even after Texas Rangers arrived to "keep order" by preventing the attendance of African American students.[100] The reason for federal inaction, historians argue, was Governor Shivers's support of the Republican Eisenhower in the presidential election. The governor's apostasy in breaking from the Democratic Solid South, in this view, earned him leeway on civil rights issues not accorded to Orval Faubus.[101] The Mansfield model did not hold, however, as centrists allied with Lyndon Johnson wrested control of the state Democratic Party that same year, marginalizing the Shivercrat right wing and its preference for massive resistance. School integration remained uneven in the state, but the drama of Mansfield would not often be repeated.

In all, the civil rights era of the 1940s, 1950s, and 1960s produced stirring victories and raised hopes for the substantial and rapid achievement of equality. The national narratives of *Brown*, sit-ins, SNCC, freedom rides, and voter registration had their Texan versions not only in victories like *Smith v. Allwright* and *Sweatt v. Painter*, and the massive resistance to integration at Mansfield, but in the parallel struggle of Mexican Americans through the Felix Longoria affair in Three Rivers and Paredes's intellectual revolt at the University of Texas.[102] The hopes generated by such an accelerated pace of change in the early postwar years created a climate ripe for frustration in instances where change was not so forthcoming. Entry into schools and voting booths did not deliver urban neighborhoods from poverty, end the corruption whereby Anglo political machines ruled the border counties, or bring the Anglo mainstream to recognize the positive value of cultural difference. Activists broached new approaches and new ideas to meet these frustrations, and the resulting atmosphere of cultural nationalism would have distinct ramifications for the Anglo-Texans' own brand of metaphorical nationality. As the vanguardist 1960s gave way to the 1970s, all Texans and "Texans" came to engage the new terrains and textures of identity, political economy, popular culture, and lifestyle, a story that will fill the remainder of this book.

In the final chapter of *Adventures with a Texas Naturalist*, Roy Bedichek described a chance meeting in the Texas Hill Country with an old man clearing the land of cedar. The primal man in the wilderness, alone on the frontier, the Texan out of the Old Rock, made Bedichek feel as if his own virility was fading. The vanishing Texan of this Hill Country cedar-chopper stands in marked contrast to the performances Cactus Pryor described at Lyndon Johnson's Western White House. Bedichek's cedar-chopper "couldn't do anything but cut cedar, since that was all he had ever done except to farm a little. I found that he was eighty-six years old and that here in this locality his father had put him to cutting cedar when he was only ten."[103] This meeting, for Bedichek, underscored his theorized connection between man, labor, and land, a life spent in relation to a specific Texas place; the Western White House bespoke spectacle, a simulacrum of the landed rancher woven around a powerful man who had found a very different place in the world from where he was born. And yet, Johnson, too, had his moments as the "Texan alone," a cedar-chopper on the verge of a political wilderness. One such night arrived on March 31, 1968, when Johnson shocked national television audiences by announcing that he would not seek a second term in office due to the pressures of the Vietnam conflict. Five days later, James Earl Ray assassinated Martin Luther King Jr. in Memphis, and the liberal center forged in the Great Depression, tested, expanded, and strained in the Great Society overseen by Johnson and the civil rights movement led by King, seemed to unravel all at once. The representation and performance of Anglo-Texan masculinity as a cipher for American national identity had served as one element in that vital center's rise and fall. Dismantling and re-visioning the hegemony of Anglo-Texan masculinity in Texas itself served as another.

Home with the Armadillo

AUSTIN'S PROGRESSIVE COUNTRY MUSIC SCENE

Lyndon Baines Johnson's political immolation in 1968 and death in 1973 punctuated a span of years that found the state of Texas, and the symbolic "Texan," in an interesting moment of transition. All history traffics in transitions, of course. The present always constitutes a pivot between past and future, defined by change rather than stasis. It is the particular textures of the transition, then, that matter. Bedichek turned to a lone cedar-chopper to express a sense of the vanishing Texan out of the Old Rock. Those present at the moment of Johnson's passing could see this consummate modern politician, who won his first Senate race traveling around the state in a helicopter while his opponent, Coke Stevenson, chatted with folks on the courthouse squares, as himself a sign of the traditional Texas fading from view.

Jan Reid's 1974 book *The Improbable Rise of Redneck Rock* charted this particular transition through the medium of Austin's progressive country music scene and the return of youthful audiences to a genre that many had rejected in the culture wars of the 1960s. The young journalist talked about much more than music, though. One chapter, in fact, opens with Reid narrating a visit to the Hill Country town of Luckenbach on the day of Johnson's funeral. "LBJ was an enigma to most Texans under thirty, an awesome figure full of stupefying contradictions," Reid wrote.[1] The year of Johnson's death held its fair share of such stupefying contradictions and strange coincidences, and the weeks surrounding his demise saw their fair share of history. Johnson died at his ranch on January 22, 1973, the same day the Supreme Court issued its 7–2 ruling in *Roe v. Wade*. Johnson's funeral cortege proceeded through the Texas Hill Country on January 25, just two days before the signing of the Paris Peace Accords between the United States and Vietnam. The war that mired Johnson's presidency died with him. As the nation became more acquainted with President Nixon, and the New Left's energies seemed to dissipate, some began to re-evaluate Johnson. For Texans, the sentiments could be quite contrarian. As Jan Reid wrote, "Many of them had cursed and hated Johnson at times, but he was still the mightiest of Texans. At times he had been an almost comic figure, an unwitting butt of those jokes that typecast Texans as blundering, foolish braggarts, but he also symbolized times that were changing, even in Texas. For all his faults, he was one of them."²

Reid failed to make it to the burial at the Johnson ranch that day, sufficiently unnerved by the spectacle to veer off the road to Luckenbach. The town proprietor and poet Hondo Crouch had turned the Hill Country hideaway into a gathering place for storytellers, musicians, and assorted misfits. Once Reid arrived, Crouch and other older area residents shared with him memories of the Johnson they had known before he became a national figure, personal reflections otherwise lost to the depths of time: "Listen, little buddy, I don't know you, but I knew LBJ all his life. The only time he ever had a lick of sense was when Court Mortimer knocked him off that jackass with a lunch pail."³ By 1977, a hit song performed by Waylon Jennings would make Luckenbach synonymous with the kind of pastoral escape Reid sought that day and found, a place to get "back to the basics of life," but here at the beginning of 1973 Luckenbach stood on the cusp of its fame, much as did the Central Texas scene as a whole.

Jerry Jeff Walker's album *Viva Terlingua*, recorded at Luckenbach and released later in 1973, stood very near the center of these events, one of a series of records that captured the developing Austin sound. The year 1973 also saw the release of Willie Nelson's *Shotgun Willie*, the first of the singer's collaborations with producer Jerry Wexler; Doug Sahm's *Doug Sahm and Band*, another Wexler production on Atlantic Records featuring all-star sidemen Bob Dylan, Fathead Newman, David Bromberg, Dr. John, and Flaco Jiménez; Waylon Jennings's *Honky Tonk Heroes*; the debut albums of Asleep at the Wheel, Kinky Friedman, and Billy Joe Shaver; B. W. Stevenson's commercial breakthrough *My Maria*; and Michael Murphey's *Cosmic Cowboy Souvenir*, an album that, for better or worse, gave the scene one of its enduring monikers. Taken together, these 1973 albums would exert a distinctive influence on the course of popular music, sketching the contours of a "progressive country" sound associated with Texas and situating Austin in an American soundscape linked to the sensibilities of Laurel Canyon country-rock, boisterous Southern rock, and the new wave of Nashville singer–songwriters.

This chapter explores the rise of Austin's music scene as a significant aural dimension of the broader cultural transformations affecting Texas in the 1970s. Popular music remains the most visible, or more to the point, audible, artifact of this rich cultural moment, literally resonating every time a classic country station plays Willie's version of "Blue Eyes Crying in the Rain" or a Jerry Jeff Walker audience sings along with "Up Against the Wall (Redneck Mother)." For this reason, I will use this chapter to explore the subject of progressive country music and its relation to Texanness before proceeding in the chapters that follow to discuss the wider milieu. The soundtrack produced here will then inform the subsequent evolution of the symbolic "Texan" in the decade, the styles, gestures, literary endeavors, and politics that situated the cowboy figure in the larger conversation of the American search for meaning in the 1970s. Those who invoke Tom Wolfe's branding of these years as the "Me Decade" tend to focus on the fixation with hedonism, celebrity, and sexuality, or what Christopher Lasch termed the era's "culture of narcissism." However, the larger thrust of Wolfe's satire aimed at the elevated role of the quest for meaning and the authentic self in the 1970s, an endeavor equally born from evangelical Christian sects and the "free to be me" counterculture.[4] Anglo-Texans' fascination with regional identity—the vocal insistence on the distinctiveness of "the Texan," accompanied by persistent fears that that distinctiveness was being erased by modernization—might seem at first glance to be far removed from this larger American frame. But just as Bainbridge in the 1960s saw in Anglo-Texan identity a kind of "Super-American," so did Texas experience a kind of "Super-Seventies" in which it continued to serve as a distorted mirror for the American zeitgeist. Progressive country's interest in place, the past, craft, and the pastoral speaks to a certain seventies sensibility that prized rootedness and tradition, even as it communicated those ideas through a ceaseless experimentation with self and performance through rituals of consumption.

The story of the modern Austin music scene's origins has been told often and well, most recently by Travis Stimeling in *Cosmic Cowboys and New Hicks: The Countercultural Sounds of Austin's Progressive Country Music Scene*. It is not my intention to supersede such tellings so much as to help place them in new contexts. By highlighting the migration and mutual influence of artists alongside the 1970s scene's celebration of "the Texan," I hope to render Austin an inextricable part of state and national historical narratives often at odds with the scene's exceptionalist bluster.[5] Austin's self-promotion can often blur its connections to outside scenes and trends. At the height of the period under study, Larry McMurtry wrote, "If I were to choose one example of the Texas penchant for ludicrously overestimating local achievement, my example would certainly be the city of Austin."[6] The critique is fair enough, and the penchant has only increased over time. Austin's significance should not be overlooked, however, as it has become an important center in the production and promotion of popular music, host to the annual South by Southwest music conference, the PBS artist showcase program *Austin City Limits*, and the self-declared "Live Music Capital of the World."

The city's meteoric ascent to this status was by no means obvious. Houston, Dallas–Fort Worth, and San Antonio were and are the state's population centers, and each possessed a more substantial musical history than Austin through the 1960s. Dallas's Deep Ellum district produced some of the earliest blues recording stars, most notably Blind Lemon Jefferson, and young white blues musicians from Dallas and Fort Worth would later cement what came to be known as the Austin blues scene.[7] Houston had long been a center of recording and performance that drew on the cotton-producing areas of the Brazos River Valley, the oilfield towns of the Golden Triangle, and the creole and Cajun Louisiana borderlands. Bill Quinn's Gold Star Records produced Harry Choates, Lightnin' Hopkins, George Jones, the Big Bopper, and Roy Head, and was among the first to record Willie Nelson's compositions in Claude Gray's version of "Family Bible" and Ray Price's rendition of "Night Life." Don Robey's Peacock Records formed in the late 1940s to record Clarence "Gatemouth" Brown, the headliner for Robey's Bronze Peacock nightclub in the city's Third Ward. After acquiring Memphis-based Duke Records, Robey's labels could count between them such stars as Bobby Bland, Big Mama Thornton, Lavelle White, the Dixie Hummingbirds, and the Mighty Clouds of Joy. San Antonio would remain the capital of tejano music, catering to a South Texas hinterland dense with musical hot spots such as Discos Ideal in Alice and Falcon Records in Del Rio. Further, San Antonio and Fort Worth easily rivaled 1960s Austin as garage rock scenes. Lubbock and West Texas, too, claim a rich musical history that encompasses an array of country and rockabilly leading lights. However, Austin came to serve as a magnet for a youth audience and a countercultural style that drew many musical artists from each of these centers, and from others nationwide.

"Onward Through the Fog!": Austin Counterculture

The state's numerically small and embattled counterculture entered the public eye, and ear, along several often-unexpected fronts. For most of the 1960s, voyeuristic critics controlled how that counterculture came to be seen. As late as 1969, H. L. Hunt's conservative radio program *Life Line* blasted hippies over the airwaves, fearing the invasion of grubby hordes during the Texas International Pop Festival in Lewisville outside Dallas. Organizer Angus Wynne III had booked Led Zeppelin, Santana, Grand Funk Railroad, B. B. King, and others just two weeks after Woodstock, and, *Life Line*'s threats aside, the concert proceeded without widespread disruption to the social fabric. National acts came to Texas, then, in the year that Woodstock Nation was born. This involved chickens coming home to roost, though, as Texas had already exported some of the counterculture's leading acts. In retrospect, Austin's musical cachet derived not just from its association with blues maven Janis Joplin. The city also served as the home of the 13th Floor Elevators led by Tommy Hall and Roky Erickson, pioneers of a searing, strange psychedelic rock with Roky's soaring vocals and Tommy's bizarre electric jug taking listeners into an auditory equivalent of the psychedelic experience. But there is much more to the Austin story than that, and the broader scene often tells us more than do its leading lights.

As fitting a beginning to the story of the Austin counterculture as Joplin's singing at the folk nights at Threadgill's or Erickson lifting the roof off of the teen club the Jade Room might be the moment in 1966 when Joe Brown, Tony Bell, and Gilbert Shelton, associated with the UT humor magazine the *Texas Ranger*, founded the Underground City Hall downtown. It was a hip "head" shop, but also the site for the fictive gubernatorial campaign of Oat Willie. Oat Willie was a large-nosed, sunken-chested, shirtless man with feet permanently fused in a bucket of oatmeal on wheels. Gilbert Shelton also created the superheroics of Wonder Warthog and the soon-to-be-famous Fabulous Furry Freak Brothers, but Oat Willie, a onetime University of Texas student of Tex-German extraction who supposedly moved to Austin during the drought of the 1950s and underwent his transformation after Kennedy's assassination, would endure as one of his odder creations. Oat Willie's ever-present rallying cry surely made sense to the growing counterculture in the state capital at a time of dizzying social and political change: "Onward through the fog!"[8]

The 1960s counterculture altered the production, presentation, and master narrative of American popular music, and Austin, Texas, claims itself as a significant site of this transformation. In the 1960s, Austin served as both a node of the New Left, with one of the nation's largest chapters of Students for a Democratic Society, and a point of origin for many developments more commonly associated with San Francisco, including the pioneering psychedelic rock of the 13th Floor Elevators, the "kozmic" blues of Janis Joplin, and the underground comics of Gilbert Shelton and Jack Jackson. As with other college communities across the country, a strong Austin–San Francisco migration stream buttressed developments in both communities. Roky Erickson, Avalon Ballroom proprietor Chet Helms, Jack Jackson, Janis Joplin, Augie Meyers, Dave Moriaty, Doug Sahm, Powell St. John, and Gilbert Shelton, among others, all participated in forging the sixties counterculture in its Haight-Ashbury crucible.[9]

Austin in the early 1960s had nurtured a small group of nonconformists who participated in a stew of folk music, civil rights activism, and left-wing politics. This conglomeration stood in opposition to the town's basic conservatism. However, the incipient hippie–redneck trope of the progressive country years also pointed a way to transcending this opposition by declaring the counterculture's allegiance to the presumably authentic expressions of Texas tradition. This sense provided one of the sparks to the folksinging nights at the much-storied venue Threadgill's, a service station and bar on the northern edge of town where proprietor and Jimmie Rodgers acolyte Kenneth Threadgill invited old friends and talented students to celebrate folk, country, and bluegrass music. Threadgill's came to be known as a space where traditional working-class Anglo musicians like Bill Neely (and Threadgill himself) consorted with University of Texas students interested in the folk revival, like folklorist Roger Abrahams, country music historian Bill Malone, musicians Lanny Wiggins, Janis Joplin, Powell St. John, and others. As Joplin's biographer Alice Echols parses the Threadgill's scene, "In more urban places like Cambridge, Berkeley, and Greenwich Village the search for authenticity led folk music mavens to seek out obscure records and songbooks. But in Austin authenticity was considerably less hard to come by. Texas was a region still alive with 'real' music, including country and western. 'It was less academic for us,' says [Threadgill's regular Stephanie] Chernikowski, 'because we were living in the past.'"[10] Tricky assertions of authenticity aside, such sentiments display the temporal–spatial dimension of American regionalism, the notion that the provinces remember what the metropolis forgot long ago.

In this, Austin developed along similar lines as other "provincial" scenes even as it dovetailed with the national narrative of the counterculture. When Bob Dylan launched his infamously ill-received electric tour in 1965, his first engagement brought him to Austin. A native Austinite of the Lone Star regionalist circles, Alan Lomax, had recoiled at Dylan's earlier electric turn at the Newport Folk Festival, writing home to Cactus Pryor that "Bobby Dillon [sic] came on stage all in motorcycle black, in front of a very bad, very loud electronic r-r band. . . . He more or less killed the festival. . . . That boy is really destructive." But the newer generations gathering around Threadgill's had a very different take. Gilbert Shelton reviewed the tour's Austin date in *The Texas Ranger*: "Dylan's imagination continues to serve him well. His voice and drive lend themselves well to rock and roll, and more importantly, he likes it and takes it seriously, like he always took his music: as art. Dylan actually is an artist."[11]

The period surrounding Dylan's visit marked a turning point in the youth culture's position in the city, as young entrepreneurs began to construct alternative institutions to serve their own community. The Vulcan Gas Company on Congress Avenue, founded in 1967, constituted the first successful space run by members of the counterculture for members of the counterculture, outflanking the teen-oriented go-go or dance clubs that had previously dominated the town's rock 'n' roll scene. That this new venue, founded by Don Hyde, Sandy Lockett, Gary Scanlon, and Houston White, could arise near the center of town, in plain sight of the state Capitol building on the city's main street, augured both the threat posed to the status quo as well as the city's cultural future. The authorities did not trust the Vulcan, and their combination of panic and puzzlement derived in part from the fact that, rather than being the product of "outside agitators," the city's own youth built the site. Don Hyde, for example, was able to make the business connections for the Vulcan's site lease and handbill production in part through his father, U. A. Hyde, a public relations consultant for the conservative Shivercrats and Republican Senator John Tower. Don Hyde's sister worked at the Bergstrom Air Force Base, where, among her other duties, she monitored the Secret Service's presumed security threats to Lyndon Johnson and let Don know when the Vulcan began to appear on the government's radar.[12]

The Vulcan showcased developments in psychedelia by regional bands such as the 13th Floor Elevators, Bubble Puppy, Conqueroo, Golden Dawn, Lost and Found, and any number of acts on the roster of Houston's International Artists record label. As was characteristic of the period, the venue mixed and matched rock with African American blues acts, including James Cotton, Sleepy John Estes, John Lee Hooker, Lightnin' Hopkins, Freddie King, Mance Lipscomb, Fred McDowell, Jimmy Reed, Big Mama Thornton, Muddy Waters, and Big Joe Williams. Johnny Winter recorded his first album, *The Progressive Blues Experiment*, in the space, and Steve Miller made early appearances there. National touring acts such as the Velvet Underground, the Fugs, and Poco sealed the site's significance for its local audiences. There were other such countercultural spaces in Texas—Love Street in Houston, for example—but the Vulcan's significance owed to the scene it set in motion, training individuals who would go on to work the city's most successful venues of the 1970s.

Across the United States, innumerable young amateur rock bands sprouted in the wake of the British Invasion, and blossomed as the Summer of Love and Woodstock Nation came into view. Austin proved no different. While the 13th Floor Elevators possessed the greatest cult appeal, the cast of musicians taking the Austin stage in the late 1960s went far to determine its 1970s moment in the sun. The Wig featuring Rusty Wier ruled the go-go clubs and covers scene. Powell St. John started the blues-rock outfit Conqueroo, which was then taken over by Charlie Pritchard and Ed Guinn when St. John departed for California. The Lubbock–Austin migration began its fruitful cross-pollination with acts such as the Hub City Movers, whose members included Jimmie Dale Gilmore, John X. Reed, Charlie Sauer, Ike Ritter, Ed Vizard, and Gerry Barnett.[13] Each of these acts contributed to the local counterculture's continued attempts to synthesize folk authenticity and the experimental, improvisational aesthetics of psychedelia. The hippie–redneck fusion attributed to progressive country in the 1970s, then, had deep roots—in the Threadgill's folk circles, Dylan's musical evolution, the psychedelic volume of the 13th Floor Elevators and the Vulcan Gas Company, and the garage-psych-folk-blues played by young acts all over town. Perhaps the most important band in managing the transition between this countercultural underground and the progressive country–helmed ascent of the scene in the city's life was Shiva's Headband, led by Spencer Perskin. A child violin prodigy, Perskin entered the conservatory at Southern Methodist University in Dallas at age nine. Later, he participated in the student folk music club overseen by Threadgill's veteran Stan Alexander at the University of North Texas in Denton that also included future Austin scenesters Steve Fromholz, Travis Holland, Michael Murphey, B. W. Stevenson, and Eddie Wilson.[14] Led by Perskin's piercing fiddle, Shiva's Headband would blend country stylings with contemporary rock and psychedelia in a similar fashion to what their contemporaries Conqueroo did for the blues, or as the Grateful Dead did in Northern California. Shiva's Headband practically became the Vulcan Gas Company's house band, playing there nearly twice as often as any other single group.

Both the Hub City Movers and Shiva's Headband prefigured the local borrowings among rock, country, blues, and folk idioms. The Hub City Movers' repertoire included such songs as Gilbert Shelton's "Set My Chickens Free"

Shiva's Headband at the Wooldridge Park Love-in, April 13, 1969. Photo © Burton Wilson. Wilson (Burton) Collection, Dolph Briscoe Center for American History, University of Texas at Austin.

(on liberating a farm's poultry under the influence of psychedelics) and George Vizard's "Bhagavan Decreed" (a mixture of Orientalist lyrics, country instrumentation, and wry hippie humor). The Shiva's Headband debut album, *Take Me to the Mountains*, popularized the counterculture pastoral in its title track and "Armadillo Homesick Blues," an early anthem addressing the sensation among Texas hippies that they belonged in Austin rather than San Francisco. The song, preceding Gary P. Nunn's similarly themed, armadillo-laden "London Homesick Blues" by a few years, detailed the sentiments that had led many of the erstwhile Texas migrants to San Francisco back home.

    The appropriation of country instrumentation and voice by the Hub City Movers and Shiva's Headband did not arise simply due to local influences. After all, the counterculture had long held the cowboy as among its many aesthetic options, and getting back to the land as a salutary goal. Even in making its case against the Southern redneck, for example, *Easy Rider* (1969) celebrated the code of the West not only in the meal the protagonists shared with an interracial Anglo and Mexican ranching family, but in the figure of

Dennis Hopper's Billy himself, all cocked hat, unruly moustache, and fringe jacket. Haight-Ashbury's purchase on the cowboy figure rested to a considerable extent on the psychedelicized Wild West fantasy of the Red Dog Saloon, a remote Virginia City, Nevada, venue founded in 1965 by the California exiles Don Works, Mark Unobski, and Chan Laughlin. "This was the Wild West, a big fantasy world where you could be whatever you wanted to be," the light show veteran Bob Cohen recalled. "That's where all the fringe and leather came from, which became a big part of that whole hippie image."[15]

The counterculture borrowed widely from country-western music, as well. In 1968, the Beau Brummels' *Bradley's Barn*, the Byrds' *Sweetheart of the Rodeo*, Buffalo Springfield's *Last Time Around*, and the Band's *Music from Big Pink* all laid the groundwork for the country-rock hybrids that would become so popular in the 1970s, switching from the outer-space predilections of psychedelia to a sometimes ironic, sometimes earnest rapprochement with an imagined American past. Countercultural bellwether Bob Dylan, too, issued the country-themed albums *John Wesley Harding* (1967) and *Nashville Skyline* (1969), the latter recorded in Nashville with performances by Johnny Cash, Earl Scruggs, Norman Blake, and session musician Charlie Daniels. Such experiments were corollaries of and strong influences on Austin's developing progressive country scene. In fact, one of the first visual glimmers of Austin's cosmic cowboy imagery appeared in a Gilbert Shelton cartoon accompanying *The Rag*'s review of *Sweetheart of the Rodeo*. Shelton's character Freewheelin' Franklin of the Fabulous Furry Freak Brothers, a countercultural cowboy that drew on Shelton's Texas roots, is shown nervously hitchhiking, thumb out, carrying a sign labeled "Nashville."[16]

Amid the aural turn to pastoralism, Austin's purported hippie–redneck confluence began to take shape. In the summer of 1970, local heroine Janis Joplin made her final visit to Austin for her mentor Kenneth Threadgill's birthday party, a concert organized by the antiwar activist Martin Wigginton and headlined by Shiva's Headband.[17] As a figure who connected the brashness of Austin's counterculture with that national counterculture's more storied locale of San Francisco, Joplin's visit stirred a great deal of interest and shaped the Austin scene's focus in a moment of transition. In the *Daily Texan*, Roger Leinert noted the changes underway. The show's audience, Leinert wrote, presented a diverse but converging "blend of longhairs and rednecks, hippies and businessmen."[18] Further, with her 1969 album *I Got Dem Ol' Kozmic Blues Again Mama!* Joplin was among those beginning to deploy the "cosmic" label to a developing hybridity of American roots music with countercultural rock. Gram Parsons's quest for a "Cosmic American Music" provides another significant antecedent, and one that flowered with a Southern California country-rock aesthetic around the Eagles, the Nitty Gritty Dirt Band, Poco, Linda Ronstadt, and others.[19] The musical counterculture's attraction to the narrative artistry and perceived authenticity of white, rural American musics gathered steam in the late 1960s. Cory Lock has noted these developments as an example of the folklorist John Coggeshall's notion of the "rustification" of American culture in the 1970s and 1980s, a retreat from the seemingly intractable challenges associated with the racialized "urban problem."[20] Further, Michael Coyle and Jon Dolan read in rock's appropriations of the folk concept of authenticity in the same period a canard that would continue to bedevil mainstream popular music. Beginning with the Lomaxes seeking after the true American song craft and culminating in the folk music scene and the critical discourses of *Rolling Stone*, the "turn of these new bands to countrified or folkified rock was meant to suggest a rejection of consumer culture, and it proved a commercially substantial gesture."[21] The developing Austin scene participated in and shaped these wider cultural fields.

"Suddenly, We've Got the Bastards on the Run": The Armadillo World Headquarters

Austin's neighborhoods south of the Colorado River traditionally consisted of working-class Anglos and Mexican Americans, both peripheral to the city's symbolic power centers: the Capitol building and University of Texas north of the river. Honky-tonks, cantinas, and dance halls were scattered among these neighborhoods, spaces for weekend or end-of-workday leisure in which musical performance meant much. George Davis's Cactus Club on Barton Springs Road was one of these spaces, yet this traditional honky-tonk was open to reaching beyond its core audience. On Thursday nights in 1970, to boost attendance, Davis ceded the venue's stage to psychedelic rock and folk acts that alternated with traditional honky-tonk. Indeed, Jim Franklin made posters for the venue that prefigured the hippie–redneck alliance with the motto "Where the heads and the necks come together." Coincidentally or no, the club burned down shortly after this campaign, but before then it provided one Austinite a chance for epiphany.[22] The manager of Shiva's Headband, while attending a Hub City Movers show on one of the Cactus Club's psychedelic Thursdays, stepped outside to relieve himself, as the venue's plumbing was not in working order. With the musicians Jimmie Dale Gilmore on one side and John X. Reed on the other, Eddie Wilson stood staring into the Austin night. Amid an auto repo lot, cafeteria, and roller rink, he spied a hulk of an abandoned structure originally designed to be a National Guard armory. Capitol Records had recently signed Shiva's Headband and included a hefty bonus to be used as seed money for similar Austin acts. As the Vulcan Gas Company, Austin's most reliable venue for psychedelic bands, had closed, Wilson had been looking for a space amenable to Shiva's performances. With this in mind, Wilson explored that abandoned structure, and shortly thereafter he and a group of collaborators dubbed the site the Armadillo World Headquarters.

The Armadillo's physical structure was far from ideal for the near-utopian imaginings it often housed. A large, open central space with inadequate roofing made for poor acoustics and precluded effective climate control. The 150-by-96-foot hall was too hot in the summer, too cold in the winter, and given to flooding in the region's intermittent storms. In the beginning, dirty carpet squares covered the space before the stage. Seating in the venue was rudimentary, and early on the tables consisted of used industrial cable spools. Around this central space, a network of rooms constantly shifted in function to meet the needs of the Armadillo's ever-changing mission—offices, makeshift apartments, art galleries, recording studios, bakeries, and arcades came and went. The venue's staff made the most of these accommodations, and a talented group of visual artists—Kerry Awn, Jim Franklin, Danny Garrett, Henry Gonzalez, Jack Jackson, Guy Juke, Ken Featherston, Bill Narum, Micael Priest, Sam Yeates, and others—created a vision of the Armadillo through posters, handbills, murals, and comics that transcended its humble physical existence. The kitchen, too, proved a constant in the Armadillo equation. Under the stewardship of Jan Beeman, former leader of a San Angelo commune dedicated to helping Vietnam veterans, and Rikke Lee Moursund, better known as the Guacamole Queen, it developed a hospitable reputation among national touring acts. An outdoor, German-style beer garden, one of the venue's most popular modifications, expanded capacity and gave the Armadillo an outside stage. In all, the Armadillo World Headquarters was an unwieldy, awkward, but charming beast that took after its namesake. An unlikely space from which to revolutionize the civic identity of the state capital, but, through the labor and imagination of a spirited legion of characters from 1970 to 1980, it worked. More than that, the Armadillo provided the spark to solidify Austin's developing music scene.

There was reason to believe in the existence of an audience for such an experiment in Austin. Countercultural performance venues and gathering spaces had briefly flourished in the past few years, but they met with daunting community opposition. The Vulcan Gas Company had shuttered its doors. The Chequered Flag, the Eleventh Door, the IL Club, the New Orleans Club, and others had provided similar spaces for folk, blues, and psychedelic rock performance. All of these operations were relatively small, however, and few stood poised to succeed in the new decade. Further, the talk of a hippie–redneck convergence became rampant by the early 1970s in a manner that would have been inconceivable to the denizens of the Vulcan Gas Company or the psychedelic rock pioneers who decamped from Austin. When asked about how the hippies and rednecks interacted in the Austin he knew, Powell St. John, among the members of the Austin counterculture who left for San Francisco early, said, "They didn't." Reflecting for a minute, he then recounted several instances of harassment and violence that constituted the whole of hippie–redneck relations in his memory of late-1960s Austin.[23] By the early 1970s, however, a number of the San Francisco migrants and other countercultural exiles began to stream back, and the Armadillo World Headquarters gave them a home. In time it became the central representation of the 1970s Austin scene. Other centers of gravitation would arise over the course of the decade with their own subcultural allegiances—blues at Antone's, a somewhat more locally oriented country-rock venue at Soap Creek Saloon, other country rivals in the Alliance Wagonyard and the Austin Opera House, punk at Raul's—but the cavernous Armadillo put Austin on the musical map and created the network of performers, audiences, and media that enabled these other nodes of the scene.

Wilson initially intended to name the place the "Armadillo National Headquarters," a tribute to the venue's military past, but Bud Shrake convinced him that, in the wake of the Vietnam War, international symbolism would play better than national—hence "world."[24] The role of the armadillo in the name has a more nuanced history, and one that, in its own way, made the strange creature a Texas national symbol. The saga began with a stable of artists including Glenn Whitehead and Tony Bell at the University of Texas humor publication the *Texas Ranger*. Jim Franklin came to the symbol independently and perfected it, making the armadillo a psychedelic genre all its own in *The Rag* and in concert posters, album covers, and comics. In Franklin's armadillo universe, the creatures counterattacked riot police, helped the UT Longhorns win football games, staged raucous music festivals, copulated with the Texas capitol building, flew over dangerous roadways, burst out of the chest of bluesman Freddie King, and, lest we forget, "balled" for Charles Manson. Jim Franklin has offered a number of reasons for the symbol's popularity, the most succinct being his late-1960s realization: "Armadillo. They dig underground. We're underground."[25] Bud Shrake drew out the counterculture–armadillo analogy further in the pages of *Sports Illustrated*:

Exactly why armadillos are taking hold as a youth symbol is a matter for speculation. Armadillos are paranoid little beasts who prefer to mind their own business. They love to sleep all day, then roam and eat all night. They are gentle, keep their noses in the grass and share their homes with others. Perhaps most significant, they are weird-looking, unfairly maligned and picked on, and have developed a hard shell and a distinctive aroma. They do far more good than harm, and yet the usual social reaction toward an armadillo is to attempt to destroy it.[26]

The symbol proliferated, and discussions ensued over pet armadillos, armadillo recipes, armadillo anatomy, armadillo races, and whether the armadillo should replace the longhorn as the mascot of the state's flagship university.[27] A resolution on this last development passed the student government, only to be met with the disdain of the university's powerful alumni. A local Houston DJ even issued a novelty record mocking the idea.[28] Author Ken Kesey visited campus and called for the organization of a politically independent Armadillo Party to carry forward the aims of the counterculture.[29]

The sensation was not yet in full effect, however, in August 1970. When the place opened, it seemed more of an ambitious experiment than a successful nightclub. Wilson became the Armadillo's "trail boss" and public face, but, from the beginning, running the place and determining its character was a collective endeavor. Artist and figurehead Jim Franklin, Vulcan Gas Company veteran Bobby Hedderman, Shiva's front man Spencer Perskin, and lawyer Mike Tolleson all brought distinct experiences and visions to the Armadillo World Headquarters' Board of Directors. Franklin became the club's emcee and artistic director, bearded and bespectacled, living in an apartment he had built just offstage at the venue. Mike Tolleson joined Franklin and Wilson in seeking something more than a mere concert hall. He championed the idea of making the Armadillo not merely a concert venue but a community arts laboratory. Recently returned from London, he hoped to model the Armadillo after the experimental Arts Lab, which endeavored to combine film, dance, theater, and music under one roof.[30]

After opening in 1970, the Armadillo World Headquarters tested the bounds of this community arts credo, hosting crafts fairs; the Underground Press Syndicate conference; the National Lawyers Guild conference; benefits for the Free Clinic, the alternative Greenbriar School, striking UT shuttle bus drivers, Vietnam Veterans Against the War, and the United Farm Workers; community rap sessions on drug abuse; the Austin Ballet Theater; musicals; lectures; and the San Francisco Mime Troupe. Politicians such as Austin Mayor Jeff Friedman, Travis County Sheriff Raymond Frank, and gubernatorial candidate

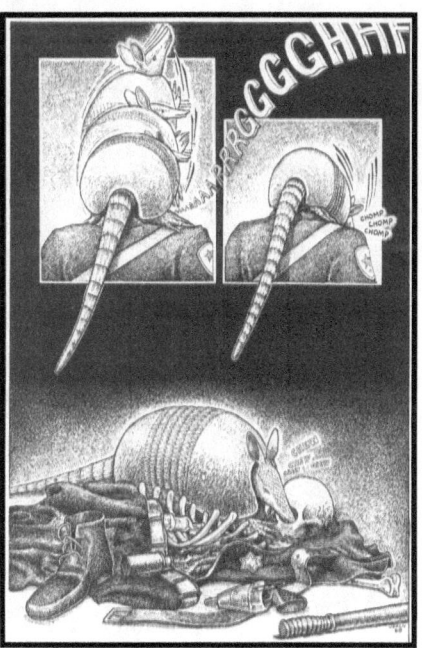

Jim Franklin, "Never Bite Off More Than You Can Chew," Armadillo Comics (San Francisco: Rip Off Press, 1971), issue 2. Originally appeared in 1969.

Frances "Sissy" Farenthold regarded the place as a significant segment of their base. Soviet delegations, Chilean exiles, and future president Bill Clinton would make notable visits.[31] A shaken Charlie Daniels, in later years known for his cantankerous conservatism, broke the news of John Lennon's murder from the stage. The odd admixture would invite a broader audience that not only nurtured the hippie–redneck and cosmic cowboy tropes, but also made the space a common destination for other figures long involved in the process of manufacturing "the Texan." John Henry Faulk and Cactus Pryor presided over events there, and they were not the only classic Lone Star regionalists with ties to the place. While covering a ballet performance at the venue for the new magazine *Texas Monthly*, Suzanne Shelton thought she saw a familiar face: "Inside the cavernous Armadillo gloom, the audience gropes its way to its seats. A polite offer of assistance to the elderly Mrs. Walter Prescott Webb, widow of the renowned Texas historian, is refused with a firm, 'Honey, I know the way. I come here to rock shows all the time.'"[32] In short, the Armadillo World Headquarters homesteaded a space for a countercultural confluence to take place, but space alone does not create the dense social network that is a scene.

Performers and audiences still had to find their reasons for gathering. At this point, in the early seventies, the social climate of Austin, which had earlier pushed a wave of countercultural migrants to San Francisco, now began to pull them home. The diffusion of the counterculture's influence and shifts to more lax enforcement of drug laws in Travis County made for a more amenable atmosphere. Doug Sahm, a Tex-Mex rocker originally from San Antonio, numbered amongst these returnees. Sahm had moved to San Francisco with his band, the Sir Douglas Quintet, following a drug bust in Corpus Christi in the mid-sixties. In the early 1970s, he followed the homesick laments of his own recordings like "Texas Me" and "Is Anybody Goin' to San Antone?" by making the return trip himself.[33] Such high-profile homecomings

The Armadillo World Headquarters logo. Drawing by Micael Priest. Logo design by Jim Franklin. Courtesy of the South Austin Popular Culture Center.

began to reverse the 1960s migration stream. As music writer Joe Nick Patoski remembers, "The back-to-the-roots album *The Return of Doug Saldaña*—whose cover featured longhaired Doug in cowboy hat, a bottle of Big Red in hand—signaled to Texans in exile that it was okay to come back home, that we wouldn't get our asses kicked for looking or being different."[34] Sahm's performative orientation toward the self, here seen in his ability to signify with only a cowboy hat and a bottle of regional soda, fit the moment well.

Michael Murphey also made the prodigal return in the period, back from a lucrative stint as a pop songwriter in Los Angeles once his career as a singer–songwriter took off with the album *Geronimo's Cadillac*. Reluctantly, Murphey gave the growing core of Texas-styled hippies its name and its anthem in the song "Cosmic Cowboy, Pt. 1." "I just wanna be a cosmic cowboy," Murphey's song proclaimed, a "supernatural country rockin' galoot" steeped in the countercultural pastoral of Lone Star Beer, skinny-dipping, steel guitars, and Western landscapes.[35] Murphey early on argued that the song satirized the scene, more than defined it, and wanted little to do with the elaboration of a subcultural iconography. Members of Murphey's band tend to concur, but have varied memories of the context surrounding the song's composition while touring in New York City. It poked gentle fun at the more counterculturally minded Texans Murphey knew, including bandmate Bob Livingston. An earnestness marked Murphey's song, too. Just prior to that trip to New York, though, Murphey had spent time with keyboardist Gary P. Nunn on his family ranch in Oklahoma, and Murphey had been enamored with the experience.[36] The song, satirical or no, became a climactic number at many festivals built on the concept it named.

Though Sahm and Murphey had greater visibility among the youth counterculture in the early 1970s, Willie Nelson played the most catalytic role in amplifying the significance of the seventies Austin scene. The Armadillo World Headquarters and other like venues scraped by in 1970 and 1971, but failure always looked to be right around the corner until Willie Nelson moved to town and cemented the much talked about hippie–redneck or progressive country alliance, joining crowds across generation and class to form a country-western music infused with the sensibilities of the counterculture's folksy, improvisational rock. The transformation began with the Dripping Springs Reunion festival of March 1972 that brought older Nashville stalwarts (Roy Acuff, Tex Ritter, Earl Scruggs) together with a new generation of songwriters (Kris Kristofferson, Willie Nelson, Billy Joe Shaver) in an event billed as a country Woodstock. The concert had mixed results, losing a substantial amount of money and creating tension between the honky-tonk and youth culture entrepreneurs involved. It created enough interest, though, that Nelson continued his pursuit of the youth crossover audiences.

Indeed, a number of scene narratives date the origins of progressive country to a single performance, that of Willie Nelson at the Armadillo on August 12, 1972. After that night, supposedly, everything fell into place for a distinctive regional country scene to develop. Indeed, the number of country-identified artists at the Armadillo World Headquarters explodes in the fall of 1972. It should be noted, however, that Nelson's country performance, while an essential catalyst to the developing scene, was not unprecedented in early-seventies Austin. Guy Clark, Marcia Ball's Freda and the Firedogs, Bill Neely, John Prine, Earl Scruggs, Kenneth Threadgill, and Jerry Jeff Walker had all taken the Armadillo stage prior to Nelson's first appearance, to say nothing of the vibrant dance halls in town such as the Broken Spoke and the Split Rail. The reception of such acts at the Armadillo, though, often ran to a folk or singer-songwriter frame, rather than the hardcore country that Willie was taken to represent upon his return to Texas. At the same time, the slippage between folk and country labels should serve notice that the hybrid nature of progressive country drew on numerous generic conventions. It repackaged and redirected, but did not eclipse, the youth counterculture's enthusiasm for folk, rock, and the blues.

Born in Abbott, Texas, in 1933, Willie Hugh Nelson had led a long itinerant life as a musician in Texas dance halls, Pacific Northwest radio stations, and, finally, the country music mecca of Nashville. By the 1960s, he had established himself there as a successful songwriter, placing hit songs with Patsy Cline, Ray Price, and Faron Young, among others. His own attempts to record his material, however, had fallen short. Willie Nelson did not look quite right for Nashville producers in the 1960s. He did not sound quite right, and many, behind closed doors, mused that Nelson, well, maybe he just was not quite right, at all. Straining against the recording sensibilities of the Chet Atkins–era countrypolitan sound, Nelson as early as 1971 recorded a concept album, *Yesterday's Wine*, that spoke to the new interests, new ideas, and new identities that Nelson was developing beyond Nashville. The album, using a number of Nelson's previously recorded songs, narrated the life of a man from birth to grave. The first track, beginning before this man was born, seemed prophetic of Nelson's impending cultural shift. Spoken voices before the music begins murmur, "You do know why you're here?" The man answers, "Yes, there is great confusion on earth, and the power that is has concluded the following. Perfect man has visited earth already. The voice of imperfect man must now be made manifest, and I have been selected as the most likely candidate." His

Micael Priest handbill advertising first Willie Nelson appearance
at the Armadillo World Headquarters, August 1972. Courtesy
of the South Austin Popular Culture Center.

interlocutors respond, "The time is April and therefore you, a Taurus, must go. And this strength, combined with wisdom and love, is the key." The music then enters, and Nelson sings, imploring God to let him get started.

The astrological references, the notion of the seeking self, and Nelson's plaintive voice combined to suggest to the listener that Willie would not be contained by Nashville's traditional order much longer. In the same year that Nelson recorded *Yesterday's Wine*, his farmhouse in Ridge Top, outside of Nashville, burned to the ground. Nelson moved back to Texas, settling first in Bandera and considering Houston before deciding that his sister Bobbie's home of Austin might provide a receptive audience.[37] His inclinations proved correct, and by 1974 Jan Reid could write that whatever "his ideology, in Austin Willie seemed to be able to do no wrong. He was as natural as dirt, and when he walked through a crowd he knew everybody who spoke to him.... And Willie acted like Texas was the center of the universe."[38] In other words, for the young, previously rock-oriented audiences of Austin, Willie Nelson embodied a Texan out of the Old Rock, and thus was extremely valuable as a figure around which to build a subculture, joining youth countercultural forms to the traditional "redneck" ways through authentic performance. The divide was at times palpable in material social spaces, such as when hard country audiences wanted the floor for dancers to move in a large counterclockwise circle, while hippies insisted on sitting or standing in front of the stage facing the performer. But the divide was much more fluid in terms of individual experience. The hippie–redneck trope developed because many young Anglo-Texans in town grew up in settings that made the markers of traditional Texas culture, "redneck" culture, second nature. While they may have rebelled against the politics or mannerisms of their home culture in adopting a countercultural lifestyle, the rejection could hardly be total. "Class" does not exactly get at the distinction, either, except for the notion of class as a social or ideological marker of the decade, shorthanded in just such terms as "hard hat" and "redneck."

Nelson had, indeed, a long record of performing in honky-tonks. He did come from hardscrabble Anglo-Texan roots and a rural upbringing. Both counted for much in establishing Nelson's experiential authenticity for young audiences in Austin. This "authentic" status stands apart from Nelson's personal ability and sincerity. In Jan Reid's words and Henry Nash Smith's formulation, these audiences identified Willie not only as an individual, but also as something of a concept and emotion fused into an image, "natural as dirt" and "able to do no wrong." As much as his musical ability or performative persona, Nelson's centrality in the progressive country scene—his aura—came from the ways he tapped a deep discursive stream transcending oppositions—hippie/redneck, urban/rural, country/rock, masculine/feminine, young/old—while also transcending the tricky terrain of generation and history by providing an embodied amalgamation of fathers and sons, tradition and change. When he arrived from Nashville, Nelson had yet to adopt the beard and flowing hair of his now-trademark image. Soon enough, though, Willie-as-icon became the archetype of the redneck–hippie, the cosmic cowboy, carrying the contradiction in the guise of his own person.

Though Willie Nelson's presence proved catalytic, he by no means anchored the progressive country aesthetic that persisted at the Armadillo, to some degree, until it closed in 1980. Nelson's relationship with the venue proved a relatively short and intense one over the years 1972 and 1973. Nelson and the Armadillo then fell out in the wake of Willie's first Fourth of July picnic over a series of financial-, entourage-, and firearm-related misunderstandings.[39] In fact, Willie Nelson supported and patronized Tim O'Connor's Austin Opera House as an alternative venue to the Armadillo World Headquarters.[40] Nelson's split with the Armadillo and the rise of the Opera House draws our attention to the fact that the progressive country movement enabled the success of an array of venues in Austin and across the state.

As with Doug Sahm, Nelson's presence ushered a return of Texas's prodigal sons. In an article for *Playboy* about his Texan friends' entreaties to return home, Larry L. King, a prominent Texas writer resident in New York and Washington, wrote that "people kept telling me Austin was the only thing happening in Jerry Ford's America other than inflation and Tupperware parties. The Texas city was represented as the new Haight-Ashbury and the new Nashville, the only wide-open-dope-and-music resort available now that students were studying again and Tom Hayden had taken to wearing neckties and kissing babies."[41] Though King was less than impressed upon his visit, the Willie Nelson mystique resonated with the developing currents of Texas chic that King was promoting in New York City.

Observers often shorthand the Austin scene with reference to the nationally successful recording artists such as Murphey, Nelson, Sahm, and Jerry Jeff Walker, but the proliferation of performance venues showcased an array of local progressive country acts who have not been similarly memorialized. While Shiva's Headband predominated in the later months of the Vulcan and the early years of the Armadillo, such groups as the band Greezy Wheels went far toward providing the soundtrack to the local scene in the mid-1970s, becoming a virtual house band to both the Armadillo and Soap Creek Saloon. The band's lead singer, Cleve Hattersley, had moved to San Francisco from

New York at the suggestion of mutual friends that he might join the 13th Floor Elevators with Roky Erickson and Tommy Hall. As the Elevators' West Coast move left the band in disarray, this did not happen. Rikke Moursund, who had attempted and failed to make the meeting happen, instead paid for Hattersley to fly to Austin in 1969. He settled there, followed shortly by a number of friends from upstate New York, including his sister Lissa. Hattersley began his Austin career by performing solo shows at the downtown blues club the One Knite before forming the Greezy Wheels with Mike Pugh, Pat Pankratz, and Tony Laier. Fiddler Mary Egan and Lissa Hattersley joined shortly thereafter.[42] The Greezy Wheels played the Armadillo World Headquarters more than twice as much as any other act, and nearly accomplished the same feat at the Soap Creek Saloon. Their sound encapsulates 1970s Austin, a scene that skewed toward country accents, but one that also typically ignored genre boundaries. According to Hattersley:

> We never considered ourselves country, for to us (especially me), writing songs was always about pushing the musical envelope, making new sounds. Anathema to true country folk.... A couple of us were kinda country, and our instrumentation automatically led folks to call us progressive country, but Lissa, Mike Pugh, and Tony Airoldi brought real jazz sensibilities into the mix. Yes, Sweet Mary was blowing things up at the end of every set with the "Orange Blossom Special," but the meat of our sets evoked everything from Hendrix to Django.[43]

The same might be said for any number of acts defining the Austin sound at the grassroots, from the seminal Freda and the Firedogs (Marcia Ball, David Cook, Steve McDaniels, John X. Reed, and Bobby Earl Smith) to a proliferation of progressive country acts in town by 1974, including Cooder Browne, Eaglebone Whistle, Plum Nelly, Uncle Walt's Band, and Velvet Cowpasture. Hattersley's evasion of the progressive country label is typical, as most of these acts, though participating in an aesthetics of the moment that privileged countercultural pastoralism and the imagined past of country music, saw "progressive country" as a marketing and formatting label pioneered by the local radio station KOKE-FM and latched onto by record companies. The label "progressive country" itself evoked the same transcendence of opposites as hippie–redneck or cosmic cowboy, providing a liberal, sophisticated gloss to a music often treated by the mainstream rock press as simplistic or retrograde. That the designation seemed a backhanded compliment may have been one more reason that artists themselves staked their distance from it. In the same vein, "progressive

Members of the Greezy Wheels backstage at the Armadillo World Headquarters, March 15, 1974. Photo © Burton Wilson. Wilson (Burton) Collection, Dolph Briscoe Center for American History, the University of Texas at Austin.

country" also played on the seventies evocation of "progressive rock" or "progressive jazz" (or, as in Johnny Winter's album recorded in Austin, "progressive blues"). Each of these carried with it the sense that they were superior, more artful and considered, than their nonprogressive variants, and this gets to the heart of the strange baggage that progressive country carried, attempting to claim an authenticity through intimate knowledge of country while also trying to maintain sufficient, ironic distance due to the stereotypes so often foisted on that music and its fans.

A distinct subcultural style developed alongside the progressive country sounds. As a journalist wrote in Austin's underground newspaper *The Rag* in February 1974:

> The image finally made sense. . . . I could understand that these people were not faking it. Behind the image was a reality, that these people were Texans, caught up with a genuine love of the hip. It's hard being a hip Texan. . . . The

image abounds in contradictions. Think now: long hair and long horns, psychedelics and porch sitting, sexy truckers punching cattle; all that. Somehow the Cosmic Cowboy image fuses those contradictions and makes them whole. Listening to everyone standing around singing Murphy's [sic] song, I felt it was a song of liberation, of people recognizing who they are and saying it out loud.[44]

The cover of that issue featured a cowboy drawn in the style of the psychedelic poster artists, winking, smiling, and, from the midst of a smoke cloud, reassuring the paper's countercultural audience that "Podnahs . . . You can be *damn* sure it ain't from Marlboro Country!" Inside, the reviewer of the "Tribute to the Cosmic Cowpeople" benefit for the Pacifica radio station in Houston felt he saw something new in this self-conscious attempt to export a musical style developed in Austin. The concert featured the progressive country artists Commander Cody, Freda and the Firedogs, Kinky Friedman, Michael Murphey, Willie Nelson, Doug Sahm, Billy Joe Shaver, and Jerry Jeff Walker. "Up until last week," the reviewer began, "I was only seeing the bad in the Cosmic Cowboys. . . . Well, my opinion has changed." He then proceeded to explain how the "image finally made sense." Some participants, then, saw in Murphey's song "I Just Wanna Be a Cosmic Cowboy" a liberation anthem, and in the cosmic cowboy an unlikely melding of the constituencies of the hippie counterculture and the Texan cowboy or redneck, shorthands for the state's traditionally minded white working class. As such, this New Left newspaper, counterculturally inflected, deployed the liberationist rhetoric of the 1960s social justice movements to describe a genre of country-rock performance that supposedly achieved a transcendence of opposites that brought wholeness amid the seventies' fracturing malaise.

The Rag here suggested the basic components of the hippie–redneck confluence over the markers of Anglo-Texan identity that was so discussed, performed, celebrated, fretted over, and maligned in 1970s Austin.[45] The fascination with the cosmic cowboy audiences of progressive country music rested in their perceived transcendence of deeply ingrained social contradictions. Participants and observers painted a picture of the counterculture coming home to roost among those spaces it had sought to escape, the generation gap closing through roots nostalgia for "the Texan" as a fictive ethnicity or metaphorical nationality. Judging from the tone of many accounts, "the Texan's" romantic attraction for young men of the period, reminiscent of that same figure constructed in the Texas Centennial, enabled such fusions. Journalists such as the reviewer from *The Rag* insisted that all of this transpired communally in spaces of live musical performance, particularly in Austin, from the coffeehouse atmosphere of clubs geared toward singer–songwriters like Castle Creek and the Cactus Cafe, to the cavernous Armadillo World Headquarters that largely produced the synthesis, to the spectacle of hip country festivals helmed by artists such as Waylon Jennings, Kris Kristofferson, Michael Murphey, and Willie Nelson in Dripping Springs, Luckenbach, College Station, and Gonzales.[46]

If the assertion of Anglo-Texan identities and the challenge to that assertion's hegemony corresponded to the maturation of Richard Flores's "Texas Modern," the performative Anglo-Texan of the 1970s spoke to the forward edge of a "Texas Postmodern." That is, even as cosmic cowboys borrowed the language of liberation in "recognizing who they are," their performance occurred as the relation between that cowboy-wheeler-dealer-oilman-Texan figure and the (sub)urban experience of the majority of real, existing Texans became increasingly unmoored. Dobie, Webb, and Bedichek had engaged in much the same project of salvage in the years surrounding the tipping point of Texan urbanization in 1950. The cosmic cowboys grew up on the far side of that divide, though many would bring memories of rural lifeways. All the more reason, then, for young Anglo-Texan men to hunger for the notion that "behind the image was a reality."

Up Against the Wall, Bob Wills: Progressive Country's Strange Bedfellows

In terms of vanishing icons of Anglo-Texan masculinity, Lyndon Johnson's demise loomed large in Central Texas, but the passing of Western swing legend Bob Wills in 1975 perhaps cast the larger shadow over Austin's progressive country scene. The following year, Waylon Jennings testified to this effect clearly in a live recording of his "Bob Wills Is Still the King" at the Austin Opera House. He introduced the song as being "about a man that has as much to do with why we're down here as anybody" before launching into verses that culminate in the chorus, "It don't matter who's in Austin/Bob Wills is still the king."[47] Western swing's syncretic embrace of the musical styles of country, jazz, polka, and *ranchera*, paired with its elaborate Western image, provided a model for thinking through the performative aspects of Texan identity. In a contemporaneous article on Jennings's performance, Nicholas Spitzer suggested that the Austin Opera's crowd "hoots and hollers on cue in a manner that . . . I would describe as self-conscious. That is, they are themselves performing in the fashion presumed to be truly Texan."[48] Somewhat ironically, then, these artists and audiences performed authenticity via an expansive genre that subverted the very notion of the pure authentic in its omnivorous, hybridizing gestures. As Travis Stimeling has written of the irony in his own treatment of the subject, "Wills was not lauded as a sophisticated, cosmopolitan bandleader who had worked diligently to make the Texas Playboys and their music accessible to a larger public. Rather, he was celebrated as a folk legend."[49]

In actuality, Western swing of the 1930s and 1940s provided less an authentic ancestor of Anglo-Texan essentialism than an apt model for the progressive country mixture of hippie and redneck, rock 'n' roll and honky-tonk. Bob Wills's band members wore Western clothing to amplify their regional image, but did so in the self-conscious, flamboyant manner of their singing cowboy peers. As a big band, they conveyed rurality by relying heavily on strings where other swing orchestras foregrounded horns. Still, their fiddles spoke in an improvisational jazz idiom, and the songs that Wills himself sang, for the most part, were blues numbers. This was a whitened jazz and blues, surely, but the performers still considered it jazz and blues of the most modern variety. Further, Central European polkas and schottisches threaded through the Western swing oeuvre. As a model of generic hybridity with wide-ranging racial, ethnic, and national origins, Western swing offered an aural reminder of the Southwest's diversity—within certain bounds. Bands and their audiences remained, for the most part, segregated by race. Though German and Czech bands like that of Adolph Hofner could cross between Anglo and ethnic European audiences, and a number of Western swing stars claimed Native American ancestry, the self-presentation of acts in performance tended toward the white, Western, and Anglo-Texan mainstream. Still, for 1970s cosmic cowboys to ground a performance of Anglo-Texan masculinity on the figure of Bob Wills connoted, at different times, either a subtle recognition or a willed erasure of the patchwork nature of that identity's cultural forms. More likely, the popularity of Western swing in the cosmic cowboy subculture encompassed both, as playful suspension of the essential and the performative, the stylized gesture and the nostalgic pang, echoed throughout the developing currents of Texas chic in the Lone Star State.

Western swing's revival in Central Texas in the 1970s involved artists such as Alvin Crow and the Pleasant Valley Boys, Asleep at the Wheel, Commander Cody and His Lost Planet Airmen, and Cornell Hurd. Of these artists, only Alvin Crow hailed from Texas (by way of Oklahoma), while the others relocated to or performed frequently in the area due to its historic association with Western swing. As such, it stands to reason that those countercultural, rock-oriented artists from outside the state who adopted the genre found its "old-time" qualities its primary fascination, its authentic communication of a rustic time and place trumping its openness to the complexity of Depression and World War II America. This perhaps sells such artists short, however, as groups such as Commander Cody and His Lost Planet Airmen reveled in the genre-jumping, freewheeling live performance that such a tool as western swing afforded them. Originally from Michigan, Cody (born George Frayne IV) had settled in the San Francisco Bay Area in the late 1960s, performing a variety of boogie-woogie, rock, and Western swing revival musics in a countercultural vein tinged with the earnest humor of Haight-Ashbury. His style played well in early 1970s Austin and made the Lost Planet Airmen very nearly a local group by mid-decade. Commander Cody played the Armadillo World Headquarters more than any other touring act, and he helped to draw national attention to the venue with the recording of 1974's *Live from Deep in the Heart of Texas*.[50]

In a variant of the migration streams that brought Texas musicians home from San Francisco and Nashville, Commander Cody's successful performance of western swing for Austin audiences led to the bookings and subsequent migrations of like-minded groups Asleep at the Wheel and Cornell Hurd to Austin from California. Both groups quickly became local institutions. Indeed, few have carried the Western swing torch or embodied the performative Texan as has the Philadelphia native Ray Benson.[51] Asleep at the Wheel performed Wills's songs faithfully, and though Bob Wills's stroke at the time of his recording sessions for the album *For The Last Time* in 1973 prevented their collaboration, a double album of Wills and Asleep at the Wheel music was released as *Fathers and Sons* in 1975, the year of Wills's death.

If Asleep at the Wheel's Western swing revivalism provided the most straightforwardly nostalgic variant of progressive country, Jerry Jeff Walker and the Lost Gonzo Band's album *Viva Terlingua* defined the sound's progressive edge. Still, the experience of its recording in Luckenbach steeped it in a similar nostalgic mode. Of the old men who became symbolic fathers on the progressive country scene, Hondo Crouch stands out as perhaps the most patently eccentric and his project of Luckenbach, Texas, a prime performative space for the Austin singer-songwriter.[52] Crouch purchased and presided over Luckenbach, a small group of buildings including a post office, general store, bar, and dance hall, in 1970. He made the site an attractive gathering space for songwriters, musicians, and artists in Central Texas, hosting an annual mud dauber festival, an all-women chili cook-off, a visit by Billy Carter, and interminable picking sessions.

In terms of progressive country, Jerry Jeff Walker and the Lost Gonzo Band placed Luckenbach indelibly on the map as the site of the live recording of

Viva Terlingua in the summer of 1973. A collection of Walker originals and the songs of other progressive country luminaries Guy Clark, Ray Wylie Hubbard, Michael Murphey, and Gary P. Nunn, the simple nature of its recording illustrated the "spontaneous" aesthetic so prized by the Austin scene, as Travis Stimeling has recently demonstrated.[53] Further, in his account of the Austin scene *Dissonant Identities*, Barry Shank selected the rendition of Guy Clark's "Desperadoes Waiting for a Train" on that album as the creative pinnacle and truest expression of the progressive country alliance, a performance steeped in nostalgia but knowingly pushing against the bounds of tradition that determine country performance.[54] Clark's song takes the point of view of a young man recounting his childhood relationship with an old man and mentor, who is in the present moment of the song recently deceased. The narrator expresses wistfulness over the old man's aging and death. Shank deftly analyzes the song as an aesthetic recognition of social change and evolution in the progressive country form, as the song begins with snatches from the fiddle tune "Red River Valley" and ends with a fade-out on guitar licks in a countercultural "jam" mode. As opposed to the Western swing revivalists, Walker's Lost Gonzo Band was much more grounded in the rock elements of the country-rock spectrum, and this placed them in creative tension with country music conventions.

However, Ray Wylie Hubbard's "Up Against the Wall (Redneck Mother)" provided the more immediately influential, even anthemic, album track from *Viva Terlingua*. Like "Desperadoes Waiting for a Train," this song effectively encapsulated progressive country's creative contradictions. In expressing a fascination with redneck masculinity, it delineated the commodified elements of the redneck style that countercultural Anglo men in Austin sought to perform, and bundled them together with a sort of satirical, countercultural self-loathing. In this instance, a mother–son relationship disrupts the generational narrative of fathers and sons that dominated discussions of Anglo-Texan masculinity. Hubbard castigates a "redneck mother" who has raised her son with traditional mores that find him drinking in a bar, "just kickin' hippies' asses and raisin' hell." In an inversion of the Cold War *Generation of Vipers* trope, here the mother replicates the hypermasculinity that threatens Austin's hippie-redneck hybridity (even as that hypermasculinity tantalizes countercultural men disparaged for their perceived abdication of same). Hubbard intended the song as satire, more obviously so than Murphey's "I Just Wanna Be a Cosmic Cowboy," though the pleasure taken in the song by audiences led Hubbard to believe that they were not typically aware of his intentions.

In performance, the song consciously tacks back and forth between countercultural and country-western allusions. The "up against the wall" echoes the militant poetry of Amiri Baraka's "Up against the wall, motherfucker, this is a stick-up," which gained wide currency in New Left sloganeering, and the "What's that spell?" shouted at the song's close refers to Country Joe McDonald's famed obscenity at Woodstock. The band nests these references in the entire song's larger conversation with the more subtle satire of Merle Haggard's "Okie from Muskogee." Musically, the songs sound quite similar. The Haggard allusion at the recording's close punctuates the effect, as the answer to the shouted query "What's that spell?" are the sung words "Muskogee, Oklahoma, USA." *Viva Terlingua* strains to close the cultural rifts that Haggard performed in 1969 by making the song's satirical bent more transparent and over-the-top, but still affectionate, in 1973. The deep, playful ambivalence of Haggard's song, as transformed and re-written by Hubbard, holds the contradictions of the cosmic cowboy subculture in careful suspension.

Like Hubbard, many Austin artists approached the project of performance through the distancing persona Philip Auslander has theorized for 1970s glam, consciously and playfully inhabiting a role rather than attempting to project an essential authenticity.[55] Progressive country, after all, shared a decade and the airwaves with David Bowie, Lou Reed, Iggy Pop, Alice Cooper, and Kiss. Youth culture's interest in progressive country and country-rock supposedly inverted such spectacles by hewing to authentic Americana, but each employed an orientation to the performative sense of self, the use of commodities, music, and fashion to declare one's place in the world. In the following chapter, we will see how practitioners of British cultural studies examined this issue amid London's punk turn, and how their thinking might be applied to Austin in the same years. For now, Kinky Friedman's performative take on the cosmic cowboy provides us with an example of the progressive country style, spectacularly performed. Friedman, though born in Chicago, was one of the few Austin-raised country artists on the scene, and he debuted his performative persona, a politically incorrect, cigar-smoking, sequin-suited Jewish cowboy, with great fanfare at Luckenbach. His song "They Ain't Makin' Jews Like Jesus Anymore" staked out the continuing tensions in the Texas hippie–redneck fusion, foregrounding Friedman's Jewishness as a factor in preventing his fusion into the cosmic cauldron. Friedman was by no means the only Jewish artist in the progressive country fold, but in keeping with the resurgence of white ethnicity, he foregrounded Jewish identity even as these other artists often effaced their origins in re-creating themselves as Anglo-Texans. The song begins with a "redneck" who insults Friedman's Jewishness even as he misrecognizes him racially as black. When Friedman balks, the redneck laments, "They sure ain't makin' Jews like Jesus anymore." In the chorus, Friedman reclaimed the redneck's insult as a masculine assertion of self-defense in which "not makin' Jews like Jesus anymore" meant "we don't turn our cheeks the way we done before." Just as Friedman penned perhaps the only cowboy song about the Holocaust in "Ride 'Em, Jewboy," he also, here, delivers a rare country song that in part echoes the Israeli nationalism sparked among American Jews by the Six Day and Yom Kippur Wars.[56]

Like Auslander's glam artists, Friedman bracketed the performative self. "'Jewboys don't jam' has been our motto," he told Jan Reid. "I play on bills with these bands, and they say come pick, let's jam. We never use the word pick when we're going onstage. . . . We're more realistic, I think, about the whole damn thing." "The word pick," Friedman's bandmate Danny Finley added, "indicates some kind of imbecilic joy at being able to get your hands on a guitar."[57] Friedman's approach contradicted the aesthetic ideology of Austin artists insofar as, according to a September 1974 *Time* article on the scene, "if the Austin sound has a common trait, it is the lack, onstage, of show business antics or, in the recording studio, of slick electronic techniques. Leading musicians concretize and make records the way they drink—quickly, while everybody is looking, with few rehearsals and fewer regrets. The more natural, unlaundered, even raunchy the result, the better."[58] Authenticity here does not derive from essential identity so much as a loose, spontaneous, nontechnical approach to the performance of country music.

Friedman, however, foregrounded the show-business artifice of performance. He argued that the "Austin nerds don't like me because I got a lot of publicity for a bogus personality. Why, I'd kill any one of them with a fork. I didn't have to hang around Kenneth Threadgill's for ten years to be cool."[59] Of course, Friedman deliberately provokes here as part of that "bogus personality" ("I don't really view hippies as people," he added), but the remarks spoke to a divergent sense of the performative self, a recognition of persona that was not nearly so forthcoming in Reid's conversations with Michael Murphey or Willie Nelson. Friedman offered an honesty regarding the celebration of Texas in the decade, as well: "I've always told people I love Texas. I love Texas, I really do. But I can't say anything good about it when I'm geographically here. I have to go elsewhere to appreciate it. Right now I'm digging New York."[60] Friedman would go on to be a key artist of the Texas chic scene surrounding the Lone Star Café in New York City, but that is a story to which we will return in chapter 5.

Beyond Progressive Country: The Diversity of the Scene

Nelson, Murphey, Walker, Hubbard, Friedman, the Greezy Wheels, and others defined the bounds of progressive country and often stand in for representations of the Texas music scene in the 1970s. The subgenre attracted national attention with features in *Rolling Stone*, *Sports Illustrated*, and *Time*. Legendary producer Jerry Wexler invested in the scene during his brief tenure overseeing Atlantic's country division with albums by Willie Nelson, Doug Sahm, and Freda and the Firedogs.[61] But musical trends moved quickly in Austin as elsewhere, and it is important to recognize the diversity of Austin music in the decade. The Texas blues scene, which would triumph nationally in the 1980s with the likes of Stevie Ray Vaughan, the Fabulous Thunderbirds, and Houston's ZZ Top, developed in parallel with progressive country and attracted some of the white counterculture's best guitarists in the 1970s. Blues, in fact, preceded country as a dominant genre at the Armadillo World Headquarters. What first distinguished the experimental bent of the Armadillo from the earlier Vulcan Gas Company was its addition of country-inflected music to the scene's mix of blues, folk, and psychedelia. Indeed, perceptions of a shift from a blues-oriented to a country-oriented mode of performance over 1973 and 1974 in the eyes of local white blues artists contributed directly to Clifford Antone's founding of a downtown club explicitly for blues acts in 1975.

Prior to the progressive country explosion, though, the Armadillo had served as a regional node of the blues revival, picking up where the Vulcan Gas Company left off and developing ongoing relationships with such Texas artists as Robert Shaw, Mance Lipscomb, and Freddie King. Freddie King, indeed, held pride of place as one of the first big names to be booked by the venue. He returned often to the "house that Freddie King built" and developed an audience there. Al "TNT" Braggs, Lowell Fulson, Etta James, Sonny Terry and Brownie McGhee, and Big Joe Turner, too, put in appearances in the early years. These musicians served as mentors for aspiring white blues artists in the local audience, including Paul Ray and the Cobras, Storm, the Fabulous Thunderbirds, the Nightcrawlers, and various other acts that nurtured the early careers of such notable blues players as Doyle Bramhall, Bill Campbell, Denny Freeman, and Jimmie and Stevie Ray Vaughan. The blues scene also served as a bridge to the segregated blues world of East Austin, and figures like W. C. Clark played in bands with both mid-century stalwarts like Blues Boy Hubbard and young guns like Stevie Ray Vaughan.

Other genre scenes developed in the shadow of country and blues. Oft unrecognized, Michael Mordecai founded Fable Records as a base for Austin's rising jazz artists, and by decade's end, the Armadillo World Headquarters became the Central Texas hub of jazz performance. The gulf between memories of Armadillo World Headquarters performances and the calendar of acts to take its stage grows widest when it comes to jazz, a genre not typically associated with the space or the larger Austin scene. And yet jazz played a major role in the venue's middle and later years. Typically, participants explain this with the change in the venue's leadership, as Eddie Wilson left amid the club's financial troubles in 1976 and turned over the reins to Hank Alrich. A musician himself in several Austin bands, Alrich had a deep and abiding interest in both classic and avant-garde jazz and immediately took to booking major jazz acts. But the rise in jazz performance did not occur out of thin air, nor was it due solely to Alrich's personal taste. In fact, jazz performance spiked a year earlier, in 1975. Over the course of that year, a number of young artists began to look to embellish rock performance with jazz aesthetics, leaning more heavily on improvisational passages and horn sections in ways that straddled the line between jazz and funk. Local bands that played together on bills and hewed to this developing jazz-rock or fusion aesthetic included Beto y Los Fairlanes, Cool Breeze, Eric Johnson's Electromagnets, the Jazzmanian Devils, the Point, Starcrost, Steam Heat (later Extreme Heat), and 47 Times Its Own Weight, many of whom joined the Fable Records roster. This scene lent weight to Alrich's later decision to book more jazz acts and suggests a consistent, though admittedly small, audience for the form.

After 1976, the calendar positively sparkles with jazz performance, ranging from legends like Count Basie, Stephane Grappelli, Sonny Rollins, and Charles Mingus to the pop jazz of Chuck Mangione, to the kind of jazz-rock perhaps more properly seen as a wing of progressive rock such as Blood, Sweat, and Tears and Nova. Bookings even extended to the more difficult reaches of free jazz and jazz fusion with John McLaughlin, Pat Metheny, Old and New Dreams, and early Weather Report. Alrich recalls that the Armadillo became one of the few venues between the coasts to book many of these artists: "When Carla Bley toured, Armadillo World Headquarters was the only Carla Bley Big Band gig between New York City and the West Coast scene. . . . I brought artists that nobody else in Texas brought. When I booked Pat Metheny almost nobody outside the northeast knew who he was."[62] The presence of a jazz contingent among the Armadillo performers surprises, in part, because it departs from the pastoralist romance that drew the Texan and American counterculture to both country and the blues.

The Fable Records roster also hybridized jazz and Latin musics and, in its predilection for horns, pointed toward yet another regional subgenre born of the cultural politics of the 1970s. As Manuel Peña has documented in *Música Tejana*, a style dubbed La Onda Chicana synthesized working-class *conjunto* (an accordion-driven polka music) with middle-class *orquesta* (a smooth, pop-oriented mix of ranchera and big band jazz) to create a new style of music that took pride in Chicano forms while also remaining conversant in contemporary mainstream rock and funk. Little Joe y la Familia served as the primary arbiters of the style and extremely popular performers of a radicalized Chicano identity. Its leader, Joe Hernandez, had spent much of the 1960s in a popular band, Little Joe and the Latinaires. He had long aspired to the crossover success of such artists as fellow tejano Sunny Ozuna, who had appeared on *American Bandstand* with his hit "Talk to Me."[63] By the 1970s, however, Hernandez's priorities outstripped Dick Clark. As his trumpeter Tony "Ham" Guerrero recalled in an interview with Manuel Peña, Little Joe "said, 'I've decided we're gonna drop the Latinaire bullshit, and we're going to *la Familia*, and we're gonna become hippies with long hair.' . . . And he became the first freak in *La Onda Chicana*. *Andaba* Little Joe with real long hair down to his ass. He looked like a cross between a hippie and a militant Chicano."[64] In their countercultural renaming, the Central Texas group Little Joe y La Familia echoed a name change in the band of that other 1970s Austin "cross" between a hippie and a redneck, in Willie Nelson and Family.

The high profile of the Chicano movement drew the attention of Austin's broader cultural scene. Over Thanksgiving weekend in 1972, for example, the United Farm Workers held a benefit concert in Austin with Steve Fromholz, Greezy Wheels, Moods of Country Music, Willie Nelson, Alfonso Ramos, Teatro Chicano, and Vida, mixing the developing sounds of progressive country with La Onda Chicana.[65] The developing connections among political officeholders, insurgent labor, and popular music point to the creative ferment of Central Texas in these years. To the extent that progressive country lived up to its branding, as an updating and revising of country style, its investment in "the Texan" stood shoulder-to-shoulder with the decade's identity politics.

Progressive country, then, did not develop in a musical vacuum. It grew out of the networks developed through the national counterculture. Young people migrated from Austin, Ann Arbor, and Philadelphia to San Francisco, or from Lubbock, Dallas, and Corpus Christi to Austin, or from San Francisco back to Austin again. As they did so, like so many of their baby boomer peers, they began to yearn amid the decade's disorientations for a rootedness that, for at least some, led to a mining of country music for authentic Americana.

Country-rock, Southern rock, folk rock, the Western swing revival, blues-rock, and La Onda Chicana all testify to the resulting marriage of pastoral imagination and improvisational hybridity in musical performance. Nor does such popular music stand apart from formal politics, or the decade's discourses of gender, race, and ethnicity, or the "thin cultural slices" through which individuals navigated the new sense of commodified lifestyles. Hippie–redneck fusions did not always succeed in this matter, and the symbolic weight of the Anglo-Texan style could strain under its contradictions. As a journalist wrote in *The Rag* even as he came to embrace the cosmic cowboy, "No one has yet developed a popular image of a Black or Chicano who is hip and Texan. Trouble is, 'Texan' just doesn't seem to mix with anything but white."[66] Situating the progressive country turn in this larger cultural context constitutes the subject of the chapter that follows.

This New Cross Between Baba Ram Dass and Sam Bass

COSMIC COWBOYDOM AND THE 1970S

In April 1975, the cover of the *Austin Sun* featured musician Ed Guinn dressed in full cowboy attire, with weathered hat, oversized armadillo belt buckle, turquoise jewelry, and two longneck beers brandished as pistols, pointed cavalierly at the viewer. The caption next to the image editorialized, "Whoa!" By the spring of 1975, readers of the *Sun*, one of the new alternative weeklies to grow out of the underground press, would have been acquainted enough with the imagery to recognize the cover's disparity. The cosmic cowboy style pictured there, after all, had become closely associated with nightlife, leisure, and music in Austin during the early 1970s, and Ed Guinn would have been well known on the scene. A veteran of the band Conqueroo and an activist associated with the *Sun*, Guinn's image ran against the grain because, simply, he was an African American dressed as a 1970s cosmic cowboy. Further, he was a black man who had protested loudly against segregation in Austin ever since fighting to become the first African American accepted into the University of Texas Longhorn marching band. Finally, in his musical career, he had objected to what he saw as the inherent reactionary sensibility of the country-western aesthetic.[1] His foray into the cowboy style here was meant to jar the viewer into recognition of the racialized nature of the subculture it represented. Jeff Shero Nightbyrd, a former leader of Students for a Democratic Society who authored this cover story, emphasized the point with a question on the issue's cover, "Too Many Cosmo Cowboys in Austin?"[2]

As the cosmic cowboy scene attained high visibility in Austin by the mid-1970s, critics seized on the obvious fissures in the tenuous performative alliances between hippies and rednecks. Jeff Shero Nightbyrd made the most high-profile critique in "Cosmo Cowboys: Too Much Cowboy, Not Enough Cosmic." He emphasized the troubling gender politics of the movement: "Who has heard of the Cosmic Cowgirl? . . . The cosmo scene consists of male tribalism. Women are relegated to spectators or hangers on." Further, he assailed what he saw as the apolitical elements of the cosmic cowboy: "It doesn't take much. Particularly it doesn't require any changes in attitude like being a hippie in the sixties did. You don't have to know anything about the war, give a damn about race, tussle with psychedelics, or worry about male chauvinism. No internal restructuring is required. . . . Cosmo cowboydom allows you to be just what you always were."[3] The questions remain, then, whether this conservative valence inheres in the set of symbols surrounding the cowboy, and whether an alternate, progressive vision of Anglo-Texan masculinity was sustainable.

Movements to expand the polity and to re-affirm the culture of previously marginalized groups called into question the hegemony of Anglo-Texan masculinity, its symbols and exercise of power. Many young Anglo-Texans sympathized with these movements and, as they did so, re-investigated their own sense of identity and ties to regional culture. Ambivalence marked their experiments. They were, on the one hand, critical of the uses of "the Texan" in shoring up Anglo-masculine authority, but also, as in the contemporaneous white ethnic revival, they took new pride in a particular, rooted identity deeply associated with such privileges. This included the purported hippie–redneck convergence of progressive influences and resurgent white Southern identities. Who were the "Cosmo Cowboys" Nightbyrd felt in overabundance in Austin by the mid-1970s? What did their appearance mean, and how did it jibe with the New Texas envisioned by African Americans, Mexican Americans, and women of all races then challenging the state's status quo? This chapter examines the elements of the synthesis, first defining the attempted progressive revaluation of Anglo-Texan masculinity in the cosmic cowboy figure before moving on to the social movements for equality with which this revaluation conversed.

The talk of collapsing boundaries between hippie and redneck identity suggested to some the retreat, exhaustion, and routinization of the counterculture, its victory rendered hollow through ubiquity. "Rednecks" could appropriate the counterculture, and vice versa, not because an Aquarian utopia free of exploitation had been created, but because such stylistic gestures as long hair and beards on men had lost their disruptive charge over time. Surely, the celebration of hippie–redneck hybridity easily got out of hand, but the critics, too, overstated their case. While Nightbyrd and others dismissed the scene as the monolithic projection of a reactionary Anglo-Texan masculinity, I propose that the identity politics of the 1970s spurred fissures in the dominant, whereby an alternate, though ultimately unstable, construction of Anglo-Texan masculinity developed around the progressive country trope. The cultural nationalism of Black Power and the Chicano movement, the gendered consciousness of feminism, and the authenticity discourses of the counterculture contributed to this reappraisal of the forms of Anglo-Texan masculinity, and that reappraisal erupted in aural and visual fashion in Austin's progressive country scene.

Certainly, not every young man who donned a cowboy hat and wore his hair long became an agent of progressive change, but, in the thin cultural slices of life, each in his own way negotiated between past and present, professing allegiance to a progressive, inclusive polity while evincing a fascination with the agrarian conservatism of the cowboy figure. It is important to recognize, at the same time, that "cosmic cowboy" was never a movement so much as a moment, and it remains a label that most of the figure's contemporaries disavow. But it does have strong explanatory purchase on the rise of a generational subculture in Texas, one that begs comparison with the scholarship issuing from the Centre for Contemporary Cultural Studies in Birmingham, England, in these years. In addition to drawing this theoretical parallel, this chapter makes its central argument through a series of examples: Bud Shrake's sartorial epiphany in the Big Thicket portrayed in his article "The Land of the Permanent Wave," the school of performance-oriented folkloristics developing at the University of Texas, social movements for equality, and the outlaw country turn of the late 1970s.

Austin's participation in, and divergence from, national trends in the 1970s go far toward explaining the curious frames of Anglo-Texan masculinity that arose in the scene's cultural productions. Nationally, pundits bemoaned the collapse of a unitary public in the 1970s as Americans supposedly retreated into the identity politics of race, gender, and ethnicity, marooned themselves on consumerist islands of lifestyle, and became exhausted with the mobilizing activisms of the 1960s. However, an attention to the local in sites such as Austin shows the limits of this rhetoric in contemporary social practice.[4] The hippie–redneck confluence also echoed the larger celebration of ethnic particularity in white Southern identities, as the Solid South became the Sunbelt South, truckers entered the pantheon of American icons, and Jimmy Carter replaced Lyndon Johnson as the country's regionally accented president.[5]

Just as Austin fit uncomfortably with a number of national narratives of the 1970s, so did the state of Texas at large. As the editor of the celebrated new regional magazine *Texas Monthly*, William Broyles, set the scene:

> Confused, introspective, plagued with doubts, our economy beset by double-digit inflation and run by single-digit politicians, we can only fumble blindly from the harsh memories of 1974 into the uncertain future of 1975. Depressing, isn't it? . . . We propose that Texans consider washing their hands of the whole mess and become (drum roll, please) the Republic of Texas. We did it once, didn't we? This time, however, instead of a thinly-populated, rough, frontier republic, we'd be the world's fifth largest petroleum producer (ahead of Venezuela and Kuwait), the thirteenth largest producer of beef and fifth of cotton, and we would rank ninth in Gross National Product among the non-Communist nations of the world.[6]

Broyles underscored the old adage that Texas was different, apart, here in the 1970s, just as in 1836 or 1936, wealthy in cotton, cattle, and oil, and cocksure over that abundance. The gulf between the American and Texan zeitgeists opened by the decade's oil crises temporarily masked the decline of regional distinctiveness as Texas rapidly suburbanized. Nevertheless, this gulf fueled the fashionable celebration of "the Texan" in a process that simultaneously reified older markers of regional distinction and modernized them through a countercultural lens.

Austin represented one of many regional exceptions to the 1970s transformation of the electorate into a conservative majority coalition whose ethos has ruled through the beginning of the twenty-first century. Changes in city politics and the state Democratic Party were not merely contemporary with the scene centered on the Armadillo World Headquarters. They were, I argue, mutually constitutive. The progressive country scene sustained the energies of the left–liberal coalition that had developed in Austin over the course of the sixties.[7] At its best, then, this confluence suggests a sort of hippie–redneck populism that confounds contemporary appraisals of political polarization on the national stage. At the same time, these "best" moments were rare, and multiple failures belied the myth of the cosmic cowboy. Where and why did these "redneck" and "hippie" audiences cohere? What conditions contributed to their successful construction as an audience, and which to their failure? How did the idea of "Texas" figure into these events, and what role did the media play in its construction and reception? These questions point us back to the cusp of the decade, to the final years of the 1960s and the origins of the hippie–redneck figure.

"The Land of the Permanent Wave":
The Sartorial Import of the Redneck Counterculture

The unlikely specter of hippie–redneck fusion, and its relation to Anglo-Texan identity, had been on the imagined horizon for some time. The period from 1968 to 1970 offered a number of glimpses of the developing trope. We have already encountered the media's portrayal of the diverse audience at Janis Joplin's last Central Texas appearance, as well as Spencer Perskin's country fiddle at the heart of Shiva's Headband's psychedelic rock. In another example from 1970, Bud Shrake spent several days exploring environmental politics in the Big Thicket of East Texas, but found himself shunned at every turn. Prospects did not look good for the article he meant to file with *Sports Illustrated*, and not only because the magazine's new owners had investments in the region's lumber concerns. Shrake's editor, André Laguerre, passed on the resulting article, and it ended up in *Harper's* instead under the title "Land of the Permanent Wave." In it, Shrake made his shunning by local residents, and his attempts to rectify the situation, the centerpiece of his narrative. Shrake's challenge was that he matched locals' visual cues of the hippie. A tall Fort Worth native with Texas accent and swagger, Shrake had spent the past several years in New York, grown his hair long, and adopted other countercultural habits. The conflicting image created no small amount of consternation. "For about five hours I had been drinking scotch whiskey and arguing with a rather nice, sometimes funny old fellow named Arch," Shrake noted, "who was so offended by my moderately long hair that he had demanded to know if I weren't actually, secretly, a Communist."[8] As it turned out, Shrake's most obvious sin in East Texas was sartorial, and the meanings projected by his hair could be easily redirected: "Then the notion struck me that I could quite simply change all this. I went to the parking lot, opened the trunk of the car, and put on a battered, well-crushed cowboy hat that I have owned for years. As I turned back toward the coffee shop, there stood the cop. His mean face slowly resolved into a baffled, respectful expression, like that of a weasel facing a trap. 'Good morning,' he said. 'Hot sumbitch today,' I said. 'Yes sir, it is.'" In donning the cowboy hat, Shrake's social difficulties disappeared. State Senator Charlie Wilson, who was with Shrake on this trip, "congratulated me on having lived for a week bareheaded in East Texas without being beaten with a tire iron. 'With this hat on, they can see your hair hanging down, but a long-haired cowboy is likely to be a dangerous man best left alone.'"[9] Shrake was not alone in discovering the guise's powers, the apparent fact that the appropriation of markers of Texanness allowed for dissenters to re-enter the community, if uneasily, even as they attempted to re-fashion what it meant to be Texan.

In this time and place, a previously besieged countercultural sensibility attained a heightened visibility and acceptance through the re-valuation of regional identity markers. The artists, texts, firms, and audiences involved all invite discussion on their own terms, but a fuller understanding requires an appreciation of their cohesion as a larger scene. Normally the notion of musical scene leans heavily on its origins in the theater, suggesting that audience, industry, venues, and cityscapes serve as a backdrop for musical performance. More than mere setting, however, a scene such as Austin in the 1970s constitutes a dense web of social, political, economic, and affective relations that give meaning to, and not merely adorn, the performance of popular music.[10] By understanding this larger subjective context, we can begin to make sense of why the Armadillo World Headquarters' Eddie Wilson remembers the "Me Decade" in the following manner: "We felt the rush of joyful and energetic optimism that comes when you realize . . . that the giant tug-of-war is beginning to shift in your favor. Voices begin to speak in unison. New power rushes from your fingers through your shoulders then down your back into your legs and suddenly we've got the bastards on the run."[11] Why would Wilson frame a pop cultural endeavor so squarely in terms of struggle? He speaks here about much more than music. His Armadillo World Headquarters visibly aligned itself with what it saw as the rising tide of new politics in Texas and briefly reconfigured mainstream representations of "the Texan" with countercultural aesthetics and progressive political concerns.

The cosmic cowboy's recombination of countercultural preoccupations and "the Texan" coincided with a period of theorizing on the cultural politics of youth subcultures across the Atlantic that helps contextualize the Texas scene. The Birmingham School's classic *Resistance Through Rituals: Youth Subcultures in Post-war Britain* (1976), edited by Stuart Hall and Tony Jefferson, and Dick Hebdige's *Subculture: The Meaning of Style* (1979) argued that British working-class youth enacted a form of symbolic revolt through well-delineated subcultural styles: teddy boy, mod, rocker, skinhead, punk.[12] Austin's cosmic cowboy approximates a subcultural figure in the Birmingham sense. Class discourses function differently than in the British case, but these authors' apt assessment of patterns of consumption and performance among young people in the 1970s speak to the Austin example. In the introductory essay of *Resistance Through Rituals*, John Clarke, Stuart Hall, Tony Jefferson, and Brian Roberts define the relations between classes in a society with the terms dominant culture, subordinate culture, parent culture, and (youth) subculture. The fourth represents a stylistic reimagining of the relation among the other three, an attempt to "resolve" the problems of class conflict on the ideological plane.[13]

The clearest of their examples concerns the early British skinheads, who, "in the resurrection of an archetypal and 'symbolic' form of working-class dress, in the displaced focusing on the football match and the 'occupation' of the football 'ends,' Skinheads reassert, but 'imaginarily,' the values of a class, the essence of a style, a kind of 'fan-ship' to which few working-class adults any longer subscribe: they 're-present' a sense of territory and locality which the planners and speculators are rapidly destroying."[14]

The skinhead example suggests an analogy with the cosmic cowboy in Texas. In the 1970s, oil-rich Texas witnessed an affluence and urbanity that brought with it rapid change. Opportunities drew many whom urbanites would term "rednecks"—members of the rural or small-town white working class—to the larger cities of Houston, Dallas, San Antonio, and Austin. New jobs simultaneously drew migrants from other regions of the country, as Texas participated in the more general pattern of seventies Sunbelt growth over and against the Northeast and Midwest. This urban turn (represented later "on the ideological plane" by the television drama *Dallas* and the movie *Urban Cowboy*) fed nostalgia for an imagined "Texanness" that both "hippies," with their concern for roots and authenticity, and "rednecks," with their strong conservative streak, feared might vanish. Moreover, the hippie–redneck dichotomy itself masks the more complex experience of individuals whose backgrounds, politics, and habits did not neatly match one or the other to begin with, but blended the two as a matter of course. Hybridity discourses assume the existence of distinct species to hybridize, but a young person growing up on the outskirts of Austin or Dallas would likely be steeped in the culture of rural Texana even as he or she was attracted to the rebelliousness of countercultural peers. Such individuals reflected their generation's experience in Texas, much as Dick Hebdige's English punks "were not only directly *responding* to increasing joblessness, changing moral standards, the rediscovery of poverty, the Depression, etc., they were *dramatizing* what had come to be called 'Britain's decline.'"[15] Punk in the United States worked in much the same fashion, playing with the apocalyptic rhetoric surrounding 1970s New York. Cosmic cowboys likewise performatively articulated social change, even if the economy of Texas (unlike New York or London) was relatively strong, dramatizing the survival of "the Texan" in a region secure from national malaise but also, in some measure, unsure of its new urban and suburban landscapes.

At the same time, the cosmic cowboy differed from the British mod or punk. The subculture's creation paralleled that theorized by Birmingham fellow traveler Stanley Cohen in his *Folk Devils and Moral Panics* (1972) in that, despite the popularity of the cowboy style, the cosmic cowboy as a clearly defined figure arose primarily through localized media accounts of the Austin scene. Critics in the press used the term more frequently than did participants in the scenes surrounding the Armadillo World Headquarters, Soap Creek Saloon, Alliance Wagonyard, Austin Opera House, the Split Rail, and like venues. The cosmic cowboy subculture hung together loosely through the homology of its fashion, music, and preoccupations. In this sense, it diverged from the British subcultures that tended to be loudly declared and vigorously defended through participants' boundary maintenance. Though constructed in part through moral panics regarding youth culture in London and Brighton, British mods and rockers declared themselves as such. Cosmic cowboys, identified largely through media accounts of a style, had a more lackadaisical definition of how their fashions fit together in a subcultural whole. Few participants talked about their cosmic-cowboyness as such, in contrast to mods or skinheads or punks. In fact, many individuals engaged in the decade's countercultural celebration of "the Texan" remain highly dismissive of the style.

Homologies: Cosmic Cowboy Field Guides

The Birmingham Centre for Contemporary Cultural Studies offered a tool kit for unpacking the significance of these developments. In particular, Paul Willis's notion of subcultural homology between "the values and lifestyles of a group, its subjective experience, and the musical forms the group adopts" fits the conversations surrounding the cosmic cowboy in Austin in the mid-1970s. The authors of *Resistance Through Rituals* developed this notion of homology as a key strategy to understand the coherence of subcultural styles. When Dick Hebdige addressed punk in *Subculture*, he argued that the stylistic "objects chosen [by punks] were, either intrinsically or in their adapted forms, homologous with the focal concerns, activities, group structure, and collective self-image of the subculture."[16] In the case of the working-class mods, Hebdige read the elements of their lifestyle—Italian suits, mopeds, continental design, amphetamines—as "a parody of the consumer society in which they were situated. The mod dealt his blows by inverting and distorting the images (of neatness, of short hair) so cherished by his employers and parents."[17] In other words, individuals advertise their lifestyles, and thus cultural allegiances, through the things with which they surround themselves. To discover the homologous nature of the cosmic cowboy subculture, how its musical tastes, fashion, and political unconscious cohered through commodities, it is necessary to single out those objects selected to express the cosmic cowboy's cultural allegiances.

Conveniently, in a piece titled "Cosmic Changeling," the *Daily Texan* set out a step-by-step guide to the style. "We went ahead and designed a How To Be a Cosmic Cowboy Course especially for all you newly arrived Eastern Establishment Liberals and carpetbaggers eager to adopt this new cross between Baba Ram Dass and Sam Bass," it began, citing the fusion as a meeting of New Age Timothy Leary confrere Dass and the legendary Texas outlaw Bass. With accompanying photographs, the article provides the following advice:

1. The prerequisites are few. No previous experience is necessary. Just begin with the stripped down model of your average student hippie.
2. Leave the jeans on. Discard the rest except the hair, then add basic Western shirt of the fancy variety, boots, and Stetson. There you be.
3. For the chrome job (very important) throw in optimals like reflective mirror shades. For mystique, coke spoon from Oat Willie's, and any kind of turquoise you can afford.
4. Fill in background with old lady in gingham dress, large dog (preferably a German Shepherd named Toke or Milo), and pickup truck. The older the better (the truck, that is).
5. You're ready to ride, buckaroo. Complete the backdrop with the most essential item—a beat-up guitar made whole with autographs from the stars. Stir in stimulants.[18]

The hippies, then, would seem to have engaged in an appropriation of the uniform of their erstwhile enemies, the rednecks. The pickup trucks and boots that once signaled the proximity of violence for Austin hippies now became fashionable paeans to the authenticity of their Texas home. Likewise, young Anglo-Texan men of rural or small-town backgrounds found a terrain on which to experiment with new countercultural lifeways. Even traditional mores came in for re-use, as the above guide displays the subculture's misogynist undertones by characterizing a woman as an accessory akin to a dog or a truck.

The resulting cosmic cowboy, though, still ostensibly possessed a difference from the "real" cowboy or redneck, as evidenced in Jack Jackson's similar "Cozmic Cowboy Identification Chart" published in the *Austin Sun* on March 11, 1976. Here, the cartoon of a hirsute cosmic cowboy stood alongside the drawing of an "authentic" cowboy, the similarities and differences of the two tabulated for comparison. They shared their Western hats, shirts, and boots, but the cosmic cowboy differed in the length of his hair, the flashiness of his clothes, and the amount of jewelry, including an earring. Interestingly, these differences hinged on heavily gendered fashion accessories, rendering the cosmic cowboy's uniform a tad glam. It is even more interesting because a primary motivation in the male hippie's appropriation of cowboy/redneck style and mores may have owed to their very claim on masculinity. The performance of machismo played well on the scene, and this may be because, just as J. Frank Dobie's "homemade fascists" had long characterized the counterculture as un-Texan and un-American, conservative Anglo-Texans also questioned the manliness of young men who wore their hair long.[19]

Texas Monthly also published a redneck identification chart to aid in the discernment of the true and the false under the title "So You Want to Be a Redneck." Editor William Broyles introduced the piece with an invocation of the state's ambivalence toward its white working class: "It is not a pretty heritage, but it is ours. Rednecks at times may be violent, ignorant, and racist, but they are also the same people we venerate as settlers and pioneers. . . . This mixed heritage—with its ethics of hard work and friendship and its prejudices of race and ignorance—is the source of much of the social confusion in Texas today." And yet, Broyles argued, there was a reason for the current fascination with the redneck, his elevation as a new American hero, as the magazine's cover proclaimed. Speaking in the language of the white ethnic revival, Broyles argued that re-inventing oneself as redneck "is arguably easier for middle-class whites than waking up one morning and deciding to be black or Indian. So, if you feel affluent and rootless and wonder if the meaning has gone out of your life, you might consider 'So You Want to Be a Redneck.'"[20] Images of two couples appeared on pages that faced each other. The first carried the caption, "This here's the cleaned-up but honest-to-God Redneck pair. Don't Mess with 'em." A middle-aged, portly man with a trucker cap and rolled-up sleeves glares ahead, while his well-made-up wife or girlfriend sits in the cab of a pickup truck. The second pair consisted, notably, of two long-haired androgynes in calculated outfits, also with a pickup truck, captioned "And this is the pseudo-Redneck couple. Note worn clothes and $1000 in Indian jewelry." The gendered content of the comparison is obvious, imputing a masculine virility to the "real" redneck male, while disparaging the fashionable accessorizing, purposive dishevelment, and dilettantish pose of the "pseudo" redneck style.

Beneath the images, a chart anthropologically documents the tastes of authentic rednecks and their cosmic replicas. According to the chart's authors, observers could discern real rednecks through their tastes for Webb Pierce, Gilley's nightclub, catfish, Budweiser beer, John Wayne, bourbon, and "Roy Clark" sideburns, while pseudo-rednecks betrayed their affectations through Jerry Jeff Walker, the Armadillo World Headquarters, Mexican food, Shiner beer, Clint Eastwood, tequila, and long hair on men.[21] Note the cosmic predilection for Mexican food and tequila that, taken from the widest angle of view, might suggest a questioning of their whiteness, but more likely commented on the cosmic cowboys' ideological alignment with a more inclusive Texas in line with the Chicano movement. Stirred together, the commodities of boots, hats, and beer, combined with long hair and other stimulants, created the type of the cosmic cowboy, and yet this updated, figurative Anglo-Texan continually attracted disdain. As a member of the satirical rock group Uranium Savages wrote to the *Austin Sun* in response to Jeff Shero Nightbyrd's 1975 "Cosmo Cowboys" article:

> Dear Sun: I read with interest your story on "Cosmo Cowboys." However, the term should be cosmetic cowboys. It takes a lot of time, money and effort to keep up with the ever changing style in Indian jewelry and custom boots. Why just yesterday it seemed a '55 pickup truck was the rage and now everyone has a '75 Dodge with a camper and big tires. By the way, where can I get a sequin cowboy suit? Cosmetically yours, O. T. Tall, Sons of Uranium Savage, Pioneers of Regressive Country Glitter.[22]

Together with the *Daily Texan*'s "Cosmic Changeling," Jackson's "Cosmic Cowboy Identification Chart," and *Texas Monthly*'s "So You Want to Be a Redneck" guide, the Uranium Savage letter evinces the regional obsession with parsing out visually the differences between hippies and cosmic cowboys, cosmic cowboys and real cowboys, and even pseudo-rednecks and real rednecks. The tone plants tongue firmly in cheek, but nevertheless points to a very real anxiety about the changing nature of Texas and the performative discourses of self in the 1970s.

In the midst of 1970s flux, in other words, Anglo-Texans repackaged markers of region and class as "lifestyle," seeking to fix subject positions through the agency of commodity consumption. Sociologist Sam Binkley, writing on the 1970s, argues that "the experience of the new is often one of disaffiliation and rupture within previously consolidated groups, but also a regrouping, an investment, emulation (or even fetishization) of identity across boundaries dividing previously competing groups."[23] The "hippie–redneck" or "cosmic cowboy" fusion exhibited these qualities in a moment heady for the denizens of Sunbelt Texas trying to find their post-1960s, post–civil rights, post-industrial footing. The Austin scene propelled a new investment in Anglo-Texan masculinity through commodities that, consumed and displayed together, constituted a lifestyle. Businesses that developed around this subcultural consumption often made the links explicit. As KOKE-FM, the radio station that pioneered the local progressive country format for the airwaves, proclaimed, "We're not just a radio station—we're a Texas lifestyle."[24] Cultural geographer David Harvey has argued that in the midst of the postmodern shift, the "assertion of any place-bound identity has to rest at some point on the motivational power of tradition. It is difficult, however, to maintain any sense of historical continuity in the face of all the flux and ephemera of flexible accumulation. The irony is that tradition is now often preserved by being commodified and marketed as such."[25] Each of the elements of countercultural Texas style followed Harvey's assertion—markers of tradition available in the marketplace, often with a fetish for the craftsmanship of pre-industrial methods.

Enter the cult of the cowboy boot. A *Texas Monthly* article of 1976 made the argument: "Perhaps even more than the cowboy hat and shirt, a pair of boots is quintessentially Texan and, by extension, quintessentially American. Until recently, this was something that a lot of native sons tried to sweep under the rug, but now, thanks to Willie, Jerry Jeff, progressive country, and—yes, even to Lyndon—it's become a source of pride rather than acute embarrassment. Texas chic, our own homegrown variety of redneck chic, is just the natural outgrowth of the cowman and the hippie being friends."[26]

Boots, like their wearers, could be assessed according to their presumed authenticity, whether they approached "the real" of function or merely served fashionable ends: "There are a few clues, though, that will help you tell the real true-grit cowboy and the rodeo star from the cheap imitation cosmic variety.... The only real problem in telling the cowboys (real and rodeo) from the cosmics is that there's been some cross-pollination between them lately. The cowboys are easing into lower heels and rounder toes while the cosmics are tottering around in high-heeled boots just like the real McCoy."[27] Buck Steiner's Capitol Saddlery, a few blocks away from the Austin Capitol building, was ground zero for this cross-pollination. In addition to being a leather-making tycoon, Steiner's family was rodeo royalty who had reportedly engaged in bootlegging during Prohibition. A bit of an iconoclast, Steiner exhibited an appreciation for the Austin counterculture, and Austin's hippies returned the favor. Jerry Jeff Walker promoted the shop and recorded a song about Steiner's master boot maker, Charlie Dunn.[28] The celebration of boots, of course, constituted only one element of the subculture. Cowboy hats came in for their share of devotion, too, especially those from local makers such as Manny Gammage, another Walker confrere. Long hair on men transformed the meanings attached to boots and hats, and, in the context of the hirsute 1970s, signified much.[29]

In addition to boots, hats, and hair, the expressive function of brand loyalty to Texas beers such as Lone Star, Pearl, and Shiner in the regional subculture should not be underestimated.[30] As late as the 1970s, the United States was still a map of fairly distinct beersheds. Indeed, the regulatory laws governing interstate commerce in alcoholic beverages, holdovers from the prohibitionist impulse, served as the basic conceit for the popular 1977 film *Smokey and the Bandit*. In Texas in the 1970s, the drinking age, like the voting age, fell to eighteen, and liquor by the drink first became available in Austin. In the beginning, the Armadillo World Headquarters did not intend to serve alcohol at all (following the example of the Vulcan Gas Company), but economics and demand intervened. Soon enough, as Armadillo employee Fletcher Clark recalled, "if music [was] the soul of the Armadillo, beer [was] certainly its blood."[31] Promotional materials would claim that only the Astrodome sold more beer than the Armadillo.[32] Accordingly, bartending became one of the most prestigious positions on the Armadillo floor and, not coincidentally, a strictly male domain. Male bartenders claimed that women did not have the discriminating taste to tell the difference between finely crafted Texas beers, each of which had its rabid partisans. As an experiment, employee Leea Mechling switched the lines to the Lone Star and Pearl taps. No one noticed for days. For all of the blustery attachment to Lone Star, Pearl, and Shiner beers, then, the attraction owed not to taste but to cultural capital, the beers' association with working-class lifestyles and country music.[33]

The Armadillo World Headquarters' early lack of a beer and wine license made for some tense near-confrontations with local authorities. In one such instance, Texas Alcoholic Beverage Commission officials burst into the offices of the Armadillo, where a small group was partaking of alcohol. Luckily for the venue's countercultural denizens, *Monday Night Football* announcer and former Dallas Cowboys quarterback Don Meredith was among them, a guest of Bud Shrake. The officers lit up upon recognizing Meredith, who put his hands on their shoulders, escorted them out the doors, and signed autographs. Eddie Wilson grabbed Bobby Hedderman by the elbow and told him to go get one of the gaudy basketball trophies they happened to have in storage under the stage. "I gave the trophy to Eddie and he took it to the stage as the band finished their set," Hedderman recalled. "Eddie relayed to the audience what had just taken place and called Don Meredith to the stage. Underneath the anemic stage lights Don accepted the trophy. 'You may not know it,' he said, 'But this is what I really always wanted.'"[34] Such prestigious contacts eased the Armadillo's way with traditional audiences and legal authorities and marked the city's evolution from the hostility shown the Vulcan Gas Company.

The interpretation of the Austin scene as a Texas lifestyle crafted from the traditional commodities of beer, boots, and hats made for a kind of folk culture that interested the scholars at the University of Texas. Just as Dobie and

Bedichek had theorized an organic Anglo-Texan nationalism joining men and land, progressive country and its attendant fashions suggested a performance of "the Texan" that often claimed a natural relationship among the homologous elements of the subculture, rather than their artifice. The notion of authenticity, though, need not be a bogeyman here, as these performances possessed a great deal of self-consciousness. Further, there may well be an "authentic" element to such musics and styles in Central Texas. As ethnomusicologist Aaron Fox has defended the concept in its relation to country music performance in nearby Lockhart, "The working-class claim on 'country music' is coherent, justified, and ethical—that is to say, 'authentic.' . . . Explaining 'country' culturally, in terms of forms of personal and communal local musical practices rather than industrially mediated processes, is not to 'folklorize' country music, or to lose sight of political economy."[35] Country music has long invited such fierce contestation over its claims to authenticity, as it conveys a certain organic relationship fusing ideas of the American nation, whiteness, and rurality.

Many young Anglo-Texans donning boots and hats in Austin in the 1970s could make claims to a rural or small-town background. Their relation to the subject position of "redneck" often made sense, but the elision of this position with the cowboy guise was often more tenuous. To the extent that they did have experiences of rurality, the referent would as likely be farming as ranching. Artists frequently heralded the cowboy in song as a handy metaphor for an older, rural Texas, but it was often an imagined Texas outside the experience of both the "hippies" and the "rednecks" gathering in Austin. Television Westerns, in particular, had a formative influence on baby boomers inside and outside the Lone Star State. Bruce Willenzik, an important figure in the Armadillo's later years and the founder of the Armadillo Christmas Bazaar, has said of some of his earliest notions of Austin formed in New Orleans that, "when I was five years old, 1952, I told my mama I was gonna live in the capital city of Texas 'cause I was watching the cowboys on TV and they lived in Texas and they met in the capital city. . . . I had to live there 'cause that's where I could wear my hat and tote my little six gun, you know, ride my little broomstick horse around and that was my dream was to come to Austin and live here when I grew up."[36] Similarly, a Texas icon like Willie Nelson has testified to the influence of the singing cowboy pictures he watched as a boy in Hillsboro. Culturally, North Texas immersed Nelson more in the cotton South than the cattle West, and his first bands leaned toward Western swing in their cowboy style wrapped around the aural core of jazz and the local accents of Czech and German polka. As his biographer Joe Nick Patoski noted, "Willie and [his sister] Bobbie fantasized about cowboys and cowgirls, horses and singing.

Their play acting did not include cotton," though their everyday life included plenty.[37] Likewise, Nelson's frequent collaborator Waylon Jennings reflected on his upbringing in Littlefield, near Lubbock: "You'd figure growing up in West Texas we'd practically be cowboys ourselves, but most of our six-gun lore came from the movies. I considered us farmers."[38] Don Graham, a leading scholar of the state's literature, grew up in Parker near the site of what would become the Ewings' Southfork Ranch on television's *Dallas*; but that, too, was cotton land, and cowboys entered these parts of Texas via movie screens, just as they did in Nelson's Hillsboro and Jennings's Littlefield and elsewhere in the United States and the world.[39]

One need not go so far as Birmingham, England, to find scholars interested in this convergence of performativity and identity. In Austin, a school of performance-oriented folklorists arose in these years among Américo Paredes's students and colleagues at the University of Texas. While this theoretical school did not quite make the mark that Birmingham did in subsequent cultural studies, its manifesto *"And Other Neighborly Names": Social Process and Cultural Image in Texas Folklore* (1981), with chapters by Roger Abrahams, Richard Bauman, Archie Green, José Limón, and Manuel Peña, has a direct relevance to the musical scene with which these scholars lived. Roger Abrahams was a fixture at the early Threadgill's folk nights. Manuel Peña was a musician on the verge of becoming the foremost chronicler of tejano musics. Many of the rest had deep connections in the social networks of the Austin scene. As Bauman and Abrahams described their endeavor at the beginning of that volume, performance-oriented folkloristics consists of three basic traits, undergirded by the now-obvious notion that "on the one hand, folklore must be observed in its living place and, on the other, in terms of its social and even political ramifications."[40] First, the performance-oriented folkloristics school is "marked by a deep personal sense of real life that goes through and beyond the nostalgia that tends, in most places, to overwhelm the study of local folklore."[41] The "in most places" phrasing here served less to distinguish performance-oriented folkloristics geographically as it did historically, contrasting the Paredes school with the Dobie school. Nevertheless, they did not completely eschew Dobie's legacy. A second "characteristic that sets these Texas folklorists apart from the mainstream of American folklore study . . . is that they have seen themselves not only as scholar–collectors of lore of their own people and region, or as authors in the purely academic sphere, but as writers for a readership that went far beyond the academy." However, this popular orientation, a positive holdover from the Dobie generation, could also crash against the dangers of Bedichek's occasional blut und boden tendencies: "When you know your group as an insider, you will also have a clear sense of who the outsiders are."[42] In short, performance-oriented folkloristics provided an intellectual analog to the aural markers of progressive country in Austin, a further theorization of "the Texan" in the decade synthesizing old and new, Dobie's nostalgic formulations and Paredes's challenge to them joined through an attention to folkloric performance. *"And Other Neighborly Names"* deployed this methodology on such subjects as dear to the cosmic cowboy as dogs, rodeo, the Chicano movement, storytelling, conjunto, and, in an influential chapter by Archie Green subtitled "Words in Collision," the cosmic cowboy subculture itself.

La Raza Unida: Cultural Nationalism in the Borderlands

The inclusion of Green's essay in a volume dedicated to Paredes gestured toward the relationship between youth culture's appropriation and re-visioning of Anglo-Texan nationalism and the wider field of progressive identity politics that enlivened the 1970s moment. In these years, an attention to cultural specificity over and against the assimilationist ideal gave rise to a nationalist model of understanding race and ethnicity. In positing metaphorical nationalism, such movements competed with the Anglo-Texans' own elaborate brand of nationalist thinking. Though cultural nationalism participated in reifying essentialisms just as the Anglo-Texans' vision did, these movements generally provoked a salutary contestation over identity that revealed Texanness as relational and constructed, rather than normative or natural. Historians should not overstate the assimilationist/nationalist or liberal/militant dichotomy in the civil rights movements of the postwar period. The NAACP had its militants, to be sure, and LULAC never advocated the complete abandonment of Spanish language or Mexican culture.[43] Rather than an evolutionary trend in which cultural nationalism follows neatly on earlier, liberal civil rights movements, the two should be seen as coexisting tendencies that have different moments of dominance in the public sphere. The late 1960s and early 1970s marked one of those periods in which radical nationalist positions came to the fore. African Americans, Mexican Americans, Native Americans, and others articulated a sense of difference whereby activists defined each group as a sort of nation-within-a-nation, distinct from the culture of whiteness that presumed itself at the center of the American experience. A growing sense of cultures as particular, and the American nation as pluralist, came into greater view in the wake of Stokely Carmichael's declaration for Black Power in 1966, and this nationalist turn possessed tremendous significance, especially for the Chicano movement, in Texas.

THIS NEW CROSS BETWEEN BABA RAM DASS AND SAM BASS

The race-as-nation rhetoric emanating from the Black Panthers, Ron Karenga's US Organization in California, and the radicalized Student Nonviolent Coordinating Committee under Carmichael and H. Rap Brown resonated with militant black groups in Dallas, Austin, and Houston. Fred Bell fronted the Black Panthers in Dallas, Austin became home to Houston transplants Larry Jackson (formerly an aide to Congressmen George H. W. Bush) and Lee Otis Johnson, and Houston witnessed some of the most dramatic confrontations of the period with uprisings at Texas Southern University and a pitched gun battle with police that killed People's Party II leader Carl Hampton in the summer of 1970.[44] The state's Mexican American activists, too, found inspiration in cultural nationalism and often posited that nationalist stance as a direct counter to the existing discourses of Anglo-Texan nationalism. Historiography aided this endeavor, as the state's public history had long vilified Mexican Americans even as it had erased African Americans. J. T. Canales could turn to Juan Cortina, and Américo Paredes could refashion Gregorio Cortez, as key individuals of the Texas national story to be contested and refigured. However, the history of African American resistance to Anglo power in the state remained more submerged in dominant narratives, its rebellions—slave revolts, Reconstruction, Populist political campaigns, the Camp Logan mutiny of 1917—shrouded in anonymity.[45] Anglos used the stories of open warfare against Mexico and Mexicans to buttress a sense of Anglo-Texan national identity, by extension proffering a public narrative to be reinvented by tejanos. By contrast, slavery and defeat in the Civil War did not redound to one-sided tales of Anglo-Texan glory, and thus were often rendered invisible in the public script.[46]

Mexican American participation in the national discourses of Texanness has an additional source. The U.S. Southwest stands out in the history of American expansionism as a product of war between revolutionary New World republics. Among tejanos, this made for variant resonances of territoriality, sovereignty, and claims to a homeland. In particular, the Nueces Strip's position as a true irredenta—a bounded territory whose sovereignty is held by an occupying power while it remains linguistically, culturally, and historically tied to a neighboring nation—accounts for the divergence. This South Texas space between the Nueces River and Rio Grande had been part of the Nuevo Santander/Tamaulipas state under Spanish and Mexican rule, rather than in the administrative district of Texas. Political leaders of the Republic of Texas and the United States claimed otherwise, and this territory directly led to the outbreak of war between the United States and Mexico in 1846. The history of conquest made South Texas a key site of territorial and cultural contestation. While the point can be overstated, the discourse of territoriality and sovereignty that figured into the more radical cultural nationalist movements of the late 1960s and early 1970s struck a responsive chord in the state's Chicano activism.

The Chicano movement combined the concerns of electoral politics and social activism as its leaders moved from a focus on inclusion as citizens to the achievement of political power in Mexican American majority areas of the state, using cultural nationalism as a mobilizing force. The Chicano movement's manifesto of 1969, "El Plan Espiritual de Aztlán," referred to a mythic homeland of the Aztecs in the U.S. Southwest prior to their migration to the central valley of Mexico. Though mythic, the rhetoric overlapped with the subjective experience of homelands lost in the Nueces Strip and Winter Garden regions of South Texas. These spaces, along with New Mexico, perhaps best fit the nationalist arguments of the Southwestern Chicano movement—irredenta in which many counties had majority Mexican American and Mexican populations.

The Mexican American Youth Organization (MAYO) provided the movement's Texas vanguard, and its successor, La Raza Unida Party, its apotheosis.[47] Though the successes of both rested in a deeply collaborative social movement, José Angel Gutiérrez became a prevailing public face for both. A working-class native of Crystal City, José Angel Gutiérrez had attended college in Kingsville. In 1967, while a graduate student in San Antonio, he joined with Juan Patlán, Willie Velásquez, Ignacio Pérez, and Mario Compean to found MAYO. Soon afterward, the organization shifted its focus from the Mexican American metropolis to Crystal City and the Winter Garden region in South Texas. The place had a singular history of bucking against the Anglo political machines that had for so long controlled the counties of South Texas. Four years earlier, in 1963, Juan Cornejo, the Teamsters, and the Political Association of Spanish-Speaking Organizations had organized among field workers and Del Monte plant workers to elect a Mexican American slate of candidates to the City Council of Crystal City. The state sent Texas Rangers to "keep order," and the Del Monte plant doubled hourly wages and went into overtime production to suppress voting. Nevertheless, Cornejo's entire United Citizens slate of five was elected, the first Mexican Americans to hold office since Zapata County's incorporation in 1910.[48] They were voted out of office in 1965, but their brief success provided a model for future campaigns.

MAYO activists made note of such prospects for electoral success, but they began their organizing in South Texas around issues of education. The Mexican American education agenda often differed from that of African American groups. Mexican American student populations suffered high levels of segregation. In areas of the state with large Mexican American populations, however, the segregationist wall often proved porous, meaning that a number of loosely integrated Mexican-Anglo schools existed. As political battles over education erupted along the border, the issues thus involved disparities within schools in addition to those between schools. Where Mexican and Anglo students shared a campus under Anglo teachers and administrators, Mexican students tended to be underrepresented in extracurricular activities, were forbidden from speaking Spanish, and were more harshly punished than Anglos for similar disciplinary infractions. MAYO ascertained these disparities through organizing in schools and called for their rectification. In addition, they demanded more Chicano teachers and administrators, and changes to the content of the curriculum, especially in Texas history. Inclusion was not so much the issue in 1969 Kingsville and Crystal City, as it had been in 1956 Mansfield; instead, it was the nature of that inclusion and the authority exercised within educational institutions that mattered. MAYO used the direct action measures of the school walkout and boycott to great effect in these situations, pressuring local school districts with the threat of reduced funding through absenteeism. MAYO initiated thirty-nine such walkouts in South Texas between 1967 and 1970.[49]

La Raza Unida Party developed out of these MAYO activities in 1970. Having mobilized support in South Texas, a number of MAYO organizers felt that the next obvious step involved forming an ethnically based political party to run against the Anglo Democratic machines that took Chicano votes for granted. While Raza Unida quickly expanded throughout the Southwest and Midwest, its most significant electoral successes and base of power always remained in Texas. Raza Unida's effectiveness on the local level there, like MAYO's, owed to its combination of militant nationalist rhetoric with pragmatic political ends. As Ignacio García, a party member and one of its first historians, has argued, they "placed importance on getting immediate results by being resilient, adaptable to shifting political winds. . . . They shunned the dogmatic approach of sectarian groups in order to avoid ideological limitations on their freedom of action and choice."[50] Nevertheless, Gutiérrez never shied from militant rhetoric. He envisioned Raza Unida as an ethnic-based, interest group party, and, in a move sure to draw attention, publicly compared it to what he saw as George Wallace's party for whites, the American Independent Party.[51] The fiery rhetoric worked, and soon after its founding in 1970, Raza Unida figured significantly in the state's political calculus.

Gutiérrez's primary objective with Raza Unida remained the pragmatic one of gaining power over taxation and the courts in Zavala County to create a local–regional model for others to follow.⁵² This attention to local control of institutions squared closely with the proposed objectives of militant nationalists—black, Chicano, Puerto Rican, and Native American—throughout the United States. But Raza Unida's tremendous practical success—they won mayoral elections in Cotulla and Carrizo Springs and control of two city councils and school boards in the first year of their existence—would not be shared by militants elsewhere. In fact, this local–regional electoral model brought Gutiérrez into conflict not only with more media-oriented and vanguardist urban radicals like Corky Gonzales's Crusade for Justice in Denver, but also with Texas compatriots like Ramsey Muñiz. Originally a moderate, relatively unknown activist with the party's Waco chapter, Muñiz's charismatic bearing as the party's gubernatorial candidate in 1972 and 1974 rendered him, in the eyes of many, the party's standard-bearer. As opposed to Gutiérrez, Muñiz believed in campaigning throughout the state, courting Anglo liberals, and basing the party in the urban barrios rather than the small towns and rural areas of South Texas. In the end, Muñiz's high profile backfired with a 1976 arrest on drug trafficking charges. The scandal damaged the party's reputation among the older, more socially conservative Mexican Americans Gutiérrez courted in small-town South Texas.⁵³ The party's strong showing in 1972 and 1974, however, had still been enough to hasten the fracturing of the Democratic coalition as the votes sapped from Democratic totals in both elections strengthened the possibilities for Republican victory statewide by 1978. Far more important, though, Raza Unida broke through the conservative Anglo political machines that ruled the border counties as personal fiefdoms in the modern period. Though Gutiérrez's militant, third-party vision did not survive past the elections of 1978, the space for political self-determination that the party created did.

In Austin, the Chicano movement's activists included politician Gonzalo Barrientos, artist Amado Peña, Raza Unida leader María Elena Martínez, and poet Raul Salinas, in addition to the developing Mexican American Studies program on the University of Texas campus, led by Paredes's colleagues and protégés.⁵⁴ The Brown Berets, too, founded in Los Angeles on the model of the Black Panther Party, established a presence in Austin under Paul Hernandez and aligned with the Berets' more forceful presence in San Antonio.⁵⁵ Contemporaneous with the developing hippie–redneck fusion among Anglos whereby the counterculture refigured the traditional iconography of "the Texan," the Chicano movement in early-1970s Austin also established a high profile, and used it to critique the traditional exercise of Anglo power. After a police shooting of a Chicano in his home in 1974, for example, Hernandez led the Brown

Berets in a protest in front of the city's central police station: "We assembled under Interstate 35, right next to the police station, and we were having our rally when we heard Mayor Roy Butler speaking from the roof of the cop shop, where there were about thirty to forty helmeted police with riot gear, automatic weapons, the works. Butler stood there with the microphone, talking down to the people. . . . And they were going to provide a microphone down there so we could talk up to him and he could talk down to us."[56] Instead of enduring this condescension, Hernandez led the marchers to Roy Butler's home in an upper-class neighborhood on the west side of town. Hernandez thus underscored the city's segregation based in the Master Plan of 1928.[57]

In addition to public protest, Austin's Chicano movement followed both the model of black officeholders in pressing for greater political representation and that of the mainstream Chicano movement in its focus on labor issues. Gonzalo Barrientos ran for state representative from Austin in 1974 carrying an endorsement from César Chávez, whose United Farm Workers organized in the Lower Rio Grande Valley.[58] As in California, the Lower Rio Grande Valley housed the factories in the field of modern agribusiness tended largely by Mexican migrant labor. Often treated as peripheral to the concerns of the capital, the UFW and other farm worker groups led marches to Austin that dramatized their concerns, as early as 1966 and deep into the 1970s.[59] In El Paso, the high-profile strike against the Farah Garment Factory brought Chicana workers to the fore of both the Chicano movement and national labor militancy.[60] Labor issues did not solely exist along the border, either. In Austin itself, a highly publicized strike at Economy Furniture from November 1968 to March 1971 became a cause célèbre for the local Chicano movement and its progressive allies. In an echo of prior struggles such as the San Antonio pecan-shellers' strike of the late 1930s, a predominantly Mexican and Mexican American workforce walked out over the nonrecognition of their union, Local 456 of the Upholsterers International. The National Labor Relations Board sided with the union soon after the vote for unionization, but manager Milton Smith resisted the NLRB, fought the order to negotiate in court, and lost.

These strikes, which electrified the Chicano movement in Texas, involved large numbers of Mexican American and Mexican women, placing them at the forefront of an activist field whose media portrayals emphasized the likes of Gutiérrez and Muñiz. The shared masculinist ground of Anglo-Texan nationalism and much of the public Chicano challenge to it made for a doubly challenging situation for women of color. This rendered the accomplishments of black women and Chicana officeholders and activists all the more impressive in the period. Barbara Jordan was foremost among African American lawmakers in the state, and the effective organization of African American welfare recipients was most often an affair conducted by women such as Velma Roberts in East Austin. Likewise, in the Chicano movement, paeans to machismo and carnalismo aside, strong Chicana leadership, from Dolores Huerta's example in the United Farm Workers to María Elena Martinez in the Austin branch of Raza Unida, shined through in the decade's labor and political militancy. The women's movement in Texas began to address the broader issues posed by the gendered nature of power disparities in the state.

Lone Star Women's Liberation

Movements for racial and ethnic equality did not always forthrightly engage the contemporaneous politics of women's liberation, but, in the spirit of the times, the two were always intertwined. The feminist elaboration of gender as a category of social inequality directly affected discourses on Texas in the 1970s. More to the point, Texas feminists engaged in material interventions that attended their discursive ones. They played a national role through both *Roe v. Wade* and the Carter administration's outreach to the women's movement, and their activities back home also resisted women's frequent erasure in the symbolic "Texan." Anglo-Texan identity had long encompassed a variant performativity for women, a frontier femininity that existed as a kind of mirror to the masculinist Anglo-Texan. Confidence, bluster, and independence associated with either the "tough prairie mother" or the "cowgirl" stereotype prevailed, from Texas Guinan, Miriam Ferguson, and Bonnie Parker to Molly Ivins and Ann Richards. Texas Guinan, "Queen of the Nightclubs" and veteran silent-film cowgirl, had gone far to establish the brashness of flapper New Womanhood in 1920s New York, and Miriam Ferguson served as the first woman governor of Texas in the same decade.[61] The visibility of such early figures provided performative models of Texas women in the public sphere, but they typically stood apart from reformist currents aimed at redressing women's second-class status in Texas. The state's ancestors of second-wave feminism, women like suffragist Minnie Fisher Cunningham, hewed more to models of middle-class Progressivism.

The new feminism born in the years following Betty Friedan's *The Feminine Mystique* (1963) developed in Texas, as in other states, not only out of frustration with the constricted lot of women in postwar America, but also from the chauvinism experienced even within the civil rights, antiwar, and student movements. In the 1960s, young Texas women primed to challenge inequality in the wider world discovered such injustice even among the movement's beloved community. Casey Hayden of Victoria and Austin proved a vital link in this chain that theorized the new wave of women's liberation for the 1970s. Together with Mary King, Hayden in 1965 penned "Sex and Caste: A Kind of Memo," an internal SNCC document instrumental in drawing attention to the movement's hypocritical record on gender.[62] As Hayden and King argued, "Having learned from the movement to think radically about the personal worth and abilities of people whose role in society had gone unchallenged before, a lot of women in the movement have begun trying to apply those lessons to their own relations with men."[63] The feminism opened up by Friedan's critique of postwar domesticity found new fire by the late 1960s in women's liberation, a shift from liberal to radical rhetoric akin to the assimilationist–nationalist shift in the racial justice movements of the period.

By 1965, Hayden had left the Austin that did so much to form her sensibilities, but the community continued to harbor an independent women's movement that left a distinct imprint on the larger city. Feminists created a series of independent institutions such as Red River Women's Press, Austin Women's Center, the bookstore Book Woman, communal houses in the neighborhoods west of the University of Texas, the publication *Texas Woman*, and University Women's Liberation. According to Frieda Werden, the peak of the movement's fervor came in 1974 or 1975, coinciding with the florescence of the city's Chicano movement and progressive country music scene.[64] These activist energies inhabited semi-autonomous spheres, to be sure, but they also overlapped in ways that expressed a desire to map a new Texas and sense of Texanness. We have already seen the rise of Chicana leadership in the decade's labor and political activism with figures such as María Elena Martínez. Progressive country, though like the Chicano movement often prone to a masculinist swagger, also had its feminist variants. Feminists fronted their own progressive country band, the Soeur Queens, and came out to cheer on Marcia Ball's ironic rendition of Tammy Wynette's "Stand by Your Man" at the Split Rail, a tongue-in-cheek performance akin to Ray Wylie Hubbard's or Kinky Friedman's inversions of "Okie from Muskogee."[65]

Some women in this scene began their own revisions and critiques of the symbolic Texan's masculine swagger. Frieda Werden was a particularly effective advocate in this regard. In 1975, she worked with both the new regional magazine *Texas Monthly* and the feminist publication *Texas Woman*. In the second of these two publications, she critiqued the first in an article titled "'Balls,' Said the Queen, or Tit for Tat in Texas," calling out what she saw as the sexist language of *Texas Monthly* and the centrality of chauvinist behavior to the performance of "the Texan." Objecting to the ever-present attribution of "balls"

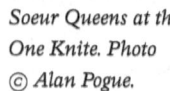

Soeur Queens at the One Knite. Photo © Alan Pogue.

to a courageous or bold act taken by a journalist, Werden sarcastically proposed such alternative editorial comments as "I dig this. Real womby," or "Pretty titsy!"⁶⁶ Her article evidences the fact that the brashness of "the Texan" need not be a male domain, and feminists could easily re-tool its ardor to make themselves heard among the traditionally conservative din of the state. Werden's tenure at *Texas Woman*, together with editors C. A. Moore, Carol Stalcup, and Carolyn Cates Wylie, brought a diverse array of topics to the fore that connected Texans to the national women's movement. *Texas Woman* also crafted a usable past for Texas feminists with articles on the Chicken Ranch in La Grange, women's prisons, nineteenth-century Texas sculptor and intellectual Elisabet Ney, and the history of women in the state's labor movement.

As with the African American and Mexican American civil rights movements, the women's movement sought candidates and allies in the formal realm of electoral politics. In a political culture marked by the exclusion of women, Austin elected Sarah Weddington as the first woman to represent the city in the Texas House of Representatives in 1972. Ann Richards managed that campaign as well as that of the African American representative Wilhelmina Delco in 1974 prior to Richards's own run for Travis County commissioner in 1976. As women entering the good ol' boy sphere of Texas politics, each had to endure discrimination and often-overt hostility. At a Texas AFL-CIO convention, for example, Weddington found herself confronted with a brash reporter. "Off the record, Mizzes Weddington, you really have beautiful legs, and they'll probably take you a long way." "That's what they said about Ben Barnes," Weddington replied, referencing the former lieutenant governor embarrassed by the Sharpstown influence-peddling scandal, "and look where he is now."[67] In another instance, Ann Richards, recently elected as Travis County commissioner, had begun to visit the local offices of the county's road crews. In one, after encountering stony silence from the men working there, she decided to break the ice by asking after a particularly ugly dog she had noticed on the way inside:

> Texas men will always talk about their dogs. Nothing. No one said a word. There was some shuffling of feet. I thought, "There must be something unseemly about the dog's name, it's the only answer." I looked around the room and they were ducking my gaze. "Let me tell you," I said, "that I am the only child of a very rough-talking father. So don't be embarrassed about your language. I've either heard it or I can top it." "So, what's the dog's name?" An old hand in the back row with a big wide belt and a big wide belt buckle sat up and said . . . "Her name is Ann Richards." I laughed. And when I laughed they roared. . . . From then on those guys and I were good friends.[68]

Such ability to absorb and redirect slights through humor to be "one of the boys" proved an effective weapon in Richards's arsenal on her path to becoming governor and a national figure in the Democratic Party.

Weddington, too, had a larger role in American history than as the first woman elected state representative from Austin. Prior to her election, the Austin feminist Judy Smith had approached Weddington, recently graduated from the University of Texas Law School, about drawing up a federal test case on abortion.[69] In the youth-oriented spirit of the early 1970s, Weddington argued the resulting *Roe v. Wade* before the Supreme Court, at age twenty-seven the youngest attorney ever to do so. *Roe v. Wade* marks one of two milestones in the women's movement that drew the nation's attention to Texas; the National Women's Conference of 1977 held in Houston was the other. In 1975, a United Nations conference in Mexico City declared "The International Year of Women," and President Gerald Ford and Congress called for a national women's conference to focus on the challenges, problems, and promise involved in the changing status of women in American society. The National Organization for Women chose Houston as the site of the conference for a number of reasons, including the pro-woman policies of Mayor Fred Hofheinz. Hofheinz had established the office of women's advocate in Houston in 1976. By 1977, when the National Women's Conference convened, the nation had come to see in Texas, and especially in the metropolis of Houston, the rising Sunbelt tide.

State conferences elected the slate of delegates to the national gathering. Though conservatives attempted to capture the delegations in a number of states, women associated with the state's feminist movement dominated the Texas proceedings in Austin in June 1977. The conference provided a watershed in mainstreaming the concerns of the women's movement and gave rise to such empowering and novel events as Lady Bird Johnson introducing the keynote speech by Barbara Jordan, who spoke of handing a gavel once used by Susan B. Anthony to New York Congresswoman Bella Abzug to oversee the conference.[70] In the end, social conservatives controlled about 20 percent of the delegates within the conference itself, and anti-ERA activist Phyllis Schlafly led a spirited coalition of counterdemonstrators in Houston. The state government came down on the side of Schlafly's group, though, with Governor Dolph Briscoe appeasing values voters by proclaiming the week of the conference "Family Week" in Texas. The state's ruling clique, and especially the wealthy white rancher governors among that group, was not quite ready for women's liberation, Texas style.[71] They shared this reluctance with a wider backlash then gaining steam nationwide.

Outlaw Masculinity: "I'm Just Mean, and I Feel Wonderful"

Like the cosmic cowboy trope, the backlash to the women's movement cannot be seen as simply cultural or simply political, nor confined to a particular medium. It transcended cultural sensibilities and formal politics and took many forms. Movements for race and gender equality reverberated in new consideration of the normative categories of white ethnicity and masculinity in the 1970s. Intellectuals, artists, and everyday folk came to ask what it meant to "be white" or "be a man," rendering both as particular aspects of identity rather than universal norms against which to define "the other." Nationally, Black Power and the Chicano movement inspired a rethinking of the multiple identities submerged in whiteness, resulting in a new attention to white ethnicity. Further, the passion for knowing the authentic self through knowing the identity of one's "people" fed not only off Black Panther militancy, but also off the rage for genealogy inspired by the television miniseries *Roots* (1977).[72] Michael Novak's book *The Rise of the Unmeltable Ethnics* (1972) had earlier crystalized a renaissance in which hyphenate-Americans came to take new pride in their Italianness, Irishness, or Polishness. "White" came to be seen as not nearly so natural as it seemed, and provoked such rethinking not merely among Northern ethnics, but also among Southern whites. For example, when Texas writer Larry L. King became frustrated at being deemed racist in the atmosphere of black nationalism on Northern campuses, he set out to write a book chronicling how he, a white Southerner, had always been a productive liberal in racial matters. The book that resulted though, *Confessions of a White Racist* (1971), with a title that would recur in one of Novak's chapters, instead acted as a kind of memoir of King's own white privilege as he came to realize how little he had really done to grapple with the weight of American racism in his own experience.

These developments provided ground for meaning and a usable past in the unsteadying 1970s. Similarly, feminism's careful theorization of the experience of womanhood sparked a bifurcated response in the decade's representations and experiences of masculinity. On the one hand, a backlash erupted that retreated into machismo, and, on the other, a movement developed that echoed the feminists' critiques by arguing for the transcendence of oppressive gender categories altogether. This movement, exemplified by works such as *The Liberated Man*, *The Hazards of Being Male*, and *The Male Machine*, made the case that society's vision of masculinity victimized men as well as women.[73] Most of these authors employed the logic of women's liberation to argue for men's need to access those aspects of themselves gendered feminine in order to exercise true freedom and create an authentic self unburdened by societal constraints. Herb Goldberg, in *The Hazards of Being Male*, argued that the "male in our culture is at a growth impasse. He won't move—not because he is protecting his cherished place in the sun, but because he can't move. . . . He lacks the fluidity of the female who can readily move between the traditional definitions of male and female behavior and roles."[74] Goldberg both overstated the ease of women's move beyond gender roles in the mid-1970s and understated the masculine impulse to defend patriarchal privilege. He did, however, raise a common perception. Marc Fasteau's *The Male Machine* also fixated on this transcendence of masculine–feminine duality: "To resolve, however temporarily, the opposing forces in society, to release the energy bound in opposing positions and make it fruitful, one must be able to accept and integrate the corresponding opposites in oneself."[75] This desire to transcend opposites echoed throughout the 1970s, and, indeed, underscores Austin's fascination with the hippie–redneck, as many Americans in the decade sought to restore a notion of the unitary American public in the midst of social strife and the assertion of particular identities. The literature on sensitive masculinity provided a venue, suffused with countercultural tropes of authenticity, for men to explore these issues in something other than backlash politics—an alternative meditation on their perceived loss of hegemony in the American mainstream.

The other version of masculine reflexivity sparked by the women's movement involved a re-investment in the masculine, rather than a desire to transcend it. This most commonly took the form of a backlash politics that shouted its defense of patriarchal privilege. The backlash did not always proceed in straightforward fashion, and texts meant as satire could often convey the message as well as those that were sincere. Take the Shel Silverstein–authored Tompall Glaser song "Put Another Log on the Fire (Male Chauvinist Anthem)" as an example. The song's protagonist catalogs a long list of chores he wishes his wife to perform—cooking, car repair, cleaning, laundry, the fetching of pipe and slippers—before reaching the subject on his mind: "Then put another log on the fire, babe/And come and tell me why you're leaving me." In recounting the tedium of housework and the easy assumption of command, the joke is, of course, on the oblivious man. The song fit, however, into a wider re-assertion of the masculine amid the wave of women's liberation, and played the part well in an album that marked both a crowning moment of and distinct transition from the progressive country sounds of earlier in the decade. In January 1976, the album *Wanted! The Outlaws*, produced by Waylon Jennings and Steve Albright in the Nashville studios of Tompall Glaser, quickly climbed both pop and country charts and became the first country album to achieve platinum status by selling a million copies.[76] All of this transpired despite the fact that the songs on the compilation had previously appeared elsewhere. The album's packaging, surely, had something to do with its success. The cover evoked the "wanted" posters of the Old West, faded and yellowed, with the artists pictured. Waylon Jennings stood at top and center with Willie Nelson, Jessi Colter, and Tompall Glaser arrayed beneath him. The album itself, like its packaging, featured Jennings most prominently, beginning with his renditions of "My Heroes Have Always Been Cowboys" and Billy Joe Shaver's "Honky Tonk Heroes," then Jessi Colter, Jennings's wife, singing "What Happened to Blue Eyes?" and "You Mean to Say," before proceeding to the Waylon duets that anchor the album, "Suspicious Minds" with Colter to end side 1 and "Good-Hearted Woman" with Nelson to begin side 2. Nelson and Glaser carry the last half of the album, with Nelson on "Heaven or Hell," the autobiographical "Me and Paul," and "Yesterday's Wine," and Glaser singing Jimmie Rodgers's "T for Texas" and Shel Silverstein's "Put Another Log on the Fire." Chet Flippo, the music journalist who had cut his teeth on the Austin scene before becoming the head of *Rolling Stone*'s New York office, wrote the extensive liner notes.

Given the focus of this study, it should not surprise that I underscore the connections of movement politics and popular culture that this tension between women's liberation and outlaw country demonstrates. The conflation of country music with a particular conservative vision of the American nation was more or less complete by the years of "Okie from Muskogee," despite a variegated past politics that had included everything from the "folk" artist Woody Guthrie to the more recent anti-chauvinist voice of Loretta Lynn.[77] "Authenticity" had long served to stake the genre's claim on a steadfast aesthetic, social, and political conservatism, the perception that a lost rural Eden should define the music in perpetuity. Country music's perennial bid for mainstream crossover success existed in an uneasy relationship with this vision, and, by 1976, had reached another of its defining moments.[78] Country's authenticity cachet attracted new fans nationally as both the white ethnic revival and countercultural discourses of self, nationalism in the bicentennial year, and the regionalized politics of backlash created a hunger for "real" American music. In this environment, Austin's progressive country scene and the new wave of Nashville singer–songwriters stood on the verge of national celebrity.

The soundtrack to late-decade Texas chic, however, was not "progressive" but "outlaw" country. Participants dispute the derivation of the outlaw label, and it seems to have sedimented over time rather than exploding in national consciousness all at once. The name's most plausible origin may have been when Lee Clayton pitched the song "Ladies Love Outlaws" to Waylon Jennings, who made it the title track of a 1972 album. Or it may have originated the following year, when Hazel Smith, the office manager of Tompall Glaser's studios at "Hillbilly Central" in Nashville, began to use the term to describe Jennings's and Glaser's music for publicity purposes. Art critic Dave Hickey became an early proponent and deployed the outlaw frame in an influential 1974 *Country Music* magazine profile of the edgier artists among the progressive country set. "Now, as you know, I'm just an old foot-tapper, bottle-thrower and freelance layabout," Hickey wrote. "I don't know much about these guys except by watching and listening. But just by watching and listening I can tell you that they're about the only folks in Nashville who will walk into a room where there's a guitar and a *Wall Street Journal* and pick up the guitar."[79] In the tradition of cultural writers from the national press, Hickey effaced the relationship between country's authentic expression and its commercial orientation. These men (and men, Anglo-Texan men, predominated in the outlaw phenomenon) were presumed to be artists who spontaneously rebelled against the bloated business strategies of Nashville. In addition to Jennings, Nelson, Glaser, and Colter, other artists the media associated with the outlaw label included Bobby Bare, David Allan Coe, Rita Coolidge, Kris Kristofferson, Billy Joe Shaver, Johnny Paycheck, Shel Silverstein, and Hank Williams Jr.[80]

What does "outlaw" signify in this context? Though the 1976 album's themes continued the decade's musical elaboration of cowboy masculinity, these artists focused on those elements of the mythos that stressed the cowboy's singular moral authority outside the law of the community. Country music's outlaw pose fit the seventies, a musically performative variant of the outlaw antihero that dominated the decade's best cinema. The outlaw stance drew on the general mistrust of established institutions inherited from the sixties and ratcheted to new levels through the Watergate scandal. From the films *Dog Day Afternoon* to *Taxi Driver* to *Network* to *Dirty Harry*, individuals who operated outside the bounds and against the strictures of bureaucratic institutions spoke to a broad anti-authoritarianism that often transcended traditional political labels of left and right.[81] Country outlaws absorbed both countercultural flair and hard-hat reaction to make their point (and their record sales), and it is this breadth, in part, that accounts for the musical subgenre's meteoric success.

As far as Willie Nelson, Waylon Jennings, and the Texas music contingent were concerned, the outlaw pose served three ends. First, as with the cosmic cowboy, the outlaw was a performative guise that successfully drew on the decade's populist anti-authoritarianism, discourses of authenticity, and libidinal charge. Dallas Cowboys tight end turned novelist Peter Gent spoofed the shift from progressive to outlaw style, even as he acknowledged its appeal, with the character Willy Roy Rogers in *Texas Celebrity Turkey Trot* (1978): "Willy Roy's act sure had changed. Instead of the smiling, sleepy-eyed, melancholy drunk he was a strutting, threatening bad guy . . . 'God I love being an outlaw.' Willie Roy grinned. 'These people need me to do their feeling. They love outlaws. I don't put up with any shit. I do and say what I want. I tell it like it is . . . I'm just mean, and I feel wonderful.'"[82] This "meanness," in part, differentiated the outlaw style from the progressive one that directly preceded it. Second, the outlaw provided an aesthetic that, while claiming a return to authentic, honky-tonk roots in its music, also cemented the country rock crossover from bases in Austin and Nashville. James Szalapski's documentary *Heartworn Highways* of 1975 demonstrates the hybridities well. For all its paeans to the country life (as represented by the depiction of Townes Van Zandt with his dogs, chickens, and guns), the film's musical performances by the likes of Charlie Daniels and David Allan Coe demonstrated the blending of country styles with rock tempos, theatrics, and volume.

The third and final element of the outlaw pose involved a declaration of independence not only from Nashville's smooth-pop countrypolitan sound, but also from the Nashville seat of production itself. Outlaw, in this sense, signified a rebellion against country's means of production along Music Row, building a cultural apparatus outside the law of the Nashville studio system.[83] To this end, Willie Nelson and Waylon Jennings exerted greater control over their creative work, looking to producers in New York, Los Angeles, and Austin, employing their own touring bands in the studio, and participating more heavily in management decisions. Nelson went so far as to construct an alternate infrastructure for recording country music under artists' control in Austin, with the venue the Austin Opera House and his own Lone Star Records imprint for Columbia at its center.

Taken together, the outlaw phenomenon continued the face-off that sociologist Richard Peterson sketched between hard-core country, often read as masculine, and soft-shell country-pop, often interpreted as feminine.[84] Nelson and Jennings framed themselves, and were framed by critics, as returning to the wellsprings of the country aesthetic, but did so largely by engaging in what Peterson terms authenticity work outside of traditional country, borrowing heavily from blues, rockabilly, and rock.[85] What constituted "the popular" in pop music influences in country in the decade depended largely on angle of view. Critics read the outlaws' forays into rock as diametrically opposed to the existing pop orientation of mainstream country, despite the fact that both were involved in crossover projects. Producers engineered the Nashville Sound to capture an adult market they felt had been vacated by the rock obsession with youth, while the outlaws sought to share in rock's youthful audience and studied hipness. In this, the outlaws had the best of both worlds, making savvy commercial decisions while maintaining outsider status.

In 1974, the same year progressive country caught fire at the Armadillo World Headquarters, the Country Music Association stirred controversy in selecting the Australian singer Olivia Newton-John as female entertainer of the year. In response, a number of traditionalists, including George Jones, Grandpa Jones, Ernest Tubb, and Tammy Wynette, briefly formed the rival Association of Country Entertainers—an organization comprising solely country artists, to the exclusion of promoters and industry moguls who held sway in the CMA—in order to "preserve the identity of country music."[86] In 1975, a visibly intoxicated Charlie Rich burned the envelope for male entertainer of the year on stage upon learning that the award went to John Denver.[87] The irony, of course, is that Rich himself first recorded with Sam Phillips's Sun Records in Memphis, the epicenter of the genre's prior authenticity crisis brought on by rockabilly. Further, Charlie Rich's 1970s albums that earned him male entertainer of the year in 1974 (thus giving him the honor of presenting the 1975 award) were themselves of the country-pop variety. Rich's crooning on *The Silver Fox* hardly echoed the plaintive wail of Hank Williams Sr. In short, by

1976 the country music industry had run up against one of its perennial authenticity battles. While countrypolitan's crossover project sputtered, outlaw's ability to reach new audiences soared, not by smoothing out the rough edges of country's sound, but by acting as if those rough edges were all that country ever was.

"The Texan" had long stood as a marker of masculinist authenticity in hardcore country music. Central Texas was indeed the place where Jimmie Rodgers spent his last years; where Ernest Tubb defined the honky-tonk sound under the tutelage of Rodgers's widow, Carrie; and where the rowdy Harry Choates, Johnny Horton, and Hank Williams Sr. played some of their final concerts.[88] Country music's authenticity claims engaged American culture as a whole in the 1970s. The atmosphere made possible the cutting edge of Robert Altman's film *Nashville* (1975) on the American dialectic of authenticity and artifice, and the desire for authentic lifestyles and experiences were in part what drew the youth counterculture to Austin's progressive country and Southern California's country-rock scenes.[89] The outlaw phenomenon of the late 1970s provided the punctuation mark that took this beyond local youth subcultures or the rock market and brought the conflict into the open in Nashville itself.

The success of *Wanted! The Outlaws* vindicated the aesthetics of the outlaw group, even as the album laid bare their contradictions. Glaser, Jennings, Nelson, and others had been pushing for country traditionalism over and against the vestiges of Atkins's countrypolitan sound. In practice, however, the tracks on *Wanted! The Outlaws* seem to have been aimed at a crossover strategy not unlike the one Atkins had in mind.[90] The countrypolitan sound arose in the wake of the rockabilly revolt within country music, as that youth-oriented form embraced African American rhythm and blues. Atkins sought to shore up the genre's respectability by securing an upscale pop audience in the face of rockabilly's vulgar thrust. Waylon and Willie sensed that, by the late 1970s, this was the wrong crossover project with which to be involved, and the "something" they found in countercultural Austin audiences in 1972 translated into a new fan base for country music. Still, Waylon Jennings and Jessi Colter's rendition of "Suspicious Minds" on *Wanted! The Outlaws* brings to mind Vegas-era Elvis rather than the Grand Ole Opry. In addition, *Wanted! The Outlaws* did not necessarily stand so far outside the bounds of establishment Nashville as it purported, with legendary producer Owen Bradley's son Jerry doing much to define the album's concept.[91] The outlaw label signified a rather unstable aesthetic difference, then, from mainstream Nashville music.

In projecting an aesthetic distance from Nashville, though, Nelson and Jennings at times focused on performative, rather than aural, strategies. Nelson did declare his independence through the spare arrangements of *Red-Headed Stranger* (1975), but it was just as common for other artists to revel in the dark imagery of the outlaw to make their point. Jennings, for one, was comfortable with the new pose and had long been aware of its popular appeal. He had ridden the rockabilly wave with Buddy Holly in West Texas and was early on marketed as an unruly outsider in the Jay Sheridan 1966 American International Pictures drive-in feature *Nashville Rebel*.[92] Outlaw recaptured the masculine swagger long associated with authenticity claims in country music, and the shift made uneasy the Austin critics invested in the peaceable *communitas* of hippies and rednecks.

The changing styles led Jan Reid to declare the "death of redneck rock" in a *Texas Monthly* article just two years after he had mythologized the genre's "improbable rise." Reid bemoaned the eclipse of the hippie elements of the hippie-redneck hybrid as the performance of stereotyped redneck behavior came to the fore. The earlier critiques of Nightbyrd and Guinn seemed to prove prescient as perceptions of distance grew between the audiences and their stars. Jeremiads arose around the local scene as its performers began to receive national recognition. As Michael Bane wrote of a visit to Nelson's home, where he encountered an imposing security system: "The gate itself is solid steel, mounted on a rolling track and, like the wall, topped with electrified barbed wire. To talk to the people's poet, you press a call button mounted on a stone post beside the gate and wait patiently while a television camera sunk into the wall gives you the once over. If that gate keeps out one person he doesn't want to see, Willie tells me later, then it's worth every cent he paid for it."[93]

Bane accused Nelson of creating a distance between artist and audience that ran against the basic subcultural dictum regarding the privileged intimacy of artist and audiences in a scene. The new distance between them ruptured perceptions of an unmediated, beloved community of artists and audiences in Austin, now supposedly and suddenly fraught with marketplace relations. According to Reid, "Outlaw country music is not just some misguided notion of the crowd. It's a sales promotion hawked by the recording industry with Madison Avenue zeal."[94] National popularity, in this reading, short-circuited the local subculture's use of music as a means of redefining "the Texan" on its own terms.

In the pages of *Texas Monthly*, Joe Nick Patoski read the decline of progressive country into outlaw bravado in the bicentennial Willie Nelson Fourth of July picnic at Gonzales. Nelson had chosen the site for his 1976 gathering due to its ties to the Texas revolt against Mexico in 1835–1836, thus collapsing the national revolutions of the United States and Texas in the bicentennial year. Prior to the revolt, the Mexican government had lent a small cannon to the people of Gonzales for defense against Comanche raids; as tensions rose between the Anglo American settlers and the government, Mexico asked for the cannon to be returned. The settlers balked, and the first battle cry of the conflict was born. The Gonzales militia brandished the diminutive cannon at the Mexican troops sent to retrieve it while flying a banner picturing a black cannon on a field of white with the phrase "Come and take it." Outlaw bravado could hardly have chosen a more fitting site for performance.

Joe Nick Patoski's review of the Gonzales picnic took a dour view of the affair: "For openers, this year's marathon heralded the artistic decline of progressive country just as the style has begun to enjoy national popularity. The only consensus hit at the picnic was old traditionalist George Jones . . . [who] wasn't the least bit impressed by progressivism, flatly stating after the show, 'Country music is going to the dogs.'" In addition to aesthetic shifts, such critics perceived a fracturing of the cosmic cowboys' beloved community: "At this affair, guns, knives, and chains seemed more plentiful than joints and coke spoons." Patoski and others saw the rise in violent behavior and hypermasculine swagger as signs that the promises of progressive country had been betrayed: "There were no violent deaths or serious shootings this year, but with the growing emphasis on armed macho posturing, it's only a matter of time."[95] Patoski here noted in 1976 fears that such critics as Larry L. King ("The Great Willie Nelson Outdoor Brain Fry and Trashing Ejacorama") and sociologist William Martin ("Growing Old at Willie Nelson's Picnic") had first raised at Nelson's earliest gatherings.[96]

There is evidence to suggest that Waylon Jennings concurred with Reid's and Patoski's assessments of Texas outlaw audiences becoming prisoners of their outsized image. The song "Don't Y'all Think This Outlaw Bit Has Done Got Out of Hand?" explored Jennings's 1977 drug bust, occasioned by the tremendous efficacy of outlaw hype in making the musicians' claims to operating outside the law seem literal. The song played on the rapid conflation of the three dimensions of the outlaw movement—cultural production, aesthetic ideology, and performative guise. For Jennings, the most significant of these involved independence in cultural production that allowed for a free hand in determining how he created music. But it was not "singing through [his] nose" in the traditional style, as he puts it in the song, that attracted the attention of law enforcement; outlaw's successful hype derived from its third leg, the staged performance of liminal criminality. This pose struck a chord in the late 1970s and invited the kind of surveillance that resulted in Jennings's bust.

Willie Nelson's Fourth of July picnic in Gonzales, 1976. Note the flags celebrating various nationalisms in the bicentennial year. Photo by Coke Dilworth. Dilworth (Coke) Photographic Collection. Di_08103. Briscoe Center for American History, the University of Texas at Austin.

Punctuating the rhetoric that had earlier surrounded progressive country, the outlaw figure demonstrated the uneasy relationship between country's counterculture and the decade's expressive identity politics. The outlaw's populist antiauthoritarianism, masculine swagger, and performance of the Texan conveyed a sense of rebellion, but against whom did these artists rebel? Nelson and Jennings aimed their barbs at the Nashville establishment of Atkins and Bradley, but they invoked the names of prior generations, Bob Wills, Hank Williams Sr., and Jimmie Rodgers amongst them, to do so, honoring an older generation in the country tradition even as they brashly gave voice to the new. As the sixties' social movements for social justice came to fruition in the seventies, a new Texas would seem to have come into view, but in country music, as across Texas culture, artists and authors mourned the perceived loss of an older Texas even as they celebrated the modern and progressive trajectory of the Lone Star State. Many seemed to feel that something was vanishing from the Texas landscape and mind-set. In this chapter, we have looked to the twinned sense of novelty and loss as expressed in the conversation between identity politics and the cosmic cowboy in the Austin scene. In the next, we continue to plumb the political dimensions of the period's nostalgic regionalism, looking to the figure of the Vanishing Texan as it plays across the terrain of formal politics in a moment of partisan realignment.

The Vanishing Texan

THE PARTY OF THE FATHERS REALIGNS

*While we digested our suppers on The Old Man's front porch . . .
[he] recalled favored horses and mules from his farming days, remembering
their names and personalities though they had been thirty or forty years dead.
I gave him a brief thumbnail sketch of William Faulkner—Mississippian, great
writer, appreciator of the soil and good bourbon—before quoting what Faulkner had
written of the mule: "He will draw a wagon or a plow but he will not run a race. He
will not try to jump anything he does not indubitably know beforehand he can jump;
he will not enter any place unless he knows of his own knowledge what is on the
other side; he will work for you patiently for ten years for the chance to kick
you once." The Old Man cackled in delight. "That feller sure knowed
his mules," he said.* ★ Larry L. King, "The Old Man"

Larry L. King's story about his recently deceased father, "The Old Man," appeared in *Harper's Magazine* in April 1971. The issue served as a swan song for the editorship of Willie Morris, formerly of the *Daily Texan* and *Texas Observer* and a friend of King's, who had become *Harper's* editor in chief in 1967. Though Morris led the literary magazine to new heights of prestige and relevance, the magazine's owners dismissed him over flagging sales.[1] It is fitting that "The Old Man" appeared in Morris's final issue. The editor had tried to pull this story out of King for some time, knowing that it touched on something that King, an Anglo-Texan who had spent most of his adult life in Washington, DC, and New York, felt deeply. But it was only in the wake of

Cyrus King's death that he felt up to the task of writing about "The Old Man." He took as his subject a road trip he and his father embarked on in his father's eighty-second year. "The Old Man" had seen neither the Alamo nor the Capitol building in Austin, wanted to do so before he died, and so the father and son set out from the plains around Midland for Central Texas.

King's article "The Old Man" engaged in reverie regarding a lost masculine self, rendered as a generational narrative that the author mapped onto the rural–urban, temporal–spatial divide: "He had a love for growing things, a Russian peasant's legendary infatuation for the motherland; for digging in the good earth, smelling it, conquering it."[2] A denizen of West Texas tied to that ground like a serf, hardly a "redneck" (King goes to great lengths to establish his father's sense of propriety), Cyrus King nevertheless possessed that element of presumed authenticity that undergirded notions of hippie–redneck confluence. Larry L. King, a liberal who had worked as an aide for Lyndon Johnson and, if no hippie, certainly of bohemian bent, wrote this piece in 1971 in much the same tones as music critics investigating the Austin scene. Further, he envisioned the rapprochement between feuding generations on the terrain of symbolic state power in the Capitol and the Alamo. King's piece sketched the older generation's perceptions of changing times with relation to war, race, and gender: "What did the Old Man think of this age of protest and revolt? 'It plagues me some,' he admitted. 'I got mad at them young boys that didn't want to fight in Vietnam. Then after the politicians botched it so bad nobody couldn't win it, and told lies to boot, I decided *I* wouldn't want to risk dyin' in a war that didn't make sense.'"[3] Larry L. King and his father reached agreement on this once most contentious of political points, regarding a war championed by King's former employer, while on a trip visiting a shrine to the Texans' martyred folly of 1836.

The cultural politics of the 1970s gave rise to renewed interest in the figures of Anglo-Texan masculinity in a way that not only attempted to refashion them for the future, but also simultaneously retrenched them. This refashioning spoke to a deep nostalgia for a Texas that always seemed to be passing, and it devised a figure I call the Vanishing Texan. To make sense of their subject position in the 1970s, Anglo-Texan men invoked themes of fathers and sons, the agrarian and the urban, and a Texas that constituted its own nation, even empire. The tone echoed Dobie's concern with "Texans out of the Old Rock," only these authors looked back to Dobie's generation rather than the state's Anglo founding fathers to make much the same arguments on the passage of time. Where the Lone Star regionalists wrote at the state's tipping point from rural to urban and its national ascendance through oil wealth, these authors and artists operated in a contrarian moment in which the Texans' imperial reach appeared at times extended by its connections to oil, and at other times foreshortened by the perceived homogenization of the American landscape. Economically prospering from energy prices even as the state passed its peak production of oil, culturally swaggering even as social change seemed to erode the state's distinctiveness, politically in limbo with the death of LBJ and dissension among the Democrats amid partisan realignment, participants wove narratives of declension to explain the change. This chapter sketches this discourse in two parts to build on the discussion of the musical counterculture and seventies identity politics that preceded it. First, I will investigate figures of Anglo-Texan masculinity in early *Texas Monthly* and the imperial rhetoric surrounding oil wealth in novels by Bud Shrake and H. L. Hunt. Second, I will extend this conversation on cultural and identity politics into formal politics to understand how this rhetoric infused the moment of partisan realignment, particularly in the capital city of Austin. The fathers-and-sons trope of the Vanishing Texan traced a filial commitment that charged the changing dimensions of the Democratic Party in the decade, in Texas as across the Solid South.

"Loyd Is an Anachronism": Anglo-Texan Masculinity in Early *Texas Monthly*

In the summer of 1970, the influential liberal publication the *Texas Observer* dedicated a special issue to the vanishing of "The Texas That Was," the cover adorned with a Russell Lee photograph of a graveyard. Bill Porterfield, a new contributing editor, led the issue off with a piece on a country store amid an array of articles on trade days in Canton, childhood homes in West Texas, the vulgarities of adolescence, conservation in the Big Thicket, and civil rights. One of the contributors, a young historian of the cattle trails named Ken Dessain, decided to return from graduate school at the University of Chicago to try his hand at being a real, live Texas cowboy. His somewhat tongue-in-cheek article on the experiment, "Why Can't I Be One?", documented his trip to Loving County, in West Texas, to do some oral history work on horseback: "'That's great,' my fellow historians-in-training said of the venture. 'You can test Webb's Great Plains thesis in an area largely unchanged by technology.'" Ken giddily recounts riding up to a stranger's ranch and being taken in, his cowboy pantomime apparently working well enough, if not to fool his hosts, at least to encourage them to play along. In several meetings on ranches over the course of the next few days, Ken plays the question "Who are these guys?" against "Why can't I be one?" and, then, in one exhilarating moment, he is allowed to work alongside them. Once he rides with the actual cowboys, he exclaims over the "reality of it! I was, in full armor, indistinguishable from a distance, even by my actions, from the rest of them; less than five miles off the old Goodnight–Loving, and I was herding cattle." The labor lends the guise its reality, its materiality: "What a great game it is, to be a cowboy, when the reality is so close and so distant. In our elaborate mimicry, we hadn't really fooled anyone. We were just playing cowboy, riding through, and these authentic cow punchers, doing it for a living, had played right along. Perhaps they, like the boys who first rode out here, knew that the range will always be a grand play, and not just a job."[4] Dessain concludes that, perhaps, these cowhands too are performing the role along with their occupation.

The *Observer* was by no means the only publication mining the Vanishing Texan vein in the 1970s. When *Texas Monthly* won a National Magazine Award in May 1974 after having been in business only a year, publisher Michael Levy crowed that the "greater significance is the simple fact that our existence and growth as a new magazine is a very real product of the state of Texas and its cultural maturation. . . . Texas has come of age. Texans are sophisticated, inquisitive, and aware."[5] The fledgling magazine's strong investigative bent chided what it saw as the state's petty corruptions in politics and business, its small-mindedness in matters of culture and education, but there existed also a soft spot for the state's provincial affectations, for that which the journalists of *Texas Monthly* felt they had lost in the very process of Levy's "cultural maturation." This loss frequently took the form of a generational narrative akin to King's. In it, fathers stood in for worlds in which journalists perceived their forebears to have moved, ruggedly, alone, taming the frontier even as they fought back the rigidifying effects of Eastern institutions.

Themes linking the vision of a supposedly nobler Texas to a narrative of fathers and sons, youth and age, identity and difference, constantly recur in the 1970s. A perusal of the cover stories of the early *Texas Monthly* reveals an anxiety over the icons of Anglo-Texan masculinity, together constituting a considerable bout of hand-wringing over the Vanishing Texan. Three cover stories, in particular, stand out. First, from September 1974, Paul Burka's "What's Happening to Texas Football?" or "The Decline and Fall of the Southwest Conference." On this cover, mourning cheerleaders gather around the casket of a uniformed football player. Second, from November 1974, there is Bill Porterfield's "The Texas Wildcatter: Endangered Species" or "The Lonely Search for Oil." Here, a cowboy-hatted oilman leans against his Cadillac, longhorns on hood, profiled against a sunset scene of derricks. Finally, from October 1975, Bill Porterfield chimes in again with "Is the Texas Cowboy Extinct?" or "In

Search of the Modern Cowboy."⁶ A bemused cowhand's taxidermied head sits on the wall, labeled *Cowboy Texanus*. Each cover story sets forth a particular iconic figure as representative of the passing distinctiveness of Anglo-Texan masculinity. The titles borrow from the environmental language of the threatened ("endangered species," "decline," "extinct"), fashion a quest for the increasingly rare ("oil," "the modern cowboy"), and suggest on the surface a general state of bewilderment with the world of the 1970s ("What's Happening to Texas Football?").⁷

Texas Monthly *covers. Upper left: September 1974. Cover photography by Ron Scott. Upper right: November 1974. Cover photography by Ron Scott. Lower left: October 1975. Cover photography by Kent Kirkley.*

It makes sense that these themes arose in the decade. Texas shared in the spoils of Sunbelt prosperity, and alongside the political clout and wealth came new migrants to the cities, new migrants to the state, and new questions over what it meant to be Texan. Of course, these questions did not merely revolve around newcomers and the specter of homogenization, the national–normative versus regional–distinctive axis. As described in the last chapter, the changing proportion of natives and newcomers within the Anglo American male demographic coincided with contestation on the part of the African American civil rights, Chicano, and feminist movements over claims on the very identity of Texan itself. The word "Texan," standing alone, had long conjured images of the icons *Texas Monthly* singled out on these covers. The seventies opened the term and its attendant symbolism to a wider range of the state's inhabitants. The notion of "who counted" politically, socially, economically, and ideologically shifted in radical ways. In this sense, the figure of the Vanishing Texan augured not the disappearance of Texanness, but also an anxiety over the new contours of that identity in the absence of Anglo-masculine normativity.

In all, *Texas Monthly* engaged in the contradictory exercise of reifying the distinctly Texan at the same time it documented the modernizing forces that fractured the monolith of the state's mythology. The three cover stories on football players, wildcatters, and cowboys sketched those contradictions in miniature. Burka's story on football appeared first, in September 1974, and on the face of it, the figure of the football player seemed to be an unlikely candidate for Vanishing Texan, the sport's association with the state still being relatively young in the 1970s. Paul Burka argued, however, that at the collegiate level a formerly competitive Southwest Conference had passed with the increasing urbanization and homogenization of the Lone Star State:

> There was a time when Southwest Conference football was more than a sport: it was a social institution, as definitive of Texas life as the oil well or the open range. Each school symbolized a different way of life, and the meeting of two football teams represented a confrontation between lifestyles . . . farmers and laborers [identified] with Texas A&M, Baptists with Baylor, Dallas socialites with SMU, West Texas farmers and ranchers with TCU. The Southwest Conference is a relic of a time when Texas was both diverse and chauvinistic, varied yet inbred. Life was simpler then; people knew who they were.[8]

Burka's vision of Texas ran against the narrative that attaches heterogeneity and diversification to the forward march of modernization. Rather, Burka perceived in the urban a flattening of social difference, at least as far as college football was concerned. He outlined a Texas that seemed to be somehow multicultural within an Anglo framework alone, organized around the concept of distinctive "ways of life." Tellingly, the article did not engage the issue of race that had become so prominent as sports teams, pragmatically and in piecemeal fashion, faced up to the challenge of racial integration. Instead, the author focused on the urban–rural divide as that which distinguished authentic, vibrant, Texan competition from the stilted games played by interchangeable parts without natural, organic constituencies. In particular, urbanization leached the supposed Texanness of college football as talent pools shifted from rural areas of East, West, and South Texas to Dallas and Houston: "But the farms are disappearing now, and so are the people: as the water table drops on the High Plains, people flee the unproductive land for the city. The best schoolboy athletes are no longer found in the small towns of West Texas, but in the bigger cities and suburbs. [The University of] Texas doesn't recruit much better in the rural areas than it ever did, but that no longer matters. The players are no longer there."[9]

College football, Burka argued, had become less organically tied to its community, and thus less engaging, as urbanization generally favored the recruiting demographics of the University of Texas. But that same rural–urban divide also stood in for the issue of race. The racial integration of college football had proceeded apace by 1974, but the origins of the struggle remained in very recent memory. The process began as much as twenty years earlier, in the year of *Brown v. Board of Education*, when University of Texas football coach Dana X. Bible ignored segregationist Regent rules for a game featuring Washington State College's African American running back Duke Washington. As late as 1969, however, Darrell Royal's Longhorns secured the dubious honor of being the last all-white team to win the national championship, and Royal subsequently carried a reputation as a conservative on racial issues. Royal unfortunately bore the brunt of the criticism of the university's slow pace of integration, a systemic problem implicating the Board of Regents and influential alumni organizations more than the university's football coach.[10]

Such issues lay beyond Burka's immediate concern. Rather, he offered a spirited defense of the collegiate game against the corruption of virtue and community he attributed to professional football. As the University of Texas achieved domination in the Southwest Conference, Burka cast Darrell Royal as a Trojan horse carrying the cold, cybernetic philosophy of Dallas Cowboys coach Tom Landry into the collegiate game. College football, Burka argued, should be collectively owned by a community of like-minded peers, preferably real, rural Texans. Professional football, on the other hand, "owns the cities today. A pro team is the natural repository for the loyalties of thousands of people who came to the city from far away.... In a rootless and anonymous environment, the professional team gives the newcomer something to identify with."[11] Again, the city, rootless and anonymous, threatened the native Anglo-Texan traditions of lifestyle-oriented football in a place where the "people knew who they were."

Texas Monthly took professional football seriously in the landscape of urban Texas, and not only because some of the state's best journalists in those years either began their careers or achieved their greatest success as sportswriters.[12] The magazine book-ended its first year of issues with cover stories on television announcer and former Dallas Cowboys and SMU quarterback Don Meredith (the inaugural issue of February 1973) and Cowboys coach Tom Landry (November 1973). That Meredith came first and Landry later may reveal where the magazine's loyalties lay in the cultural struggle that has been mapped onto the two men: Meredith a spirited, good-timing good ol' boy, and Landry the straight-laced fundamentalist and cybernetic statistician. Gary Cartwright began the conversation with a cover story, "Tom Landry: Melting the Plastic Man," that announced itself in the caption: "In Landry's presence you do not feel the plastic and computers you might expect. You feel something more visceral. You feel fear."[13] Here, the stern, silent brand of frontier masculinity, adorned in a fedora rather than a Stetson, evoked threat rather than nostalgia, and some observers nationwide mapped this same sensibility onto the seventies designation of Landry's Cowboys as "America's Team." In this regard, Texas's imperial reach seemed ascendant, as Dallas and its Western-themed team represented the nation.[14]

Following Lyndon Johnson's political demise, one might have expected the nation's hand-wringing over the stereotypical uncouth, trigger-fingered, drawling Texan as political player to have faded somewhat, but the state continued to loom large in the minds of those who saw something sinister in the much-discussed Rust Belt/Sunbelt dichotomies of those years. The "America's Team" moniker suggested the shifting locus of national identity south and west, as well as an entire discursive arsenal that flashed into view when the Dallas Cowboys played representatives of the Northeastern industrial core such as the Pittsburgh Steelers.[15] One of the highest-profile critiques of the Sunbelt phenomenon, in fact—Kirkpatrick Sale's *Power Shift* of 1975—summed up the whole series of demographic, economic, political, and cultural changes in the country as a struggle for power between the "Yankees" of the Eastern Establishment and the "Cowboys" of the Southern Rim: "There is a broadly metaphorical but rather apt way of describing these rival power bases ... as the yankees and the cowboys. Taken loosely, that is meant to suggest the traditional, staid, old-time, button-down, Ivy-League, tight-lipped, patrician, New England–rooted WASP culture on the one hand, and the aggressive, flamboyant, restless, swaggering, newfangled, open-collar, can-do, Southern-rooted Baptist culture of the Southern Rim on the other."[16] And while Sale did not mention the Dallas Cowboys by name, he saw it as no coincidence that football's popularity rose along with the fortunes of the region with which it had become increasingly identified. He argued that:

> it is bizarre but not at all fanciful to see football as the objective correlative of the third major characteristic of the Southern Rim: repression. No other sport is inherently so rigid, so autocratic, so brutal, so anti-individualistic. No other sport combines one-man rule on and off the field, systematic and sanctioned violence, automatonism as a clear virtue, established and elaborate plays and patterns, and the orderliness of a set field of play and an inflexible clock. No other sport surrounds itself with such patriotism and piety, such spectacle and militarism, such mechanization and organization. And no other sport is so beloved, associated with, and characteristic of, the Southern Rim.[17]

These same elements made some Anglo-Texan men cringe, too. A Larry L. King article titled "Coming of Age in the Locker Room" accompanied Paul Burka's jeremiad to Southwest Conference football in the September 1974 issue. In it, King extensively documented a series of extreme yet commonplace brutalities visited on high school and college athletes by coaches.[18] King preferred anecdotes of extreme and grotesque hazing to Sale's ideological ax-grinding, but their accounts produced much the same effect.

As with the issue of racial integration in sports, Coach Royal gave a public voice to the dehumanizing vision of football with such attributed aphorisms as his definition of the game as "meat on meat, flesh on flesh, and stink on stink."[19] A disgruntled former University of Texas player, Gary Shaw, assailed Royal's program with much the same language in *Meat on the Hoof: The Hidden World of Texas Football* in 1972, opening up a genre of exposé and thinly veiled fiction regarding Texas football during the decade. Former Cowboys tight end Peter Gent and journalist Dan Jenkins carried these critiques to the professional level and burlesqued the practices of modern football in the novels *North Dallas Forty* (1973) and *Semi-Tough* (1972), further rendering the Texas football player as a sort of tragic hero, a man–child who participated in the systematic destruction of his own body for the love of playing a game.[20] Perhaps we are supposed to feel that the player whose funeral is staged on the September *Texas Monthly* cover has been put out of his misery. Yet these authors remained fans of the game while declaiming a sordid loss of dignity in the modern arena with the routinization of the players' charisma, and the remove that separated local Texas boys from their natural Texas fandoms in college and professional football. The anxieties themselves ring untrue in light of the sport's continued high profile in the state, but the virtuous hometown hero, in Burka's and King's eyes, became one instance of the Vanishing Texan.

At the time, the Houston Oilers and Dallas Cowboys represented the state on the national stage as its two professional football teams. *Texas Monthly* journalist Bill Porterfield did not address football for the magazine in these years, but he did explore both of these symbols, oilers and cowboys, and the men who lived in and through their iconography. The oil-field wildcatter, like the football player, seems at first an odd figure to be tagged as a Vanishing Texan.[21] Texas swagger in the 1970s, after all, owed a good deal to the resurgence of the petroleum industry in the decade. In "The Lonely Search for Oil" of November 1974, though, Bill Porterfield lamented the demise of what he found to be organic, spirited, and wheeler-dealerish in the wildcatter's profession. These frontier virtues that had supposedly formed the core of Texanness came under threat in the face of federal environmental oversight, the consolidating corporate powers of the oil majors against the independents, and the burgeoning production and market control of foreign fields.

In the article, Porterfield accompanied the second-generation wildcatter Loyd Powell Jr. through several days of his ventures in West Texas. For a man like Loyd, those outside, bureaucratic forces of the federal, the corporate, and the foreign had reduced the room for maneuver, the frontiers to be exploited, the optimum habitat. In short, Porterfield wrote, "Loyd is an anachronism. In his manner and dress, in his ideas and values, he is a swashbuckler of the Texas Fifties. He looks like he just stepped off a Trans-Texas prop plane from Austin, where he had been closeted at the capitol with Governor Shivers and Price Daniel (the old man, not the boy), plotting to keep the Texas tidelands and throw Harry Truman out of office."[22] As anachronism, Loyd provided an interesting type. In the wider cultural manifestations of the Vanishing Texan, talk usually turned to comparisons of fathers and sons, the Vanishing Texans typically portrayed as Dobie's "Texans out of the Old Rock." Here, we have a young man acting the role of a Texas icon whose heyday has passed. But Loyd, too, held his father as model and avatar: "He wanted action, not soul-searching psychology. Life was to conquer, not to contemplate, and Loyd's head was full of stories of his father's heyday. It seemed a bolder, more adventurous time, more manly, somehow, than his own, and for a while there Loyd felt cramped at every turn of his growing maturity, a Gulliver in a land of Lilliputians."[23] Porterfield put these words into Loyd's head, but they echo not only through these three cover stories and, indeed, much of 1970s *Texas Monthly*—"a bolder, more adventurous time, more manly, somehow, than his own"—but through much of Texas culture in the decade. *Texas Monthly*'s journalists, overall, did not engage in rigid worship of the past. Rather, the publication remained reflective and self-aware of the nostalgia it communicated, making its accounts useful in thinking through old and new conceptions of masculinity and their relationship to Texan identity in the 1970s.

In Burka's football article, nostalgia appeared in a narrative of *gemeinschaft/ gesellschaft* decline, the corruption of organic communities through the rapid movements of people induced by modernity and urbanization. The wildcatter of Porterfield's piece, on the other hand, thrived in the rapid displacements of early modernity. The wildcatter did not exist in an organic community that gave him purpose. Rather, it is the very advent of purposeful society—environmental regulations, the geopolitical body of nations, the risk-averse nature of corporate bureaucracy—that hems him in. The wildcatter is not some village agrarian, in other words, but the embodiment of the lone frontier gambler. The focus on such a figure as iconic of the masculine recalls the early equation of women and the arrival of "society" on the nineteenth-century frontier.[24] In the context of the 1970s, revisited masculine icons of the Texas frontier were overlaid with the rhetorical challenge of a resurgent feminism. Porterfield fell back on no less a masculinist Anglo-Texan authority than Dobie to fend off claims to a frontier mythology on the part of Texas women, in the 1970s just as in the 1870s.

> J. Frank Dobie, that deceptive cowboy of campus and chaparral, once summed up the oilman's contribution to the American spirit. In the Old World, he said, the legends that persisted with the most vitality were legends of women— Venus, Helen of Troy, Dido, Guinevere, Joan of Arc. But in the New World, men have been neither lured nor restrained by women. . . . Into this world, women have hardly entered except as realities; the idealizations, the legends, have been about great wealth to be found, the wealth of secret mines and hidden treasures, a wealth that is solid and has nothing to do with ephemeral beauty.[25]

This trope of the Vanishing Texan ran deep in the cultural politics of the 1970s. The profusion of such symbols bore the weight of a perceived or threatened loss of mastery on the part of Anglo-Texan men in the wake of the ongoing civil rights and feminist revolutions in the 1970s. The legends of Anglo-Texan men, according to Porterfield's parsing of Dobie, had always been of something "solid," but the seventies unmoored these past certainties with regard to social order and Texan identity. The ground that had yielded Anglo-Texan men so much wealth seemed to shift rapidly beneath their feet. The 1970s brought with it the prospect of fluid and multiple identities that challenged the "solidity" of Anglo-Texan masculinity.

No iconic Texan saw greater deployment amid these rhetorical struggles than the cowboy, a core figure of imagined American masculinity, and Bill Porterfield provided one of the more sophisticated examples of the Vanishing Texan genre in the October 1975 cover story "Is the Texas Cowboy Extinct?" or "In Search of the Modern Cowboy." Here, finally, we would seem to have an up-front lamentation over the loss of a literal frontier, though Porterfield's narrative is hardly that straightforward. His story of the modern cowboy trumpeted the value of adaptation. Porterfield may have bemoaned the industrialization of cow-work, but he also praised new developments in the continuing enterprise. "With millions at stake, the hand-crafted, horse-driven West has had to give way to the realities of efficient mass production and distribution. Computers are more important than cowboys," but "it was always economics, then and now."[26] Porterfield tells the story through profiles of three separate ranches that exemplify different trajectories in the industry: the "Santa Berta in South Texas because it represents the Mexican heritage of the cowboy; the Waggoner in Northwest Texas because it is a traditional Anglo institution; and the Circle K outside Dallas because it is a modern, experimental ranch."[27]

Porterfield here offered the first instance in this series of articles to join the iconic figures of Texanness to a discussion of race and ethnicity, the first acknowledgement of African American and Mexican American claims on an expanded vision of the state's basic iconography. Porterfield did not draw the reader's attention directly to race, but matter-of-factly paired the well-known Mexican genealogy of the cowboy with an investigation of a contemporary Mexican American–owned and –managed ranch.[28] Also, the only old-time cowboy with connections to the late-nineteenth-century trail drives he mentions, Pluck Smith, was an African American man who retired to farming in East Texas. Even as he investigated the cowboy's legendary resonance, Porterfield employed small details to portray a more complicated, varied cowboy reality.[29]

Such investigative work is important, for cowboys appeared as figurative forms of slander and promise in settings that far outstripped such realities. When Kirkpatrick Sale defined the dichotomy of Eastern Establishment and Southern Rim through Yankees and Cowboys, he oddly chose to climax *Power*

Shift with a portrayal of President Nixon as king of the Cowboys ("The Nixon Presidency was the culmination of cowboy influence in American affairs").[30] When Carl Oglesby, like Sale a veteran of the Students for a Democratic Society, wrote his appraisal of the Rust Belt/Sunbelt divide against the backdrop of the Kennedy assassination, he titled the work *The Yankee and Cowboy War* (1976). Even further afield, Nixon's national security adviser, Henry Kissinger, first publicly sketched the now familiar contours of "cowboy diplomacy" in a 1972 interview with Oriana Fallaci, explaining that "the cowboy doesn't have to be courageous. . . . All he needs is to be alone to show others that he rides into town alone and does everything himself. . . . This amazing romantic character suits me precisely because to be alone is part of my style."[31] Porterfield, again, subverted such solipsistic manifestations of the cowboy by sticking close, as the best ranching historians have typically done, to the occupation itself, with its wellspring of communal endeavors, technical knowledge, and basic drudgery.

In fact, in all of this *Texas Monthly* cover talk of endangered species and extinctions, Porterfield shifted attention to ongoing transformations, the move from lariat tricks and cowboy games to pickup trucks and innovative business practices. Porterfield showed less interest in the fading away of the old-timers than in the likes of John Waggoner, an urbane stockbroker who had returned to family land to take up the trade. If authenticity reared its head in the rhetoric of the piece, here as elsewhere it was used to distinguish the appropriation of the occupation's symbols by outsiders from the changing nature of the occupation's actual requirements. The Southwest Conference failed to remain competitive, and so was reorganized. The rules to garnering quick wealth through independent, domestic oil exploration changed, and so the wildcatter lost much of his purchase on the public imagination. The cattle industry became more industrial, scientific, and advanced, and so the cowboy changed to fit the new scene. His purchase on the public imagination and Texas identity, however, remained undimmed.

Texas Monthly's home base of Austin, with its cosmic cowboys, provided an interesting comparison and counterpoint to the Vanishing Texan figure that Burka, Porterfield, King, and others explored. As Bill Porterfield put it, while ruminating over the progressive country music then bubbling up in the capital city, it "is a curious hallucination. Cosmic cowboys around counterfeit campfires, breathing burning grass and drinking longnecks, listening to the lowing of Darrell Royal's Longhorns."[32] The cosmic cowboy or hippie–redneck fusion among Austin youth, symbolized by the music of Willie Nelson and Jerry Jeff Walker and locales such as the Armadillo World Headquarters and the Soap

Creek Saloon, participated in these same currents of nostalgia for a certain vision of Anglo-Texan masculinity. But the young men of Austin must have re-tooled the iconography a little too much for the tastes of Burka, Porterfield, and the like. The cosmic cowboys' attraction to these passing icons as repositories of authenticity seemed to share much with the journalists of *Texas Monthly* questing for the Vanishing Texan, but the magazine's writers frequently disparaged the cosmic cowboys in articles that mourned the passing of a certain type of masculine authenticity. Willie Nelson and other artists associated with the style got a cover story of their own on occasion, but the youth subculture that formed these artists' primary audience seemed to irk these authors, even as the journalists traveled in similar circles. Another example comes in Larry L. King's *Texas Monthly* article "Redneck!": "Now, the Rednecks I'm talking about are not those counterfeit numbers who hang around Austin digging the Cosmic Cowboy scene, sucking up to Jerry Jeff Walker and Willie Nelson, wearing bleached color-patched overalls and rolling their own dope, saying how they hanker to go live off the land and then stay six weeks in a Taos commune before flying back on daddy's credit card. Fie and a pox on such fakers; may such toy Rednecks choke on their own romantic pretensions."[33]

But the magazine's relationship to the Austin scene was by no means wholly adversarial. An article in *Texas Monthly*, after all, generated Jan Reid's classic chronicle of seventies Austin music, *The Improbable Rise of Redneck Rock* (1974). Still, when these journalists invoked the Vanishing Texan, that figure's rhetorical power was predicated on a notion of authenticity that precluded the kind of role playing, the re-habitation or re-tooling through the style and art of older models of Texas identity, that the counterculture represented. Porterfield and King both used the word "counterfeit" in their descriptions of the Austin scene, and they were by no means alone in doing so. Both were savvy enough to recognize "the Texan" as a persona, but some form of essentialism still crept into their best works.

If these cosmic cowboys seem less serious or accomplished to us now than their sometime chroniclers in *Texas Monthly* do, they nevertheless may have had a better grasp of the seventies zeitgeist. In *1973 Nervous Breakdown*, Andreas Killen argues that "if the sixties emphasized being, the seventies were about becoming."[34] Dessain's adventure in the *Texas Observer*, his insistent "Why can't I be one?", finally arrived at this conclusion, that he could pantomime the role to some extent because it had performative dimensions even for "those guys," the real cowboys. The Vanishing Texan required a vision of authenticity rooted in the essence of what one has always been, while the cosmic cowboy's flirtation with supposedly outmoded ways of life, returning consciously to a set of symbols that may not fit his or her everyday reality, was a means of consciously, visibly becoming Texan. The cosmic cowboys had no monopoly on this strategy. Porterfield's wildcatter Loyd may have been an anachronism, but he became one through a series of choices. His sartorial and professional replication of his father's lifestyle involved an avoidance of that lifestyle's other, as represented in the photographer who accompanied Porterfield for the *Texas Monthly* story: "Gary, on the other hand, looks like a male model's version of a chic *Cosmo* or *Playboy* photographer, all old denim and elegant equipment. Handsome and long-haired, he is in every way a man of the Seventies."[35] Though the retrenchment in the organicism of the cowboy figure might seem worlds away from the denaturalizing gestures of punk or glam, they share the Me Decade's recognition of the self as a project and stylized performance for others' consumption. The Vanishing Texan, then, might have as his counterpart a sort of Sartorial Texan, who becomes such through a conscious figuration of these iconic roles, rather than through the simple matter of his or her upbringing. In the rhetorical corridors of Texas identity, there remains a fetish of nativity-as-destiny, but a vigorous and truthful exploration of "the Texan" will always generate other possibilities, recognizing the plastic, performative nature of personal identity.

"Great Luke Never Had Enough": The Appetites of Imperial Texas

The anxiety surrounding the Vanishing Texan, the notion that essential identities tied to concrete spaces were passing, came along in a moment when the notion of an imperial Texas also waxed and waned. Though originally established as the capital of the independent Republic of Texas, Austin was familiar with such imperial concerns. In 1838, Vice President of the Republic of Texas Mirabeau Buonaparte Lamar stood near the north bank of the Colorado River and declared that the site would serve well as the "seat of a future empire." He won the presidency soon thereafter, succeeding his rival Sam Houston and intent on using his new position to further an alternative to Houston's annexation agenda. Lamar envisioned Texas in imperial terms as an independent, expanding, continental power with the potential to rival the United States. The city of Austin sprang from that endeavor.[36] Events did not play out in support of Lamar's bluster, but this imperial conceit did not die so easily in representations of Texas and Texanness. The idea erupts periodically when the Lone Star State is on the minds of those debating the larger constructs of American power and character. The discourse of generational crisis evident in Anglo-Texan popular culture in the 1970s marks one such instance.

In 1969, with a conspicuously Texan figure recently departed from the White House, cultural geographer D. W. Meinig defined this notion of an imperial Texas in a thin, but instructive, volume of the same name. For Meinig, the state's claims to the status of empire rested in the parallels it shared with that particular form of historical polity, the fact that Texas possessed "a history of conquest, expansion, and dominion over a varied realm, and not only an outward movement of people, but the thrust of a self-confident aggressive people driven by a strong sense of superiority and destiny."[37] Anglo-Texans' imperial conceit hardly sets them apart from Americans as a whole, and, in fact, provides a key site for investigating representations of Texas as a kind of displaced self of the American nation. As Meinig saw it, what proved so distinctive about Texas was the extent to which its dominant Anglo class insisted on its own distinctiveness, all evidence to the contrary. Meinig did not stand alone in this evaluation. John Bainbridge's *The Super-Americans*, a classic in this line of thought, argued that despite how it is viewed by and presents itself to Americans, Texas serves as exemplary, even super-exemplary, of the American national character.

Both Bainbridge and Meinig identified the oil industry as a key element in perpetuating this Anglo-Texan sense of distinction. Meinig viewed the early twentieth-century oil strikes as a means of artificially perpetuating the trope of frontier individualist in wildcatter guise. Bainbridge, too, saw in the stereotypes of oil wealth an exaggerated figure of the self-made man. Oil gave rise to new visions of Texas's imperial reach. As an industry based on the extraction of a crude natural resource, petroleum at first served to demonstrate the state's provincial and underdeveloped nature, but Texas soon elaborated the industrial (refining, pipelines, exploration) and post-industrial (finance, research in new technologies) infrastructures that have made the state the center of the global petrochemical field.[38] Texas's extraction of oil from its own soil reached its peak in the 1970s. However, Texans no longer extracted wealth from oil simply by selling a commodity stumbled on by wildcatters; they drew it from a global web of scientific models and transnational flows of capital and expertise. Imperial Texas survived in this sense, taking on the characteristics of empire described by Michael Hardt and Antonio Negri, in which the authors claimed that the postmodern world would witness the resurgence of empire not as a bundling of conquered territories, but as an entirely new form of transnational sovereignty in the wake of the decline of the nation–state.[39] The corporations of Big Oil have that kind of reach.

To invoke empire, though, commits to a certain fatalistic historicity in which a brash, virile, triumphalist period of expansion boils over into inevitable decline attended by corruption and fey decadence. As the imperial conceit relates to Texas, it is in this last stage of the course of empire—corruption, decadence, and brash and bodily vulgarity—that the idea of Texas often served as America's abject other. The powerful Anglo-Texan can serve as America's displaced self in positive terms, as in the unfettered, can-do frontiersman, but the displaced self trope more commonly surfaces as a form of displaced self-abnegation: the representative Texan as the grasping, violent, vulgar wheeler-dealer. Think of the representations of LBJ as the corrupt, corny-folksy, warmonger Texan. The image speaks to a larger type. The nouveaux riches who seemed to spring up from the earth as quickly as the roughneck boomtowns of the Golden Triangle and Permian Basin played a preponderant role in each of these three modes of national thinking through the idea of Texas (as rival empire, displaced self, and abject other) in the middle of the twentieth century. The decade of the 1970s, with its contestation over older notions of stable patriarchal authority, provides a significant hinge moment in this imperial metaphor. As President Nixon noted, while speaking at the National Archives Building in 1971, "Sometimes when I see these columns I think of seeing them in Greece and in Rome. And I think of what happened to Greece and Rome, and you see only what is left of great civilizations of the past—as they became wealthy, as they lost their will to live, to improve, they became subject to the decadence that destroys the civilization. The United States is reaching that period."[40] Mid-century visions of grandeur thus gave way to narratives of Watergate-inflected corruption and Vietnam-imposed decline. The idea of Texas could simultaneously signify the cause of this imperial decline (in Johnson's perceived arrogance on the world stage) and its remedy (Sunbelt prosperity amid industrial malaise).

These ideas—Texas as empire, displaced self, and abject other—play across the state's postwar literature, including a few curious texts I wish to profile here, Bud Shrake's *Strange Peaches* (1972) and *Peter Arbiter* (1973), and H. L. Hunt's *Alpaca* (1960). They are novels, but to describe either of these authors as primarily a novelist is to ignore much of what is compelling about the two as cultural–historical figures. Shrake, who has entered our story before, was a journalist who also wrote a body of solid historical fiction. "Novelist" proves an even trickier category in which to fit Haroldson Lafayette (hereafter H. L.) Hunt, oilman, America's first billionaire, and prolific right-wing propagandist at the time he penned his first and only novel, the utopian romance *Alpaca*. Though *Alpaca*'s publication in 1960 places it earlier than the representations of *Texas Monthly* and Bud Shrake in this chapter, Hunt's death in 1974 brought renewed attention to his family's wealth, politics, and place in the Texas mythos, and it re-inserted him into conversations over the Vanishing Texan.

The novel *Strange Peaches* features Shrake's narrator and alter ego, John Lee Wallace, a television star of the popular Western *Six Guns Across Texas*. Wallace has tired of the state's stereotypical portrayal on-screen and retreated to his home turf of Dallas to make a documentary to "tell people what the place was about as we lived it, not the crap people were supposed to believe if they watched *Six Guns Across Texas*."[41] Wallace's diverse social circles in the Dallas of 1963 challenge his attempts to do so. On the one hand, he associates with bohemians, dancers, and roustabouts the likes of Buster Gregory (née Gary Cartwright), Jingo (née Jada), and Jack Ruby. On the other, his celebrity status leads him to spend time with the city's ultraconservative elites. The narrative thus follows Shrake's own experience in Dallas in the months surrounding the Kennedy assassination. As a sports journalist, he had entrée to the Murchisons and Hunts, who owned the city's rival football teams in the Cowboys and the Texans. At the same time, he roomed with fellow young journalist Cartwright and had run cross-wise with Ruby over dating his star dancer, Jada. Such autobiographical details fill the raucous text, including some that recall the Shrake we have already encountered in "Land of the Permanent Wave." Upon seeing Wallace's style when he returned to Dallas, an acquaintance exclaims, "John Lee, this is Dallas, not Hollywood. They'll kick you to death for having hair like that. You better wear a cowboy suit and claim you're Buffalo Bill."[42] Wallace struggles to get others to sign on with his attempts to document the experience of modern, diverse Texas, finding at every turn that the city's inhabitants prefer the kind of myth his California producers broadcast on television. As he argues with his agent over the need to make Westerns more realistic, the agent answers with a near-perfect encapsulation of "the Texan" that so often obscures the Texas that both the character Wallace and the author Shrake seek to represent:

> In our show, here's what you find week after week—good is stronger than evil, shooting and fighting don't really hurt ... women are pretty unless they're old and then down deep they're warm-hearted, whores don't put out for bad guys, the landscape is beautiful, Mexicans are picturesque, Negroes are loyal and polite, Indians are either innocent or evil, a man is free to make up his own mind about anything and change his destiny, nobody is poor and hardly anybody is rich, everybody is violent except for yellow chickenshits, and if something is wrong a good man will come along to straighten it out. Americans believe this stuff about themselves, John Lee. They don't want the story changed.[43]

Moreover, this vision pertains to nouveaux riches as much as to the middle- and working-class Anglo populists, as it trumpets the frontier individualism that overshadows the need for collective solutions to modern problems. Here, Shrake's critique echoes the Walter Prescott Webb of *Divided We Stand*, as frustrated in his 1972 portrayal of 1960s Texas as Webb had been in the 1930s over resistance to the New Deal. *Strange Peaches* delights in these contradictions and satirizes the elites who hold such frontier ideals so dear.

The year following the publication of *Strange Peaches*, Shrake's *Peter Arbiter* adapted Petronius's *Satyricon* to the setting of contemporary Texas in a fictional city that amalgamates Dallas and Austin. The imperial conceit, and implicit critique, of Anglo-Texan wealth proves difficult to miss. *Satyricon* charted the picaresque adventures of four characters: a young man, Encolpius; his companion, Ascyltos; their servant boy, Giton, who serves as the object of their desire; and an older poet and con man, named Emolpus. Shrake updated these four characters, adopting as his narrator and alter ego a pansexual interior designer by the name of Peter Arbiter. His roommate, Albert, stands in for Ascyltos, Guy-Guy for the servant boy, and the elderly poet appears as a bohemian named Sidney Hulmes. Shrake followed the basic conventions and episodes that propelled Petronius's picaresque, but did so in a manner that magnified parallels between the imperial strata of nouveaux riches of late twentieth-century Texas and first-century CE Rome. Where Petronius focused on the class of freedmen who had attained wealth and sought to boast publicly of it, Shrake unleashed a panoply of rags-to-riches, up-by-their-bootstraps oilmen and their various attendants.

For each author, a feast provided the central episode for the display of vulgar excess. In Shrake's re-telling, this feast took place at the mansion of Dallas oilman and football team owner Billy Roy Eanes, a surreal and grotesque evening that featured pastries in the shape and texture of baby possums, meats bursting from a roast pig's belly to replicate entrails, and the sexual organs of animals cooked as representations of the zodiac. The event climaxed with a mock-funeral for the host, who declares that he wants a burial monument that features chiseled likenesses of great men he has known: "Roosevelt, Churchill, Hitler, Mussolini, Sinatra, Lombardi, Lyndon, Ike, old Curt LeMay, Duke Wayne, old man Hunt, guys like that—sitting on their thrones welcoming me to heaven with Shirley Temple giving me an armload of roses. . . . Put up a big neon sign that says this is billy roy eanes's tomb—his heirs don't own it."[44] Eanes's pantheon projected a vision of robust masculine wealth, power, and authority, an interlocking directorate of U.S. presidents, European dictators, and full-blooded American right-wingers.

The gorging goes on for what Peter Arbiter reckons to be several days and nights, and Shrake used the opportunity to display alongside these gaping maws a brand of shallow right–populist politics. He begins with a cue from Petronius, having the dinner guests discuss supernatural events. General Enos Taylor tells the story of encountering a werewolf while on counterinsurgency maneuvers in Paraguay. What provokes horror in Taylor's audience, however, is not the invocation of lycanthropy, but Taylor's further disclosure that the very same man who had transformed into a wolf before his eyes later turned out to be a leader of the troublesome miners' union: "'Not only was the son of a bitch a werewolf, he was a goddam Communist!' The crowd gasped." The other attendees followed with diatribes concerning the need for military intervention in Central America, the rising costs of labor, the general decline in morals, and the increasing difficulty of purchasing the services of a loyal congressman.

Peter Arbiter's plot advances through such parties, and to describe them, Shrake employed the device of serial naming to invoke a sense of almost obscene plenitude in portraying the breadth of empire and the fruits it yielded to its ruling class. Food provides the best example, as on walking through a meat freezer Peter sees "the carcasses of cattle, pigs, sheep, goats, ducks, quail, pheasants, blue jays, doves, and deer," or was served "barbecued ribs, chicken, cole slaw, barbecue sauce, potato salad, pinto beans, jalapeño peppers, red chilis, sliced onions, scallions, pickles, garlic bread, hot sausages, beef tacos, boiled shrimps, fried quail, and oysters on the half shell."[45] On topics of discussion at a party, Shrake listed "baseball, bowling, moon shots, duck hunting, pipelaying, television, quarterhorse racing, cockfights, chili, beer, and Bermuda grass." On people, Shrake envisioned the ruling Anglo-Texan class and its retainers as "actors, dancers, museum patrons, university professors, oil men, politicians, electronics tycoons, violin players, landscape architects"; "a football player, a university horticulturist, and an astronaut." Finally, amid these absurdities, Shrake forthrightly described a 1973 newscast: "Wars. Riots. Strikes. New weapons. Kidnappings. Arson. Murder. A Politician's birthday party. Hunger march. Rebellion. Dope raids. American Legion rally. A brief report on polluted rivers."[46] The lists serve as shorthand in this brief novel to survey and tabulate, often through homologous commodities, the Texas that Shrake sought to describe, and, despite the good humor with which he engaged in the descriptions, also hoped to indict. Race figures here in interesting ways. African Americans and Mexican Americans appeared wholly in servile roles to the super-rich, a historical inaccuracy for the Texas of the early 1970s but one that Shrake used to suggest a set of organic hierarchies tinged with paternalism that is nothing if not imperial in its pretense. The non-Anglo subjects of the novel speak as if from behind the masks of these roles, casting sly judgment on the foibles of the arriviste elite they serve.

And there is much to judge in Shrake's portrayal. *Peter Arbiter* sketched the late imperial impulse as an inability to maintain control of appetites, a deadly penchant for excessive consumption that finds its most obvious manifestations in the desires for food and sex. When the ribald character "Great Luke," who entices Peter and Guy-Guy to his ranch with a trip on his private plane, perishes after being thrown off his yacht, his tombstone reads "Great Luke never had enough/He couldn't help it."[47] The words echo the Billy Joe Shaver lyric quoted in the introduction ("Too much ain't enough"), a phrase that would also recur on a banner stretched across the front of Manhattan's Lone Star Café by the late 1970s, advertising the outsized appetites of "the Texan."

Great Luke's epitaph might serve as well to describe any number of Shrake's characters in *Peter Arbiter*, as well as the historical figures on which he based them. As the central figure of eccentric excess, Billy Roy Eanes combines characteristics of assorted true-to-life wheeler-dealers and right-wing oilmen, including Clint Murchison Jr., Edwin Walker, and Lamar and H. L. Hunt. A satirized Hunt family appeared even more clearly in *Strange Peaches*. There, John Lee Wallace lunches with the oilman Big Earl, and, over the course of the meal, enough bizarre details emerge to identify Big Earl with the historical H. L. Hunt—the all-liquid diet; the penchant for spontaneously breaking out into Tin Pan Alley sing-song; the belief in alternative health therapies, ESP, and the merits of crawling on all fours as a means of rejuvenation; and, finally, an interest in the medicinal properties of aloe vera that Hunt made the last of his entrepreneurial endeavors.[48] Now, to be fair, a number of these qualities might be rightly considered Dallas folklore, perhaps even folklore that Shrake himself had a hand in inventing, but the 1960 novel *Alpaca* leaves no doubt that Hunt was a very eccentric man indeed. To explore the biographies of the oil rich in twentieth-century Texas is to encounter the very real possibility that the Bud Shrake behind *Peter Arbiter* and *Strange Peaches* possessed less the skills of a clever satirist than those of a shrewd documentarian.[49]

The oilman H. L. Hunt, born in Illinois in 1889, had already made and lost fortunes in oil in Arkansas and real estate in Florida before prospering as a wheeler-dealer in the East Texas oil-field strikes of the 1930s. To promote his rags-to-riches story and the national ethos to which he attributed it, H. L. Hunt oversaw a conservative media empire instrumental in the early growth of the 1960s New Right, including the radio programs *Freedom Forum* and *Life Line*. From this position, Hunt proved one of Joseph McCarthy's staunchest Texas defenders in the fifties and supported editorial attacks on the civil rights movement and counterculture in the sixties.

Alpaca appeared in 1960 as a small, fifty-cent paperback for distribution by the H. L. Hunt Press. On one level, it seems to be far removed from the gross display of excessive appetites found in *Peter Arbiter*, and even farther from Shrake's indictment of Texas as an overweening empire. At the same time, *Alpaca* outlines the political desires of a member of the arriviste class that serves as Shrake's subject. The book sets out to construct the perfect constitution for the fictional Latin American nation of Alpaca. Hunt's dashing alter ego, Juan Achala, buries himself in the libraries of the European capitals and organizes a brain trust of the world's best political and economic minds, whom Hunt insists on giving names and roles that to him signified the height of exoticism (Orlando Tasso, the Roman lawyer; Sir Gerald Ripney of England; Joset Holbecht, the Austrian autodidact; Jan Wankowski, Polish exile; Andre Marchillon, tax genius; and Robert and Betty Brown, the American department store clerk and factory worker who "had dealt with life in its actuality rather than theory").[50] Hunt hoped to sweeten the didactic pot by marrying this constitutional quest to a romance between two political exiles, Juan Achala and his fellow Alpacan, the opera singer Mara Hani. The romance of Juan and Mara never approaches the heated level of Peter and Guy-Guy in *Peter Arbiter*, its steamiest episodes dulled by Hunt's awkwardly wielded arsenal of clichés.[51] Though the love interest Mara's actions communicate some surprising positions for Hunt regarding gender parity, she just as often serves as an ideological straight man, cooing in Juan's ear, "Now tell me more about the work you're doing to free Alpaca from dictatorship. That is far more important than anything I have ever tried to accomplish."[52] In all, *Alpaca* reads like a Ross Perot invective disguised as an Ayn Rand novel, wrapped up in Voltaire's *Candide* by way of a censored Harlequin romance.

For Hunt, the essential notion of good governance, the key to a future utopia for Alpacans, rests in graduated suffrage. This means that an individual's vote in national affairs should be, must be, defined relative to that individual's personal wealth, property holdings, and tax contributions. Hunt, apparently, was willing and eager to pay such taxes if they yielded him a constitutionally defined influence in national affairs. After all, in "efficiently operated corporations, the larger stockholder naturally has the greater voting power. This was one of the clinching arguments in favor of the graduated voting power favoring the larger taxpayers who in effect are the largest stockholders in the national entity."[53] For the wheeler-dealer, the civic sphere should not operate on principles separate from those of private enterprise. The purchase of liberty is rigid hierarchy: "To operate successfully, a government must have a ruling class far above the average of its citizenry. The average, and particularly the lower class, of its citizenry are incapable of efficiently conducting their own affairs."[54] This organic conception of hierarchy echoes those stratifications so apparent in *Peter Arbiter*, and though Hunt's language is tame and prim, his ideal republic begins to resemble that imperial Texas spelled out around the feasting table of Billy Roy Eanes.

Here, too, race intruded in interesting ways, as Hunt borrowed from his McCarthyite toolkit regarding aliens to get at the need for the protection of borders. Aliens, Juan Achala says, "are there to practice espionage, to entice and enlist gullibles and dupes; they consort with intellectuals to build and join subtle organizations intended to pave the way for the overthrow of their host government . . . the aliens toil indefatigably for the national ruin and the ruin of all that these queer citizens are supposed to hold dear."[55]

Though Texas does not serve as an explicit referent in *Alpaca*, its presence is implicit, as in this section on border-crossing "aliens." Hunt's utopia does not meet the definition of empire as centralized rule over a diverse group of nations, but graduated suffrage and the explicit, constitutional recognition of class privilege do speak to Hunt's own vision of the Texas wheeler-dealer as the ideal of the displaced American self, of the supposedly unfettered entrepreneurial climate of the Lone Star State as a model on which the rest of the nation should remake itself. This sensibility has become political common sense in the state's dominant Republican Party, but such was not necessarily the case at the time of Hunt's *Alpaca*. The Democrats remained the arbiters of political power in Texas in the 1960s, their fortunes tied to a man, Lyndon Johnson, whose political philosophy could not be further from Hunt's. Within the next ten years, much would change.

The Bifurcation of Southern Democracy

A generational feud over primacy figured in the formal politics of the Texan 1970s as in its cultural politics. Changes lay on the horizon for the vaunted "party of the fathers," the solid Democracy that had ruled the South since the collapse of Reconstruction in the 1870s. Regional cracks in the Democratic coalition dated back at least to the infighting over the New Deal and through the fractures of the Homer Rainey affair.

Cyrus King, Larry L. King's "Old Man," spoke to the Democrats' ability to maintain their base among rural voters. He may have been reluctantly antiwar by 1971, but, in most senses, a conservative Texan he remained. When his son asked if he had ever voted Republican, though, he answered, "Yeah, in 19-and-28. Voted for Herbert Hoover. And he no more than put his britches on the chair till we had a depression. I promised God right then if He wouldn't send no more depressions, I wouldn't vote for no more Republicans."[56] The death of the fathers paved the way for a struggle over their political party with new generations of voters in an expanded Texas electorate, precipitating a wholesale partisan realignment in the Solid South.

The anxious ferment surrounding the figure of the Vanishing Texan traced a cultural moment and a significant shift in the realm of formal, electoral politics in the state capital in Austin. In such an atmosphere, hand-wringing over the compromised hegemonic force of Anglo-Texan masculinity registered anxiety over changes in regional identity. It also raised concerns over the issue of political representation in legislative bodies and the rights of legally constituted subjects and citizens. As African Americans, Mexican Americans, and women of all races contested the nature of political and cultural authority in the 1970s, the terrain of their struggle increasingly became entangled with partisan alignment in a state where the Democrats had ruled since the collapse of Reconstruction. Over the latter half of the twentieth century, the South's monopoly "party of the fathers" yielded to a competitive two-party system with Republicans in the ascendant, pivoting in the 1970s. The remainder of this chapter charts that change by looking to the legacies of Lyndon Johnson and the careers of his protégés, the history of the modern Republican Party in Texas, the rhetoric of Texas liberalism, and municipal politics in Austin. While the upheaval did not necessarily signify a substantive ideological shift in Texas—a conservative bloc set the basic agenda before and after the partisan change—the movement of politicians and voters from the Democratic to the Republican Party did draw on the charged relations among class, race, gender, region, and the state in the 1970s.

Conservatism's continuity in Texas politics should not preclude recognition of the state's equally persistent populism. Texans have long voiced a full-throated suspicion of the concentration of power, whether in the federal government, private corporations, or various incarnations of "outside" interests. The earliest Anglo settlers of the 1820s and 1830s suffused the Republic's early politics with a Southern-accented Jacksonian Democracy that privileged the interests of the common man. Jackson's protégé Sam Houston followed this creed. He broke from many of his peers, though, when he chose union over slavery, and was forcibly ejected from office to make way for secession. The Republican Party entered the picture following the Confederacy's defeat, with Radical Reconstruction's brief Texas phase being overseen by Governor Edmund Davis. Davis's defeat in 1873 yielded only a small respite for the Texas Regular Democrats seeking to restore the antebellum status quo, however, as the Farmers' Alliances that would birth the national Populist Revolt also convened in the 1870s. Governor James Hogg appropriated much of the Populist rhetoric, however, blunting their most radical contentions while expanding the role and function of state government. In one of the country's earliest articulations of the regulatory state, Hogg established the Texas Railroad Commission to monitor the "foreign," which is to say, "un-Texan" railroad corporations.

In the years that followed, the first half of the twentieth century witnessed the defeat of the Populists and Debsian Socialists, the rise of Progressives and Prohibitionists, and successful demagoguery from the likes of Governors Jim Ferguson and W. Lee O'Daniel. Increasingly, the political fights in which such figures engaged seemed to derive from feuding personalities in a one-party state. Even in this context, though, policy did matter. Our concern here, the struggles between modern liberals and conservatives in the mid- and late twentieth century, arose over divergent conceptions of the state embodied in the New Deal, as described in chapter 1. The pendulum swings, and apparent partisan and ideological continuities, mask bitter political conflicts that have unfolded in Texas over time.

From another angle of view, the transformation of the national Democratic Party in the 1970s involved an attempt to square the differences between corporate liberalism, an ideology in which the government smoothed over the worst contradictions of free-market capitalism, and humanist liberalism, an ideology aimed at maximizing liberty and dignity for the largest body of citizens. The Great Society's expansive government required partners and patrons in the private sphere, and Johnson loyalists like the Brown & Root corporation, which had supported LBJ since the New Deal efforts to dam the Colorado River, could easily back expanded government spending on infrastructure. Such corporate partners could not balk at, and indeed lobbied hard for, the federal largesse that subsidized Sunbelt growth. But the War on Poverty and Johnson's civil rights initiatives also linked his success to insurgent social movements that desired a more equitable society, anathema to the oilmen who funded much of Texas politics. The balancing act required firm leadership of the state Democratic Party by a cohort of centrists loyal to Johnson in Texas. This group had won control of the party from the pro-Eisenhower, massive resistance Shivercrats in the mid-1950s around the time that Johnson became Senate majority leader, and would hold onto that power until the Sharpstown influence-peddling scandal embarrassed their leading figures in 1972.[57]

A moderate Democratic congressional delegation from Texas strengthened Johnson's hand in passing the flurry of legislation that constituted the Great Society—the Civil Rights Act (1964), the Economic Opportunity Act (1964), the Food Stamp Act (1964), the Immigration and Nationality Services Act (1965), the Voting Rights Act (1965), the Elementary and Secondary Education Act (1965), the Higher Education Act (1965), the Bilingual Education Act (1968), and the creation of VISTA (1964), Head Start (1964), the National Endowment for the Arts and National Endowment for the Humanities (1965), Medicare and Medicaid (1965), the Public Broadcasting Service (1967), and many others. The same centrist wing of the party also held the major state offices in Austin. Johnson's longtime associate John Connally served as governor from 1963 to 1969. Protégé Ben Barnes held the office of speaker of the Texas State House of Representatives from 1965 to 1969. Frank Erwin oversaw matters at the University of Texas as chair of the Board of Regents from 1966 to 1971. At the federal level, J. J. Pickle held down Johnson's old tenth congressional district, which included Austin, from 1963 to 1995. These associations outlasted Johnson's presidency and structured, at least initially, the state's post-1968 politics. Ben Barnes rose to lieutenant governor (1969–1973), Johnson's friend Roy Butler became mayor of Austin (1971–1975), and a number of Johnson's advisers taught at the LBJ School of Public Affairs at the University of Texas, while Erwin continued on at the Board of Regents.

The presence of Johnson's political machine, as well as the state's hybrid Southwestern identity, complicates the narrative of partisan realignment in Texas. During Johnson's presidency, 1963–1969, his allies maneuvered conservative Texas politics to keep the state visibly aligned with his national agenda, or at least rendering it incapable of embarrassing his larger initiatives. Change accelerated after Johnson's retirement, however, and not in ways that brought the Great Society vision closer to fruition in a New Texas. Without Johnson's ability to distribute patronage at the highest levels, a substantive realignment began to appear inevitable. In May 1973, John Connally—among the highest-ranking and longest-serving of LBJ's many protégés, the man who had engineered LBJ's earliest runs for the Senate, had been shot alongside John Kennedy in the Dallas motorcade, and had acted as Johnson's key lieutenant as governor of Texas—switched to the Republican Party at the height of Watergate. Connally's change of partisan loyalties owed something to personal ambition, but it also highlighted the changing regional and ideological coalitions being reworked between Republicans and Democrats.

The remainder of this chapter attends to such shifting loyalties in Texas politics, then, but it also situates this electoral calculus in a social network and cultural context, spatializing realignment, as it were, in the capital city of Austin, where this political process took on human scale. The concerns of this study—Texas identity, counterculture, new politics, popular music, performance, gender, race, and partisan shift—converge in 1970s Austin in discrete, material ways. The casts of characters in Austin's narratives of politics, popular music, and regional identity overlapped considerably. A brief example will demonstrate the larger point. One day in Luckenbach, as Craig Hillis, a guitarist for Jerry Jeff Walker and Michael Murphey, recalls, the members of the Lost Gonzo Band were playing poker with University of Texas football coach Darrell Royal. After a while, Royal looked at his watch and abruptly excused himself. "Boys, I gotta go," he said. "Gotta play golf with the president"—that is, the retired LBJ, who lived in the neighborhood.[58] Such juxtapositions were not random or taken lightly. They suggested dense social networks and meaningful relationships that made for a thicker level of politics. The Austin scene generated a number of such unlikely meetings. Willie Nelson played Chicano movement rallies and caused mischief in Jimmy Carter's White House. A Soviet journalism delegation listened to Texas music at the Armadillo World Headquarters, and voters elected a "hippie mayor," Jeff Friedman, to Austin's City Hall.[59] These lines of influence form the significant backdrop of the more arcane level of political maneuvering that must first garner our attention.

These overlapping social networks did not make for a monolithic political culture. Indeed, they resulted in a stew of competing residual, dominant, and emergent formations contained within a single, largely unopposed Democratic Party. Countercurrents, idiosyncrasies, and tensions marked the Democrats' long monopoly of power. To be a Southern Democrat in the post-Reconstruction, pre-Nixon era was to belong to a bloc whose chief rationale for partisan allegiance lay in the fact that the Democrats were not the odious Republicans who had attempted to establish racial justice in the South following the Civil War.[60] This tenuous loyalty could spark temporary schizophrenia, leading to the phenomenon of "presidential Republicans" who voted conservative Democrats into office locally while casting a ballot for the Republicans' presidential candidate. In 1928, Texas engaged in its first rebellion along these lines, as Cyrus King noted, choosing Republican Herbert Hoover over Democrat Al Smith to protest Smith's urban ways, wet politics, and Catholicism. Democratic Texas likewise selected Dwight Eisenhower over Adlai Stevenson in 1952 and 1956. The Eisenhower loyalties owed much to the leadership of Allan Shivers, a conservative who objected to the liberalism of the national party on race and the paramount Texas issue of state control of tidelands.

This bifurcation in partisan behavior accelerated apace in the 1940s and 1950s, as the Democratic monolith began to fracture through much of the Jim Crow South. Traditional conservatives or "Regulars" continued to elect Democrats on the local level but often voted for Republicans on the federal, while those denoted liberal or national Democrats supported the broader ideological aims of the party. The state's Republicans, in post-Reconstruction years primarily a vehicle of federal patronage, benefited from this split as voters and candidates began to consider it a party of protest and, perhaps, the standard-bearer for a conservatism that would limit federal authority.

The notion of realignment has a long history in political literature. In short, realignment holds that the parties in the American political system consist of disparate interest groups joined by an electoral calculus. At key moments of political strain, those interest groups rearrange their partisan loyalties. The labels Republican and Democrat remain constant after the 1860s, but they signify ever-shifting coalitions. The election of 1860 and the Civil War set up a regional partisan dynamic with the new Republican Party of Northern capital, farmers, and abolitionists over and against the agrarian South. The Populist Revolt of the 1890s shook much of the agrarian Midwest and Mountain West from its Republican moorings, making 1896 a realignment election. By the time of the New Deal, the Democratic coalition became an umbrella comprising organized labor in the Northern cities, white ethnic immigrants, African Americans, white Southern conservatives, and Western farmers. Though ideologically disparate—J. Frank Dobie called it "one of the oddest compromises the political world has ever known"—the New Deal's broad scope appeased each in some manner.[61] Meanwhile, the Republicans became a rump opposition party of Northern capital. The South remained solidly in this Democratic fold into World War II.

In Texas, conservative Republican Bruce Alger's election to the U.S. House of Representatives from Dallas augured the impending partisan shift as early as 1954, not coincidentally the year of the Supreme Court's decision in *Brown v. Board of Education*. John Tower's election to the U.S. Senate in 1961 provided the next important sign, as he filled the seat vacated by Johnson's move to the vice presidency. The Johnson years kept Austin a firmly Democratic city within and without the Capitol dome. At the same time, Johnson's balancing act on the national stage and the state's Senate delegation split between conservative Republican Tower and liberal Democrat Ralph Yarborough sketched the outlines of the partisan shift to come. Johnson's elevation to the presidency, together with his political acumen and able lieutenants back in Austin, slowed these developments. In fact, Johnson's landslide election in 1964 seemed at first to push back the Republican beachhead, with Alger's defeat wiping out the only Texas Republican foothold in the U.S. House. Political fallout over Vietnam and unrest in the cities soon eroded the apparent liberal consensus of 1964, however, and the late 1960s brought the election of three Republican

U.S. representatives from Texas: Robert Price from the Panhandle, James Collins from Dallas, and George H. W. Bush from Houston. From there, partisan realignment in Texas from a one-party Democratic state to a predominantly Republican one occurred slowly over a number of years. The passage of the 1960s into the 1970s set the stage for a decade of substantial jockeying over partisan allegiances among voters and politicians, beginning with the Sharpstown scandal of 1972, proceeding through Connally's party change in 1973, and culminating in the Republican William Clements's watershed gubernatorial victory in 1978.[62]

Still, Republicans did not hold a majority in the Texas Senate until 1997, in the Texas House until 2002, or in the federal congressional delegation until 2004. This echoed the shift in the wider South. Rather than a wholesale switch of partisan allegiance, change involved fits and starts that reconfigured the priorities of both Democrats and Republicans in the region.[63] Nixon's Southern strategy of bringing conservative, anti–civil rights whites into the Republican fold did not meet with immediate success. In fact, the strategy's clumsy deployment led to the defeat of Nixon's preferred Southern congressional and gubernatorial candidates in 1970.[64] The early failure of Nixon's strategy and the success of Southern Democratic centrists in the elections of 1970 made the discrediting of those centrists a key Republican strategy in Texas by 1972. Given this back-and-forth context, it becomes apparent that the political changes of the post–World War II era were continuous, and arguments over the pivotal nature of a single decade can oversimplify the nature of history's persistent unfolding. Nevertheless, the 1970s constitute a tipping point in this narrative of political realignment, as the Republican Party then gained unprecedented legitimacy in the Southern states.[65]

The changes in Texas and the South existed in close dialogue with the national environment of the 1970s. In political terms, as in cultural ones, "the seventies" is a polysemic notion, not given to the kind of quick characterizations that judge decades as dominated by a particular political consensus. So, observers often attempt to securely place "the sixties" as the decade of the left, "the eighties" the decade of the right, and throw up their hands when it comes to the years in between.[66] In part, this gesture unintentionally recognizes the complex character of the moment, one that established the viability of left alternatives and consolidated the civil rights revolutions of the 1960s, even as the right successfully employed the social movement tactics and rights rhetoric elaborated in the prior decade for different ends. In general, the period's political discourse shifted from a focus on social problems to the doctrine of individual responsibility, from an appreciation for the instrumentality of government to an anxiety about the unintended consequences of reform. Finally, a base distrust of constituted authority dominated these years and provided a shared thread between the decade's populist voices of left and right.[67] They had reason to enjoy one another's company.

At the same time, the South's position in the nation changed substantially. Historians differ on the nature of this shifting relationship between nation and region. On the one hand, Bruce Schulman, following John Egerton, has posited a "thoroughgoing southernization of American life" in the decade as national political debate hewed toward the region's small-government conservatism and evangelical religion.[68] On the other, a new wave of historians sees in the Seventies not a "southernization" of American life so much as a nationalization of the South and a suburbanization of the region's politics, convergent with the United States at large. Matthew Lassiter, Joseph Crespino, and Kevin Kruse, in particular, fit the Southern political narrative of the post–civil rights moment more neatly to the arc of white flight and urban divestment in the North as set out by Thomas Sugrue in *The Origins of the Urban Crisis*.[69] As Lassiter argues, "The ascendance of the metropolitan Sunbelt played a crucial role in the fading of Southern distinctiveness and the national collapse of the New Deal Order, a process of regional convergence marked by the parallel suburbanization of southern and American politics."[70] Though in many ways distinct within the region, on this point Texas looked like the rest of the South and, indeed, the nation. As seen in previous chapters, this convergence provides one of the primary motive factors in the celebration of regional difference regarding both Texas and the South in the 1970s. Whether its causes involved regional convergence or Southern ascendance, the significance of the partisan realignment cannot be missed.

Realignment, in practice, hinged on the politics of race amid the civil rights movement. Drawing on the ideological deployment of a skewed historical memory, the Republican Party had been anathema in the South due to the party's association with the Civil War and Reconstruction.[71] In addition to re-orienting views of the South's development in the later decades of the twentieth century, Crespino, Kruse, and Lassiter, together with historians such as Jason Sokol and Randy Sanders, have mapped a new vision of race, politics, and the post–civil rights South. These authors document the ways that a Southern politics of race became coded into a more moderate-sounding rhetoric trumpeting law and order, private property, or the rights of white citizens, as the nation came to revile, and Southern elites came to be embarrassed by, the openly voiced politics of white supremacy.

Texas politics, in the West of the New South, differed in some small degrees from developments in the Deep South. With one of the proportionally smaller African American populations of Southern states, the white–black racial dyad, though significant, had not driven politics in quite the same way in the state. Indeed, political theorist V. O. Key, an Austin native and graduate of the University of Texas, argued in his classic *Southern Politics in State and Nation* that Texas would prove the most fertile ground in the South for the development of a two-party politics that hinged on issues of class and economics, rather than racial demagoguery.[72] In Texas, race acted as one wedge issue among a number of broader arguments over federal authority. Also, the effects of the African American civil rights movement operated in tandem with the Chicano movement to bring substantive change to the Texas Democratic Party in the 1970s by virtue of Raza Unida's third-party ascendance in the border counties. Raza Unida's defeat of the Anglo political bosses in that region removed a primary bloc of conservative power-brokers from influence in the Democratic Party. The counties with political bosses who had delivered border votes to state and national candidates in return for political favors now represented districts that required campaigning on issues much as the rest of the state.[73]

Simultaneously, African American influence in the state's Democratic Party rose as black electoral strength and constitutional rights finally found protection in law. This included a black congressional delegation taking its place in the state Capitol for the first time since Reconstruction. By 1974, the black caucus in the Texas legislature would include Eddie Bernice Johnson and Sam Hudson of Dallas, G. J. Sutton, Senfronia Thompson, Craig Washington, Mickey Leland, Paul Ragsdale, and Anthony Hall of Houston, and Wilhelmina Delco of Austin. But the acceptance of such black officeholders was by no means immediate. When up-and-coming Comptroller Robert S. Calvert publicly referred to Eddie Bernice Johnson as that "n——r woman," it was obvious that the nominal victories of inclusion in the political process constituted only a beginning.[74]

Shifting politics in the 1960s and 1970s derived from many causes in addition to the salient one of race and divergent opinions regarding the federal government's sanctioning of racial justice. Contemporaneous accounts such as Richard Scammon and Ben Wattenberg's *The Real Majority* and Kevin Phillips's *The Emerging Republican Majority* traced the shift toward a generalized mistrust of government and a turn from understanding issues in terms of the social to the lionization of individual responsibility for private success or failure.[75] In *The Real Majority*, Scammon and Wattenberg, centrist Democratic strategists, predicted the move from economic and workplace issues to an electorate's concern with "the social issue," and especially "law and order." Both registered as code for racial anxiety, but conservatives could also spin them into a broader politics with a wider, though typically white, audience. In *The Emerging Republican Majority*, American regionalism came to the fore with Kevin Phillips's introduction of the terms "Southern strategy" and "Sunbelt" to describe the Republican need to pursue the ideological outliers of the Democratic coalition. While Phillips remained cautious over the advisability of such a strategy, the idea caught on among influential segments of the Republican Party. By mid-decade, Kirkpatrick Sale agreed with Phillips's regional assessment even as he bemoaned the successful Republican inroads in the South: "This power shift is more than a passing phenomenon," Sale argued. "It is a way of comprehending modern America. An understanding of its sweep and pattern helps to make sense out of the recent past."[76] Each of these authors focused on a singular element to describe a series of shifting political moods (region, race, values), but the logic that connected them one to another remained the collapse of mid-century liberalism as the vital center of American politics.

Realignment's logic made for strange bedfellows. By the 1970s, the progressive *Texas Observer* had been promoting the fortunes of the Republican Party as a means of realigning the state's politics for at least a decade. Southern liberals argued that forcing conservatives into the Republican Party would create a competitive two-party system, incidentally following the road map provided by V. O. Key. Southern liberal support for conservative Republicans promised a space for political choice outside of the Democratic primary elections that had a rather predictable dynamic in Texas, one unfavorable to the party's liberal faction. Since the eruption of the liberal–conservative split in the state party during the New Deal, statewide Democratic primaries often featured a crowded field of conservatives and a sole liberal. With the conservative vote thus divided in the initial primary, a run-off often resulted between the leading conservative candidate and the lone liberal. While this emboldened state liberals by keeping their candidates in the spotlight despite their minority status, it also produced perennial disappointments. The liberal faction almost always fielded a strong gubernatorial candidate who achieved statewide name recognition through the primaries—Ralph Yarborough in the 1950s, Frances "Sissy" Farenthold in the 1970s—but Democrats from the party's liberal wing would not win that office until the victories of Mark White in 1982 and Ann Richards in 1990.[77] That is, liberal Democratic candidates did not prevail until the exodus of conservatives made the Republicans relevant and recalibrated the state's electoral politics and primary system.

The strategy of liberal support for conservative Republicans goes back at least to John Tower's Senate campaign in 1961. In that election, the *Texas Observer* endorsed Tower against the conservative Democrat William Blakely, stating that liberals "want to free their party from the dead weight of the Dixiecrats. . . . Republicans want to reorient Texas conservatism into a source of greater state prestige. At the intersection of these two basic objectives lies a vote for John Tower."[78] Republicans accomplished little to expand on these initial victories in the 1960s. Just as the Republican Party found its conservative voice and Southern audience with Barry Goldwater's candidacy in 1964, Johnson's victory that year temporarily reversed the Republican tide in Texas. Just six years later, Lloyd Bentsen's defeat of Ralph Yarborough in the Democratic primaries signaled the temporary nature of 1964's liberal watershed. Afterward, a number of *Observer*-associated liberals founded the Democratic Rebuilding Committee to promote the defeat of conservative Democratic candidates at the hands of Republicans, thus facilitating the growth of a two-party system. They took their name from a John Kennedy quote regarding the health of the Massachusetts Democratic Party: "Nothing can be done until it is beaten . . . badly beaten. Then there will be chance for rebuilding."[79] It was not until 1972 that liberal Democrats and conservative Republicans made further progress along these lines.

Political consensus shifted in ways that belie easy divisions of left and right, and this rhetorically murky middle challenges the assessment of late-sixties and seventies politicians. For example, though law-and-order rhetoric maligned the strident elements of student antiwar protest, public opinion as a whole had turned largely against the Vietnam War by the early 1970s. Texas Democrats felt compelled to chart a middle ground on the issue. Bob Eckhardt, a liberal congressman from the Houston area, wrote that the "reaction that I have indicated to me from letters sent to my office has been very adverse to the Cambodian intervention [of 1970]. And I don't even come from a particularly dovish district."[80] This led liberals such as Eckhardt to deploy the state's history and iconography to frame political points in this uncertain atmosphere. In arguing for a withdrawal from Vietnam, for example, Eckhardt suggested that discretion might be the better part of valor, since in "the South, names like Stonewall Jackson and Robert E. Lee stir our blood, but they fought for a cause as questionable and for a victory as unattainable as that in Vietnam. . . . [James] Fannin's men were no less heroic for fighting in the clearing, under orders, rather than taking to the woods" during the revolt against Mexico.[81] The heroic complex embedded in Anglo-Texan masculinity, he suggested, was not compromised by the logical need to retreat from Vietnam, nor was the heroism of American troops in question for fighting a "losing" battle, as Fannin's men had at Goliad.

The attempt to give Texas shape to the philosophies of liberal Democrats extended to the quest for a symbolism to match Eckhardt's stance on the war:

> I'm not a dove, I'm not a hawk. I suppose I'm a paisano. "Paisano," you know, means two things in Spanish. It means a kind of southwestern bird, a roadrunner, and it means a "countryman." I think we should keep our feet on the ground: we must keep our Anglo-American pragmatism.... I don't think we can "coo" our way out of responsibility for a situation that did not come about without our participation. Also, I am sympathetic with the position of "the countryman," opposing those who would block his aspirations toward nationalism.[82]

Eckhardt thus appealed to local knowledge to forge a middle way using the bird that was J. Frank Dobie's totem, and, in the process, he even deployed the Spanish vernacular of the Southwest to bolster "our Anglo-American pragmatism." He framed his paisano position as based in patriotism, pragmatism, and, by extension, the nationalist aspirations of the Viet Cong. These attempts at a middle-way liberalism, a transcendence of the oppositions marked by hawk and dove, required such Texas accents, as individuals like Eckhardt sought to push the state party leftward without invoking political labels then becoming unpopular with voters.

Bob Armstrong, a candidate for state land commissioner in 1972 who would bring environmental issues to the fore at the General Land Office, trod lightly on this issue of political labeling. While attending a program sponsored by the Texas AFL-CIO that featured liberal legislators in Houston, Armstrong resisted the label that came from his association with the group. As the *Houston Chronicle* wrote, while "Armstrong has since received organized labor's endorsement for the land commissioner post, he claims this does not make him a liberal, for he also had the help of former governors John Connally and Allan Shivers."[83] In other words, Armstrong garnered support not only from the liberals, but also from the right wing of LBJ's centrists (Connally), and, indeed, from the far right of the Democratic Party (Shivers). Texas politicians in the 1970s perhaps missed an opportunity to construct a populist coalition around this center that maintained broad support outside the major cities. Their attempts to hold onto the language of agrarian populism and the symbols of Anglo-Texanness, however, ultimately fell short. These developments closely paralleled those at the Armadillo World Headquarters across the Colorado

River, which allowed for young adherents of the new politics to celebrate and re-imagine the traditional symbols of rural Anglo-Texan masculinity.

Sharpstown and Watergate

While John Tower's election to the Senate in 1961 augured the coming realignment, the denouement of the Yarborough–Connally feud within the state Democratic Party more effectively traced realignment's 1970s pivot. In 1970, Senator Ralph Yarborough, the most significant politician ever elected out of the liberal wing of the Texas Democratic Party, lost to South Texas rancher Lloyd Bentsen in the Democratic primaries. Bentsen went on to defeat Republican George H. W. Bush in the general election, and Bush moved over to a consolation prize as chairman of the Republican National Committee. George Norris Green, whose seminal *The Establishment in Texas Politics* appeared in the late 1970s, argued that Yarborough's defeat, as well as his earlier electoral successes, owed more to the national political climate than the rise or fall of liberal sentiment among Texas voters. Throughout the postwar period, liberal Democrats pressed the argument that the state was surely trending in their direction with urbanization, industrialization, unionization, and the civil rights movement. Green, rather, suggested that Yarborough won in 1958 due to a recession blamed on Republicans and in 1964 on the coattails of a wider liberal wave. In 1970, however, the shifting political discourse of "law-and-order" issues on which voters perceived Yarborough as weak doomed his campaign against the upstart Bentsen.[84] The defeat shook the *Texas Observer*'s confidence that the state was primed for modern, urban liberalism under Yarborough's leadership, and the paper reacted viscerally with the post-primary headline "The Yarborough Defeat: Anti-nigger, Anti-Mexican, Anti-youth."[85] For a politician whose career had been built on the notion of "putting the jam on the lower shelf so the little man can reach it," the collapsing fortunes of liberal egalitarianism hit hard.[86]

Lyndon Johnson recognized the changing political landscape, and by 1970 devoted his remaining energies in his home state not to Great Society liberalism, but to shoring up the centrist bloc he saw as the Democratic Party's only chance for remaining dominant in Texas. Back in 1964, Johnson had not only endorsed Yarborough as a key legislative ally, but also made it known in Texas that he did not want any other Democrat running against the incumbent senator. In 1970, the retired president conspicuously refused to endorse a candidate in the Yarborough–Bentsen contest.[87] Circumstances validated Johnson's concerns over the centrist bloc's fortunes. John Connally left the Democratic Party during his time as Treasury secretary in the Nixon White House. Nixon put a great deal of stock in Connally's counsel, in part due to the charisma he exercised by playing "the Texan" in Nixon's presence. As Henry Kissinger said of Nixon's estimation of Connally, "There was no American public figure Nixon held in such awe. Connally's swaggering self-assurance fulfilled Nixon's image of how a leader should act."[88] With Johnson retired, Yarborough defeated, and Connally ensconced in the opposition party, the leadership vacuum among Texas Democrats left them vulnerable to the perfect storm of scandal that hit the party at the dawn of the seventies.

The Sharpstown scandal that scattered Johnson's centrists began to unfold in January 1971, as LBJ's Democratic allies were inaugurated to statewide offices. Investigators alleged that Frank Sharp of the Sharpstown State Bank and National Bankers Life Insurance had issued lenient loans to a number of Democratic politicians. Sharp then instructed the politicians to invest that money in stocks of the National Bankers Life Insurance Company, vote for banking legislation amenable to Frank Sharp's business interests (thus increasing their stock value), and sell their stocks at a profit. The scandal directly implicated Governor Preston Smith, state Democratic chair Elmer Baun, Texas House Speaker Gus Mutscher, Fort Worth Representative Tommy Shannon, and Mutscher aide Rush McGinty. Lieutenant Governor Ben Barnes, though not technically guilty of his colleagues' improprieties, found himself caught in the cross fire in the election year of 1972. Both liberal Democrats and energized Republicans raised the flag of reform, as a disparate coalition of state representatives dubbed the "Dirty Thirty" placed LBJ's centrist wheeler-dealers in their crosshairs. Sharpstown accelerated partisan realignment, as it closed the period in which Johnson's centrists, who had taken control of the state apparatus from the Dixiecrat-leaning supporters of Allan Shivers in 1956, guided the party.

Despite Johnson's retirement, the Texan profile remained high in national politics, if not always quite as visible or evocative. By the end of 1972, Robert Strauss and George H. W. Bush, both Texans, had been named national chairmen of the Democratic and Republican Parties, respectively.[89] In addition, Anne Armstrong, another Texan, served as co-chair of the GOP from 1971 to 1973 and, like Connally, had the ear of the Nixon White House. As knowledge of the Committee to Re-elect the President's dirty tricks and unconstitutional cover-up unfolded, Texans headed both major parties, and another Texan, John Connally, hoped to benefit politically from Nixon's fall. His partisan switch originated in part from a belief that he could win the Republican Party's nomination for president. The larger air of political maneuvering around Watergate drew Nixon's attention to events in Texas, as the state's bloc of electoral votes and its close association with LBJ made it a coveted prize in the Southern strategy.[90] As Attorney General John Mitchell told President Nixon, "Where, I think, you have a prime and vital interest is the politics in Texas. As you know, this Sharp thing has just about destroyed the Democrat Party down there, and will continue to as this thing builds up."[91] Ben Barnes maintains that Nixon's political interest in Sharpstown drove the aggressive federal investigations that cut short the careers of moderate Democrats like himself not directly linked to improprieties. If Barnes overstates the extent to which Sharpstown was among Nixon's dirty tricks—the core defendants were, after all, guilty—it is nevertheless true that Nixon's interference served partisan ends and diminished the political legacy of his predecessor, Johnson, in his home state.

Sharpstown brought the most reform-minded Democrats to the fore even as the party still held broad voter loyalty among rural conservatives as well as urban liberals. In the short term, Frances "Sissy" Farenthold stood among the biggest winners in this development, a state representative from Corpus Christi who ran stirring, but ultimately unsuccessful, campaigns for the Democratic gubernatorial nomination. Earlier in her career, Farenthold had envisioned herself working behind the scenes in politics, but the women's movement inspired her to come into her own as a candidate. "I was going to be a student of it and work in politics," she recalled to a newspaper reporter, "but I didn't expect to be elected. This is part of those low expectations (of women)."[92] First elected to the Texas House of Representatives in 1968, Farenthold sought the Democratic nomination for governor in 1972 and 1974, both years in which she faced off with, and lost to, the prominent Uvalde rancher Dolph Briscoe.[93]

Farenthold energized a liberal base that believed the modernization of the state, its "cultural maturation," in publisher Michael Levy's words, had finally delivered them their moment in the sun. The *Texas Observer*'s endorsement of Farenthold for governor in 1972, written by Molly Ivins and Kaye Northcott, made the case, if in self-deprecating terms: "OK, so white liberals are a bad joke. OK, so Texas liberals are a national laughingstock—petty, disorganized, and more prone to fight one another than the perverted priorities of the people who call themselves conservatives in this state. We don't give a damn. get up off your butts and move. This woman is worth fighting for."[94] Ivins's enthusiasm mirrored John Connally's consternation over Farenthold's popularity. The Secretary of the Treasury described Sissy Farenthold to President Nixon with the exclamation, "And hell, this woman—this Sissy Farenthold, who's for legalized abortion, who's for legalized marijuana, who's for this, who's for that, a very radical woman!"[95] And, in Texas Democratic circles, she did come close to earning the label. In the Texas House of Representatives in 1969, she

Frances "Sissy" Farenthold, 1974. Photo © Alan Pogue.

cast the only vote against commending Lyndon Johnson's presidency in order to protest the Vietnam War, and she did propose a bill making marijuana possession a misdemeanor. In the gubernatorial campaigns, Farenthold cast her lot with the farm workers' union and, in a heretical move, called for the abolition of the Texas Rangers.[96] Still, as a statewide candidate Farenthold had to work to distance herself from the liberal label in Texas, echoing Eckhardt and Armstrong in framing herself as an insurgent populist. According to a *Dallas Morning News* article, "While Anne [Armstrong, the prominent Texas Republican and Nixon adviser] is prone to drink Dubonnet on the rocks with a lemon twist, Sissy was apt to pop a can of Budweiser after a tough day on the campaign trail. Philosophically, Sissy has been tagged a liberal, although she prefers to call herself an 'insurgent.'"[97] Farenthold also pushed back against the notion of liberals as "soft," combining the tough prairie-mother archetype with feminism's new assertiveness. As Calvin Trillin described in the *New Yorker*, one of her patented applause lines during the campaign referred to Dolph Briscoe's refusal to meet her in debate as "unmanly."[98] While her liberalism might have caused voters uneasiness, this beer-accented populism played well in the context of the Texan 1970s.[99]

If Nixon's political machinations seemed to pull the rug out from under the Johnson centrists in Austin, they simultaneously helped to propel the career of another Johnson acolyte. The televised impeachment hearings of the House Judiciary Committee made the Houston congresswoman Barbara Jordan a household name. In this, Jordan was the rare Johnson-supported politician to survive the 1970s with her reputation intact. *Texas Monthly* editor William Broyles imagined that the outcome would have pleased Johnson: "So far as Johnson could tell, both Connally and his protégé Ben Barnes had inherited the skills but none of the heart. Barbara Jordan was different . . . In the King Lear fantasies of his final year, with John Connally a Republican, Barnes' political career in ruins, and Nixon dismantling the Great Society, she was the one child who never wavered, who kept his legacy and promised to carry it on when he died."[100]

Further, Broyles mused, both Connally and Jordan "had LBJ's backroom magic, but Connally had Lyndon's poor-boy materialism, and she had Lyndon's New Deal heart. Blended together, they made a pretty good LBJ."[101] Jordan's rise, and Connally's partisan switch, signified a rupture in what had been formerly portrayed as a unitary, organic body politic. In this view of political decline, no Texan could combine or transcend the contrarian qualities of traditional Texanness and modern liberalism as had LBJ. Savvy, Jordan did not read this rupture as a move away from Texan identity, but a step toward its reconfiguration. Indeed, she publicly embraced the state. "I am a Texan. . . . My roots are there," she wrote in the Texas-themed issue of *Atlantic Monthly*. "'Texan' frequently evokes images of conservatism, oil, gas, racism, callousness. In my judgment, the myths should be debunked, or at the least, should include the prevalent strains of reasonableness, compassion, and decency."[102] A number of Texas voters, in a variety of locales, came to similar conclusions.

All Politics Is Local: Austin Municipal Elections in the 1970s

This hunger for transcending Texan stereotypes while retaining a sense of place and tradition, of course, also stood behind the hippie–redneck, cosmic cowboy performances at the Armadillo World Headquarters. Willie Nelson's success, in this case, served in part as an antidote to the "vanishing" of LBJ, combining iconic Texanness and the airs of modern progressivism as he did. Further, LBJ himself let his hair grow a little longer upon moving back home. An early 1970s comics insert into the *Daily Texan* by Richard Hoffman, titled "The Day the Freaks Took Austin," played with this sense of inversion, imagining a time when the counterculture took the reins of Austin government. The hippies' victory forced the former figures of the Texas establishment to live off the land. The final panels of the comic end with the narration, "And finally, the mightiest men took to the road to rediscover their country," and a drawing of a smiling, long-haired, Stetson-wearing LBJ hitchhiking out of town.

Austin serves well as a laboratory for examining the intersection of national, state, and local politics, as the capital city of the Sunbelt South's largest state and home territory of a retired president. As sociologist Anthony Orum wrote in his political history of the city, the "early 1970s were a time not only for the small revolts of American youth. They were a time when challenges to the normal routine of political life were breaking out everywhere."[103] But youth did have something to do with it, as the University of Texas's experience of the sixties student movement carried over into the changing municipal politics of the 1970s. The *Daily Texan*, along with the university's Young Democrats and Student Action Committee, advocated for the mobilization of the University of Texas student vote in local elections as early as 1973 and analyzed the returns at length to determine the efficacy of the student bloc. The study concluded that student precincts, with high turnout, could deliver a significant swing vote to liberal candidates. In the city council elections of April 7 of that year, though, most student-supported, new politics candidates lost (the exception being "hippie councilman" Jeff Friedman in Place 5).[104]

By 1975, however, the student precincts had sufficiently mobilized to force a realignment of sorts in Austin city politics: "University students turned out *en masse* in 1975 to elect one of the most liberal city councils in Austin's history: a chicano, a black, two women (one liberal, the other conservative), a blind millionaire, another woman who campaigned on a 'think trees' platform, and a Jewish mayor in his thirties. . . . Molly Ivins said it 'looked like an affirmative action program gone berserk.'"[105] Young local politicos delighted in the new political landscape. As the *Austin Sun* editorialized in 1975, the year of Austin's city council shift, "Lyndon is dead, Ben Barnes rejected, John Connally disgraced, and now local kingpin Roy Butler has been reduced to just another car dealer."[106] In place of LBJ confrere Roy Butler arose the left-leaning Jeff Friedman, a product of the mobilized student voters who also formed the basis of the Armadillo World Headquarters audience. Friedman had risen to prominence in the local demonstrations following Kent State and provided a face to that left–liberal coalition that furthered the movement politics of the 1960s into the electoral politics of the 1970s. The local press, from the centrist *Austin American-Statesman* to the progressive *Austin Sun*, kept a close eye on the unfolding of Friedman's countercultural pose.

> Image is the key to understanding Friedman. Jeff Friedman obtained his image in 1971 as a mustachioed, shaggy councilperson elected at a time when such foliage was not quite yet in. As the city has grown increasingly more polarized, younger and hipper, Friedman has gained in acceptability. Mayor Butler and rightist journalist Wray Weddell . . . helped Friedman's image along with snide loaded remarks about Austin's "hippie councilman" and "New Left" politician. . . . The fact is that Friedman is a liberal—but a liberal moderating rapidly with time.[107]

Friedman, like Farenthold, recognized the value of the Armadillo World Headquarters as a base. He held campaign fund-raisers there and, as emcee, shared the stage in 1976 with the bands Balcones Fault and the Uranium Savages, artist Jim Franklin, magician Harry Anderson, and dancer Chastity Fox.

In 1975, the year of Friedman's election as mayor, Austin also hosted the National Conference on Alternative State and Local Public Policies, an event aimed at exploring the paths out of the New Left and into electoral politics represented by the city's rising political stars.[108] Barbara Cigianero, a former United Farm Workers organizer who served in the 1970s on the Texas State Board of Paroles and Corrections, addressed the logic of the activists' turn to existing institutions. "You no longer think you can somehow personally end the war or that you'll be on the cover of *Time*. . . . People with experience in the Movement have learned that they can make a difference. They are less likely to be overcome by the sense of futility that bureaucracies nurture."[109] While many media accounts in the 1970s focused on the degeneration of the New Left into farce embodied by the Symbionese Liberation Army's 1974 kidnapping of Patty Hearst, numerous movement politicos shifted toward local left–liberal electoral coalitions with less public fanfare. The *Austin Sun* derided Friedman as a "liberal moderating rapidly with time," but learning the lessons of Lyndon Johnson's half-a-loaf politics—you cannot always get what you want—proved valuable amid the oft-contracted municipal horizons of the 1970s. These developments deepened and diffused the new politics in ways that rendered them less visible and audible, but more efficacious, than the prevailing rhetoric of seventies exhaustion.

This transition occurred through the mechanism of elections, but also transpired in the leisure spaces described elsewhere in this study. These shared spaces and the scenes they engendered did not merely involve a series of coincidental meetings between random individuals or places for letting off steam after the politicking was done; they represented dense social networks that forged affiliations and influenced decisions. The work/leisure divide does not describe the mechanisms of political life in a state capital. The "personal is political" aphorism that migrated from feminist circles across any number of discourses in 1970s life had as its unlikely corollary in a place such as Austin the recognition that the political—the lives of legislators in a lawmaking town, campaigning in municipal elections amid a politicized youth culture, enjoying music and the arts that traffic in the same symbols that enable political leadership—is personal. The operation of formal, electoral politics involved affective relationships by which the cultural and political scenes of the city more than merely coincided; they proved mutually constitutive.

Sociologist Sam Binkley's "thin cultural slices of life" come into play here, too, as illustrative of the intimate cultural–political continuum in Austin. Eddie Wilson recalls Bob Bullock's decision to pursue the office of comptroller as he described it in the Armadillo World Headquarters Beer Garden. Wilson asked Bullock if he had decided what office he was running for in 1974: "Yup, just now, and you'll be the first to know. I've learned that my liberal friends don't trust me enough to want me as treasurer. I've also learned that they don't know what comptroller means, so I'm going to take that one and shove it up their ass."[110] Obviously, though Bullock had friends among them, he did not see himself as exactly aligned with the left–liberal forces that dominated the Armadillo scene, nor did they necessarily return the favor. Later, while running the bar The Raw Deal, Wilson, at Ann Richards's request, marketed T-shirts referring obliquely to Bullock's well-documented orneriness: "Idi Amin for Comptroller."[111] Ann Richards also became involved in one of these less heralded struggles that made for those "thin cultural slices" of the city's cultural–political fabric, as she lobbied Wilson in a feud with former mayor Roy Butler over whether the Armadillo World Headquarters should stock Coors beer. The reactionary politics of the Coors family of Colorado led Richards to push a boycott (declared nationally by the AFL-CIO and gay rights advocates) despite the brand's popularity. Butler, a local beer lobbyist and friend of the Coors family, argued otherwise. As Wilson put it, his "best defense about Coors' politics was claiming the Budweiser family was a bunch of former Nazis and even worse than the Coors family."[112] The row over beer points to the developing politics of consumption as expressive of social values.

"A Man on Horseback to Lead This Nation": Carter, Clements, and the Conservative Turn

On the national level, the presidential election of 1976 promised to reverse the Republican gains from earlier in the decade. Just as Johnson's victory in 1964 closed the Republican window opened in Texas by Bruce Alger and John Tower, Democrats in 1976 felt that Richard Nixon's resignation and Gerald Ford's bumbling had exhausted the political capital yielded the Republicans by the law-and-order issue and Southern strategy. Indeed, to read editorials from the period is to get a sense that the Republican Party would never recover from Watergate. To underscore the point, the Democrats went back to their moderate Southern wing for the 1976 candidate, Jimmy Carter, who, like Johnson, carried deep regional inflections in his public performance. Texas joined in the Democrats' attempted Southern resurgence. *Texas Monthly* published two articles on the subject in September 1976, one chronicling the continued high profile of Texas Democrats in the national party at the New York convention, "All's Fair in Love" by Richard West, and, opposite, one covering the continuing feuds between liberal and conservative Democrats in the state party back home, "And War," by Paul Burka. The first celebrated Democratic Texas in the post-Johnson era, while also foregrounding the performance of "the Texan" in New York:

> Why, then, five days later—after the Reverend Martin Luther, Sr.'s benediction—was New York City Mayor Abe Beame, standing five-foot-two on the bandstand of the Rainbow Room atop Rockefeller Center, looking like Yosemite Sam in a twenty-gallon Stetson, thrusting a hook-'em-horns sign toward the roof, telling of his love for the hundred or so gathered Texans. . . . The whole convention was a love-in, as everybody has heard by now ad nauseam. But the biggest love-in of all turned out to be New York for Texas and vice versa. Who would have thought it, after all, thought that those old antagonists, the melting pot and the frontier, would have finally got together and picked each other out to love and honor, out of all the states in the USA?[113]

Despite, or perhaps because of, New York's bankrupt doldrums and Texas's oil-driven swagger, the two outsized spaces, "empire states," stuck close to each other at the Democratic convention.

Texans' success at the national convention in 1976 did not reflect the bitter struggle over authority within the state party's Democratic Executive Committee. This locus of leadership proved the primary battleground between liberals trying to cement their control of the party in a realigned Texas, and those conservatives attempting to maintain the party's centrist course. Paul Burka, surveying the scene in the state convention, observed that things had been:

> different under John Connally. For his six years as governor, beginning in January 1963, he was in total control of the state party. With Lyndon Johnson lending his weight from the White House, conservative Democrats were at the apogee of their power; liberals could seldom muster more than 10 of the 62 votes on the SDEC. But Briscoe is in the unenviable position of needing help from the outside . . . to avoid an embarrassing defeat, not from his veteran political rivals, but at the hands of a bunch of political novices, and liberal novices at that. It didn't use[d] to be this way.[114]

This comes across as a declension narrative, the organic unity and patriarchal authority exercised in the party fractured into shrill dissent by the rising power of the liberals and their attempts to shunt the conservatives from leadership. Burka then outlined the history of prior party feuds, including Lyndon Johnson versus Coke Stevenson in the 1940s, Johnson versus the Shivercrats in the 1950s, Ralph Yarborough versus John Connally in the 1960s, and Sissy Farenthold versus the Sharpstown Gang in the 1970s: "This one is different. Everyone's in this one: the governor, all the high-ranking state officials, labor, blacks, browns, career liberals, a congressman or two, the Democratic presidential nominee. This is not just one faction against another; this is an entire political party playing musical chairs."[115] The combatants sought to stake out the party's identity and its position on the prospects of partisan realignment. By 1976, events had vastly reconfigured the Yarborough left/Johnson center/ Shivers right calculus. McGovern's new politics wave, represented in Texas by Sissy Farenthold, crashed against rural conservatism, and Carter's moderating New Democrats were on the rise in the South. This vulnerability finally produced an opening for the Republican Party on the state level in the gubernatorial election of 1978.

That election brought Bill Clements to power, the first Republican governor of Texas in the century since Reconstruction. Richard Nixon declared Clements's election as "the nation's most significant Republican victory in a generation."[116] It also marked the passing of the Raza Unida tide, as the RUP candidate Mario Compean earned lower than the 2 percent threshold required to secure future state money for primary elections. Still, Clements beat the Democratic candidate, Texas Attorney General John Hill, with fewer than 20,000 votes out of 2.5 million cast. Compean had polled 14,000 votes, and a Socialist Workers Party candidate 4,500, that otherwise might have tightened the race. Clements's victory followed the pattern established by presidential Republicans on the national level, as he did not extend coattails of any significant length to local officeholders. For the time being, Texas voters continued to vote Democratic (and conservative) on the local level, while placing a Republican in a statewide executive position.[117]

Though pivotal, Clements's victory by no means sealed the Republican ascendance in the state. After a single term, Democrat Mark White defeated Clements for governor in 1982, when the independent party challengers (Libertarian Party and Constitution Party) lay to the right, rather than the left (Raza Unida and Socialist Workers), of the insurgent Republicans. The 1982 elections, in fact, suggested a revival in the fortunes of the liberal wing of the Democratic Party with the victories of Ann Richards for state treasurer and

Jim Hightower for agriculture commissioner. The *Observer* thesis regarding the salutary effects of realignment for liberal Democrats and conservative Republicans seemed to be vindicated. The pendulum continued to swing, though, as Clements returned to take the governor's office back from White in 1986. The election of 1982 proved a temporary reprieve for the liberals. Their desire to have the Democratic Party to themselves and create a competitive two-party system had, thus far, created mixed results, but the party's future marginalization seemed far from assured in the 1980s.

If electoral politics on the state and national level shifted rightward, the legacy of the New Left had a greater effect in the "thin slices of cultural life" that can be traced through local and municipal politics. It was at this local level that the new calculus of identity politics and civil rights prevailed with the 1975 Austin City Council elections. Moreover, in the 1970s, the officeholding class on the local, state, and federal levels at last began to look a little more like the population as a whole. Though the performance of "the Texan" in its traditional, Anglo-cowboy guise would remain a popular position in the state's politics, it was no longer the prerequisite performance it once was.

However, Texas often still signified, in the national imagination, traditional gendered dichotomies and frontier values. The political fluidity of the 1970s, its digestion of the new politics and countercultural impulses of the 1960s, would soon give way to the New Right ascension nationwide in the 1980s. Here, too, cowboys signified the political aspirations of a certain segment of the American electorate, placing the United States high in the saddle again with a president, Ronald Reagan, who thought best "with a horse between [his] knees."[118] The Sunbelt political imagination had long sought to conjure such a politician. At a White House luncheon for newspaper executives in October 1961, Ted Dealey, publisher of the *Dallas Morning News*, spoke to those assembled, including his host, JFK: "We need a man on horseback to lead this nation and many people in Texas and the Southwest think that you are riding Caroline's tricycle. The general opinion of grassroots thinking in this country is that you and your administration are weak sisters."[119] The tragedy in the Dallas plaza named for the Dealey family would seem to have delivered such "grassroots thinking" its first shot at such a vigorous cowboy president. Johnson's failure in Vietnam, in the views of theorists like Sale, would seem to have given them another cowboy in Nixon.[120] And, as the 1970s came to a close, a decade of hybridities and questioning of old verities, of hippie–rednecks and androgynous glam and nuanced debates over constitutional law, it seemed as if the wide-open possibilities had contracted, and the strict binaries of male and female, left and right, and right and wrong would have to be asserted once again through the American national symbol of the cowboy. McMurtry's "god," it seemed, was due another round of resurrection, and many Texans stood poised to play their parts. In spaces like Gilley's in the Houston suburb of Pasadena, or in Manhattan's Lone Star Café, or the Broadway stages or outlaw country concerts or television or cinematic screens that projected these images, the cowboy rendered counterculturally cosmic at mid-decade was reclaimed by the forces of political backlash.

You a Real Cowboy?

**TEXAS CHIC IN THE
LATE SEVENTIES**

The movie screen fills with the bottom of a pair of blue jeans, and the camera pans up to a large belt buckle and Lone Star longneck held at the side, across the field of a blue Western shirt, to find as the object of our gaze a clean-shaven John Travolta, aka Bud, leaning against a bar in Gilley's nightclub in a black cowboy hat. The band strikes up a number of country songs, time passes, and to the tune of Johnny Lee singing Michael Murphey's "Cherokee Fiddle," Debra Winger's character, Sissy, approaches to pose a question that resonates across this study, as well as across the broader ranges of national identity, gender, region, race, and power. "You a real cowboy?" she asks. "Well, depends on what you think a real cowboy is," Bud answers.[1]

While this question and its answer play across a long history of American perceptions of cowboys real and true versus those performed and false, the appearance of the film *Urban Cowboy* in 1980 lends to this question and its answer a specific, rather than a general, historical resonance, sitting as it does between the zeitgeists of decades. The litmus test both sums up the ambivalence over the 1970s countercultural interpretations of the cowboy, and previews Reagan's coming counterrevolution on horseback. A figure of archetypal opposites, like the virgin–mother or the hippie–redneck, the urban cowboy contained within his person the most basic tropes and contradictions of the American nation, an assertive masculine hero who might tame that machine in the garden or, at the very least, the mechanical bull in the world's largest honky-tonk.

Where Jimmy Carter's New South moderation drew on, as well as fed, what Bruce Schulman has called the cultural "reddening of America" in the 1970s, the Reagan revolution of the 1980s reinvigorated Barry Goldwater's earlier Westering of the imaginary of Sunbelt realignment. Where much of the present study focuses on events in Texas itself, this chapter sketches nationally projected representations of "the Texan" that accompanied and influenced these shifts in the late 1970s and early 1980s. A shared moment of "Texas chic" once more amplified the state's ongoing self-examination through popular forms into a tool for the nation's own cultural–political signifying. The trend drew on the local countercultural re-imagining of the cowboy at the Armadillo World Headquarters or Soap Creek Saloon, but frequently contradicted or erased that figure's tentative progressive dimensions. Rather, the cowboy's masculinist, Americanist core dovetailed nationally with the rising politics of backlash. Where the cosmic cowboy subculture of the early and mid-1970s attempted the refiguring of the Texan in the face of the shifting raced and gendered discourses of the decade, the purveyors of Texas chic tended to deploy it as a bulwark against the new identity politics, rather than their extension. The cosmic cowboy subculture emanating from Austin helped spark the larger faddishness of Texas chic, but its originators did not control the national (and international) diffusion of the image.[2]

The shifting perspective takes us from the Armadillo World Headquarters in Austin to Gilley's nightclub on the outskirts of Houston and the Lone Star Café in Manhattan, and envelops such texts as the musical *The Best Little Whorehouse in Texas* (Broadway 1978, film 1982), *Urban Cowboy* (article 1978, film 1980), and the prime-time soap opera *Dallas* (1978–1991). As with the country's perennial fascination with the dialectic of cowboys real and false, Texas chic spoke to contemporary anxieties over gender, race, desire, nation, and empire. In the 1970s environment of perceived corruption and malaise, the Sunbelt's swagger and, in particular, the Texan connection to oil, made the Anglo-Texan cowboy figure attractive for Americans at large.

TINYs; or, Texans in New York

As noted in the introduction's nod to *Midnight Cowboy* and reinforced by the antics described at the 1976 Democratic National Convention, seventies narratives often set Texas and New York as instructive sites of comparison and contrast. Indeed, New York City itself had long served as a stage for performative Texans. The "cowboy pianist" A. O. Babel of Seguin delighted audiences there in the 1880s. In 1922, fiddler Eck Robertson, costumed as a cowboy, showed up unannounced at New York's Victor Recording Company to make what are considered some of the first country music recordings. Likewise, Vernon Dalhart parlayed a theatrical career there into country stardom based on his Texan roots, and Texas Guinan injected brashness into New York flapperdom through her performance of the frontier guise.[3] Such performances were self-conscious and, in the 1970s, continued to take on organized and self-parodying forms as Texans in New York (or TINYs, as some of them came to call themselves) gathered in the Lone Star Café or wrote paeans to one another in the TINY newsletter, the *New York Texan*. The decay that marks representations of New York City in the period stands in stark contrast to the swagger of Texas's cultural production. Nationwide, New York's financial collapse marked the pinnacle of seventies corruption and decadence, projected in the decade's New Hollywood cinema through gritty films such as *Serpico, Mean Streets, Dog Day Afternoon, The French Connection, The Warriors,* and *Taxi Driver*. When a bankrupt New York went to the federal government for aid in the mid-1970s, the White House balked. The *New York Post* infamously headlined President Gerald Ford's refusal: "Ford to City: Drop Dead!" The symbolism of New York's moral and financial bankruptcy resonated throughout the American culture of the 1970s.

"The Texan" rode in to the city to right its troubling malaise, symbolized in figures of hale confidence, the Joe Buck naïf now rendered the spirit of can-do Americanism that pundits feared had fled the Rust Belt. This infusion was in some instances literal. For example, the organization formed in 1976 to get the city's finances in order, New York's Municipal Assistance Corporation, was headed by Houstonian Eugene Keilin.[4] At other times, "the Texan" offered metaphorical aid. In 1978, a delegation from Luckenbach offered to help set New York City on better financial ground. "'Everybody is somebody in Luckenbach,' city spokesman Jack Harmon wired Ed Koch, in announcing the Luckenbachians were coming to his aid. 'And we feel the same about other folks—even those as far away as New York City. We'll meet with you anytime in the mornings or afternoons and tell you how Luckenbach has coped with urban expansion.' Luckenbach recently installed its second parking meter for added revenue." The three official citizens of Luckenbach, together with a brace of armadillos, supposedly boarded a train for the Big Apple shortly thereafter, though no evidence exists that they were able to meet with Mayor Koch.[5]

In this atmosphere of financial anxiety, danger, grime, and corruption, a banner waved atop Mort Cooperman and Bill Dick's Lone Star Café when it opened at Fifth Avenue and Thirteenth Street in 1976, proclaiming "Too Much Ain't Enough."[6] From the late 1970s through the late 1980s, the venue served as the capital of Texas chic, an embassy of "the Texan" to communicate the shared bluster of two of America's largest, and symbolically salient, states. Kinky Friedman decamped to the Lone Star as a scene more conducive to his ironic take on country music than the earnestness of Austin. Judy Buie, owner of the first modern Western wear store in Manhattan, held Texas fashion shows there heavy on boots and hats. Strange assortments of prominent people came through its doors over the years, lending it a voyeuristic, performative air: Mick Jagger and Johnny Paycheck, Abbie Hoffman and Doug Sahm, Grace Jones and Liz Carpenter, John Connally and Jerry Garcia, Julian Schnabel and Tommy Tune. In some ways, the Lone Star Café played a similar symbolic role in transcending oppositions as the hippie–redneck confluence in Austin, only in New York closing the imaginative gulf between socialite and Sunbelt celebrity.

New Yorkers, Texans, and tourists could easily identify the Lone Star Café by the enormous iguana sculpture that sat atop it. In the iguana's creator, artist Bob "Daddy-O" Wade, the Lone Star Café found a perfect imaginative diplomat of "the Texan." Son of a hotel manager, Wade spent his childhood across Austin, Galveston, San Antonio, Marfa, and El Paso. After earning a master's in painting at the University of California at Berkeley in the late 1960s, Wade returned to Texas to teach and make art in Waco, Dallas, and Denton, successively. As Wade had said of his time in Dallas with like-minded artists in Oak Cliff such as George Green, Jim Roche, and Jack Mims, "We weren't rednecks with MFAs; we just felt there was an aesthetic that needed to be explored that had its roots in Texas."[7] With a sensibility geared toward a populist, frenetic, and occasionally surrealist regionalism, Wade became a significant figure promoting the state to the larger world in the Texas chic moment. In his *Texas Mobile Home Museum* for the 1977 Paris Biennale, Wade filled a classic Spartan trailer with plastic bluebonnets, stuffed armadillos, rattlesnakes, and a two-headed calf, and set up speakers to blare Waylon Jennings at Parisian passersby.[8] At the San Francisco Museum of Modern Art in 1976, he re-created an entire Texas dance hall in a museum gallery, installing wood floors and scattering sawdust, lowering the ceilings and spraying them with glitter, and putting in an old jukebox filled with Texas honky-tonk music, while in a show in Los Angeles, he mounted a full taxidermied bucking bronco (dubbed Funeral Wagon) horizontally from a gallery wall.

He engaged in similar diplomatic endeavors between Texas and the New York art world. In 1975, filmmaker Ken Harrison, in conjunction with Dallas public television, documented one of Wade's trips collecting Texana materials for an art show in SoHo. The resulting film, *Jackelope*, provided a snapshot of

Lone Star Café in Manhattan. Photo from the collection of Bob Wade.

artistic Lone Star regionalism in the 1970s. After sections treating fellow Texas artists James Surls, a sculptor and founding figure of Houston's Lawndale Art Center, and the idiosyncratic George Green, Harrison charted Wade's travels in which the two met with Chicano movement artist Mel Casas, hatmaker Manny Gammage, taxidermist Byron Jernigan, and, for redneck frisson, a group of Wade's old friends he referred to as the "Waco Boys" who liked to shoot up and detonate old cars out in the country. His "Texan" was not simply the mythic and heroic figure of the American West. Wade burlesqued the figure, fixating on the excessive and colorful and weird, traits that distinguished Texas, in his mind, from the homogenizing herd. As he stated about his trip making *Jackelope*, "Even though the Texas landscape was beautiful, I was taking pictures of weird trailer trash and dude ranch signs."[9] Operating in the art world, Wade collapsed the distinctions of high and low in his performance and creation of "the Texan," whether for French galleries, New York nightclubs, or Dallas public television.

If the Lone Star Café became Texas chic's Armadillo World Headquarters, and Bob Wade its diplomat from Texas artist circles, Larry L. King was perhaps the phenomenon's leading light, its exhibit A. *Rolling Stone*'s New York bureau

Bob Wade poses with the Waco Boys on the set of Ken Harrison's Jackelope. Photo composed by Bob Wade and James King. Wade stands on far left. © Bob Wade.

chief, Chet Flippo, declared King the pioneering and undisputed leader of the TINYs. King sold "the Texan" through social performance:

> Larry could good-ol-boy it better than any man, dead or alive. His voice, tempered by decades of "whuskey" and tobacco intake, was a rumble that could shake glass. And he was the real thing. He had actually worked for LBJ. . . . Yankees, my first night in New York, actually crouched at his feet and marveled aloud as he sipped from his bottomless tumbler of whiskey and told marvelous lies with such gravelly charm that even me and Elaine believed him. But he could bullshit anybody and come out ahead. So he was the number-one TINY.[10]

Larry L. King has admitted as much. As his rationale, King offered that "long after I knew that the Texas of my youth dealt more with myth than reality, and long past that time when I knew that the vast majority of Texans lived in cities, I continued to play cowboy. This was a social and perhaps a professional advantage in the East; it marked one as unique, permitted one to pose as a son of yesterday, furnished a handy identity among the faceless millions."[11]

As Larry L. King led the TINY faction, it makes sense that a Broadway play he wrote served as one of the central expressions of Texas chic in New York. The Broadway production of *The Best Little Whorehouse in Texas* premiered on June 19, 1978. It told, loosely, the true story of the closing of a notorious house of prostitution in Texas in 1973. Marvin Zindler, a Houston crusader of the burgeoning action news genre, took it on himself to expose the Chicken Ranch, a brothel that had been operating in plain sight in La Grange since at least 1905. Responding to Zindler's pressure, in August 1973 Governor Dolph Briscoe and Texas Attorney General John Hill forced the Chicken Ranch to close.[12] Larry L. King saw a perfect vehicle to exploit the current rage for outsized, outsexed Texanness in New York City and began developing the story into a musical, adapting a *Playboy* article on the Chicken Ranch fracas. Fellow TINY Tommy Tune handled the music.

The musical followed aging Chicken Ranch madam Mona in her clash with the Zindler character and the sheriff, her paramour, torn between his love for Mona and his duty to enforce the law. A *gemeinschaft/gesellschaft* theme appears even here, and one that inverts stereotypes of urban/rural moralities. Here, it is the city of Houston and the policing that its anonymous population requires that sanctimoniously misunderstands the basic social arrangements that—in *The Best Little Whorehouse*'s fantasy, at least—make the Chicken Ranch a functioning element of the La Grange community. The Chicken Ranch had a high profile in Texas culture at large prior to the musical. *Texas Monthly* even advertised commemorative tin plates and wall hangings when it closed.[13] Houston's blues-rock trio ZZ Top scored a hit single amid the controversy in 1973 with "La Grange." The *Daily Texan*, the student newspaper of the University of Texas, published a rather straightforward review of the place and its services as late as 1971, and the feminist *Texas Woman* provided an insider's account that seemed to view Madame Edna Milton's practices as salutary when compared to those of urban sex workers.[14] The establishment's posthumous fame, however, reached its height with the 1982 feature film starring Burt Reynolds and Dolly Parton. The film furthered Texas chic but is not the movie most associated with the aesthetic. For that distinction, we turn to another film adaptation of a magazine article based on a popular nightlife venue: Aaron Latham's *Urban Cowboy*.

"America's Search for True Grit": *Urban Cowboy*

John Burnett of Galveston founded the city of Pasadena, Texas, on the south shore of the Houston-area Buffalo Bayou in 1894. He thought he saw past the bayou's swampy exterior to a lushness, a vibrancy, that reminded him of nothing so much as Southern California, hence the new settlement's name. Pasadena broke out in a rash of strawberry farms around the turn of the century, but its future, like much of the state's, soon superseded these pastoral origins. With the dredging of Buffalo Bayou in the early decades of the twentieth century, the rise of the Houston Ship Channel, and Houston's efforts to surpass Galveston in the wake of the devastating 1900 hurricane, Pasadena became linked to the industries surrounding port traffic. In the beginning, this meant the factoring of cotton; the first ship to leave the port of Houston via the ship channel carried the South's most traditional export. Soon, however, the oil companies that had been building small empires in East Texas saw the value of Houston as a port, and several refineries came into operation by 1920. By 1948, Houston consistently ranked in the top five American ports by tonnage shipped. By 1980, the port of Houston and its attendant ship channel surpassed New York City in tonnage of foreign trade.[15]

The ports and industrial refineries along the Texas coast set them apart from the rest of the state. Politically, the specter of labor radicalism at Port Arthur had nearly jettisoned liberal Ralph Yarborough's career as early as 1956.[16] This difference makes it all the more curious that in 1980, the year in which Houston first topped the nation's ports in foreign trade, *Urban Cowboy*, a film set in Pasadena about the figure of the cowboy, would amplify an ongoing national passion for all things Texan. The film, and the fad, has a prehistory. Gilley's was a nightclub in Pasadena set among the refinery communities that ring Houston. Opened by Sherwood Cryer, the club carried the name of local entertainer and impresario Mickey Gilley. By then, Gilley had had a long and uneven career, and it seemed that the kind of fame that his cousins and boyhood pals Jerry Lee Lewis and Jimmy Swaggart had achieved was beyond him. Texas chic, *Esquire*, and a John Travolta film changed all that.[17]

Gilley's anchored a distinctive honky-tonk scene that nourished a similar set of artists and aesthetics to those found at Austin's Armadillo World Headquarters (both would claim Southern rock icon Charlie Daniels as a patron saint). But Gilley's emphasized the "hard-core" elements and "redneck" end of the hippie–redneck spectrum.[18] Progressive country as such did not predominate here, though its sounds and styles did come into play. Consider the iconic scene with which this chapter began, when Bud and Sissy meet to the sound of Gilley's house vocalist Johnny Lee performing Michael Murphey's "Cherokee Fiddle," Sissy asks Bud to dance, and as they begin to do so, the volume of the song increases, and Lee sings of the confusion that happens as Indians start dressing up like cowboys and cowboys take to leather and turquoise.[19] The song echoes Austin's hippie–redneck narratives, associating hybridity with modernity and bearing witness to the corruption of the supposedly separate authenticities of "Indians" and "cowboys" scrambled sartorially through cowboy wear, leather, and turquoise. The song encapsulates the film's fascination with cowboy authenticity in Houston's industrial exurbs.

Intriguingly, this scene's adaptation to the big screen began through Bud's birth in the pages of the upscale men's lifestyle magazine *Esquire*. Before there was Bud Davis on the screen, there was his prototype, a man named Dew. Aaron Latham's article of September 1978, "The Ballad of the Urban Cowboy: America's Search for True Grit," centered on the figure of Donald Edward "Dew" Westbrook, foam insulator of pipelines by day, urban cowboy at Gilley's by night. Latham found the scale and spectacle of Gilley's to be an obvious object of fascination to *Esquire* readers and used Dew as a native guide to the club's romantic–erotic entanglements, adventures concerning a mechanical bull, and the divides between rough labor and tough leisure, men and women, machine and nature in the late 1970s Sunbelt.[20] On the one hand, Latham drew each of these dichotomies starkly—the leisured universe of Gilley's stood as a world apart from the industrial refineries, where alienated workers transformed themselves into iconic frontier cowboys (as in the film's tag line, "Hard hat days and honky-tonk nights"). On the other hand, even within the preserve of Gilley's, the borders between these traditional dichotomies collapsed or were subverted. In this sense, the retreat into Gilley's did not constitute a successful escape from the mechanized world of the refinery. Despite patrons' desires, Gilley's could not serve as pastoral other to the workplace, and the mechanical bull became a dangerous adversary that subverted the cowboy's presumed ties to nature (more unpredictable than a live bull because the rider could not watch the head to see which way the bull would turn). Linked to the theme of the collapsing borders between machine and nature in the guise of the mechanical bull, the urban cowboy's parallel retreat into that traditional subject position of American masculinity, the cowboy, did not constitute an effective defense against the presumed contentiousness of women's liberation and the more fluid perceptions and projections of gendered identities in the seventies.[21]

Dew met his ex-wife Betty at Gilley's, though their marriage likely broke on the back of the mechanical bull. Betty wanted to ride. Dew did not approve. Betty rode anyway, and her skills on mechanical bull-back outpaced Dew's. The marriage ended. At the time of Latham's article, Dew was with his new Gilley's girl, Jan, a frailer, more feminine character than Betty. This conflict points to a central concern of *Urban Cowboy*, as article and film, with traditional masculinity and its perceived castration at the hands of women's liberation.

For his national audience, Latham suggested that even Gilley's of Pasadena, a site *Esquire* readers would likely identify as a last-stand redoubt of pre-1970s masculinity, existed as a world of inversion continuous with American society at large in the late 1970s.

In the article even more than the movie, the hybrid figure of the mechanical bull ushered in the confusion. Several times in the eight-page essay, Latham felt compelled to mention that the reason the women (not only Betty, but Betty prominent among them) had begun to outcompete men on Gilley's mechanical bull rested in the lack of a phallus, that it was the bull's power to castrate that threatened the urban cowboy's sense of masculine mastery. Several comments appeared along these lines: "Put your left nut in your right hand and hang on"; "Hurts your nuts, don't it?"; "He crashed back onto the bull's back, his sexual organs taking a beating"; "Breaking an occasional arm, leg, or collarbone. Sometimes it crushes something worse. A honky-tonk cowboy has to risk his manhood in order to prove it." And, most plainly but also suggestive of the gendered power dynamics that are a constant subtext here: "As the cowboys around the bullring put it: 'a woman has nothing to lose.'"[22] The animal–machine castrated men physically, and competitive women did so metaphorically. In the context of Gilley's, Dew's strikingly offensive pick-up line to Jan, "When are you going to take me home and rape me?", made sense only in light of this perceived gender inversion amid what first seemed a virtual shrine to American masculinity. Readers and viewers were meant to see the cowboys thwarted in their escapist leisured endeavors at Gilley's by ambitious women even as they were in their dangerous jobs by callous bosses. The hemmed-in nature of the urban cowboy's range, the threats on all sides, were supposed to be such that the act of violence against women was presented to readers and viewers as at least understandable if not defensible. It was not, and the film weakly made its apologies through a more enlightened Bud at the end.

As with any adaptation, the film departed from the article in a number of particulars, though it also drew on Latham's writing and his informants' wit for its basic vocabulary. Latham was very much involved in the screenplay and filming under director James Bridges, and a number of details survived, though given a different life on-screen. The film traced a different narrative arc in the relationship of Bud (née Dew) and Sissy (née Betty). Jan is not the new, fragile girlfriend, but is represented by a slumming socialite, Pam, and the wedge that the bull drove between Bud and Sissy is exacerbated by the fact that the bull operator is a smoldering ex-convict named Wes who bests Bud in a fight and takes Sissy in when the star-crossed lovers temporarily split. The pathos of Latham's article lies in the fact that Dew and Betty are portrayed as still loving one another, but divided by the bull, whereas the film reconstitutes the union of Bud and Sissy after Bud has put their disparity to rest by mastering the mechanical bull in the contest at film's end. The triumph of the good is furthered by Bud's thwarting the robbery of Gilley's by Wes while extracting vengeance for Wes's physical abuse of Sissy, figured as a displaced defeat of his own abusive tendencies.[23]

The gendered competition over the back of the mechanical bull is not the only inversion testing these urban cowboys. The article and film both related the men's anxiety over the mechanical bull to their own objectification and domestication in the marketplace of Houston. The film, even more than the article, brought out themes of the place of working-class men in the newest version of the New South. The uncertainty attaining to the position of men like Bud in this brave new petrochemical world is such that the inversions over the meanings of manhood and mastery slip into confusions not only over gender roles but also, in a rhetorical sense, over the categories of man and animal, man and machine, reducing working-class men to either brute creatures or cogs. The mechanical bull appears all the more threatening in this context. The theme becomes clear in the scene where Bud gets his refinery job. The boss says that they contract out most of their insulation work, for which Bud is qualified, but that there may be a gopher position available:

"Do you know what a gopher is, boy?"
"I think it means, ya know, go for things. Or, could mean you're an animal," Bud jokes.
The boss nods sternly, "Yeah, well around here, they're on the same level."

Or, in another scene, the socialite Pam, who has picked Bud up at Gilley's to bring him back to her downtown Houston penthouse, describes her daddy's views on cowboys as dumb brutes. As Pam explains, "I have a thing about cowboys, just drives my daddy crazy. . . . I told daddy most men today are just too complicated. . . . I like a man with simple values. . . . 'You mean dumb,' he said." And finally, there is the scene in which Aunt Corrine, visiting Bud and Sissy's trailer, comments, "Y'all live like pigs, Bud." Bud brings the point up later with Sissy, prodding her into one of their frequent confrontations, but once the argument is underway it becomes clear that its subject is not their surroundings' porcine nature, but the fact that Sissy had been missing that afternoon when Bud had fallen from the scaffolding at the refinery and hurt himself. In the argument, the metaphorical animalization of the couple's living space crashes up against the uncertainty associated with Bud's position as a sort of expendable beast of burden. Now that he has broken his arm, the plant lets him go without recompense. And Sissy's absence following the injury of her man–animal, of course, was due to the fact of her recent flirtation with the machine–animal, the mechanical bull at Gilley's with which she had furtively spent the afternoon.

Even as these strains on the animal nature of the cowboy set him apart from urban civilization, the anxiety is not that he is an outsider in the city, but that he is not, in fact, authentically of the land, the "real cowboy" of Sissy's query. Latham, in both article and film, focused on the transformation that these urban cowboys undergo and the sartorial artifice that underlies Sissy's query regarding the reality of Bud's guise:

> He was ready to turn into an urban cowboy. He exchanged his hard hat for a black felt cowboy hat with toothpicks stuck in the band and his name spelled out in small gold letters on the back. (No country cowboy ever decorated his hat with gilt lettering.) He traded dirty bell-bottom blue jeans for clean bell-bottom blue jeans that had just been ironed. (No country cowboy ever wore anything but unironed, straight-legged jeans.) Then he swapped his work sneakers for cowboy boots with a flat, rubber heel designed for a range made up mostly of asphalt, sidewalks, and linoleum. (No country cowboy ever wore anything but high, pointed leather heels designed to let a cowboy dig in his heels if he roped something mean.) And his workingman's T-shirt was replaced by a cowboy shirt with mother-of-pearl snaps and short sleeves. (If a country cowboy wore short sleeves, his arms would be scratched off the first time he passed a mesquite tree.)[24]

In the end, the effect is a sort of cowboy drag, an urban workingman trapped in a grueling, oppressive job, finding an escape in the fantasy of the open range through costuming. But he does not escape the industrial order for agrarian utopia through this transformation. Gilley's greets him with an enclosed economy of scale that mocks myths of the open range. He rides machines rather than animals, and even fights a machine in the guise of a mechanical punching bag. The bag, like the bull, has a tendency to beat these men, with blood left on it by night's end. The urbanization that seems to promise change and class mobility instead delivers dangerous work escaped only through ritualized leisure in contests that cannot be won—with mechanical bulls, mechanical punching bags, or affairs with women.

According to Latham, the sartorial transformation brought with it a certain orientation toward the world: "When a city cowboy dons his cowboy clothes, he dons more than garments: He dons cowboy values." This value system proves their undoing, Latham suggests, by creating the chivalric conditions that welcome competition from women: "And yet the values represented by the cowboy hat prevailed. The cowboys did not try to exclude the cowgirls from the bullring, for that would have violated their code of openness. . . . I could tell, though, that they weren't happy with the way things were turning out."[25] The cowboy's sullen gender politics, as Latham frames it, then, are not due to a misplaced pride in chauvinism but to their own perceived victimization as the women find their weakness in the chivalric code. The gendered inversions played out on the bodies of Gilley's regulars as interpreted by Latham: "She wore pants, not having worn or even owned a dress for years," or "An urban cowboy doesn't have to know how to rope or hog-tie or bulldog . . . but he does have to know how to dance."[26] This echoes the postmodern sense of identities as performative guises that played across glam and punk, but here transferred to the Sunbelt South.

The soundtrack carried the urban cowboy phenomenon into the wider world as much as did the film itself, and underscored how the whole affair was only nominally about Texas, or about the convergence of Texas culture and a mass-mediated mainstream. The soundtrack gestured toward Austin favorites, with tracks authored by Rusty Wier ("Don't It Make You Want to Dance") and Michael Murphey ("Cherokee Fiddle") performed by other artists. Charlie Daniels ("Fallin' in Love for the Night" and "The Devil Went Down to Georgia"), Jimmy Buffett ("Hello Texas"), and Linda Ronstadt ("Hearts Against the Wind"), all prominently featured, had put in their time in Austin. The Gilley's scene anchored the album, with songs by Mickey Gilley and Gilley's house vocalist Johnny Lee, but the remainder issued from the country-rock and country-pop fusions so popular in the decade: the Eagles, Joe Walsh, Anne Murray, Bob Seger, Kenny Rogers.[27] The aural hybridity of the soundtrack echoed the hybrid identities on-screen: urban/rural, agrarian/industrial, man/woman, man/animal, country/rock. Thus, even though the attraction of the cowboy symbol would seem to have issued from a nostalgia for its purity, the use of the guise as a defense against the fluidity of identities in the 1970s, the urban cowboy participated in these same currents.

Charlie Daniels's hit "The Devil Went Down to Georgia" provided one of the soundtrack's highest-profile singles and aurally conveyed the dichotomies *Urban Cowboy* explored. The song's narrative involves the Devil, loose in Georgia, challenging a backcountry good ol' boy to a fiddling contest and losing. The Devil's solo in the song consists of a flight from the organic authenticity that cloaks Johnny's playing. As he takes center stage, the Devil, in the words of Peter Shapiro, "was joined by a band of demons who played a pretty mean disco-funk vamp over the top of which Beelzebub improvised some evil Psycho-style string gashes." Johnny, on the other hand, beats the Devil with traditional Southern homilies, singing of chicken, baking, grannies, and dogs. Just who is being demonized here? As Shapiro concluded, "The implicit antidisco message of the song couldn't have been clearer."[28]

The song's prominence on *Urban Cowboy*'s soundtrack carries this message into the heart of a film that echoes, answers, and contests an earlier movie often held responsible for the national disco craze, *Saturday Night Fever* (1977). More than the cinematic tropes of class mobility, leisure, desire, and dance join the two films. Latham latched onto the connections from the beginning. The 1978 *Esquire* cover announced the article as "Saturday Night Fever, Country & Western Style," and, of course, there is the shared presence of John Travolta. *Saturday Night Fever*, like *Urban Cowboy*, built on journalistic foundations, in this case Nik Cohn's *New York* article "Tribal Rites of the New Saturday Night."[29] The two narratives match each other in conventional ways. In each, a leisured dance space (Odyssey, Gilley's) figures as a way station between a peripheral class position and geography (Brooklyn, Spur) and the wealth and prestige of the metropolis (Manhattan, Houston). Indeed, the urban cowboys of Latham's article fit better to Cohn's disco dancers than one might imagine. In contrast to the cinematic Gilley's of 1980, Latham's 1978 article revealed a countercultural flair that placed the urban cowboys in greater continuity with seventies dance floor fashion: bell-bottoms, long-haired men, braless women.

The films diverged in significant ways, though. The social-climbing ambition of Tony Manero's dance partner, Stephanie, pulls him along, rather than intimidating him, as Sissy's assertiveness tends to do to Bud. The viewer is left with a sense that Bud and Sissy's love is true and lasting, the two having learned their lesson through a series of assaults, robberies, and sexual indiscretions, but their peace always seems fragile. *Urban Cowboy* the film thus catches Bud in a different narrative arc than does Latham's article. It ends not in a heart-wrenching love triangle, but with Bud and Sissy together, driving away from Gilley's in a pickup truck, Bud having carefully placed Sissy's vanity license plate in the back windshield alongside his own, and heading, if not into the sunset, at least into the dawn's early light as they speed away from the world's largest honky-tonk. It is Bud who has resolved the film's conflict in his defeat of Wes and his magnanimous apology for physically abusing his wife. *Saturday Night Fever*, too, climaxes with assault, Tony holding the threat of masculine power over the ambitious woman. Tony, too, recognizes his error and apologizes for his violence, but in following her to Manhattan, Tony also defers to her lead.

YOU A REAL COWBOY?

It is easy to overstate the distinction between the subcultural resonances of the original cosmic cowboy and his urban cowboy successor in Texas. Both were, in fact, enacted in the urban landscape; both were, sartorially, of the seventies. *Saturday Night Fever*'s portrayal of disco, however, seems to mistake the genre's origins. It assumes as disco's originary group the very bridge-and-tunnel crowd that the genre's black, Puerto Rican, and gay originators decried as gate-crashers. The film gives a partial nod to the black and Puerto Rican roots of New York disco during the climactic dance contest, but shies from the topic of gay liberation. Yet fascination with performative hypermasculinity joins the discourses one to another through the cowboy signifying in gay culture, from Joe Buck's closeted character in *Midnight Cowboy* at the beginning of the decade to the cowboy's camp apex with the Village People.

Urban Cowboy also differed from *Saturday Night Fever* in its basic relation to the incipient culture wars of the 1970s. The film projected an image of the Gilley's cowboy distinct from the photographs accompanying Latham's article. As the film, rather than the Gilley's scene, came to define the style in its new national projection on the cusp of the 1980s, we witness an erasure of the countercultural hybridities that had been stirring in seventies Texas. *Saturday Night Fever*'s national projection of disco also involved erasure, in this case of the style's gay, black, and Latin roots, but Tony's anger at being given the trophy over the more deserving Puerto Rican couple provides for a return of the repressed. Finally, the temporal lag between the two films is significant. At the end of 1977, *Saturday Night Fever* propelled the national popularity of disco, a genre that had been developing in New York, Chicago, Miami, San Francisco, and Philadelphia nightclubs and recording studios since the early 1970s. Even if late seventies discomania effaced the roles of blacks, Puerto Ricans, gays, and women, they could not be entirely denied. Disco's popularity did amplify voices in the culture that would have been difficult to imagine ten years prior: the drag falsetto of Sylvester, the assertive sexuality of Donna Summer, the empowering defiance of Gloria Gaynor or Grace Jones, to say nothing of the Village People's barely disguised, hugely popular celebration of gay subculture. These artists found the spotlight, in part enabled by the civil rights movements of the 1960s and 1970s.

By the year of *Urban Cowboy*'s release in 1980, disco's inclusiveness over the airwaves and on the dance floors had already provoked a sizable backlash, especially among young white men invested in 1970s guitar rock. This backlash often took on outlandish forms, as in the anti-disco riot held between the two games of a double header at Comiskey Park in July 1979. There, Chicago disc jockey Steve Dahl, a leading popularizer of "disco sucks" rhetoric, marshaled his supporters in the destruction of disco albums. Dahl, like a number of disco's angry critics, claimed that his ire had nothing to do with the identity or body politics of disco or the voice it gave to previously disfranchised subject positions. However, as disco historian Tim Lawrence argued in *Love Saves the Day*, Dahl's argument "holds significantly less water than Lake Michigan."[30] *Urban Cowboy* stood firmly on the other side of this divide, retrenching a pre-disco masculinity. Its popularity constituted an attempted retreat from contentious debates over identity politics, crowning the recent rise of Texas chic.

Latham latched onto the connections and contrasts with disco from the beginning in a diary that he composed during *Urban Cowboy*'s production. Through this, we know a good deal about how Latham saw the film in relation to both the political and social settings of the time and, specifically, to *Saturday Night Fever*. Both Latham and Travolta worried about the film's effect in typecasting Travolta, that people would not believe him as a Texas cowboy, urban or no. This anxiety heightened when the film's entourage—Latham, director Bridges, producer Irving Azoff, and Travolta—journeyed to Dew Westbrook's apartment outside Pasadena. While the group watched *Rockford Files* together and discussed the project, Dew objected strenuously to Travolta, who was meant to portray Dew on-screen: "He's disco. He'd never go over in a cowboy place." This anxiety suffused how Bridges, Latham, and Travolta crafted the film and extended to questions over the soundtrack. If they did not program a soundtrack of "real" country music, no one would believe Travolta as a "real" cowboy, connecting the film to the artifice of Travolta's depiction as a disco New Yorker. "We had to be especially honest, especially authentic, in a country music movie starring John Travolta," Latham wrote. "Because a lot of people were out there just waiting . . . [to] call John the disco cowboy."[31] As the film's vision of country and the urban cowboy lifestyle stood as the antithesis to disco—Southwestern opposed to Northeastern, authentic opposed to artificial, masculine opposed to feminine—such an elision through Travolta's presence could not be tolerated. According to Latham, these discussions with John over country music began to make him think that Travolta got it, easing Latham's anxieties over his inclusion in the project. A specific conversation over class politics sealed the deal: Latham asked Travolta what he thought of Jane Fonda. "He said that the way she lived bothered him. She was a rich girl who tried to ape the working class. He said he really was working class. And he felt he owed it to other working class people to spend his money and live well—that kept the American dream alive." After this, Latham felt more comfortable with Travolta as his lead cowboy. The collision of classed and gendered politics, as exemplified by this discussion over Fonda, would be central to the film.[32]

In this same vein, Latham's marriage to journalist Lesley Stahl places *Urban Cowboy*'s production in a larger political network. Best known for her work as a television journalist on *60 Minutes*, in 1979 and 1980 Stahl served as a White House correspondent in the midst of the Carter administration. Latham's time in Hollywood and Houston thinking about the meaning of the Gilley's scene, then, is punctuated by gatherings on the New York and DC party circuits, and friends or acquaintances such as Carl Bernstein, Tommy Corcoran, Jim Lehrer, Jann Wenner, Bob Woodward, and various Carter officials come into and out of the diary entries in which he agonizes over the story he is trying to tell on film. *Urban Cowboy* is not a movie, then, made at the periphery of late seventies politics and culture, but in some ways very near its center. And Latham's central concern, at that center, seems to be the issue of gender. As in the *Esquire* article written for public consumption, Latham is rather explicit about anxieties over gender when recording his private thoughts in the diary. Once, for example, Latham found himself seated on an airplane between Stahl and Gloria Steinem: "I was caught in a soft, feminine vise that threatened to crush me at any moment. I think I may have been sitting between the two most powerful women on the planet." Latham sounds excited at the prospect, but, with the wider context of the full diary, article, and film, also a little nervous.[33]

The film wrestles with women's liberation in fairly explicit fashion, but its simultaneous contention with gay liberation proves more subterranean. The push-and-pull between Latham and *Urban Cowboy*'s openly gay director, James Bridges, figures into this struggle. In his diary, Latham bristles at the cultural politics of gay liberation, and Latham's theme of the unmanning of American cowboys seems joined to a fascination with, or anxiety over, the notion of a gay chic perpetuated by disco. Throughout, Latham remarks on incidents that highlight Bridges's gay identity and flings constant innuendo toward Travolta's entourage. When Travolta becomes friendly with a Gilley's cowboy named Bubba in order to work on his accent, mannerisms, and dance moves, for example, Latham continually refers to Bubba as his new boyfriend. The notion of gay chic fuels cocktail party and movie set conversations as it relates to the *Urban Cowboy* project. Latham even brings Carl Bernstein into the mix. At a DC party, Latham recalls, "Carl [Bernstein] said he had noticed that the gay world was having a disproportionate effect on the heterosexual world. Gays used to pretend to be straight. Now it is almost as though straights were pretending to be gays." The high profile of queer politics in Latham's diary echoes the same dichotomies that would form his major theme, and that assert the equation of the masculine, the authentic, the real, and the natural in a place like Texas, counterposed to a panicked appraisal of the fey degeneracy and artifice of the East, as exemplified by disco. But all of this is undermined by the film's very premise, the contradictory figure of an urban cowboy, which, in itself, constantly invokes the tension between authenticity and artifice and the pretense of lifestyle consumption.[34]

Perhaps no document better sums up *Urban Cowboy*'s erasures of local figurations of the cosmic cowboy than a diagram published in the *Daily Texan*. A layout diagrammed the urban cowboy style, titled "Kicking a Dead Horse" because this was one in a long series of cowboy style guides that had appeared in the *Daily Texan* and other publications over the course of the decade as conflicts erupted as to just what a cowboy looked like in the cosmic cowboy's hometown. The *Daily Texan*'s previous foray into such matters had been the "Cosmic Changeling" (see chapter 3), documenting the transformation of a hippie into a cosmic cowboy (much as the oilfield worker becomes the urban cowboy). A full-page diagram instructs on urban cowboy style, including the following tips:

> Belt buckle—Accentuates your leather belt with a shiny, garish touch. Best varieties feature longhorns, beer brands and scenes from the Old West.
> Longneck—Nowhere else but Texas. Good for sippin' or smashin'.
> Hairstyle—Cowboys are not hippies! Hair must be kept off the collar and above the earlobes. Sideburns and moustaches are optional, but don't forget a two-day stubble for that macho look.[35]

As *Wanted! The Outlaws* and *Urban Cowboy* seized on and amplified the Texas chic ignited by Austin's cosmic cowboy, the progressive content of the style rapidly waned. By 1980, the owner of West World in Austin could argue that "the country and western trend is tied in somehow with America's current situation in world affairs. 'With the Iranian crisis, people are definitely more to the right. People are more patriotic.' And the cowboy, he said, is a truly American symbol."[36] National and local media viewed the *Urban Cowboy* phenomenon through a curiously amnesiac lens concerning the cosmic cowboy of just a few years past. Even within the context of the film, the neater style of Travolta's urban cowboy erases the cosmic, as the transformation that produces the iconic image with which this chapter began involved Bud shaving off his beard and trimming his hair. In the film, these markers are meant to connote his "hayseed" status fresh from Spur in West Texas, but their effect also purges the pastoral hippieness of the cosmic cowboy.[37]

The distinction marks the distance not only between the Austin scene and the projection of Texanness on national film screens, but also that between the

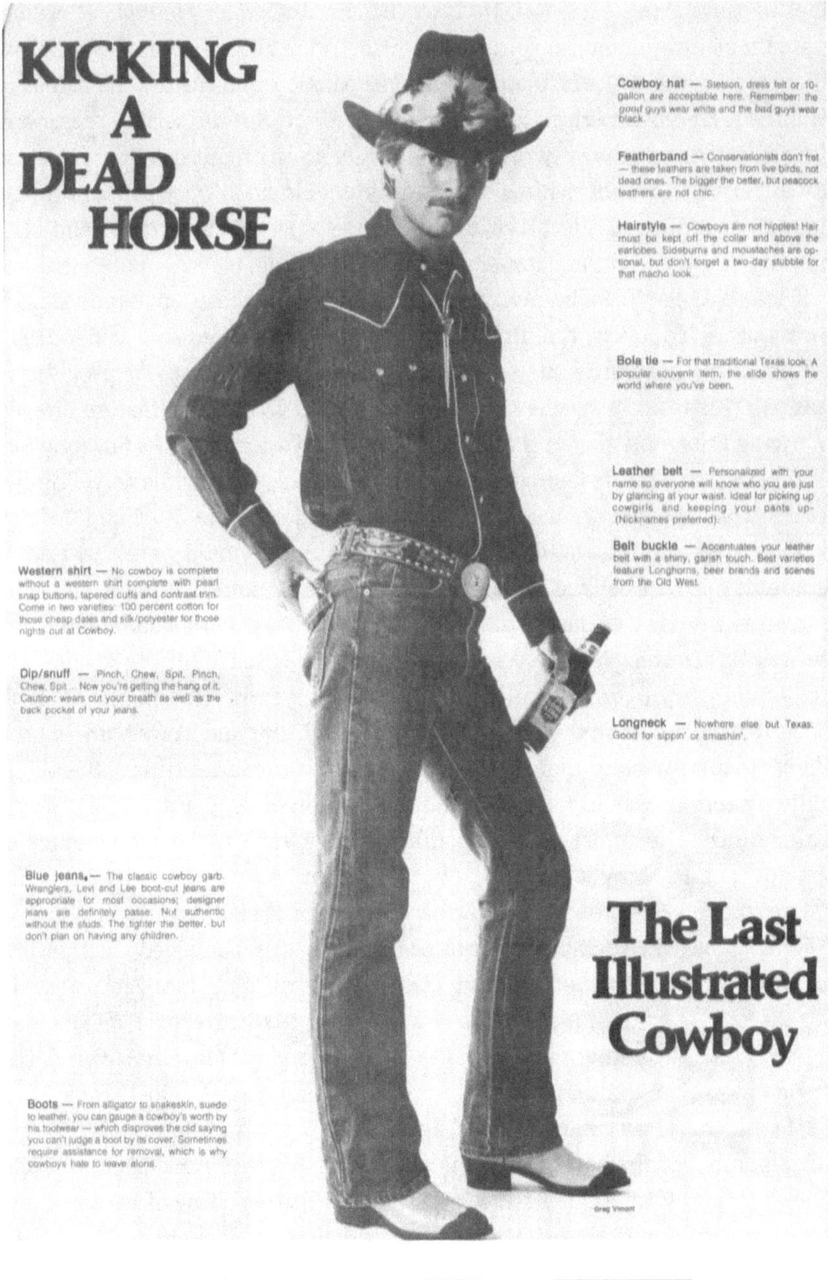

KICKING A DEAD HORSE

Cowboy hat — Stetson, dress felt or 10-gallon are acceptable here. Remember: the *good* guys wear white and the *bad* guys wear black.

Featherband — Conservationists don't fret — these feathers are taken from live birds, not dead ones. The bigger the better, but peacock feathers are not chic.

Hairstyle — Cowboys are not hippies! Hair must be kept off the collar and above the earlobes. Sideburns and moustaches are optional, but don't forget a two-day stubble for that macho look.

Bola tie — For that traditional Texas look. A popular souvenir item, the slide shows the world where you've been.

Leather belt — Personalized with your name so everyone will know who you are just by glancing at your waist. Ideal for picking up cowgirls and keeping your pants up. (Nicknames preferred).

Belt buckle — Accentuates your leather belt with a shiny, garish touch. Best varieties feature Longhorns, beer brands and scenes from the Old West.

Western shirt — No cowboy is complete without a western shirt complete with pearl snap buttons, tapered cuffs and contrast trim. Come in two varieties: 100 percent cotton for those cheap dates and silk/polyester for those nights out at Cowboy.

Dip/snuff — Pinch, Chew, Spit. Pinch, Chew, Spit... Now you're getting the hang of it. Caution: wears out your breath as well as the back pocket of your jeans.

Longneck — Nowhere else but Texas. Good for sippin' or smashin'.

Blue jeans. — The classic cowboy garb. Wranglers, Levi and Lee boot-cut jeans are appropriate for most occasions; designer jeans are definitely passe. Not authentic without the studs. The tighter the better, but don't plan on having any children.

The Last Illustrated Cowboy

Boots — From alligator to snakeskin, suede to leather, you can gauge a cowboy's worth by his footwear — which disproves the old saying you can't judge a boot by its cover. Sometimes require assistance for removal, which is why cowboys hate to leave alone.

"The Last Illustrated Cowboy," Daily Texan, *August 11, 1980.*
Courtesy of the Briscoe Center for American History,
University of Texas at Austin.

cities of Austin and Houston. In 1969, David McComb's *Houston: A History* treated the entrepreneurial spirit of the place prior to its final ascension. Both cities arose in the wake of the revolt against Mexico, and carried the names of prominent Anglo American leaders of that conflict. But the service sector employment of the University of Texas and state government gave the midsized city of Austin a bucolic white-collar cast, while Houston's petrochemical base made it an industrial site given to the kind of spectacular growth and class mobility that marked the boom–bust economies of oil.

Though Gilley's, in its own way, participated in the hippie–redneck hybridity of 1970s Texas, the film *Urban Cowboy* contributed to a wider 1980s restoration of normative masculinity incipient in the tensions of progressive country. This rears its head as early as the Latham article, as a feature directly following the article shows Ralph Lauren's new Western line. As Suzanne Slesin reports, "'It's not fashion, it's life,' insists Lauren, who while traveling out West last year in search of cowboy clothes found none he liked and decided to create his own. 'I gave the style what I thought it should have. . . . I did it because it's what I believe in, it's the way I want to express myself. This look represents my way of being part of the world today. It reflects me and my life-style.'"[38] Lauren definitely speaks to a seventies sensibility here, and one that would carry over forcefully into the coming years. Though less likely to encounter such ideas in the pages of *Esquire*, Bud Davis and Tony Manero both express themselves and their beliefs through these seventies rituals: the obsession with self and changing selves, the articulation of segmented lifestyles via commodities. The underlying attraction of the *Urban Cowboy* phenomenon was not that any cowboy could be urbanized, but that every urbanite could play cowboy in Houston, Austin, Dallas, Seattle, or Detroit.

Urban Cowboy's slick commercial packaging deftly conveyed such performativity, but portrayals of working-class Texans running more to realist regionalism also had their place in the late 1970s. In 1978, director Eagle Pennell and producer Lin Sutherland made *The Whole Shootin' Match* in Austin.[39] The movie follows the trials and travails of two working-class Anglo-Texans, Loyd and Frank. Lou Perryman played the role of Loyd, while Sonny Carl Davis, also a member of the band the Uranium Savages, played Frank. Shot in black-and-white, and with a tone that echoes *The Last Picture Show* of earlier in the decade, the time period of the piece is nevertheless indeterminate. Loyd is an amateur tinkerer and entrepreneur, and Frank his drinking buddy and hanger-on. The film details their wistful dreams of making it big with Loyd's schemes in chinchillas, frog farms, flying squirrels, and polyurethane, and his following a self-help mantra learned from one J. Paul Winfield, which becomes the film's tagline: "You've got to get your mind right."⁴⁰ Loyd wheels and deals and assures Frank that they can make it. "We can get rich, just like all these other people," he says. Much of the early part of the film, though, follows them in their carousing around town, through Frank's troubled marriage and family life, and the eccentrics that the two meet in Austin's bars. However, when one of Loyd's inventions, a mop dubbed the "Kitchen Wizard," is finally brought into production, things look to turn around. But the mail-order firm that does so cheats Loyd of his share of the proceeds, which he has signed away for a pittance. The film is very much a product of the decade's fixation on "the Texan." Pennell saw himself operating in J. Frank Dobie's lineage, insistent on a regional cinema that took the culture of its characters seriously. He also based the original short that first introduced the *Whole Shootin' Match* characters, *Hell of a Note*, on equal parts of Larry L. King's *Texas Monthly* article "Redneck!" and the murder of the poster artist Ken Featherston at the Armadillo World Headquarters.⁴¹

The Whole Shootin' Match fits between *Saturday Night Fever* and *Urban Cowboy* not only in its release date, but also in its less sanguine assessment of the traps facing the American working class in the late decades of the twentieth century. Toward the film's close, Loyd seems to have given up: "This something was mine! Those bastards stole it from me! Hell. Ever since I grew up in the damn river bottoms, been thinking I was gonna be someone else. Just couldn't wait to get out of there and come to the big city and get rich and be somebody. All I got to show for it is a bunch of half-baked projects. Know what? I'm just an ignorant country boy. All the schemin' ain't gonna do nothin' about that." He then suggests his only recourse might be to go to Alaska, at which Frank pipes up about it being the "new frontier." The two then meet midway and decide to go after a rumored treasure of Indian gold west of town on Mount Bulverde, a feint toward one of Dobie's folkloric obsessions, here embraced with a kind of tragic giddiness.⁴² They supposedly have a map, but get lost and give up. Frank wanders off and attempts to kill himself with the rifle they brought along. The film ends with the two re-assuring themselves and re-affirming their relationship: "Hell, it's a good thing they took that money from us. Shit, we're lucky. Hell, if we'd had that money, I would've moved off in the suburbs, livin' with electric dishwashers. I would've been bored. You wouldn't be able to go drinkin' in all your favorite places. You'd have to go drinkin' in a discotheque. Hell, boy. We been working together a long time. We got strong backs, and good arms and legs." The tragic arc of the film belies their confident words, however, and we are reminded that this is, after all, the late 1970s. The conservative populism of Reagan's "Morning in America" had not yet dawned.

Saturday Night Fever and *Urban Cowboy* traffic in similar frustrations over the place of the working class in seventies America. Tony Manero does leave his situation to make the move to Manhattan, but in the final scenes Stephanie challenges him with the question of what he will do next. "What'd you do?" Tony responds. "You came in, you couldn't do nothin'." "I could type, when I came." Tony rejoinders with bravado, "Big deal. I'm an able person, I can do these things," but the frustration in his voice and face betray his words. In *Urban Cowboy*, Bud regales Pam with his hopes of returning to the country and buying land with the wages he has earned from the refinery, but Pam, bored, suggests that every cowboy she has known in the city has said the same thing, and they never make it back from whence they came. Both films close these differences over with romantic attachments between men and women, though we are left with Tony and Stephanie as a platonic couple. In *The Whole Shootin' Match*, Pennell leaves us, rather, with the solidarity of these two working-class men. Despite this solidarity, the film lays bare the class divide about to re-open as Fordism enters its free fall. A tension between the characters' bluster and despair in their respective situations joins the three films to the decade's contrarian blue-collar cultural politics, a moment ably described and aptly titled in Jefferson Cowie's history *Stayin' Alive: The 1970s and the Last Days of the Working Class*. In this context, too, *Saturday Night Fever* and *Urban Cowboy* both underscore the plasticity of identity, the ability to re-make and construct the self. They also, alongside *The Whole Shootin' Match*, suspect that such freedom to determine one's self-image through commodities does not equate to the American Dream of social mobility and the self-made man. Frank tried to re-invent himself when he came into some money, buying a new Western suit, Stetson, and convertible, and re-introducing himself to a female acquaintance as an oilman ("I'm not just a cedar-scrubber out there, a handyman. Me and Loyd are what you might call independent oilmen"). The guise did not provide for much but temporary escape.

In these moments, *The Whole Shootin' Match* affects a realism over issues of class, but it also offers an essentialism concerning class and regional identities ("Ever since I grew up in the damn river bottoms, been thinking I was gonna be someone else. . . . I'm just an ignorant country boy. All the schemin' ain't gonna do nothin' about that"). This belies the notion of the created self, the lifestyle mantras of the decade. In the tugs between authenticity and artifice, though, the film remains curious in its black-and-white aesthetic that mimics mid-century Westerns.[43] Even the many scenes shot on the streets of downtown Austin efface the city's complexity in the decade. When characters step into the scenes wearing contemporary dress, as opposed to pearl-snap shirts and cowboy hats, we are meant to see class difference. Regional authenticity for Pennell, then, evoked more than one notion of place, gesturing both toward the country from which these characters sprang and the idea of class as a distinct place in the social order that held those regional cultural differences intact. In swirling together physical space and class, in ways similar to both *Urban Cowboy* and *Saturday Night Fever*, authenticity and artifice stand in relation to sense of place as well as political economy. Social mobility, then, may also require physical mobility. In one conversation over their money troubles, Loyd says to Frank, "You can always go to Dallas, where every house is a palace." Dallas had signified wealth for a generation or more of Texans, but it would soon do so for Americans at large, as well.

Two Ways Out: *Dallas* as Western Capitalist Simplicity; Maoists at the Alamo

In September 1978, the same month Latham's urban cowboy article appeared in *Esquire*, a new prime-time soap opera premiered on CBS for its first full season. Among Texas chic's most popular vehicles, the television program *Dallas* chronicled the travails of the Ewings, a fictional clan of the oil-rich.[44] Texas's place in the 1970s cultural imaginary owed something to the fact of continued prosperity, abundance, and indulgence read onto the landscape despite the economic limits imposed by the end of the long postwar boom. As Texas stood to gain from the rising fortunes of oil, however, the cultural productions taking the state as their theme often exhibited an ambivalence, envious of its affluence while simultaneously critical of its materialism. *Urban Cowboy* critiqued, if obliquely, the burgeoning oil industry. *Dallas* might be seen in this light, too, deploying the Manichean schemes of the soap opera to highlight the corrupting influence of oil wealth. But it also gloried in the organicism of an industry connected by kinship, handshakes, and backroom deals, as if the transparent corruptions of robber-baron modernity made the public relations smokescreens thrown up by the postmodern corporation seem especially duplicitous. As Alan Coren, editor of the British magazine *Punch*, saw it, the Texas of *Dallas* was the "zenith of Western capitalist simplicity.... The genius of *Dallas* is that it pays constant homage to the mythic past while it incessantly tosses its people about in the rootless, relationship-oriented world of the Singles Apartment Scene. *Dallas*'s past is vintage patriarchal frontiership, the legend of the empire builder." *Dallas* animated Bainbridge's *The Super-Americans*, making the case that these outsized Texans were merely consumers like everyone else, or, as Alan Coren put it, "just like us ... booze-sodden, nymphomaniac swindlers; guilt-crazed, greed-ridden psychopathic junkies; homicidal, schizophrenic dropouts."[45] *Dallas* definitely trafficked in such excess, a world in which it is difficult to escape the sense that the fix is in, and no more noble cowboys ride the range.[46]

Dallas follows the Ewing family, who reside outside of, but do business in, Dallas. The newly wealthy Jock Ewing married into Ellie's Southfork Ranch and the older wealth of cattle. Jock and Ellie's sons J.R. and Bobby have taken over Ewing Oil. This setup is, of course, a fable that takes place in the mythological geography of Texas long posited by Hollywood. The physical site of Southfork outside Parker, Texas, had more often been cotton, rather than cattle, land, marked by the South more than the West. The series' titular city of Dallas, too, offered discrepancies between image and reality. Settled by itinerant traders and French utopians in the early nineteenth century and a key site of Populist revolt and union organization in the late nineteenth century, Dallas's civic leaders in the twentieth century worked hard to promote an image of the city defined by free enterprise and unfettered industry. Robert Lee Thornton's Dallas Citizens Council of local businessmen trumpeted this new vision of Dallas through the 1936 Centennial and the luxurious commodities on display at Neiman Marcus. This was the "Super-American" city that so interested Bainbridge, and, as Harvey Graff has noted, was ruled by an elite that declared the place a "city with no history," a metropolis born of continuous self-invention among self-made men.[47] The television series *Dallas* echoed the city's boosters, who equated the city with freewheeling American enterprise, even as the program attempted to ground this rootless image in the broader agrarianism of the Texas myth.

The fable, though, resonates with reality. The Ewing–Barnes feud central to the series' early plots echoed, in part, the origins of the Hunt oil fortune. H. L. Hunt and Columbus "Dad" Joiner had pioneered the East Texas oil fields of the 1930s. Joiner sold his stakes to Hunt at a deep discount and later regretted it, just as the broken Digger Barnes of *Dallas* blamed Jock Ewing for his misfortune.[48] Yet Hunt's story as fodder for the Ewing saga goes deeper. In 1955, Lyda Bunker Hunt, Hunt's wife of forty-odd years, passed away. Two years later, Hunt remarried to Ruth Ray, his secretary, and adopted her four children. Hunt later revealed that these children were his own, from their long-running affair. Hunt's last years, between 1970 and 1974, seemed to accelerate, rather than slow, the drama. There were battles over matters of inheritance, with Hunt's will granting most of the fortune to his second family with Ruth Ray, and corporate chicanery at Hunt Oil in the early 1970s ended up drawing in private investigators, the FBI, Richard Nixon, the Libyan government, and the Palestinian Liberation Organization.[49] Meanwhile, in 1975, a third wife, Frania

Tye, came forward. Hunt and Tye had married in Florida in 1925. When Tye discovered Hunt's other family in the 1930s, Hunt spirited her away to New York and provided trust funds for their four children. Given Hunt's résumé, it is easy to see how a soap opera could sprout in such fertile soil.[50]

Neither Jock Ewing/H. L. Hunt, nor Digger Barnes/Dad Joiner, nor their union in Bobby Ewing's and Pam Barnes's marriage, however, would have made for a series so resonant with the late-1970s zeitgeist. *Dallas* captured the world's attention through the character J. R. Ewing as portrayed by Larry Hagman.[51] J.R. embodied and performed the excesses of the wheeler-dealer ethos, a reckless, ruthless, but effective variant of capital accumulation that made a mockery of Weber's Protestant ethic and fit the developing cult of flexible capital in the late 1970s. The "Who Shot J.R.?" episode of November 21, 1980, remains one of the most viewed in the history of television. Locally, the episode served—indeed, the series served—to partially exorcize the aura of the JFK assassination. Just as J.R.'s shooting recalled that other violence in Dallas, the show eclipsed the city's prior association with murder in the national imaginary. Southfork replaced Dealey Plaza as the number-one tourist destination in Dallas as J.R. marginalized, and even fictionalized, the JFK assassination. As journalist Gary Cartwright had said of that initial day in Dallas, "All I know is that until the assassination, everything in my world seemed clean, transparent, and orderly. Nothing has seemed clean, clear, or orderly since."[52] By 1980, it did not seem to figure for much in the city's image.

Rather, *Dallas* reconstructed the American vision of the city. The opening credits begin with a roving aerial view by helicopter of yellowed grasslands, panning left to two highways and the Dallas skyline. This view then dissolves into a close-up of the skyline before the credits take on their pattern of triptych bars that pass across the screen from left to right, with images that alternate, largely, between urban and rural spaces: oil pumpjacks, then cattle on the hoof, the skyline, then farmland, then the skyline again, a rural road, a tractor, the Dallas Cowboys home field at Texas Stadium, and closing on the skyline. Next, the introduction features the series' actors, again in triptych form, typically with an establishing shot of their character in the center, flanked by the character in a formal business or home setting, and an outdoor shot in an active or ranching setting. This sequence underscores the series' focus on the continuing juxtaposition of the urban and the rural, of Dallas and Southfork Ranch. In this, it departs from similar visualizations that foreground the seemingly inevitable historical movement from the country to the city.

Urban Cowboy, for example, opened with a cinema verité–style shot, as the viewer witnesses a traditional farmhouse breakfast, from across the home, through the dining room door. Bud says good-bye to his family, packing his things into his truck outside Spur. His mother insists that he take farm produce along with him, as "you just can't get good vegetables in Houston." Bud then drives away, and the camera pulls back to show off the expanse of agricultural fields. The image fades out, and we catch up with Bud hours later in a shot with a wide-angle view of the Houston skyline that echoes that of *Dallas*. The pilot episode of the live music performance series *Austin City Limits* featured a similar device, as the sound check for Willie Nelson and Family played over a series of images that began with the pastoral of the hill country before viewing Austin on the horizon. The name of the series itself, invoking the line between city and country, fits to the iconic image of the city limit sign, which was in and of itself an inspiration for the series. Once inside Austin, pictures of the city's spaces for live music performance, where the country pastoral has met modern musical production, appear one after another: Threadgill's, the Cotton Exchange Saloon, Castle Creek, One Knite, Split Rail, Broken Spoke, Texas Opry House, Soap Creek Saloon, the Armadillo World Headquarters.

Ken Harrison's *Jackelope* does not begin with such imagery, but ends with it. Bob Wade's journey collecting artifacts for his New York gallery show closes with the footage of the Waco Boys detonating a car body with a shotgun. After the reaction to the explosion, the scene shifts to the streets of New York, the open spaces outside Waco traded for crowded, noisy avenues. While discussing his exhibit's elements with the gallery owner, Wade explains what a jackelope is, ending with the rumor that "the jackelope sings at night in a voice that sounds almost human." A view of a mounted jackelope head is then accompanied by a sound that is part theremin, part steel guitar, part human moan. The film shifts to the street outside, a canyon of high-rises, a thoroughfare sluggish with traffic. The camera pans up, and we begin to hear crickets. The negative space of sky between the tops of the buildings fades out, and the camera fades in on a Texas country road, panning up to see the flat, empty horizon of road over grassland. The crackle of a car radio joins the sounds of the crickets and the jackelope wail. The camera zooms in on the horizon to show that there is indeed seemingly limitless space in that Texas countryside. An advertisement in Spanish blares on the radio, then the station changes to find a radio evangelist shouting "Hallelujah!" Then the title appears, and the image fades out, the organic Texas pastoral achieved.

In 1982, the British punk band the Clash brought their brand of revolutionary chic to Austin to film the video for the hit single "Rock the Casbah." The video takes the same country-to-city arc as the Texas productions described above. It begins with a nod to the city's countercultural past with an armadillo waddling up to the band as they break out into song before a working oil pumpjack. The armadillo then scurries to a roadside scene of a hitchhiking Arab sheik being picked up in a 1970s model Cadillac convertible adorned with longhorn horns on the hood, driven by an Orthodox Jew. Together, the adversaries drive around the capital of Texas, the home of the Texas Railroad Commission that gave the Saudis the model for OPEC, dancing to the beat of an English punk song ostensibly about censorship in revolutionary Iran. The duo's fantastic romp through the city culminates with their attendance at the Clash concert at City Coliseum. Where *Dallas*, *Urban Cowboy*, and *Jackelope* highlighted the contrasts between Texas and other places, the Clash here seem effortlessly to situate it in a larger global field.

By the mid-eighties, *Dallas*, though it spoke to the decade's cultural fascination with elite lifestyles, became a bit of a fantasy, as well. As the bottom fell out of crude oil prices, so did the boom of Texas chic turn to bust. The same currents buffeted the world inhabited by the real, live urban cowboys. In 1985, Aaron Latham revisited his subject in the pages of *Texas Monthly* with the article "The Return of the Urban Cowboy."[53] By that year, Gilley's had expanded, yet again, but the fortunes of its patrons had sharply contracted. The fates of the characters are predictable, and the downturn in oil especially hurt the fortunes of Dew Westbrook, on whom the character Bud Davis was based. The effects on Texas chic were clear. Romance with Wall Street finance had caught the rest of the nation up in the boom economics that had yielded Texas its 1970s aura, and the collapse of oil prices sent even the region's wheeler-dealers into other ventures. When T. Boone Pickens made the cover of *Time* in 1985, it was as a cowboy corporate raider more than an oilman.[54]

The tendency to periodize historical change by decades has its limitations, but the corporate raider 1980s differed substantially from the decade that preceded it. Incidentally, years ending in zero spark journalistic reflection on the spirit of the times. As 1979 passed into 1980, the *Daily Texan*, which had expended so much ink parsing out the sartorial distinctions between the counterculture and cowboys, printed the prevailing new wisdom that fashion "in the 1980s will probably return to the 'preppie' look of the 1950s, with a definite trend toward buying clothes based on their investment value." This was something new, the student newspaper no longer an advocate of the new politics, the city it described no longer the province of a prolonged sixties zeitgeist. Then again, the next day's paper carried an article titled "Revolutionary Maoists Scale Walls of the Historic Alamo," so the seventies' long digestion of the sixties may not have yet ridden into the sunset: "A group calling itself the Revolutionary May Day Brigade scaled the walls of the historic Alamo, removed the U.S. and Texas flags, raised their own banners, and threw down leaflets protesting the 'vicious oppression of the Chicano people.'"[55] The preppie article's focus on investment value pointed the way forward to a zeitgeist and discursive focus for the new decade. In contrast, Damian Garcia, "one of the three revolutionaries who raised the Red Flag over the Alamo," was killed in a skirmish in an East LA housing project on April 22, 1980.[56] In a manner similar to the first-time-as-tragedy-second-as-farce rhetoric seen in the relationship between the Weather Underground and their successors in the Symbionese Liberation Army, this dramatic last gasp of sixties radicalism in Texas appeared in the press as a mere curiosity rather than a portent of revolution.

In 1986, Texas engaged in a flurry of memorialization to commemorate the sesquicentennial of the war for independence from Mexico. Fifty years had passed since the Centennial Exposition in Dallas, and the state found itself in economic doldrums akin to its experience of 1936. The Texas of the 1980s was a far cry from the state marketed during the centennial of 1936, however. Where the latter strove to convince the nation of the state's modernity and its normality, the former had to work hard to continue to trumpet its sense of Southwestern distinctiveness. By the 1980s, Texas had become a great deal like the rest of the nation, even as the rest of the nation had become a lot like Texas. Still, similarities between 1936 and 1986 persisted. Amid the downturn in the price of oil and the savings and loans crisis, Texas again faced the future with trepidation masked by bravado. As in that earlier moment, Texans remained in the center of America's political and cultural life. Where Vice President John Nance Garner groused at Roosevelt's New Deal liberalism in 1936, however, another Texan now in the office, George H. W. Bush, could applaud the conservative ascendancy of Republican Ronald Reagan. And that conservatism had largely captured the ground of "the Texan" so contested in the 1970s.

Conclusion

In September 2004 in New York City, President George W. Bush accepted the Republican Party's nomination to run for a second term. In speaking to the assembled convention delegates, Bush focused on the war on terror, his plans for an ownership society, and his commitment to education reform. Near the end, he lightened the mood by joking that despite all his accomplishments, some flaws remained. His mangled English occasionally required correction, he admitted, and then there was the matter of his presumed overconfidence. "Some folks look at me and see a certain swagger, which in Texas is called 'walking.'"[1] Few combined the themes of the latter twentieth-century "Texan" I have discussed—Kirkpatrick Sale's Yankee–Cowboy dichotomy, Bill Porterfield's meditation on fathers and sons and men and oil, the lure of the sports world, the stylized projection of the cowboy—as Bush did. He brought all these icons within himself to cut the figure of Anglo-Texan masculinity. His relative success in doing so illustrates the type's performative nature, its existence as a set of symbols that can be embodied as second nature. Inexplicably clearing brush in the wilderness for journalists just as Glenn McCarthy had fondled oil, drawling more strongly as the years in Washington passed, and threatening to "smoke out" America's dastardly enemies abroad, Bush once more placed "the Texan" near the center of American political discourse at the turn of the twenty-first century.

He did so in a manner that reveled in the symbol's conservative valences born again in the national imagination with the *Urban Cowboy–Dallas* turn of the late 1970s. Texans who did not agree with the man might dismiss his authenticity with the notion that he was, after all, a Connecticut Yankee in King LBJ's Stetson crown. But the attempted progressive re-visioning of "the Texan" in the 1970s that might have served as Bush's counter had crashed against the political realignments of the late twentieth century, its momentum spent nearly as soon as it arose. That Bush's first gubernatorial victory came against incumbent Ann Richards in 1994 symbolizes this exhaustion. Born near Waco, Richards, too, played "the Texan" in service to politics, drawing on the sense of fair play, toughness, and wit presumably born of the state's frontier experience to argue for inclusiveness and social justice. Richards participated in and drew on the regionally accented Lone Star liberalism ascendant in the 1970s. However, she would seem to be among the last of that generation's Democrats to wield statewide power.[2] It was not as if the non-native Bush gave a false sense of the state's conservative mainstream. His birthplace matters less than his own Anglo-Texan subject position formed in youth. In a blog entry whose title, "8th Grade Texas History, LBJ, Larry L. King, Davy Crockett, Jim Bowie, Sam Houston, Big Foot Wallace, John Wayne, The Alamo, and Texas Rangers," perhaps said it all, Austin-born author Gary Carson stated that "somebody made the comment that Bush wasn't really a Texan because he was born in Connecticut rather than Texas." However, he concluded, "if you took Texas history in Midland, Texas as a 13 year old boy, then as far as waging war goes you're a Texan. I don't give a shit if you went to Yale later or not."[3] Carson overstates the case, perhaps, but "the Texan" continues to serve as a powerful performative site implicated in subject formation, and we must be attentive to the arenas—politics, popular culture, education, advertising, sports—in which such "Texans" continue to be created.

The public has not fully exhausted the type. Bush's successor as governor, Rick Perry, perhaps surpassed him as a performative Texan. Where Bush cleared brush, Perry shot coyotes while jogging, railed against the federal government, and shouted Texas's ability to go it alone, even secede. It is in just such settings that "Texas" stands up and walks like a man. In his own brief, error-prone bid for the 2012 Republican presidential nomination, Perry could tout the exceptional "Texas miracle" amid the country's economic doldrums, noting that the state produced a majority of the new American jobs generated between 2009 and 2011.[4] The governor attributed this to the state's low-tax, low-regulation, low-service model and the idea that entrepreneurialism unleashed served the interests of all. Never mind that government itself helped

CONCLUSION

produce a significant share of those jobs or that the geological accident of oil wealth, as in the 1970s, had helped Texan fortunes diverge from those of the nation. Perry's celebratory air would also appear to ignore the fact that the state ranked near last in any number of quality-of-life indicators. Such notions did not contradict the Texas miracle and its libertarian triumphalism in its proponents' minds; they were simply beside the point. As Kris Kristofferson and Janis Joplin reminded us long ago, after all, freedom is just another word for nothing left to lose.

Bush's and Perry's high profiles re-invigorated the cottage industry of Texas national character literature. Liberal authors wrung their hands, asking, to paraphrase Thomas Frank's work on Kansas, "What's the matter with Texas?" The stakes were higher in this case, perhaps, than in Frank's Midwestern portrait. Bush's presidency brought a distinctly Texan cast to the corridors of power in Washington, and Governor Perry and former House majority leader Dick Armey did the same for the conservative insurgency of the Tea Party. This new wave of authors, in works such as Robert Bryce's *Cronies: Oil, the Bushes, and the Rise of Texas, America's Superstate*, Bryan Burrough's *The Big Rich: The Rise and Fall of the Greatest Texas Oil Fortunes*, and James McEnteer's *Deep in the Heart: The Texas Tendency in American Politics*, took the long historical view and a top-down approach, demonstrating the ongoing influence of a Texas elite joined through Washington politicians and businessmen attached to Texas-oriented firms including Brown & Root, Halliburton, and Baker Botts. A consistent cast of characters march, often in performative Texan mode, through these texts that connect the Johnson and Bush White Houses, consistently railing against services provided by the federal system even as they enriched themselves on government largesse.

New York Times columnist Gail Collins's *As Texas Goes . . . : How the Lone Star State Hijacked the American Agenda* may well provide this school's polemical apotheosis, one that explored not only Texas's exceptional sense of self, but also how that exceptionalism drove American policy on deregulation, education, anti-environmentalism, and a range of other matters. Collins does not find the state's outsized influence altogether salutary. Citing the Texas Legislative Study Group's 2011 "Texas on the Brink" report, Collins demonstrates the tension between claims of a Texas miracle predicated on a wide-open business climate, and the quality of life that proceeds from the state's large-scale divestment from the public sphere. The Lone Star State stands dead last or next to last in the percent of population with a high school diploma or covered by Medicaid, per capita spending on mental health, percent of women with health insurance, and workers' compensation coverage; it leads in executions, carbon dioxide emissions, toxic chemicals released into the water, and carcinogens released into the air.[5] Like Kirkpatrick Sale, Collins reads the Texan influence into a Manichean American conflict, not between Yankees and Cowboys, but between the politics attached to those who live in the country's "empty places" and "crowded places." In such a formulation, in its own way like Walter Prescott Webb's rendering of America's frontiers in *Divided We Stand*, culture derives from the materiality of a physical space, but that culture also becomes overly invested in the mythos it weaves. The idea of Texas-as-American-frontier enlivens this culture, even as it forecloses a wide range of pragmatic solutions for existing social problems. A degraded, sound-bite political discourse seizes on this cultural frame.

Where some saw a Texan bête noir bedeviling American liberalism, another, somewhat counterintuitive, set of perspectives rendered Texas not as social conservative vanguard, but as progressive sleeping giant. In a July 2012 campaign visit to Austin, for example, President Barack Obama crowed that the changing nature of Texas would soon make it a battleground state. When he did so, as a politico blog noted, "he was echoing the beliefs held among Democrats that the state's changing demographics make the transition from red to blue inevitable."[6] A similar vein of chatter about an impending blue Texas attended San Antonio Mayor Julian Castro's keynote speech at the Democratic National Convention that August. Texans of a certain ideological stripe had been proclaiming that inevitability for some time. They had been doing so for so long, in fact, that the premise runs the risk of growing tired. The *Texas Observer*, the State Democratic Rebuilding Committee, and their allies and descendants saw it in Senator Ralph Yarborough's 1957 election, in the boost that Senator John Tower's 1961 election provided a competitive two-party system, in the dismantling of Jim Crow through the Civil Rights and Voting Rights Acts in 1964 and 1965, and in Raza Unida's defeat of the border political machines. Each of these events augured a new Texas that, many thought, would turn from its conservative, agrarian past to an urban, diverse, pragmatic future. In this line of thought, the state's surging Latino population and in-migration from abroad would soon produce a more varied ideological landscape, a political diversity that would draw Texas closer to the moderate center. Such were the predictions.

Historians, too, have participated in this conversation, salvaging a usable past, a "forgotten radical heritage," among the state's many Populists, Socialists, Communists, feminists, unionists, and black and tejano left–liberal activists. Lawrence Goodwyn's *Democratic Promise* of 1976 stands as a classic of the genre, identifying the state's surly agrarian radicals as the seedbed for the

CONCLUSION

Populist Revolt of the 1890s, and thus the root impulse that fed the progressive statism of the New Deal and Lyndon Johnson. A suspicion of centralized power has been consistent in the state's history, but that healthy fear has borne more than one ideological stripe, aiming its barbs at corporations just as it has at governments. More recent authors have concluded much the same, from the collection *The Texas Left: The Radical Roots of Lone Star Liberalism*, edited by David O'Donald Cullen and Kyle Wilkison, that yielded the above "forgotten radical heritage" quote, to Michael Lind's *Made in Texas: George W. Bush and the Southern Takeover of American Politics*. Lind sought to break the Texas monolith by importing the kind of Yankee–Cowboy, empty places–crowded places binaries into the strata of the Texas elite itself, tracing a long-running division between pragmatic modernists (Lyndon Johnson, Ross Perot) and traditionalists (Lloyd Bentsen, the Bushes, Tom DeLay, Dick Armey). In articulating this other, modern Texas, Lind hoped to point the way forward: "By the beginning of the twenty-first century, unfortunately, Texas was once again what it had been in the early 1900s: a symbol, to the rest of America and the world, of callous capitalism and primitive religion, of demagogic politics and conspicuous consumption, a global leader only in executions, pollution, and corporate crime. . . . Fortunately there is another Texas, with a nobler tradition."[7] The optimism of this school of Texas liberals seems to crash again and again into the apparent realities of the state's cultural politics, and progressive-minded Texans so often seem to be tilting at Panhandle wind farms.

This study, too, traffics in the notion that there is another Texas, and another "Texas," that bubbles beneath the dominant discourse, one that might yet make of Texas a progressive country. I began with a fascination for the cultural moment in which "hippies" and "rednecks" supposedly shared much, and in which the seventies political spectrum possessed a breadth now nearly unimaginable. In light of Bush's and Perry's performance of "the Texan," what happened to that progressive re-visioning of Texanness through countercultural style and country music in the 1970s? Was it untenable? Was it progressive at all, or was it a retreat into traditional symbols amid uncertain times, a circling of the wagons whereby men among the "hippies" and the "rednecks" celebrated and defended their shared privilege in the face of the civil rights and women's movements? In the course of this book, I have repeatedly referred to the developments surrounding the cosmic cowboy as an "attempted" re-visioning of traditional Anglo-Texan identities and symbols. The type did have progressive seeds, responding to the new identity politics sparked by the cultural nationalism of African Americans and Mexican Americans and the attention to gender brought to the fore by the women's movement. The institutions of the Austin progressive country scene aligned themselves explicitly with these movements, supporting the Economy Furniture strike and the United Farm Workers, giving a stage and votes to Sissy Farenthold and Ann Richards. But, as Jeff Shero Nightbyrd charged, the performance of "the Texan" might also mean simply allowing Anglo-Texan men to be just who they always were, still shrinking from the challenge of confronting the deeply imbued privileges of whiteness and patriarchy. The movements for racial and gender equality in an inclusive polity moved all Texans forward, but did the scene around the cosmic cowboy do the same?

The swagger of progressive, and later, outlaw, country could indeed serve as an excuse for deeply misogynistic and ethnocentric behavior. But this was not the case in the best of the progressive country scene centered on the Armadillo World Headquarters, which may well have taken as its motto the mid-century humorist Mary Lasswell's focus on "change and adaptability" as the progressive cornerstone of "the Texan." The countercultural youth gathered in that place sought to expand the circle of "the Texan," whether in forcing Lone Star Beer to record radio spots with Freddie King and Sunny Ozuna or holding benefit concerts for striking workers or Vietnam Veterans Against the War, drinking beer and having fun all the while. In the end, I admire the artists, entrepreneurs, and audiences who made up the scene and take pleasure in their countercultural production of "the Texan." The world would be much impoverished in the absence of Willie Nelson's *Shotgun Willie* or Jerry Jeff Walker's *Viva Terlingua*.

The new millennium's first decade demonstrated one thing. Embodied in Bush's "swagger" of 2004 and Perry's "fed up" pretensions of 2011, "the Texan" persists as a performative site of exclusionary renditions of American nationality. These symbols will not leave us anytime soon. We may combat them or divest from them, but we cannot wish them away. Why not, then, contest them again, re-fashion and re-figure them to render "the Texan" more thoroughly conversant in its historical *tejanidad*, geared toward interpreting its frontier past in terms of inclusion, adaptability, and equality, rather than combativeness, persecution complexes, and insularity? Moreover, this endeavor to reclaim "the Texan" from its martial meanings involves more than mere strategy or pose. In addition to "Texans," there are, of course, Texans. As in Aaron Fox's argument concerning the relation between the working class and country music, the claims to Texan identities on the part of the state's inhabitants are "coherent, justified, and ethical." Those of us who call ourselves Texans identify with the territory's messy history, even as we look toward a future less tied to cotton, cattle, and oil, and more toward the service sector and

CONCLUSION

transnational flows of capital; a future less rooted in an inflexible Anglo projection of the state's image, and more open to a diversity consonant with Texas history and the larger global community.[8] In this, I would like to say that I join my voice to a growing chorus of those who would argue for a new vision of Texas, but the preceding pages have demonstrated that that chorus has always been present, but rarely, if ever, heard in full consort. Texas has a progressive, populist tradition, and a population that is diverse, urban and suburban, and increasingly mobile. To conclude from this, as V. O. Key did in the 1940s, or the Democratic Rebuilding Committee did in the 1970s, that the state verges on a competitive two-party system that can be home to a vigorous, ever-changing debate on statecraft and governance, may well be mistaken.

But if the temporary symbolic victories of the cosmic cowboy subculture do not always convince us of the possibility of further contesting, and complicating, "the Texan" in our own time, then perhaps the cosmic cowboys' material victories in the city of Austin do so convince. Birmingham School theorist Angela McRobbie regarded youth subcultures as training grounds for future life, and tracing the arcs that participants took out of the Austin scene validates that claim.[9] The generation of 1970s Austinites who came up through independent music venues, alternative publications, bands, and activist organizations now stand in significant positions in the culture industry, business, and politics of the city and have gone far toward establishing their civic identity and national reputation. This scene can still speak in Texas accents, but it is not imprisoned by the type, more given to Lasswell's adaptability than Bush's stonewalling resolve.

The power of the symbols of Texanness, however, persists for Austin's cultural producers just as it does for the state's politicians. The city's newer waves of indie and experimental rock, of visual arts, filmmaking, and technology, may seem at a remove from these themes. They do, however, continue to invoke them, often with the love–hate ambivalence reminiscent of Ray Wylie Hubbard's "Up Against the Wall (Redneck Mother)." Singer–songwriter Bill Callahan, who has often performed under the band name Smog, moved to Austin in 2004. In an animated video for his song "America!" off the 2011 album *Apocalypse*, visual artists Sterling Allen, Ryan Hennessee, and Peat Duggins of the Austin-based collective Okay Mountain painted a dreamscape of the nation's abundance, wrapped, even drowned, in the vibrant colors of its myths. The video begins with a pair of disembodied cowboy boots striding across a keyboard to a dark, insistent beat and a thrum of guitars that evokes railroads and highways. Callahan interjects in his deadpan baritone, "America, you are so grand and golden," before beginning a slow catalog of the nation's qualities, and Callahan's relation to and commentary on them. The beat occasionally breaks for an interlude, in which the video shows a cartoon rendering of a musician's back and a desert Western landscape, as snatches of guitar evoking Woody Guthrie's "Pastures of Plenty" play. The entire song and video trace the tension between abundance and want, the martial and the pacific, the mundane and heroic, in the American national character. Though sites and landmarks from across the country appear throughout the video, Southern and Western imagery figure prominently, and the artists' home base of Texas figures most of all. After a scene in which infinite fast food seems afloat in an endless ocean, Callahan repeatedly sings "Ain't enough t'eat," followed by a close-up drawing of a Texas belt buckle. The video's imaginative deployment of boots, hats, lasso, buckle, and a little boy playing cowboy against the backdrop of Callahan's melancholy lyrics and music all allude to a hunger for meaning sated neither by empty invocations of Texas myth, nor by the illusions of plenitude amid staggering economic disparity. In this sense, too much simply ain't enough, and the state's young cultural producers must find new ways of re-visioning Texas for our moment.[10] Woody Guthrie's spectral presence here, an Okie who spent part of his formative Dust Bowl years in the Texas Panhandle, suggests another way, the continuing value of progressive rootedness linked to a politics of populist insurgency.

Such interconnections between the persistent imaginary of "the Texan" and the politics that continue to be carried out in its name demonstrate that culture matters. Culture and its relation to sense of place matter. Culture and its contributions to identity politics matter. And they do not stand apart from, or constitute a false consciousness that obscures, the material world of political economy. Rick Perry, Gail Collins, Michael Lind, and Okay Mountain all argue over what kind of place Texas is, and that sense of place always sits at the intersection of an imagined, mythic Texas and the physical spaces within the borders of the Lone Star State. Again, the two are not always distinct from each other. As Henry Nash Smith has reminded us, myth sometimes has "a decided influence on practical affairs," and such is the case as twenty-first-century Texans continue to contemplate the complexion of the body politic, its relation to everyday life, economics, federalism, and identity.[11] The hyper-mediated politics of the twenty-first century privileges the instant communicability of such symbols, but this does not mean that the ideas they evoke are themselves shallow.

I contend that progressive country provides one historical model for understanding these issues. Further, the Austin progressive country scene of the 1970s, though the guiding spirit of this study, was but one node of its broader

Sterling Allen, Ryan Hennessee, and Peat Duggins of Okay Mountain, stills from Bill Callahan's video for "America!"
© *2011.*

investigation of "the Texan's" projection through Anglo-Texan masculinity, and the challenges to and revisions of Anglo-Texan symbolic authority in the twentieth century. Among its larger cast of characters, Texas and "Texans" have proved to be moving targets, the source of a set of symbols that can be mobilized for multiple ends. Dobie, Bedichek, and Webb nostalgically celebrated the Anglo "Texan out of the Old Rock" even as they lambasted the structures of power that hampered modern development and liberty in the state; Américo Paredes, La Raza Unida, Sissy Farenthold, and Barbara Jordan challenged the Anglo–masculine authority that these Lone Star regionalists represented even as they expanded on their own political project of an inclusive, egalitarian Texas. And in the Austin, New York, Houston, Nashville, and Dallas of the 1970s, Willie Nelson, Waylon Jennings, Eddie Wilson, and Doug Sahm; Bud Shrake, Larry L. King, Aaron Latham, and Bob Wade; and *Texas Monthly* and *The Whole Shootin' Match* all tackled "the Texan" in this troubled and exhilarating moment and, through progressive revisions and conservative salvages, created a body of works, songs, institutions, and ideas whose legacy continues to delight and frustrate, entertain and intrigue, instruct and inform.

Notes

Introduction

1. "Texas," *Atlantic Monthly*, March 1975, 26.
2. Jennings, *Waylon*, 195–196; Nelson, *Willie*, 171.
3. *Armadillo Country Music Review*, August 1973, video, collection of Eddie Wilson.
4. Throughout, I use "the Texan" in quotation marks to denote that symbolic register whereby actors perform or artists invoke qualities stereotypically associated with the state, whether in the mass-mediated texts of film or music or in everyday social interactions.
5. Frum, *How We Got Here*, xxii. Frum did not choose the Dayton housewife randomly. The selection alludes to an example from the influential political treatise by Richard Scammon and Ben Wattenberg, *Real Majority*, 70–71.
6. Like "the Texan," both terms stand in quotes here, a gesture toward their status as figurative labels rather than descriptions of definable populations. In short, "redneck" here connotes a member of the Southern, white working or agrarian class, typically seen as possessing conservative social and racial views. "Hippie" references adherents (again, largely white, but not by definition as in redneck) of the 1960s counterculture, typically seen as socially progressive or at least iconoclastic. These shorthand definitions efface much, including the traditional masculinist qualities of each. Both labels could also be used to designate the undesirable outside of the middle-class mainstream, though their shared white privilege rendered this outsiderness a bit tenuous. Finally, "redneck" and "cowboy," another key term here, carry very different resonances nationally, one Southern, deviant, and retrograde, the

other Western, romantic, and closely tied to American national identity. In Texas in the 1970s, the two labels accented different qualities, but were often applied to the same social groups, again typically stereotyped as traditional, rural, or conservative whites.

7. I consciously use "Anglo" as a gloss for the racial category of "white" throughout, following a Texas convention delineating the binary of "Hispanic" and "Anglo" in the state. The state's descendants of European immigrants are, of course, quite diverse, particularly due to an early and strong Central European migration of Germans, Czechs, and Poles. A prolonged tension between cultural autonomy and assimilation marks each of these immigrant groups, but in the larger history of ethnoracial definitions in the state, "Anglo" tends to subsume these other distinctions and serve as a synonym for whiteness. I use it in part because of this Texas accent the word carries, but also because it better foregrounds the artifice of racial and ethnic distinctions than the more naturalized category of "white."
8. Conversation with author, November 2, 2008.
9. Barnes, *Barn Burning, Barn Building*, 147–150.
10. Ibid., 153.
11. Jim Franklin, "The Armadillo Looks at Manson," *The Rag*, August 17, 1970, 1, 3.
12. Clemons, *Branding Texas*, 1.
13. The theoretical heft of performance studies informs this endeavor, but largely through the lens of authors who deploy performativity in close readings of popular music. In particular, I follow the adaptations of performance studies found in Auslander's *Performing Glam Rock*. Auslander turns classic theorists of performativity and gender, including Judith Butler and Erving Goffman, to the topic of 1970s glam. The genre of David Bowie, T. Rex, and the New York Dolls may seem far afield from Austin's progressive country scene in its privileging of notions of artifice over authenticity. However, the popular musics of the 1970s exhibited a broader continuity than is often appreciated concerning the notions of self, subjectivity, lifestyle, and performance. The ethnomusicologist Aaron Fox, in his study of working-class bar culture in Lockhart, Texas, *Real Country*, comes even closer to the textures I explore here.
14. Stimeling, *Cosmic Cowboys and New Hicks*, 26.
15. McMurtry, *In a Narrow Grave: Essays on Texas*, 18. Both *Horseman, Pass By* and *The Last Picture Show*, too, addressed the theme of the vanishing patriarch that looms large in public discourses of Anglo-Texan masculinity. McMurtry recognized and engaged the tensions that the nostalgic register introduced into his work, stating in the *Atlantic Monthly*'s Texas issue that, "in the years I have been writing about Texas, I have always found that my initial, and my hardest, task has been to convince myself that the Texas I have lived in and in some sense known was as legitimate and as worthy of attention as the Texas that existed before my time." Larry McMurtry, "The Texas Moon, and Elsewhere," *Atlantic Monthly*, March 1975, 29.
16. Raymond Williams's *The Country and the City* parses these larger Western themes

well in a British cultural studies context, but one could also cast further back to the *gemeinschaft/gesellschaft* theorizing of Ferdinand Tönnies's *Community and Civil Society*.
17. McMurtry, *In a Narrow Grave*, 20–21. "Old Man Goodnight" refers to rancher Charles Goodnight; "Teddy Blue" to Teddy Blue Abbott, author of the cowboy memoir *We Pointed Them North: Recollections of a Cowpuncher*; and "Uncle Johnny" to McMurtry's uncle, Johnny.
18. Texana literature in many instances remains wedded to this romantic–nationalist vision of the state's past, and the "new histories" of the 1960s and 1970s took some time to enter the state's historiography. A volume edited by Walter Buenger and Robert Calvert, *Texas Through Time*, collected the threads of such new histories as they matured, and issued a clarion call for new lines of research. *Beyond Texas Through Time*, edited by Walter Buenger and Arnoldo De León, has extended this line of argument further.
19. Fehrenbach, *Lone Star*, xvi.
20. Smith, *Virgin Land*, xi. Smith's student Leo Marx mined similar ground in *The Machine in the Garden*. Finally, Richard Slotkin developed the themes further in his trilogy, *Regeneration Through Violence*; *The Fatal Environment*; and *Gunfighter Nation*, the publication of which began in the 1970s in the wake of America's defeat in Vietnam.
21. Smith, *Virgin Land*, xi.
22. Barthes, *Mythologies*, 158.
23. Dorman, *Revolt of the Provinces*, 94.
24. "King of the Wildcatters," *Time*, February 13, 1950.
25. For that matter, so does the cover of the issue of *Time* in which the McCarthy story appeared. The painted image contains a Western-suited McCarthy in the foreground while, behind him, an anthropomorphized oil well strides across the landscape with boots, cowboy hat, and flexing biceps.
26. Paredes's classic work is *With His Pistol in His Hand*. For a wide-ranging, incisive theorization of Paredes's career, see Saldívar, *Borderlands of Culture*.
27. Carroll, *It Seemed Like Nothing Happened*, xiii.
28. Schulman, *The Seventies*, xii.
29. Killen, *1973 Nervous Breakdown*, 2.
30. In addition to those of Carroll, Frum, Schulman, and Killen, other key texts include Bailey and Farber, *America in the Seventies*; Berkowitz, *Something Happened*; Cowie, *Stayin' Alive*; Echols, *Hot Stuff*; Hoeveler, *Postmodernist Turn*; Inness, *Disco Divas*; Jenkins, *Decade of Nightmares*; Lawrence, *Love Saves the Day*; Miller, *Seventies Now*; Perlstein, *Nixonland*; Schulman and Zelizer, *Rightward Bound*; Shapiro, *Turn the Beat Around*; Waldrep, *Seventies*; and Zaretsky, *No Direction Home*.
31. Harvey, *Condition of Postmodernity*.
32. In part, OPEC's salutary effect on Texas owed to the organization's origins in the Texas Railroad Commission. OPEC modeled itself on the regulatory example

of the TRC's stabilization of oil prices in the 1930s. In 1945 the government of Saudi Arabia sent Abdullah Tariki to study the oil business at the University of Texas at Austin. Tariki quickly earned his master's degree in geology and interned at the Texas Railroad Commission. Upon returning to Saudi Arabia, the government named Tariki the country's first oil minister in 1955, and in 1959 Tariki created an informal "yacht club" including the oil ministers of Saudi Arabia, Kuwait, Iran, Iraq, and Venezuela. This organization was the foundation of OPEC, a cartel Tariki based on the TRC model. While Texas benefited from the spike in energy prices born of the Arab–Israeli wars and the Iranian Revolution, the rising power of OPEC also signified the eclipse of Texas in the realm of oil production as well as the power of the Texas Railroad Commission to regulate world markets. In the short run, however, the oil crises treated Texas quite well. See Bryce, *Cronies*, 34–36.

33. Binkley, *Getting Loose*, 9.
34. This study expands on and is informed by existing works concerning the Austin music scene, Austin politics, and social movements at the University of Texas. The four with which I most engage are Reid, *Improbable Rise of Redneck Rock*; Rossinow, *Politics of Authenticity*; Shank, *Dissonant Identities*; and Stimeling, *Cosmic Cowboys and New Hicks*. Others include Dugger, *Our Invaded Universities*; Frantz, *Forty-Acre Follies*; Long, *Weird City*; Macor, *Chainsaws, Slackers, and Spy Kids*; Orum, *Power, Money, and the People*; and Swearingen, *Environmental City*.
35. Indeed, works such as David Montejano's *Quixote's Soldiers*, on developments in San Antonio in the 1970s, have already pointed the way.
36. *Midnight Cowboy*, directed by John Schlesinger (United Artists, 1969), based on the novel by James Leo Herlihy.
37. Fehrenbach, *Long Star*, xv. The most significant general histories are Campbell, *Gone to Texas*; and Haley, *Passionate Nation*.
38. Examples include Bryce, *Cronies*; Lind, *Made in Texas*; and McEnteer, *Deep in the Heart*. Bryan Burrough's *The Big Rich* and Gail Collins's *As Texas Goes* . . . can also be seen as products of this impulse.

Chapter 1

1. Ragsdale, *Centennial '36*, 247.
2. Meinig, *Imperial Texas*, 7.
3. The line begins Hofstadter's *Age of Reform*, 1.
4. Campbell, *Gone to Texas*, 405. Of course, the designation did not always meet our contemporary sense of what constitutes a city, as a population of 2,500 made an area "urban" in the censuses of 1920 and 1950.
5. Harvey, *Condition of Postmodernity*, 126–140.
6. Fordism refers to the political economy pioneered by Henry Ford, which combined mass production with wage laborers compensated on a scale to consume the

products they manufactured. The Italian theorist Antonio Gramsci elaborated the notion of Fordist production and its relation to Americanism in *Selections from the Prison Notebooks* as an "ultra-modern form of production and of working methods—such as is offered by the most advanced American variety, the industry of Henry Ford" (280–281).

7. James Conaway, "Oil: The Source," *Atlantic Monthly*, March 1975, 66.
8. On Dies, see Fried, *Nightmare in Red*, 47–56. On Faulk, see Burton, *John Henry Faulk*. See also Carleton, *Red Scare!*
9. On the history of the early oil industry in Texas, see Hinton and Olien, *Oil in Texas*.
10. Bryan Burrough traces the national fascination with the figure of the wealthy Texas oilman to two specific magazine features, in *Life* and *Fortune*, that appeared in April 1948. See *Big Rich*, 167.
11. The weaving of a larger-than-life sense of Texanness goes back, at least, to the events of the 1830s that the Centennial commemorated, was ratified by the war with Mexico in the 1840s, and found magnification during the period of the cattle drives following the Civil War. The pulp articulation of the figure aided throughout. An important early work in this genre is Charlie Siringo's memoir *A Texas Cowboy*.
12. Flores, *Remembering the Alamo*, 1–12.
13. Works on the Comanche in Texas include Anderson, *Conquest of Texas*; Cavanaugh, *Comanche Political History*; Gwynne, *Empire of the Summer Moon*; and Hämäläinen, *Comanche Empire*. T. R. Fehrenbach also wrote a history of the Comanche in the vein of his triumphalist *Lone Star*, titled *Comanches: The Destruction of a People*.
14. Johnson, *Revolution in Texas*. See also Ribb, "José Tomás Canales and the Texas Rangers." As for the relationship between this rebellion and the Mexican Revolution of the same years, see Raat, *Revoltosos*.
15. The key work on race, class, and the changing nature of cotton tenancy is Foley, *White Scourge*.
16. On the Populist revolt in Texas and its Socialist echoes, see Cantrell, *Feeding the Wolf*; Goodwyn, *Democratic Promise*; Green, *Grass-Roots Socialism*; Wilkison, *Yeomen, Sharecroppers, and Socialists*; and Barthelme, *Women in the Texas Populist Movement*.
17. Ragsdale, *Centennial '36*, 3, 4, 10, 99.
18. Boyd, *Dance All Night*; Boyd, *Jazz of the Southwest*; Townsend, *San Antonio Rose*; La Chapelle, *Proud to Be an Okie*.
19. Hegeman, *Patterns for America*, 113–114, 120–125, 134–141. The equation of the Midwest with essential American identity finds an influential example in Helen and Robert Lynd's *Middletown*, which took Muncie, Indiana, as the American microcosm.
20. Goetzmann and Goetzmann, *West of the Imagination*, 409–434.
21. Twelve Southerners, *I'll Take My Stand*. See also Maxwell, "Heritage of Inferiority."
22. Hegeman, *Patterns for America*, 138–146.
23. Michael Denning traces the multiform manifestations of the regionalist impulse,

split between the Nashville Agrarians' rearguard defense of Southern tradition and the proletarian regionalism that sought working-class mobilization by establishing the American credentials of radical politics. See *Cultural Front*, 132–133. Denning figures here, too, in his assessment of the Popular Front moment as an origin of American Studies. See "Special American Conditions." That origin story has its own Texas variant, as it was Dobie who, according to Henry Nash Smith in the preface to his seminal *Virgin Land*, "first opened my eyes to the significance of the West in American society" (xi). For a discussion of the "salvage" aspects of American regionalism, literature, and anthropology, see Hegeman, *Patterns for America*, 32–37.

24. Graham, "J. Frank Dobie"; McMurtry, *In a Narrow Grave*, 53–77; Larry McMurtry, "Ever a Bridegroom: Reflections on the Failure of Texas Literature," *Texas Observer*, October 23, 1981, 1.
25. Other regionalist expressions that arose between the 1920s and 1940s included the cowboy memoirist Teddy Blue Abbott's *We Pointed Them North*; Marquis James's Pulitzer Prize–winning biography of Houston, *The Raven*; Eugene Barker's *Life of Stephen F. Austin*; and the influential syndicated comic strip by Jack Patton and John Rosenfield Jr., *Texas History Movies*. For a broader history of American regionalism, see Dorman, *Revolt of the Provinces*.
26. Limón, *American Encounters*, 38–43, 62–68.
27. Lomax, *Cowboy Songs and Other Frontier Ballads*; Lomax, *Adventures of a Ballad Hunter*; Lomax, *Land Where the Blues Began*.
28. J. Frank Dobie to Walter Prescott Webb, October 3, 1923, Box 2M254, Folder Classified Correspondence, Walter Prescott Webb Papers.
29. J. Frank Dobie to Walter Prescott Webb, October 30, 1923, Box 2M254, Folder Classified Correspondence, Walter Prescott Webb Papers.
30. Limón, *Dancing with the Devil*, 60–75.
31. González, *Border Renaissance*, 37–39.
32. Perry, *Texas*, 11.
33. Autobiography, Box 2M245, Folder Biographical Records, Walter Prescott Webb Papers. *Divided We Stand* has not attracted wide attention, but historians who have covered it include Dorman, *Revolt of the Provinces*, 159–162, 221–225; and Carleton, *A Breed So Rare*, 188–192. Webb also comes in for substantial discussion in McCaslin, *At the Heart of Texas*.
34. Webb, *Divided We Stand*, 3. I employ the expanded 1944 edition because of the material it contains that had been censored out of the 1937 edition for fear of libel suits. Of the authors explored here, Webb most deeply engages a regional, rather than merely Texan, vision, but even in Webb's most expansive moments, as in his world historical synthesis *The Great Frontier*, he remains rooted in Texana. *The Great Frontier* treats the histories of the Australian Outback and the South Sea Bubble, but he cannot help but include the Texas Rangers' discovery of the Colt six-shooter as a key turning point in global affairs.

35. Here, Webb came close to those authors that Michael Denning, parsing Benjamin Botkin, identified as reactionary regionalists who "identified regional culture with a particular way of life, and thus took 'a certain social background for granted and a certain social order as final.'" Denning, *Cultural Front*, 133.
36. Webb, *Divided We Stand*, 114.
37. Limerick, *Legacy of Conquest*; White, *"It's Your Misfortune and None of My Own."*
38. However, Dobie's support of Roosevelt and the New Deal had evolved from open disdain to devout loyalty over time. Steven Davis traces this evolution well in *J. Frank Dobie*, 98–99, 148–49.
39. In a 1938 letter to Roy Bedichek from Rome, for example, Lomax stated that "I've run into Il Duce twice. There is absolutely no idleness in Italy; nobody begs, and nobody looks hungry. . . . I wonder if you are still so bullish on Roosevelt?" John Lomax to Roy Bedichek, April 11, 1938, Box 3Q9, Subject Classified Files Letters Lomax, J. A. 1932–1941, Roy Bedichek Papers.
40. Remembered long after John's death in a letter from J. Frank Dobie to John Henry Faulk, September 7, 1964, Personal and General Correspondence, Box 3E169, John Henry Faulk Papers.
41. Roy Bedichek to Walter Prescott Webb, undated, Box 3Q15, Subject Classified Files Letters, Webb, Walter Prescott 1937–1943, Roy Bedichek Papers.
42. One of the most evocative portrayals of Hill Country drudgery before rural electrification remains Robert Caro's account in the first volume of his Lyndon Johnson biography, *Path to Power*, 502–511.
43. For Webb, these "material benefits" were even more personally evident. "By the time the city and the University had finished their program," Webb writes in an unpublished autobiographical sketch, "the New Deal had come forward with a program of assistance to local authorities in public works and both groups continued expansion. Also with the New Deal, Austin, as the capital, became an administrative center and many new federal offices opened. Austin grew steadily throughout the Depression, was comparatively in a boom, and almost doubled its population between the census of 1930 and 1940." Consequently, Webb began to invest heavily in real estate that stood in the five-block divide between the state capitol complex and the university, most notably a Lutheran church that Webb de-sanctified and rented to the Texas State Department. Box 2M245 Folder Biographical Records: Autobiography, Walter Prescott Webb Papers.
44. Autobiography, Box 2M245, Folder Biographical Records: Autobiography, Walter Prescott Webb Papers.
45. Letters from Walter Prescott Webb to family, October 12, 1942, and November 14, 1942, Box 3Q15 Subject Classified Files Letters, Webb, Walter Prescott 1937–1943, Roy Bedichek Papers.
46. J. Frank Dobie to Roy Bedichek, November 5, 1945, Box 3Q3, Folder Subject Classified Files Dobie, J. Frank, Roy Bedichek Papers.
47. Though, again, one must look largely to his speeches, newspaper columns, and

letters, rather than his books, to get a sense of this development. *A Texan in England*, Dobie's account of his time abroad, is odd in its rather charming portrayal of the English countryside in the midst of total war, with only a few interruptions in which he talks about Texas politics after he has returned stateside: "I write from a plot of ground, delightful in itself, against the campus of the University of Texas at Austin. Here on this campus, believers in the right as well as the duty to think are combating a gang of fascist-minded regents: oil millionaires, corporation lawyers, a lobbyist, and a medical politician, who in anachronistic rage against liberal thought malign all liberals as 'communists,' try with physical power to wall out ideas, and resort to chicanery as sickening as it is cheap. My mind is paralyzed by this manifestation of 'the American way of life'" (262).

48. The Rainey affair was one of a series of such events in the South as that region's politicians increasingly soured on the politics of the New Deal. The University of Georgia underwent a similar purge under Governor Eugene Talmadge. See Lassiter, *Silent Majority*, 56. The political battles within the University of Texas had many fronts. In 1936 J. Evetts Haley led not only the university history department's Centennial activities, but also the anti–New Deal "Jeffersonian" faction of the state Democratic Party. The university dismissed Haley the same year, and he claimed that the firing was political in nature, positing himself as a casualty of the left-wing department rather than the right-wing Board of Regents. See B. Byron Price, "J. Evetts Haley" entry, *Handbook of Texas Online*, www.tshaonline.org/handbook/online/articles/HH/fhahj.html (accessed June 12, 2008).

49. In Dobie's mind, the significance of 1936 was such that he would cite it in his *Houston Post* editorial on the JFK assassination as the moment when Americans began to show disdain for federal authority. "I saw hatred for our President begin about the time of the second election, in 1936, of Franklin D. Roosevelt. I saw some men become monomaniacs in their hatred for President Roosevelt. I have seen this hatred spread from the man who is President to the office of President." J. Frank Dobie, "Sowers and Reapers of Hate," *Houston Post*, December 1, 1963.

50. The Regents sought to dismiss a group of pro-labor economics professors who spoke out in favor of abolishing the school of social work as a breeding ground for socialists, and of removing the third volume of John Dos Passos's *USA* trilogy from an English department reading list. For more on the Rainey affair, see Green, *Establishment in Texas Politics*, 86–87. See also Rossinow, *Politics of Authenticity*, 26–27.

51. J. Frank Dobie to Roy Bedichek, March 13, 1945, Box 3Q15, Roy Bedichek Papers.
52. J. Frank Dobie to Roy Bedichek, July 24, 1945, Box 3Q3, Roy Bedichek Papers.
53. Roy Bedichek to Walter Prescott Webb, May 30, 1946, Box 3Q15, Roy Bedichek Papers.
54. Rossinow, *Politics of Authenticity*, 29.
55. Roy Bedichek to John Lomax, September 26, 1946, Box 3Q9, Roy Bedichek Papers.
56. Roy Bedichek to J. Frank Dobie, July 31, 1940, Box 3Q3, Roy Bedichek Papers.

57. "My Texas," *Dallas News*, September 7, 1941, 12.
58. Undated notes for a proposed 1950 speech on patriots and patriotism, Box 3Q27, Folder Literary Productions and Speeches, Roy Bedichek Papers.
59. Historians of Texas letters typically give more credit to John Graves than Roy Bedichek as a kind of proto-ecologist, but Bedichek's earlier *Adventures with a Texas Naturalist*, though at times given to romantic language, often addressed modern environmental concerns more forthrightly than did Graves's later *Goodbye to a River* on the damming of the Brazos River. Either way, Graves flows neatly in the currents of Lone Star regionalism addressed here.
60. Bedichek, *Adventures with a Texas Naturalist*, 94–113; and *Karankaway Country*, 225–281.
61. Bedichek, *Adventures with a Texas Naturalist*, 12–19, 26–31, 263–264.
62. Ibid., 196–199. "In Texas the accidents of history have brought four racial groups together—whites, American Indians, Mexican Indians and Negroes. Anything black is likely to be called 'nigger,' as nigger-head, nigger-goose, and so on. Anything noticeably small or stunted will probably earn the 'Mexican' prefix, and I think there is a dash of genuine racial prejudice in this. On the other hand, folks all over America quickly forgave the American Indian and converted him into a pleasant legend. It is easy to forgive the exterminated: the greater their prowess, the greater glory of the exterminator. We hold no grudge against the grave, but the Negro and the Mexican persist as elements of the populations, and it is here that folk psychology in the naming of natural objects seems loath to idealize and even reluctant to be just" (196).
63. "Moreover, as a theory of art, regionalism was not significantly different from *Blut und Boden*—and indeed, by the time the United States declared war against Germany, it was already something of a commonplace of art criticism to consider regionalism fascist." Hegeman, *Patterns for America*, 143.
64. J. Frank Dobie to John Henry Faulk, October 1, 1956, Box 3E169, John Henry Faulk Papers.
65. Lasswell, *I'll Take Texas*, 368–369.
66. Ibid., 323.
67. Ibid., 306.
68. Bainbridge, *Super-Americans*, 6. A late entry in this field of literature, David Nevin's *The Texans*, echoes this point in its epilogue: "The Texans. Good and bad, cruel and kind, some of them hungry and some of them rich—they are Americans in prototype, outlining in their raw extremes the lives of us all. They are the product of their past and their past is that of all America, if told in louder voices and brighter colors. . . . The Texans come in extremes; and in their extremes they delineate the larger nation, and that is why they are important" (217).
69. Bainbridge, *Super-Americans*, 45.
70. *Texas Observer*, August 10, 1955; Lauchlan, "Texas Liberal Press and the Image of White Texas Masculinity."

71. J. Frank Dobie, "Fake Cowboy," *Fort Worth Star-Telegram*, July 23, 1958.
72. Roy Bedichek to J. Frank Dobie, undated, Box 3Q3, Folder Letters Dobie, J. Frank 1950–59, Roy Bedichek Papers. More on the Blakely–Yarborough race can be found in Cox, *Ralph W. Yarborough*, 153–161.
73. Brammer, *Gay Place*, 325.
74. Dallek, *Flawed Giant*, 625.
75. Cactus Pryor to John Henry Faulk, May 7, 1963, Box 3E170, John Henry Faulk Papers.
76. Paredes, *Between Two Worlds*, 35–36. Translation quoted here from Saldívar, *Borderlands of Culture*, 221.
77. González, *Border Renaissance*.
78. Thompson, "Long Revolution (Part 1)," 33.
79. Campbell, *Grass-Roots Reconstruction in Texas*.
80. Goodwyn, *Populist Moment*, 122–123, 188–189; Williamson, *Rage for Order*, 82, 192.
81. Montejano, *Anglos and Mexicans in the Making of Texas*, 32–33, 36, 117–119, 121, 125; Johnson, *Revolution in Texas*.
82. A number of books address the relationship between the civil rights struggle and the international context of the Cold War, including Borstelmann, *The Cold War and the Color Line* and Von Eschen, *Race Against Empire*.
83. Pete Daniel treats the relationship between the collapse of tenancy and twentieth-century movements for civil rights in the urban South as a whole, rather than Texas in particular, but his argument applies. See *Breaking the Land* and *Lost Revolutions*, 7–11.
84. Carroll, *Felix Longoria's Wake*, 119. See also Richard Ribb, "José Tomás Canales and the Texas Rangers."
85. Johnson, *Revolution in Texas*, 183–184.
86. J. T. Canales to J. Frank Dobie, January 16, 1950, Box 2M254, Folder Classified Correspondence J. Frank Dobie, Walter Prescott Webb Papers.
87. Paredes, *With His Pistol in His Hand*, 33.
88. Ibid., 17. The Webb quote comes from *Texas Rangers*, 14. Paredes follows this passage with another infamous Webb line on the Texas Mexican, "whose blood, when compared with that of the Plains Indian, was as ditch water." This comes from Webb, *Great Plains*, 125–126.
89. "Texans Comment on Webb," *Daily Texan*, March 10, 1963, 1.
90. Saldívar, *Borderlands of Culture*, 117.
91. Paredes, *George Washington Gómez*, 270–275.
92. Saldívar, *Borderlands of Culture*, 118.
93. While Paredes adopted an attitude of antagonism toward Webb and neutrality toward Dobie, it is important to note that others within the University of Texas's regionalist faction supported Paredes's endeavors. Mody Boatright, a folklorist in

the Dobie circle, had served on Paredes's doctoral committee. When Paredes took up an academic position at Berkeley in the late 1960s, Boatright wrote a letter of introduction to Henry Nash Smith. "Americo Paredes will be visiting professor of folklore at your university during the winter and spring terms. I don't remember whether or not you know him; I assure you that he is well worth knowing." Box 3M509, Folder Correspondence 1966–1967, Mody Cogin Boatright Papers. Further, Paredes worked closely with the pioneering folklorist Stith Thompson, who had also initiated Dobie into the field.

94. Garcia, *Mexican Americans*; Carroll, *Felix Longoria's Wake*, 123–128.
95. Johnson, *Revolution in Texas*, 185–94.
96. To these two Texas cases should be added the critical *Hernandez v. Texas* (1954), the first case regarding Mexican American rights to be heard before the Supreme Court, argued by the San Antonio attorney Gus Garcia. The case established that "non-Caucasians" must be included in juries under the equal protection clause of the Fourteenth Amendment. See Foley, *Quest for Equality*, 135.
97. Blue, *Dawn at My Back*, 51, 75–87.
98. On the long history and legacy of *Brown v. Board of Education* in Texas, see Foley, "Black, White, and Brown."
99. A precedent had been set for this case when African American Ada Sipuel sought admission to the University of Oklahoma Law School, resulting in the Supreme Court case *Sipuel v. Board of Regents of Oklahoma* in 1948. Oklahoma, like Texas, hastily set up a separate law school. The gambit failed, as in Texas, and the Supreme Court ordered the University of Oklahoma to admit Sipuel. Thurgood Marshall argued this case as well, and, incidentally, Page Keeton was the dean of that law school at the time of Sipuel's admission. Goldstone, *Integrating the 40 Acres*, 20–30.
100. Glasrud and Smallwood, *African American Experience in Texas*, 178.
101. Dobbs, *Yellow Dogs and Republicans*, 138–141.
102. In 1949, the body of Felix Longoria, a Mexican American soldier killed in combat in the Philippines during World War II, was scheduled to return to his hometown of Three Rivers, Texas. The local funeral home refused to let him lie in state, as "the whites would not like it." Felix's widow, Beatrice Longoria, implored the undertakers and, when they would not relent, relayed her story to Héctor García of the American GI Forum. Garcia, in turn, mobilized the local tejano community and issued a series of telegrams on the incident to influential national and state figures. The Longoria affair drew national attention to Anglo prejudice against Mexican Americans in Texas and elevated the careers of both activist intellectual Dr. Héctor Garcia and the freshman senator Lyndon Johnson. See Carroll, *Felix Longoria's Wake*.
103. Bedichek, *Adventures with a Texas Naturalist*, 284.

Chapter 2

1. Reid, *Improbable Rise of Redneck Rock* (new ed.), 89.
2. Ibid., 91.
3. Ibid., 110.
4. Wolfe, "The 'Me' Decade and the Third Great Awakening," *New York*, August 23, 1976, 26.
5. See John Nova Lomax, "Finding Austin," *Houston Press*, June 8, 2011, 1.
6. Larry McMurtry, "The Texas Moon, and Elsewhere," *Atlantic Monthly*, March 1975, 32.
7. On the cohort of young white bluesmen that came of age in Dallas–Fort Worth in the 1960s and migrated to either Austin or Southern California, see Patoski, *Stevie Ray Vaughan*.
8. See http://oatwillies.com/ (accessed June 25, 2012).
9. The documentary *Dirt Roads to Psychedelia: Austin, Texas, During the 1960s* (directed by Scott Conn, 2008) showcases excellent interviews with a number of key players in the Texas counterculture of the period.
10. Echols, *Scars of Sweet Paradise*, 53.
11. Alan Lomax letter to John Henry Faulk, July 30, 1965, Folder Personal and General Correspondence, Box 3E169, John Henry Faulk Papers; Gilbert Shelton, "Message Music and Rock and Roll: Bob Dylan on the Concert Tour," *The Ranger*, November 1965, 14–15, 31–32. Still, Shelton later remembered the audience listening quietly, even religiously, to Dylan's rock numbers, and sitting "like toads." Interview with Gilbert Shelton, March 18, 2010.
12. Interview with Eddie Wilson, September 11, 2008.
13. Many of Gilmore's compositions typically remembered as Flatlanders songs made their first appearances in the performances of the Hub City Movers (or before that, in the T. Nickel House Band with Joe Ely). Gerald Barnett, e-mail correspondence with author, January 31, 2011.
14. Reid, *Improbable Rise of Redneck Rock* (new ed.), 57–58.
15. Echols, *Scars of Sweet Paradise*, 115–116.
16. *The Rag*, November 18, 1968, 11.
17. Echols, *Scars of Sweet Paradise*, 53–58; Reid, *Improbable Rise of Redneck Rock* (new ed.), 17–25; Rossinow, *Politics of Authenticity*, 253–255.
18. Roger Leinert, "Celebration for Western Musician Becomes Fun-Filled Minifestival," *Daily Texan*, July 16, 1970, 12.
19. Doggett's *Are You Ready for the Country* provides an account that highlights the Southern California scene as a motor of these developments. The latter chapters of La Chapelle's *Proud to Be an Okie*, 197–207, also treat the development of the country-rock sound in the context of Southern California's country music history. The documentary *Heartworn Highways*, directed by James Szalapski in 1976, places 1970s Austin and Nashville side by side to highlight the new styles and sensibilities infusing each.

20. Lock, "Counterculture Cowboys," 16.
21. Coyle and Dolan, "Modeling Authenticities, Authenticating Commercial Models," 30.
22. Wilson, "Armadillo World Headquarters."
23. Interview with author, September 11, 2008.
24. Wilson, "Armadillo World Headquarters," 41.
25. Jim Franklin in ibid., 31.
26. Bud Shrake, "An Armored Force on the March," *Sports Illustrated*, January 4, 1971, 52–53.
27. Compton, *Armadilla*; Franklin, *Armadillo Comics*.
28. "Hornadillo Mascot Debate: Sold for a Song," *Daily Texan*, January 24, 1972, 1.
29. Tom Kleinworth, "Kesey: Author Fights Political System by Organizing Armadillo Party," *Daily Texan*, March 1, 1972, 1.
30. Wilson, "Armadillo World Headquarters," 32.
31. Interview with Bruce Willenzik, Armadillo Oral History Project, January 12, 2010, http://kut.org/2010/07/bruce-willenzik/ (accessed March 10, 2011).
32. Suzanne Shelton, "Armadillos in Toe Shoes," *Texas Monthly*, October 1973, 88.
33. Reid, *Texas Tornado*, 37.
34. Joe Nick Patoski, "Doug Sahm: We Remember," *Texas Monthly*, January 2000.
35. Murphey, *Cosmic Cowboy Souvenir*.
36. Aaron Brown interview with Bob Livingston, September 10, 2008; Aaron Brown interview with Gary P. Nunn, August 26, 2008. See also Stimeling, *Cosmic Cowboys and New Hicks*, 41–42.
37. Patoski, *Willie Nelson*, 212.
38. Reid, *Improbable Rise of Redneck Rock* (new ed.), 229.
39. Patoski, *Willie Nelson*, 269.
40. Ibid., 283. The venue began as the Texas Opry House. When Tim O'Connor and Willie Nelson took over the space in 1975, they re-named it the Austin Opry House, or, alternately, the Austin Opera House. I use this latter designation throughout the text. Ibid., 310–311.
41. Larry L. King, "The Great Willie Nelson Commando Hoo-Ha and Texas Brain-Fry," *Playboy*, November 1976, 100.
42. E-mail correspondence with Cleve Hattersley to author, March 7, 2011.
43. Ibid.
44. Danny Schweers, "The Kosmic Kowboys," *The Rag*, February 18, 1974, 1, 10, 14. Schweers's connection of the cosmic cowboys to liberation politics jibed with *The Rag*'s editorial stance, perhaps motivated in part by the role of the music venues as sources of advertising. The official by-line on the article is "Danny." Contextual clues and participants point to Danny Schweers as the author.
45. By the late 1960s, the counterculture became a cause célèbre in the trade press, with a cottage industry of works trumpeting its utopian nature. Two key books on the edge of the 1970s are Roszak, *Making of a Counter Culture* and Reich, *Greening of America*.

46. For more on the operation of these progressive country festivals, see Stimeling, *Cosmic Cowboys and New Hicks*, 118–132.
47. Jennings, *Waylon Live*.
48. Spitzer, "Bob Wills Is Still the King"; Shank, *Dissonant Identities*, 68–69.
49. Stimeling, *Cosmic Cowboys and New Hicks*, 98.
50. This may be the most significant of the live recordings at the Armadillo World Headquarters, though it is closely rivaled by Frank Zappa and Captain Beefheart's *Bongo Fury* (1975) and much of Freddie King's *Larger Than Life* (1975). The Armadillo World Headquarters had an in-house recording system that also produced a number of albums regionally by the blues artists Bugs Henderson, Paul Ray and the Cobras, and Triple Threat Revue with Stevie Ray Vaughan, the singer–songwriter Shawn Phillips, and the local rock favorites Too Smooth. More recently, the New Riders of the Purple Sage released *Armadillo World Headquarters, Austin, TX, 6/13/75* (2005), which had been recorded at the venue.
51. For Asleep at the Wheel's path to the Western swing revival, see Stimeling, *Cosmic Cowboys and New Hicks*, 100, 101.
52. Patterson, *Hondo*; Heck and Hilliard, *Celebrated Luckenbach Texas*.
53. Jerry Jeff Walker's recordings did proceed rather spontaneously, in a sense, but they were far from unmediated. On *Viva Terlingua*, Gary P. Nunn led the Lost Gonzo Band in performing his iconic "London Homesick Blues" before a live audience for the first time. On the album, Nunn begins the song about being homesick for Texas while alone in London with the spoken remark, "Gotta put myself back in that place, again." A listener might interpret the remark as Nunn's attempt to put himself in the frame of mind he had while writing the song in London. In fact, however, this was the second take of the song—the sound crew missed catching the first—and Nunn is merely trying to re-orient himself to the beginning of the song to start again. Aaron Brown interview with Gary P. Nunn, August 26, 2008.
54. Shank, *Dissonant Identities*, 63–64.
55. Auslander, *Performing Glam Rock*, 98.
56. Jacobson, *Roots Too*, 164–170. Friedman drove the point home in promotional photos and performances in which he wore the Israeli flag as a cape accompanying his cowboy garb.
57. Reid, *Improbable Rise of Redneck Rock* (new ed.), 237.
58. "Groover's Paradise," *Time*, September 9, 1974.
59. Reid, *Improbable Rise of Redneck Rock* (new ed.), 238.
60. Ibid., 190.
61. The Freda and the Firedogs album would not be released until much later, though, in 2002.
62. E-mail correspondence with author, May 13, 2010.
63. Peña, *Música Tejana*, 156–157.
64. Ibid., 164.
65. *The Rag*, November 13, 1972; November 20, 1972.
66. Schweers, "Kosmic Kowboys," 14.

Chapter 3

1. "An Inconqueroos Interview," *The Rag*, July 11, 1968, 15.
2. Jeff Shero Nightbyrd, "Cosmo Cowboys: Too Much Cowboy, Not Enough Cosmic," *Austin Sun*, April 3, 1975, 13, 19. In another addition to his multiform career, Guinn appeared as the truck driver at the end of Tobe Hooper's *Texas Chainsaw Massacre* (1974).
3. Nightbyrd, "Cosmo Cowboys," 13, 19. Nightbyrd, too, pragmatically rethought the meaning of militancy by the mid-1970s. In a 1976 *Texas Monthly* article detailing the career trajectory of sixties radicals, Nightbyrd said of his time with the *Sun*, "I expect there'll be big movements again, and I'll organize again. But right now I'm in business." See Thorne Dreyer, "What Ever Happened to the New Generation?" *Texas Monthly*, November 1976, 232.
4. On the counterculture and the development of "lifestyle" in the 1970s, see Binkley, *Getting Loose*. As for jeremiads regarding malaise, exhaustion, and decline, see Lasch, *Culture of Narcissism*; Novak, *Rise of the Unmeltable Ethnics*; and Tom Wolfe, "The Me Decade and the Third Great Awakening," *New York*, August 23, 1976. See also Schulman, *The Seventies*, 76–77.
5. On the high cultural profile of truckers in the 1970s, see Hamilton, *Trucking Country*, 220–224.
6. William Broyles, "Behind the Lines," *Texas Monthly*, January 1975, 5.
7. For the general debate concerning the relation of liberal universalism to identity politics, see Gitlin's *Twilight of Common Dreams* for the jeremiad's side, and Kelley's *Yo' Mama's Disfunktional!* for a spirited rebuttal.
8. Bud Shrake, "Land of the Permanent Wave," *Harper's*, February 1970, 81.
9. Ibid.
10. In his work on Austin, Barry Shank has defined the notion of scene as an overdetermined web of participation and identification whereby popular music becomes much more than the music itself, an "intoxicated celebration of identification and subjective transformation, of the construction of one's identity out of musicalized fragments of the past." *Dissonant Identities*, 192. Stirring these discussions together invokes Raymond Williams's classic formulation of a "structure of feeling" as "social experiences in solution . . . distinct from other social semantic formations which have been precipitated and are more evidently and immediately available." *Marxism and Literature*, 133–134.
11. Wilson, "Armadillo World Headquarters," 1.
12. Subsequent scholars have criticized the Birmingham School for its focus on the public performative behavior of exceptional young men to the exclusion of young women, private behavior, and in-depth biography and history. See Thornton and Gelder, *Subcultures Reader*.
13. John Clarke, Stuart Hall, Tony Jefferson, and Brian Roberts, "Subcultures, Cultures, and Class," in Hall and Jefferson, *Resistance Through Rituals*, 32.
14. Ibid., 48.

15. Hebdige, *Subculture*, 87.
16. Ibid., 114.
17. Hebdige, "The Meaning of Mod," in Hall and Jefferson, *Resistance Through Rituals*, 93.
18. The pseudonymous Lyndon Berry and Earl Scheib, "Cosmic Changeling," *The Pearl* supplement to the *Daily Texan*, January 1975. Note the similarity to the *Texas Observer*'s tabulation of the politician's cowboy guise discussed in chapter 1.
19. Or the femininity of women who performed outside of gender norms, such as Janis Joplin. Alice Echols traces the theme well in *Scars of Sweet Paradise*.
20. William Broyles, "Behind the Lines," *Texas Monthly*, August 1974, 8.
21. Richard West, "So You Want to Be a Redneck," *Texas Monthly*, August 1974, 57–58.
22. *Austin Sun*, April 17, 1975.
23. Binkley, *Getting Loose*, 29.
24. *Austin Sun*, May 1, 1975.
25. Harvey, *Condition of Postmodernity*, 303.
26. Brad Cooper, "Texas on My Feet," *Texas Monthly*, September 1976, 97.
27. Ibid., 98.
28. Walker, *Gypsy Songman*, 135–136.
29. Henry Wells, "Barbers Suffering over Hair 'Shoulder Length and Longer,'" *Daily Texan*, April 17, 1970, 9. There was a kerfuffle in the letters column of the *Daily Texan* over the suspension of the UT swimmer Frank Salzhandler over hair length, "Long Hair Associated with Riots, Molotov Cocktails, VD?" September 27, 1970, 5; David Shannon, "Showdown at Dodge City," over hippies challenging the "No Hippies or Long Haired Men Served" rule at the local Dodge City Steak House, October 3, 1970; "Firefighters Seek Change in Hair Length Standard," June 30, 1975, 2; Steven McBrearty, "Long Hair Grows from Rebellious Roots," February 10, 1976, 1.
30. "Texas Beer Trilogy," *Pearl* supplement to the *Daily Texan*, October 1974, 11–12.
31. Eddie Wilson interview with Fletcher Clark, January 1981, author's collection.
32. However, Eddie Wilson confesses that the Astrodome statement was based on his intention to have patrons think of the two venues together without missing a beat, rather than on any hard data. The counterculture, too, had its savvy wheeler-dealers. Interview with author, September 11, 2008.
33. Interview with author, August 1, 2007.
34. Bobby Hedderman in Wilson, "Armadillo World Headquarters," 60–61.
35. Fox, *Real Country*, 31.
36. Interview with Bruce Willenzik, Armadillo Oral History Project, January 12, 2010, http://kut.org/2010/07/bruce-willenzik/ (accessed March 10, 2011).
37. Patoski, *Willie Nelson*, 25.
38. Jennings, *Waylon*, 24.
39. Graham, *Cowboys and Cadillacs*, 5.
40. Abrahams and Bauman, "Doing Folklore Texas-Style," in *"And Other Neighborly Names,"* 3.

41. Ibid., 4.
42. Ibid., 4–5.
43. For a key work in rethinking the liberal/radical, assimilationist/nationalist dichotomies in the early and mid-1960s, see Tyson, *Radio Free Dixie*.
44. Minutaglio, *In Search of the Blues*, 26–29; Rossinow, *Politics of Authenticity*, 200–201; Glasrud and Andrews, "Confronting White Supremacy," 178.
45. Blue's *Dawn at My Back* provides a vivid account of cultural memory and the construction of counternarratives in the African American communities of Texas.
46. Indeed, Gregg Cantrell has argued that the turn away from the state's Southern, Confederate past to a history of Mexican colonialism and the Republic was a fairly conscious one around the years of the 1920s. See "Bones of Stephen F. Austin" in Cantrell and Turner, *Lone Star Pasts*.
47. Key works include Navarro, *Mexican American Youth Organization*; Navarro, *La Raza Unida Party*; Garcia, *United We Win*; Gutiérrez, *Making of a Chicano Militant*; and Montejano, *Quixote's Soldiers*.
48. Garcia, *United We Win*, 37–39.
49. Navarro, *Mexican American Youth Organization*, 125–148; "Walkout in Crystal City," *Texas Observer*, January 2, 1970, 5.
50. Garcia, *United We Win*, 54.
51. Ibid., 60.
52. Garcia, *United We Win*, 189. Further evidence of Gutiérrez's effective, and often sarcastic, radical style arises in his *Gringo Manual on How to Handle Mexicans*, a satirical handbook printed in English and Spanish telling the history of the movement and educating in the tactics activists might expect Anglo institutions to use against them.
53. Garcia, *United We Win*, 198.
54. The university community's interest in the Chicano movement was widespread. See Ben Sargent, "Chicano Third Party Underway in the Valley," *Daily Texan*, February 1, 1970, 4.
55. Montejano, *Quixote's Soldiers*.
56. Paul Hernandez, "Defending the Barrio," in Janes, *No Apologies*, 129; "Across the Great Divide," *Daily Texan*, October 14, 1974.
57. Orum, *Power, Money, and the People*, 175–176.
58. Barrientos campaign advertisement in *Daily Texan*, November 5, 1974.
59. One of these marches so shook Governor Connally, who feared embarrassment in Austin, that he went to meet with the farm workers in New Braunfels as they neared the capital. The fact that he pulled up to the march in an air-conditioned limousine did not help to build rapport; indeed, the publicity caused Connally just the kind of embarrassment he sought to avoid. Barnes, *Barn Burning, Barn Building*, 90–93.
60. Cowie, *Stayin' Alive*, 54–57.
61. Berliner, *Texas Guinan*; Brown, *Hood, Bonnet, and Little Brown Jug*; McArthur, *Creating the New Woman*; McArthur and Smith, *Minnie Fisher Cunningham*.

62. Evans, *Personal Politics*, 98–100; Rossinow, *Politics of Authenticity*, 302–303; Echols, *Scars of Sweet Paradise*, 30–34.
63. Hayden and King in Evans, *Personal Politics*, 99.
64. Frieda Werden, "Adventures of a Texas Feminist," in Janes, *No Apologies*, 204.
65. The tale of the Soeur Queens, from their performances at the One Knite to the National Women's Political Convention, can be found in Gail Caldwell's memoir *A Strong West Wind*, 105–107.
66. Frieda Werden, "'Balls,' Said the Queen, or Tit for Tat in Texas," *Texas Woman*, April–May 1974, 26.
67. Lela Hinkle, "Women's Work: Texas AFL–CIO Convention," *Texas Woman*, August 1973, 13.
68. Richards, *Straight from the Heart*, 165.
69. Rossinow, *Politics of Authenticity*, 329–330.
70. Levine and Thom, *Bella Abzug*, 204.
71. Prudence Mackintosh, "The Good Old Girls," *Texas Monthly*, January 1978.
72. Jacobson, *Roots Too*, 41–46.
73. Farrell, *Liberated Man*; Fasteau, *Male Machine*; Goldberg, *Hazards of Being Male*.
74. Goldberg, *Hazards of Being Male*, 4.
75. Fasteau, *Male Machine*, 208.
76. Colter, Glaser, Jennings, and Nelson, *Wanted! The Outlaws*.
77. La Chapelle's *Proud to Be an Okie* demonstrates this transition excellently in the context of Southern California.
78. Jensen, *Nashville Sound*; Malone and Neal, *Country Music, USA*; Pecknold, *Selling Sound*; Peterson, *Creating Country Music*; Tichi, *High Lonesome*.
79. Dave Hickey, "In Defense of the Telecaster Cowboy Outlaws," *Country Music Magazine*, January 1974. Hickey rose through the 1960s Austin scene as manager of the gallery A Clean Well-Lighted Place, whose first show featured Jim Franklin, before decamping to New York as executive editor of *Art in America*.
80. Hickey included Townes Van Zandt and Kinky Friedman among their number, and Michael Bane added Jennings's brother-in-law, influential producer Jack Clement. These were each impressive creative presences in their own right, but did not necessarily strike the outlaw pose in the same manner as the artists listed above. Jessi Colter and Rita Coolidge contrasted with the masculinist cast of the outlaw label, but their marriages to Waylon Jennings and Kris Kristofferson, respectively, linked them to the same performance circles.
81. Schulman, *The Seventies*, xii. On these themes in film, see Biskind, *Easy Riders, Raging Bulls*. Indeed, one of the early American films in this wave, *Bonnie and Clyde* (dir. Arthur Penn, Warner Brothers, 1967), was a Texas-centric movie filmed on location that had its premiere in the North Texas college town of Denton.
82. Gent, *Texas Celebrity Turkey Trot*, 186–187.
83. Elizabeth Harris, "Country Stars Happy in Adopted Home," *Daily Texan* supplement *Images*, April 19, 1976, 26: "Jennings said his main gripe with the Nashville people was 'artistic control' over his music. 'We just weren't understood. All we

want to do is play music our way. We're not trying to build anything or destroy anything.'" Willie: "Nashville won't miss us. . . . They're doing pretty good business without me and Waylon. We're just going to do everything we can to lure all the musicians down to Texas." This differs in some small degree from Austin's progressive country moment in that the artists who operated under the outlaw label tended to be individuals who had a past record in Nashville and who used the Texas scene to distance themselves operationally from Music City.
84. Peterson, *Creating Country Music*, 137–155.
85. Ibid., 230.
86. Malone and Neal, *Country Music, USA*, 374–375; Jennings, *Waylon*, 227.
87. Doggett, *Are You Ready for the Country*, 339–340.
88. The Horton and Williams concerts were held at the Skyline Ballroom, just north of Austin, in a building that would house, in the 1970s, a later incarnation of George Majewski and Carlyn Majer's progressive country-oriented Soap Creek Saloon. Choates, a pioneer in Cajun music and the first to record the classic "Jole Blon," died in a Travis County jail cell during a period in which he worked for Lyndon and Lady Bird Johnson's radio station in Austin.
89. Pecknold, *Selling Sound*, 228–237.
90. In fact, when Chet Atkins and Waylon Jennings worked together prior to the outlaw years, one of their first collaborations aimed at a crossover with the collegiate folk revival, the 1966 album *Folk-Country*. Further, Jennings's home base in the span between the Buddy Holly and Chet Atkins years, the club J.D.'s in Phoenix, aimed at bringing together "long-haired college students, executives, and Arizona cowboys" with an upstairs honky-tonk and basement rock venue. Denisoff, *Waylon*, 101, 102, 122, 125.
91. Flippo, *Everybody Was Kung-Fu Dancing*, 290–292.
92. The film's tagline: "With a guitar in his hand, a gal on his arm, and a talent for trouble in his fists, he battled his way from the backwoods to the bigtime the only way he knew how."
93. Bane, *Outlaws*, 146.
94. Jan Reid, "Who Killed Redneck Rock?" *Texas Monthly*, December 1976, 210.
95. Joe Nick Patoski, "It Was No Picnic," *Texas Monthly*, September 1976, 22. Guns had long driven a wedge between the countercultural and traditional camps of the cosmic cowboy/progressive country scene. Hip capitalists often did not understand the practical nature of honky-tonk musicians carrying weapons to ensure payment in some of the dodgier venues they were forced to play on the road. In fact, it was this issue that occasioned the Armadillo's break with Willie Nelson and his subsequent backing of a rival venue, the Austin Opera House. See Patoski, *Willie Nelson*, 269.
96. King, *Of Outlaws, Con Men, Whores, Politicians, and Other Artists*, 139–157; William Martin, "Growing Old at Willie Nelson's Picnic," *Texas Monthly*, October 1974, 94.

Chapter 4

1. King led a walkout of writers, including Norman Mailer and William Styron, to protest Morris's firing. See King, *In Search of Willie Morris*, 140–149.
2. King, *Old Man and Lesser Mortals*, 12.
3. Ibid., 19
4. Ken Dessain, "Why Can't I Be One?" *Texas Observer*, July 10, 1970, 5–8.
5. Michael Levy, "From the Publisher," *Texas Monthly*, June 1974, 1.
6. Paul Burka, "The Decline and Fall of the Southwest Conference," *Texas Monthly*, September 1974, 58–65, 100–106, 110; Bill Porterfield, "The Lonely Search for Oil," *Texas Monthly*, November 1974, 62–68, 109–110; Bill Porterfield, "In Search of the Modern Cowboy," *Texas Monthly*, October 1975, 58–64, 88–96. The dual titles reference the blurb that accompanies the cover image in addition to the article's title in the issue's table of contents.
7. The magazine's cover stories portraying Texas women (typically Anglo) provide further evidence of this anxiety and of *Texas Monthly*'s uneven ability to project these new identities in progressive fashion. Some examples include October 1973, "World's Oldest Profession Hits the Road," on the closing of the Chicken Ranch house of prostitution in La Grange with a cover that alludes to Jerry Bywaters's painting *Oil Field Girls*. In October 1974, the cover featured a Miss Texas dressed in janitorial gear asking, "Me? A Beauty Queen?" "The New Woman? Returning to Submission" of June 1975 foregrounded *Texas Monthly*'s take on women's liberation with a cover presenting a made-up, smiling model with deep cleavage wearing a metal collar, handcuffed to a ball-and-chain. Other icons of femininity appeared: a December 1975 "War in the Sky" on competition in the airline industry, illustrated as a brawl among leggy stewardesses; an October 1977 cover story "Is Cheerleading Really Necessary?" that inverted the doleful tone of the earlier cover of the football player. And two covers featured Anglo women with African American maids: from January 1977, "Fitting into the South: How to Make It in Jimmy Carter's America," and "Made for Each Other: The Private World of Women and Their Maids." This is by no means to indict any kind of *Texas Monthly* agenda. The covers do their work well, grabbing the casual viewer's attention in provocative fashion. The articles inside do much the same. Their exaggerations, like the magazine itself, successfully combine ethnographic detail and philosophic musings to evoke a kind of fun-house mirror of the Anglo-Texan middle class's concerns of the decade.
8. Burka, "Decline and Fall of the Southwest Conference," 59.
9. Ibid., 65.
10. Goldstone, *Integrating the 40 Acres*, 115–122; Royal, *Coach Royal*, 33–34; "Royal Fights Racist Image," *Daily Texan*, November 16, 1972, 7; "Racist Image Puzzles Royal," *Daily Texan*, November 17, 1972, 5. For the defense of Royal in the face of this larger systemic prejudice, see Gary Cartwright, "Orange Peril," *Texas Monthly*, November 1976, 124–128.

11. Burka, "Decline and Fall of the Southwest Conference," 64.
12. Steven Davis covers this material excellently, as he does so many other aspects of the literary milieu recounted here, in *Texas Literary Outlaws*.
13. Gary Cartwright, "Tom Landry: Melting the Plastic Man," *Texas Monthly*, November 1973, 64–69.
14. For further explication of the Dallas Cowboys saga, see Patoski, *Dallas Cowboys*.
15. This was especially true when the Cowboys and Steelers met in the Super Bowls of 1976 and 1979, both won by the Steelers.
16. Sale, *Power Shift*, 13.
17. Ibid., 170.
18. Larry L. King, "Coming of Age in the Locker Room," *Texas Monthly*, September 1974, 80–99.
19. Cartwright, "Orange Peril," 128.
20. Gent, *North Dallas Forty*; Jenkins, *Semi-Tough*. Gent's work deals rather explicitly with the Dallas Cowboys. Gent, a former player highly critical of Landry's methods, made *North Dallas Forty* semi-autobiographical. He foregrounded the relationship between the lead characters Phil Elliott and Seth Maxwell, bearing a more than incidental likeness to the friendship between Gent and quarterback Don Meredith. The *Friday Night Lights* franchise (book, film, and television series) provides a contemporary echo of this genre. See Bissinger, *Friday Night Lights*.
21. Briefly, a wildcatter is an independent operator who seeks to strike oil in unproven fields.
22. Porterfield, "Lonely Search for Oil," 64.
23. Ibid., 65.
24. See Pascoe, *Relations of Rescue*; Johnson, *Roaring Camp*.
25. Porterfield, "In Search of the Modern Cowboy," 65. The reference is from the introduction to Dobie, *Coronado's Children*, xxi.
26. Porterfield, "In Search of the Modern Cowboy," 58.
27. Ibid.
28. On the Mexican genealogy of the cowboy, see Terry Jordan, *North American Cattle Ranching Frontiers*. A nuanced evolution of the cowboy figure can also be found in the work of Américo Paredes, who argued that after the Anglo-Texan borrowing of the cowboy from the Mexican vaquero, the cowboy's projection from Hollywood, in turn, re-entered and refigured the Mexican vaquero and conceptions of Mexican masculinity. See "United States, Mexico, and Machismo."
29. A study that exemplifies this positive trend in current historiography is Moore, *Cow Boys and Cattle Men*.
30. Sale, *Power Shift*, 207.
31. Hoff, *Nixon Reconsidered*, 153.
32. Porterfield, "In Search of the Modern Cowboy," 59.
33. Larry L. King, "Redneck!" *Texas Monthly*, August 1974, 18.
34. Killen, *1973 Nervous Breakdown*, 154.

35. Porterfield, "Lonely Search for Oil," 64.
36. Campbell, *Gone to Texas*, 172–173.
37. Meinig, *Imperial Texas*, 7.
38. This frontier model of oil wealth speaks to the historical record of wildcatting, but it also, as is so often the case in the case of the "frontier," effaces the cooperative nature of oil exploration, the deep subsidies provided to the industry in the form of the depletion allowance, and the key role of the regulatory mechanisms of the Texas Railroad Commission in guiding oil-field prosperity. See Hinton and Olien, *Oil in Texas*, 64: "Thus, though the high visibility of successful wildcatters created the impression that oilmen were solitary heroes, those who succeeded in the high-risk end of the industry, exploration, learned that partnerships, business circles, and cooperative relationships with each other and large integrated oil companies were all requisites of survival and growth on the geological frontier." See also Goodwyn, *Texas Oil, American Dreams*.
39. Hardt and Negri, *Empire*, xi–xvii, 9.
40. Nixon quoted in Schell, *Time of Illusion*, 160.
41. Shrake, *Strange Peaches*, 4.
42. Ibid., 25.
43. Ibid., 213.
44. Shrake, *Peter Arbiter*, 55.
45. Ibid., 31.
46. Ibid., 17.
47. Ibid., 93. *Peter Arbiter* echoed Norman Mailer's novel *Why Are We in Vietnam?* Mailer's answer to the question is, in short, Texas. The book recounts, often in the stream-of-consciousness interior monologues of its teenage protagonist, D. J. Jethroe, a bear-hunting trip in Alaska undertaken by two wealthy Texans and their sons.
48. Shrake, *Strange Peaches*, 94–107.
49. See Burrough, *Big Rich*.
50. Hunt, *Alpaca*, 45.
51. The literary critic Don Graham, one of the few scholars to address the novel, singled out a particularly saccharine line regarding their honeymoon: "The world stood still, and did not move at all." See "Alpaca," *Texas Monthly*, October 2000, 26.
52. To be fair, Juan Achala had his moments of vulnerability with Mara, as well: "I am putty in your hands—direct me, my diva." Hunt, *Alpaca*, 40.
53. Ibid., 57.
54. Ibid., 143.
55. Ibid., 85.
56. King, *Old Man and Lesser Mortals*, 19.
57. The "Shivercrats" were the Texas followers of former Governor Allan Shivers, conservatives akin to the wider regional "Dixiecrats." See Dobbs, *Yellow Dogs and Republicans*.

58. Interview with author, July 24, 2008.
59. Interview of Micael Priest, Armadillo Oral History Project, December 1, 2009, http://kut.org/2010/07/micael-priest/ (accessed July 19, 2012).
60. The classic account of this development is Key, *Southern Politics in State and Nation*. The key works on the historical dynamics of Texas politics in the middle of the twentieth century are Green, *Establishment in Texas Politics* and Davidson, *Race and Class in Texas Politics*.
61. Clipping, Box 10, Folder 5, James Frank Dobie Papers.
62. On the electoral successes of the Republicans in Texas by the late 1970s, see Knaggs, *Two-Party Texas*, 201–231.
63. Bridges, *Twilight of the Texas Democrats*, 129–130. Republicans had won the governor's office in Arkansas (Winthrop Rockefeller) and Florida (Claude Kirk) in 1966. Georgia lagged behind the rest of the South in this regard, electing a Republican governor and U.S. senator only in 2002.
64. This political moment is dealt with in Sanders, *Mighty Peculiar Elections*. Matthew Lassiter also argues the point in *Silent Majority*, 251: "Instead of the next stage in an inexorable Republican realignment, the midterm elections of 1970 demonstrated the intellectual bankruptcy of the Southern Strategy in the electoral climate of the Sunbelt South. The hard shift to the right orchestrated by the White House opened the political center for a group of New South Democrats who rejected the divisive racial politics of the past."
65. Interest in conservatism's electoral rise during what Sean Wilentz terms the "Age of Reagan" has drawn much recent attention to the subject. See Wilentz, *Age of Reagan* and Schulman and Zelizer, *Rightward Bound*.
66. "The very term *the Sixties* conjures a whole set of political, social, and cultural associations," the decade's historian Bruce Schulman argues. "So does *the Eighties*. References to a 'Sixties veteran' or an 'Eighties outlook' evoke knowing nods and clear, if stereotyped, images. But the term *Seventies sensibility* evokes only laughter." *The Seventies*, xii.
67. Jenkins, *Decade of Nightmares*; Frum, *How We Got Here*, 115–123.
68. Schulman, *The Seventies*, xiii–xv, 256.
69. Crespino, *In Search of Another Country*; Kruse, *White Flight*; Sokol, *There Goes My Everything*; Lassiter and Lewis, *Moderates' Dilemma*; Lassiter and Crespino, *Myth of Southern Exceptionalism*; Sugrue, *Origins of the Urban Crisis*.
70. Lassiter, *Silent Majority*, 3.
71. The reigning historical consensus on Reconstruction as an era of corrupt misrule had been authored by William A. Dunning, whose protégé Charles Ramsdell was a founder of the Southern Historical Association and prominent University of Texas at Austin history professor. See Novick, *That Noble Dream*, 230, 236.
72. Davidson, *Race and Class in Texas Politics*, 3–6.
73. For the workings of the border political machines, see Anders, *Boss Rule in South Texas*.

74. Jack Keever, "Sole Brothers," *Texas Monthly*, January 1975, 20. There are many Robert Calverts of note in the Texan 1970s, and it is worth distinguishing them one from another in this scandalous instance. Robert A. Calvert was a historian at Texas A&M University, trained at the University of Texas at Austin. Robert S. Calvert served as comptroller during the decade, while Robert W. Calvert was a Texas Supreme Court justice and chair of the state constitutional convention in the 1970s.
75. Scammon and Wattenberg, *Real Majority*; Phillips, *Emerging Republican Majority*.
76. Sale, *Power Shift*, 15.
77. New Dealer James Allred (1935–1939) provides a partial exception, as his election as governor in 1934 occurred prior to the deepening of the liberal–conservative divide over Roosevelt's Second New Deal, the Homer Rainey affair, and African American civil rights. On Ann Richards's election, see Tolleson-Rinehart and Stanley, *Claytie and the Lady*.
78. "A Vote for Tower," *Texas Observer*, May 20, 1961.
79. Ad for the Democratic Rebuilding Committee, *Texas Observer*, June 26, 1970, 7.
80. Text of undated speech given in Memphis, "Brief History of U.S. Involvement in Vietnam," Box 95–147/33, Bob Eckhardt Papers. For more on Bob Eckhardt, see Keith, *Eckhardt*.
81. Text of speech given in Houston on Vietnam Moratorium Day Program, October 15, 1969, "We Cannot Win the War by Proxy," Box 95–147/33, Bob Eckhardt Papers.
82. Text of speech given in Austin in April 1967, Box 95–147/33, Bob Eckhardt Papers.
83. *Houston Chronicle*, January 17, 1971, 2.
84. Green, *Establishment in Texas Politics*, 202, 203.
85. Ronnie Dugger and Kaye Northcott, "The Yarborough Defeat: Anti-nigger, Anti-Mexican, Anti-youth," *Texas Observer*, May 15, 1970, 1.
86. Cox, *Ralph W. Yarborough*, 156.
87. *Houston Chronicle*, July 25, 1970.
88. Kissinger, *Years of Upheaval*, 386. See also Connally, *In History's Shadow*. The charismatic, extroverted Connally acknowledged the difference between the two men in something of a backhanded compliment while puzzling over Nixon's political success: "In a world where charisma is regarded as a priceless asset, and extroverts are the rule, [Nixon] has been an anomaly. Basically a humorless man, and extremely private, almost antisocial, he nevertheless went against the trend and the grain" (256).
89. Al Reinert, "Bob and George Go to Washington," *Texas Monthly*, April 1974, 52.
90. In addition to the advice of Connally and Anne Armstrong, Nixon had received substantial monetary and other contributions from Texas oilmen dating back to his career as a fervent anti-Communist in the 1950s. Their support earned Texans cameos in a number of dubious milestones of Nixon's career. In Nixon's 1952 "Checkers" speech, the vice-presidential candidate responded to claims of financial

impropriety by saying that the only improper gift he had ever received was the family dog, Checkers, which came from a political supporter in Texas. The "smoking gun" recording detailing Nixon's and H. R. Haldeman's complicity in the Watergate cover-up involved their discussion of laundered money from "the Texans."

91. Mitchell–Nixon recording quoted in Barnes, *Barn Burning, Barn Building*, 209.
92. Carolyn Barta, "Sissy, Anne Hooked on Politics," *Dallas Morning News*, July 15, 1973, 18. Anne Armstrong gave the keynote speech at the Republican National Convention in 1972 and served as co-chair of the Republican National Convention from 1971 to 1973, chief counselor in the Ford and Nixon administrations, and U.S. ambassador to the United Kingdom from 1976 to 1977. Armstrong and Farenthold were classmates at Vassar.
93. For more on Dolph Briscoe, see his memoir written with Don Carleton, *Dolph Briscoe*. Briscoe did not have to work hard to affect the cowboy guise, as he was one of the state's more prominent ranchers. He was also something of a reluctant politician and John Nance Garner protégé only loosely affiliated with the ideological factions of 1970s Texas politics.
94. Kaye Northcott and Molly Ivins, "Texas Needs Farenthold," *Texas Observer*, March 3, 1972.
95. Connally–Nixon recording quoted in Barnes, *Barn Burning, Barn Building*, 217.
96. Calvin Trillin, "U.S. Journal: Texas Reformer," *New Yorker*, June 17, 1972, 78.
97. Barta, "Sissy, Anne Hooked on Politics," 18.
98. Trillin, "U.S. Journal," 78.
99. The Farenthold–McGovern comparison is a valid one. Farenthold played a pivotal role in the 1972 Democratic National Convention as the first woman to be put competitively in nomination for the position of vice president. The floor fight over the issue was contentious, as feminist support kept Farenthold a close second to Thomas Eagleton on several ballots. The voting drew out the televised convention and forced George McGovern's acceptance speech to the wee hours of the morning, when few Americans were awake to see it.
100. William Broyles, "The Making of Barbara Jordan," *Texas Monthly*, October 1976, 199.
101. Ibid., 200.
102. Barbara Jordan, "How I Got There: Staying Power," *Atlantic Monthly*, March 1975, 39.
103. Orum, *Power, Money, and the People*, 290.
104. David Powell, "Campus, Austin Voters Differ," *Daily Texan*, April 17, 1973, 3.
105. "UT Activists: Former Radicals Move Towards Political 'Centre,'" *Daily Texan*, April 26, 1977, 1.
106. Michael Eakin, "River City Round-Up," *Austin Sun*, January 22, 1975, 4.
107. "This Pledge Must Be Kept," *Austin Sun*, April 3, 1975, 1.
108. Other examples of New Left or countercultural figures who became invested in electoral politics in the 1970s include John Froines of the Chicago Seven, a state health official in Vermont; Tom Hayden in California state politics and Hunter

Thompson in Aspen politics; Sam Brown as Colorado State treasurer; and Paul Siglin as mayor of Madison.
109. Thorne Dreyer, "What Ever Happened to the New Generation?" *Texas Monthly*, November 1976, 98.
110. Wilson, "Armadillo World Headquarters," 229.
111. Bullock held the office of comptroller from 1975 to 1991 and reinvigorated the role of what had previously been considered a moribund office by seizing on its powers to increase tax revenues. Bullock would similarly reinvigorate the office of lieutenant governor, which he held from 1991 to his death in 1999. The centrist Democrat Bullock's close relationship with Governor George W. Bush also contributed to the latter's reputation as a bipartisan leader. For more on Bullock, see McNeely, *Bob Bullock*.
112. Wilson, "Armadillo World Headquarters," 215.
113. Richard West, "All's Fair in Love," *Texas Monthly*, September 1976, 102.
114. Paul Burka, "And War," *Texas Monthly*, September 1976, 103.
115. Ibid.
116. Green, *Establishment in Texas Politics*, 209.
117. The elections of 1978 also tempered the shifts in Austin city politics. Voters elected Carole Keeton McClellan the first woman mayor of Austin. Carole McClellan was the daughter of liberal Republican law dean W. Page Keeton, and though she remained ambivalent about party affiliation then as later, her agenda evinced a business-oriented progressivism wrapped in the tough prairie-mother guise. McClellan served as mayor until 1983, when Governor Mark White appointed her to the State Board of Insurance. She changed her partisan affiliation in 1986 in order to run as the Republican candidate for the seat of Democratic Congressman J. J. Pickle, and later ran as an independent for governor in 2006 after serving as state comptroller.
118. Reagan quoted in Bailey and Farber, *America in the Seventies*, 26.
119. Parmet, *George Bush*, 92. Bud Shrake would paraphrase the quote in the speech of one of his rich Texans in *Strange Peaches*, 18.
120. Barry Goldwater of Arizona, too, fits this political cowboy lineage.

Chapter 5

1. *Urban Cowboy* (dir. James Bridges, Paramount, 1980).
2. I do not intend to make the claim that Austin's cosmic cowboys possessed greater aesthetic or political value as originators over and against the dilution of the cowboy figure as it comes to be amplified on the national stage. That is, the cosmic cowboys do not have a greater claim on 1970s cowboyness because they preceded the national urban cowboy phenomenon. This line of argument privileging stylistic originators dates to the origins of contemporary subculture studies in Hebdige's *Subculture*: "Each subculture goes through a cycle of resistance and defusion. . . . Subcultural deviance is simultaneously rendered 'explicable' and meaningless in

the classrooms, court, and media at the same time as the 'secret' objects of subcultural style are put on display in every high street record shop and chain-store boutique" (130). The counterargument, positing that subcultural style is valid in terms of the users' experience whether they are originators or late adopters of the style, can be found in the introduction to Thornton and Gelder, *Subcultures Reader*; and Clarke, "Defending Ski-Jumpers."
3. Karl Hagstrom Miller speaks to this phenomenon more broadly, seeing New York City as a specific performative stage for Southerners and Southernness in the early years of the recording industry. See *Segregating Sound*, 121–155. See also Jasinski, "A. O. Babel."
4. Richard West, "Texas Monthly Reporter," *Texas Monthly*, November 1976, 80.
5. "Luckenbach to Hit the Road: Texas Frolics and Financial Advice for the Big Apple," *Daily Texan*, August 11, 1978, 14.
6. The line is from the Billy Joe Shaver song "Old Five and Dimers Like Me," though it also echoes Great Luke's tombstone from Shrake's *Peter Arbiter*, 93.
7. Wade, *Daddy-O*, 56.
8. Ibid., 80.
9. Ibid., 63. This was more or less contemporaneous with a trip to New York that the Armadillo World Headquarters chief Eddie Wilson took in his capacity as TYNA/TACI (Thought You'd Never Ask/The Austin Consultants Inc.) consultant for Lone Star Beer, providing further tinder for the coming Texas chic inferno.
10. Flippo, *Everybody Was Kung-Fu Dancing*, 118.
11. Larry L. King, "Playing Cowboy," *Atlantic Monthly*, March 1975, 43, 44.
12. Hutson, *True Story of the Best Little Whorehouse in Texas*.
13. *Texas Monthly*, October 1974, 36.
14. Rita O'Brien, "The Spy in the House (Part II)," Box 3W58, Frieda Werden Papers.
15. McComb, *Houston*, 120.
16. Cox, *Ralph W. Yarborough*, 114–121.
17. Guralnick, *Lost Highway*, 176–185.
18. The closer equivalent of the Armadillo World Headquarters in Houston was Mike Condray's Liberty Hall. The Houston venue Love Street might also be seen as an analogue for Austin's Vulcan Gas Company.
19. Various artists, *Urban Cowboy Soundtrack*.
20. Aaron Latham, "The Ballad of the Urban Cowboy: America's Search for True Grit," *Esquire*, September 1978. Latham, too, has moments where he takes on the native guide role for himself as a Texan born in the town of Spur, an origin he transfers to Bud in the film.
21. Critical scholars have often overlooked *Urban Cowboy*, but a few have recognized its value as a rich text for understanding the late 1970s/early 1980s moment. Among these, the strongest reading that situates both the Latham article and film in the period's cultural politics and representations of Texanness is Lock, "Waltz Across Texas."

22. Latham, "Ballad of the Urban Cowboy," 26. Latham underscored the point later in a diary he kept during the production of *Urban Cowboy*, where he recounts a conversation with the director, James Bridges, to the effect that this "movie was about balls. And what balls really mean." Latham's *Urban Cowboy Diaries*, February 7, 1979, http://www.aaronlatham.com/ (accessed June 21, 2008).
23. Latham did not prefer this ending, which he found too traditionally Hollywood. An alternate ending that he conceived would have neatly tied up the "You a real cowboy?"/"Well, depends on what you think a real cowboy is" exchange that begins the Bud/Sissy relationship. In that film, the last lines of dialogue would have been Bud saying to Sissy, "I'm not a cowboy, I just thought I was," to which Sissy would reply, "I didn't want a cowboy, I just thought I did." *Urban Cowboy Diaries*, September 20, 1979.
24. Latham, "Ballad of the Urban Cowboy," 23.
25. Ibid., 28.
26. Ibid., 24.
27. That the soundtrack reflected California country-rock as much as it did the Gilley's scene owes something to its production by Irving Azoff, an agent who loaded the album with artists he represented. See Latham's *Urban Cowboy Diaries* entry for August 8, 1979, among others. The critic Stephen Holden aptly referred to the soundtrack's style as "Sunbelt Pop." See Denisoff, *Waylon*, 300.
28. Shapiro, *Turn the Beat Around*, 245.
29. Nik Cohn, "The Tribal Rites of the New Saturday Night," *New York*, June 7, 1976. Cohn's article on which the film is based is itself a sort of fraud, as he has admitted his *New York* profile actually chronicled the 1960s mod scene in Britain rather than the 1970s disco scene in New York, about which he knew little.
30. Lawrence, *Love Saves the Day*, 377.
31. Aaron Latham's *Urban Cowboy Diaries*, August 8, 1979.
32. Ibid., February 17, 1979, and July 3, 1979.
33. Ibid., January 13, 1979.
34. Ibid., December 31, 1978.
35. Steve Davis, "I Just Want to Be an Urban Cowboy," *Daily Texan*, August 11, 1980.
36. Martha Grisham, "Country Western Chic Arrives in Austin," *Daily Texan*, June 20, 1980, 7. Other articles from the *Daily Texan* in this vein include Ray Ydoyaga, "Urban Cowboy Dies with Boots On," June 9, 1980; Scott Campbell, "Northerners Gag on Texas Bull," June 11, 1980; "Western Music Attracts Tourists," June 20, 1980, and "Collegiate Cowboy," August 5, 1980. These urban cowboy–themed pieces coincided with hand-wringing over the impending closure of the countercultural Armadillo World Headquarters and the end of the decade in "The '70s in Retrospect: A Decade of Change," January 14, 1980; Gardner Selby, "Armadillo Landlord Plans Sale of Concert Hall Site," February 6, 1980; Gardner Selby, "Armadillo Relocation Probable," February 20, 1980; Debbie Hendrixson, "'60s Cultural, Political Revolutions Discussed: 'Cowboys and Indians' Attractive to

Counter-Culture, Says University Instructor," March 27, 1980; Cindy Widner, "Goin' Home with the Armadillo," April 28, 1980; Jeff Whittington, "Where Have All the Rebels Gone?", June 9, 1980; Alisa Hagan, "Zoning Decision Threatens Armadillo Future," June 27, 1980; Kent Anschutz, "City Council Sides with Developer over Armadillo," July 16, 1980; Ron Seybold, "Armadillo World Headquarters: Hotel, Parking Garage to Replace Humble Home of Austin's Music Roots," August 5, 1980; and Jody Denberg, "Armadillo to Close, But Its Spirit Will Live On," September 5, 1980.

37. Both Latham and Travolta recognized the repercussions of cinematic images in creating fashions and subcultures outside the life of the film. In his diaries, Latham commented on seeing the film *The Warriors*, about a near-future, gang-ruled New York City, that the "kids are so deeply into fantasy lives that they cannot tell their own lives for the movies. So they have gang-fights at gang-fight movies. Where does the screen stop and the audience start?" (February 16, 1979). Travolta remarked to Latham upon studying the film's wardrobe and the Ralph Lauren spread that accompanied Latham's *Esquire* article, "We could start a whole new look. And these clothes are even more interesting than the *Saturday Night Fever* clothes." (February 7, 1979). See Latham's *Urban Cowboy Diaries*.

38. *Esquire*, September 19, 1978.

39. *The Whole Shootin' Match* (dir. Eagle Pennell, 1978). Watchmaker Films released a restored version in 2006.

40. Sonny Carl Davis drew on memories of some of his father's own moneymaking schemes in Texas for the part. Interview with the author, July 20, 2012.

41. Macor, *Chainsaws, Slackers, and Spy Kids*, 50–51. In other connections, *Hell of a Note* filmed its climactic scene in the Soap Creek Saloon with Butch Hancock's band playing.

42. That Pennell's Dobie homage is conscious, though unstated, can be seen in the fact that the home where Loyd and Frank first encounter the story of the lost treasure is Dobie's Hill Country house on the Paisano Ranch. Lou Perryman DVD commentary to *The Whole Shootin' Match* (Watchmaker Films, 2008).

43. And, also, the French New Wave, which influenced Pennell just as it had Bogdanovich's *Last Picture Show* and Arthur Penn's *Bonnie and Clyde*.

44. Parenthetically, it only took two episodes before the Ewings found themselves at the opening night of the Braddock disco Sky Blue, while it would be several episodes before they danced the cotton-eyed joe at Southfork.

45. Coren quoted in Graham, *Cowboys and Cadillacs*, 66.

46. The show drew an especially remarkable international audience and, in turn, a scholarship surrounding the foreign reception of the show. See Ang, *Watching Dallas*, on Dutch and European reception and Katz and Liebes, *Export of Meaning*, on Israeli and Japanese. In Fiske, *Understanding Popular Culture*, the author stresses the role of the program in the developing field of American cultural studies and communication studies in the 1980s.

47. The civic erasures of the classed and raced contestation over power in Dallas have been traced in Hill, *Dallas*; Phillips, *White Metropolis*; and Graff, *Dallas Myth*.
48. Hinton and Olien, *Oil in Texas*, 173–174.
49. In short, private investigators looking into disagreements over Hunt's will revealed wiretapping within Hunt Oil, which they traced back to two of Hunt's sons. As it turned out, the spying concerned internal investigations over embezzling rather than H. L. Hunt's will, and prosecution followed. Sentencing was delayed, however, as the Nixon White House tried to broker a deal for Hunt Oil's intelligence regarding Al-Fatah agents in the United States, whom Hunt feared due to the jockeying over his oil fields in Libya, recently nationalized by PLO ally Muammar Qaddafi. See Bill Porterfield, "H. L. Hunt's Long Goodbye," *Texas Monthly*, March 1975, 63.
50. Ibid.
51. J. R. Ewing's name signifies the tendency of mid-century Texan oilmen to use their initials, most notably with the Ewing model in H. L. Hunt. J.R. may also allude to the initials for Jett Rink that festooned the ballroom in Rink's hotel grand opening in *Giant* (itself an allusion to Glenn McCarthy's grand opening of the Shamrock Hotel in Houston). Finally, there was J. R. Parten, a real-life oilman who, like H. L. Hunt, made his initial oil fortune in the Dorado fields of Arkansas. Parten, however, provided something of an antithesis to J. R. Ewing in his devotion to philanthropy and liberal political causes, including being one of the primary financial backers of the progressive *Texas Observer*. See Carleton, *A Breed So Rare*.
52. Cartwright, *Turn Out the Lights*, 1.
53. Aaron Latham, "The Return of the Urban Cowboy," *Texas Monthly*, November 1985, 148–155, 236–255.
54. "The Takeover Game: Corporate Raider T. Boone Pickens," *Time*, March 4, 1985.
55. Clara Tuma, "'Preppie' Fashion Return Forecast," *Daily Texan*, March 20, 1980, 15; "Revolutionary Maoists Scale Walls of the Historic Alamo," *Daily Texan*, March 21, 1980, 3.
56. David Stitt, "Alamo Revolutionary Slain in LA," *Daily Texan*, April 29, 1980, 5.

Conclusion

1. "President Bush's Acceptance Speech to the Republican National Convention," *Washington Post*, September 2, 2004.
2. Reid, *Let the People In*.
3. "8th Grade Texas History, LBJ, Larry L. King, Davy Crockett, Jim Bowie, Sam Houston, Big Foot Wallace, John Wayne, The Alamo, and Texas Rangers," http://americantradition.blogspot.com/2006/12/8th-grade-texas-history-lbj-larry-l.html (accessed February 28, 2009).
4. Collins, *As Texas Goes . . .* , 147.
5. Ibid., 233–246.

6. Charles Mahtesian, "Obama's Texas Battleground Prediction," July 18, 2012, http://www.politico.com/ (accessed July 26, 2012).
7. Lind, *Made in Texas*, 184. See also Cullen and Wilkison, *Texas Left*; Moser, *Blue Dixie*.
8. Fox, *Real Country*, 31.
9. McRobbie, "Shut Up and Dance," 412.
10. Callahan, *Apocalypse*. Video by Okay Mountain (Sterling Allen, Peat Duggins, Ryan Hennessee), produced by Dave Bryant.
11. Smith, *Virgin Land*, xi.

Bibliography

Archival Materials

Austin History Center (Austin, Texas)
    Gary Cartwright Papers, 1963–1984
    Edwin Allen Jr. ("Bud Shrake") (Biography File)
Briscoe Center for American History, University of Texas at Austin (Austin, Texas)
    Armadillo World Headquarters Records, 1971–1980
    Roy Bedichek Papers, 1897–1957
    James Frank Dobie Papers, 1923–2008
    Bob Eckhardt Papers, 1931–1992
    Frances Tarlton Farenthold Papers, 1913–2008
    John Henry Faulk Papers, 1881, 1936–
    Soap Creek Saloon Archives, 1966–1989
    Texas Observer Records, 1952–1990
    Walter Prescott Webb Papers, 1857–1966
    Frieda Werden Papers
Southwestern Writers Collection, Texas State University (San Marcos, Texas)
    J. Frank Dobie Papers, 1898–1988
    Texas Monthly Magazine Collection

Books, Monographs, and Articles

Abbott, Teddy Blue, and Helena Huntington Smith. *We Pointed Them North: Recollections of a Cowpuncher*. New York: Farrar and Rhinehart, 1939.

Abernethy, Francis Edward, ed. *What's Going On? (In Modern Texas Folklore)*. Austin: Encino Press, 1976.

Abrahams, Roger, and Richard Bauman, eds. *"And Other Neighborly Names": Social Process and Cultural Image in Texas Folklore*. Austin: University of Texas Press, 1981.

Alexander, Stan. *George Sessions Perry*. Austin: Steck-Vaughn, 1967.

Allen, Michael. "'I Just Want to Be a Cosmic Cowboy': Hippies, Cowboy Code, and the Culture of a Counterculture." *Western Historical Quarterly* 36:3 (2005): 275–300.

———. *Rodeo Cowboys in the North American Imagination*. Reno: University of Nevada Press, 1998.

Allen, Ruth. *Chapters in the History of Organized Labor in Texas*. Dallas: Clements Center for Southwest Studies, 2006 [1941].

Anders, Evan. *Boss Rule in South Texas: The Progressive Era*. Austin: University of Texas Press, 1982.

Anderson, Gary Clayton. *The Conquest of Texas: Ethnic Cleansing in the Promised Land*. Norman: University of Oklahoma Press, 2005.

Ang, Ien. *Watching Dallas: Soap Opera and the Melodramatic Imagination*. New York: Routledge, 1982.

Anzaldúa, Gloria. *Borderlands/La Frontera: The New Mestiza*. San Francisco: Aunt Lute Books, 1987.

Auslander, Philip. *Performing Glam Rock: Gender and Theatricality in Popular Music*. Ann Arbor: University of Michigan Press, 2006.

Bailey, Beth, and David Farber, eds. *America in the Seventies*. Lawrence: University Press of Kansas, 2004.

Bainbridge, John. *The Super-Americans: A Picture of Life in the United States, as Brought into Focus, Bigger Than Life, in the Land of the Millionaires, Texas*. Garden City, NY: Doubleday, 1961.

Bane, Michael. *The Outlaws: Revolution in Country Music*. New York: Doubleday, 1978.

Barker, Eugene. *The Life of Stephen F. Austin: Founder of Texas, 1793–1836*. Nashville: Cokesbury Press, 1926.

Barnes, Ben. *Barn Burning, Barn Building: Tales of a Political Life, from LBJ to George W. Bush and Beyond*. Albany, TX: Bright Sky Press, 2006.

Barr, Alwyn. *Black Texans: A History of African Americans in Texas, 1528–1995*. Norman: University of Oklahoma Press, 1996.

Barthelme, Marion, ed. *Women in the Texas Populist Movement: Letters to the Southern Mercury*. College Station: Texas A&M University Press, 1997.

Barthes, Roland. *Mythologies*. Translated by Annette Lavers. New York: Noonday Press, 1972 [1957].

BIBLIOGRAPHY

Bedichek, Roy. *Adventures with a Texas Naturalist*. Austin: University of Texas Press, 1961 [1947].

———. *Karankaway Country*. Garden City, NY: Doubleday, 1950.

Berkowitz, Edward. *Something Happened: A Political and Cultural Overview of the Seventies*. New York: Columbia University Press, 2006.

Berliner, Louise. *Texas Guinan: Queen of the Nightclubs*. Austin: University of Texas Press, 1993.

Bernstein, Irving. *Guns or Butter: The Presidency of Lyndon Johnson*. New York: Oxford University Press, 1996.

Binkley, Sam. *Getting Loose: Lifestyle Consumption in the 1970s*. Durham: Duke University Press, 2007.

Biskind, Peter. *Easy Riders, Raging Bulls: How the Sex-Drugs-and-Rock 'n' Roll Generation Saved Hollywood*. New York: Simon and Schuster, 1998.

Bissinger, H. G. *Friday Night Lights: A Town, a Team, and a Dream*. Boston: Addison-Wesley, 1990.

Black, Earl, and Merle Black. *The Rise of Southern Republicans*. Cambridge, MA: Belknap Press, 2003.

Blackwelder, Julia Kirk. *Women of the Depression: Caste and Culture in San Antonio, 1929–1939*. College Station: Texas A&M University Press, 1984.

Blue, Carroll Parrott. *The Dawn at My Back: Memoir of a Black Texas Upbringing*. Austin: University of Texas Press, 2003.

Boorstin, Daniel. *The Genius of American Politics*. Chicago: University of Chicago Press, 1953.

Borstelmann, Thomas. *The Cold War and the Color Line: American Race Relations in the Global Arena*. Cambridge: Harvard University Press, 2001.

Boyd, Jean. *Dance All Night: Those Other Southwestern Swing Bands, Past and Present*. Lubbock: Texas Tech University Press, 2012.

———. *The Jazz of the Southwest: An Oral History of Western Swing*. Austin: University of Texas Press, 1998.

Brammer, Billy Lee. *The Gay Place*. Austin: University of Texas Press, 1995 [1961].

Brennan, Mary. *Turning Right in the Sixties: The Conservative Capture of the GOP*. Chapel Hill: University of North Carolina Press, 2007.

Bridger, Bobby. *Bridger*. Austin: University of Texas Press, 2009.

Bridges, Kenneth. *Twilight of the Texas Democrats: The 1978 Governor's Race*. College Station: Texas A&M University Press, 2008.

Briscoe, Dolph, with Don Carleton. *Dolph Briscoe: My Life in Texas Ranching and Politics*. Austin: Center for American History, 2008.

Brown, Norman. *Hood, Bonnet, and Little Brown Jug: Texas Politics, 1921–1928*. College Station: Texas A&M University Press, 1984.

Bryce, Robert. *Cronies: Oil, the Bushes, and the Rise of Texas, America's Superstate*. New York: Public Affairs, 2004.

Buenger, Walter, and Robert Calvert. *Texas Through Time: Evolving Interpretations.* College Station: Texas A&M University Press, 1991.

Buenger, Walter, and Arnoldo De León. *Beyond Texas Through Time: Breaking Away from Past Interpretations.* College Station: Texas A&M University Press, 2011.

Burrough, Bryan. *The Big Rich: The Rise and Fall of the Greatest Texas Oil Fortunes.* New York: Penguin Press, 2009.

Burton, Michael C. *John Henry Faulk: The Making of a Liberated Mind.* Austin: Eakin Press, 1993.

Busby, Mark. *Larry McMurtry and the West: An Ambivalent Relationship.* Denton: University of North Texas Press, 1995.

Bush, Johnny, with Rick Mitchell. *Whiskey River (Take My Mind).* Austin: University of Texas Press, 2007.

Butler, Judith. *Gender Trouble: Feminism and the Subversion of Identity.* New York: Routledge, 1990.

Butler, Mike. "'Luther King Was a Good Ole Boy': The Southern Rock Movement and White Male Identity in the Post–Civil Rights South." *Popular Music and Society* 23:2 (1999): 41–61.

Caldwell, Gail. *A Strong West Wind: A Memoir.* New York: Random House, 2006.

Calvert, Robert, Randolph Campbell, and Donald Chipman. *The Dallas Cowboys and the NFL.* Norman: University of Oklahoma Press, 1970.

Calvert, Robert, Gregg Cantrell, and Arnoldo de León. *The History of Texas.* 4th ed. New York: Harlan Davidson, 2007.

Campbell, Randolph. *Gone to Texas: A History of the Lone Star State.* New York: Oxford University Press, 2003.

———. *Grass-Roots Reconstruction in Texas.* Baton Rouge: Louisiana State University Press, 1997.

Canales, J. T. *Bits of Texas History in the Melting Pot of America.* 2 vols. Brownsville: Artes Graficas, 1950, 1957.

———. *Juan Cortina: Bandit or Patriot?* New York: Arno Press, 1974 [1951].

Cantrell, Gregg. "The Bones of Stephen F. Austin: History and Memory in Progressive-Era Texas." In *Lone Star Pasts: Memory and History in Texas*, ed. Gregg Cantrell and Elizabeth Hayes Turner, 39–74. College Station: Texas A&M University Press, 2007.

———. *Feeding the Wolf: John B. Rayner and the Politics of Race, 1850–1918.* New York: Harlan Davidson, 2001.

Cantrell, Gregg, and Elizabeth Hayes Turner, eds. *Lone Star Pasts: Memory and History in Texas.* College Station: Texas A&M University Press, 2007.

Carleton, Don. *A Breed So Rare: The Life and Times of J. R. Parten, Liberal Texas Oil Man, 1896–1992.* Austin: Texas State Historical Association, 1998.

———. *Red Scare! Right-Wing Hysteria, Fifties Fanaticism, and Their Legacy in Texas.* Austin: Texas Monthly Press, 1985.

Caro, Robert. *The Path to Power.* New York: Knopf, 1982.

BIBLIOGRAPHY

Carroll, Patrick. *Felix Longoria's Wake: Bereavement, Racism, and the Rise of Mexican American Activism.* Austin: University of Texas Press, 2003.

Carroll, Peter. *It Seemed Like Nothing Happened: America in the 1970s.* New Brunswick: Rutgers University Press, 1990 [1982].

Cartwright, Gary. *Confessions of a Washed-Up Sportswriter.* Austin: Texas Monthly Press, 1982.

———. *Turn Out the Lights: Chronicles of Texas During the '80s and '90s.* Austin: University of Texas Press, 2000.

Cavanaugh, Thomas. *Comanche Political History: An Ethnohistorical Perspective.* Lincoln: University of Nebraska Press, 1996.

Ching, Barbara. "Where Has the Free Bird Flown? Lynyrd Skynyrd and White Southern Manhood." In *White Masculinity in the Recent South*, ed. Trent Watts, 251–265. Baton Rouge: Louisiana State University Press, 2008.

———. *Wrong's What I Do Best: Hard Country Music and Contemporary Culture.* New York: Oxford University Press, 2001.

Clarke, Gary. "Defending Ski-Jumpers: A Critique of Theories of Youth Subcultures." In *On Record: Rock, Pop, and the Written Word*, ed. Simon Frith and Andrew Goodwin, 81–96. New York: Routledge, 1990.

Clemons, Leigh. *Branding Texas: Performing Culture in the Lone Star State.* Austin: University of Texas Press, 2008.

Cohen, Lizabeth. *Making a New Deal: Industrial Workers in Chicago, 1919–1939.* New York: Cambridge University Press, 1990.

Cohen, Stanley. *Folk Devils and Moral Panics: The Creation of the Mods and Rockers.* London: MacGibbon and Kee, 1972.

Collins, Gail. *As Texas Goes . . . : How the Lone Star State Hijacked the American Agenda.* New York: Liveright, 2012.

Compton, J. R. *Armadilla.* Dallas: Brown Dog, 1974.

Connally, John, with Mickey Herskowitz. *In History's Shadow: An American Odyssey.* New York: Hyperion Press, 1993.

Cowie, Jefferson. *Stayin' Alive: The 1970s and the Last Days of the Working Class.* New York: New Press, 2010.

Cox, Patrick. *Ralph W. Yarborough: The People's Senator.* Austin: University of Texas Press, 2001.

Cox, Patrick, Michael Collins, and Kenneth Hendrickson Jr., eds. *Profiles in Power: Twentieth-Century Texans in Washington.* Austin: University of Texas Press, 2004 [1993].

Coyle, Michael, and Jon Dolan. "Modeling Authenticities, Authenticating Commercial Models." In *Reading Rock and Roll: Authenticity, Appropriation, Aesthetics*, ed. Kevin Dettmar and William Rickey, 17–34. New York: Columbia University Press, 1999.

Crespino, Joseph. *In Search of Another Country: Mississippi and the Conservative Counterrevolution.* Princeton: Princeton University Press, 2007.

Cullen, David O'Donald, and Kyle Wilkison, eds. *The Texas Left: The Radical Roots of Lone Star Liberalism*. College Station: Texas A&M University Press, 2010.

Cunningham, Sean. *Cowboy Conservatism: Texas and the Rise of the Modern Right*. Lexington: University Press of Kentucky, 2010.

Dallek, Robert. *Flawed Giant: Lyndon Johnson and His Times, 1961–1973*. New York: Oxford University Press, 1998.

———. *Lone Star Rising: Lyndon Johnson and His Times, 1908–1960*. New York: Oxford University Press, 1991.

Daniel, Pete. *Breaking the Land: The Transformation of Cotton, Tobacco, and Rice Cultures Since 1880*. Urbana: University of Illinois Press, 1985.

———. *Lost Revolutions: The South in the 1950s*. Chapel Hill: University of North Carolina Press, 2000.

Davidson, Chandler. *Race and Class in Texas Politics*. Princeton: Princeton University Press, 1990.

Davis, Steven. *J. Frank Dobie: A Liberated Mind*. Austin: University of Texas Press, 2009.

———. *Land of the Permanent Wave: An Edwin "Bud" Shrake Reader*. Austin: University of Texas Press, 2008.

———. *Texas Literary Outlaws: Six Writers in the Sixties and Beyond*. Fort Worth: Texas Christian University Press, 2004.

Denisoff, R. Serge. *Waylon: A Biography*. Knoxville: University of Tennessee Press, 1983.

Denning, Michael. *The Cultural Front: The Laboring of American Culture in the Twentieth Century*. New York: Verso Press, 1997.

———. "'The Special American Conditions': Marxism and American Studies." *American Quarterly* 38:3 (1986): 356–380.

Dobbs, Ricky F. *Yellow Dogs and Republicans: Allan Shivers and Texas Two-Party Politics*. College Station: Texas A&M University Press, 2005.

Dobie, J. Frank. *Apache Gold and Yaqui Silver*. Boston: Little, Brown, 1939.

———. *The Ben Lilly Legend*. Boston: Little, Brown, 1950.

———. *Coronado's Children*. Austin: University of Texas Press, 1978 [1930].

———. *The Longhorns*. Boston: Little, Brown, 1941.

———. *On the Open Range*. Dallas: The Southwest Press, 1931.

———. *Rattlesnakes*. Boston: Little, Brown, 1965.

———. *Some Part of Myself*. Boston: Little, Brown, 1967.

———. *Tales of Old Time Texas*. Boston: Little, Brown, 1955.

———. *A Texan in England*. Boston: Little, Brown, 1945.

———. *Tongues of the Monte*. Garden City, NY: Doubleday, 1935.

Dobie, J. Frank, with John D. Young. *A Vaquero of the Brush Country*. Dallas: Southwest Press, 1929.

Doggett, Peter. *Are You Ready for the Country: Elvis, Dylan, Parsons, and the Roots of Country Rock*. New York: Penguin Books, 2001.

Dorman, Robert. *Revolt of the Provinces: The Regionalist Movement in America, 1920–1945*. Chapel Hill: University of North Carolina Press, 1993.

BIBLIOGRAPHY

Drummond, Paul. *Eye Mind: The Saga of Roky Erickson and the 13th Floor Elevators, the Pioneers of Psychedelic Sound*. Los Angeles: Process Media, 2007.

Dugger, Ronnie. *Our Invaded Universities: Form, Reform, and New Starts*. New York: Norton, 1974.

———. *The Politician: The Life and Times of Lyndon Johnson*. New York: Norton, 1982.

———, ed. *Three Men in Texas: Bedichek, Webb, and Dobie*. Austin: University of Texas Press, 1967.

Echols, Alice. *Daring to Be Bad: Radical Feminism in America, 1967–1975*. Minneapolis: University of Minnesota Press, 1990.

———. *Hot Stuff: Disco and the Remaking of American Culture*. New York: Norton, 2010.

———. *Scars of Sweet Paradise: The Life and Times of Janis Joplin*. New York: Owl Books, 1999.

———. *Shaky Ground: The Sixties and Its Aftershocks*. New York: Columbia University Press, 2002.

Eckhardt, Nadine. *Duchess of Palms: A Memoir*. Austin: University of Texas Press, 2009.

Endres, Clifford. *Austin City Limits*. Austin: University of Texas Press, 1987.

Engler, Robert. *The Politics of Oil: A Study of Private Power and Democratic Directions*. New York: Macmillan, 1961.

Evans, Sara. *Personal Politics: The Roots of Women's Liberation in the Civil Rights Movement and New Left*. New York: Vintage Press, 1980.

Farrell, Warren. *The Liberated Man: Beyond Masculinity*. New York: Random House, 1974.

Fasteau, Marc Feigen. *The Male Machine*. New York: McGraw-Hill, 1974.

Fehrenbach, T. R. *Comanches: The Destruction of a People*. New York: Knopf, 1974.

———. *Lone Star: A History of Texas and the Texans*. Boston: Da Capo Press, 2000 [1968].

Fiske, John. *Understanding Popular Culture*. Boston: Unwin Hyman, 1989.

Flippo, Chet. *Everybody Was Kung-Fu Dancing: Chronicles of the Lionized and the Notorious*. New York: St. Martin's Press, 1991.

Flores, Richard. *Remembering the Alamo: Memory, Modernity, and the Master Symbol*. Austin: University of Texas Press, 2002.

Foley, Neil. "Black, White, and Brown." *Journal of Southern History* 70:2 (2004): 343–350.

———. *The Quest for Equality: The Failed Promise of Black–Brown Solidarity*. Cambridge: Harvard University Press, 2010.

———. *The White Scourge: Mexicans, Blacks, and Poor Whites in Texas Cotton Culture*. Berkeley: University of California Press, 1997.

Fox, Aaron. *Real Country: Music and Language in Working-Class Culture*. Durham: Duke University Press, 2004.

Franklin, Jim. *Armadillo Comics*. San Francisco: Rip Off Press, 1971 [1969].

Frantz, Joe. *The Forty-Acre Follies*. Austin: Texas Monthly Press, 1983.

Frantz, Joe, and Julian Ernest Choate Jr. *The American Cowboy: The Myth and the Reality*. Norman: University of Oklahoma Press, 1955.

Fried, Richard. *Nightmare in Red: The McCarthy Era in Perspective*. New York: Oxford University Press, 1990.

Friedan, Betty. *The Feminine Mystique*. New York: Norton, 2001 [1963].

Frith, Simon, and Andrew Goodwin, eds. *On Record: Rock, Pop, and the Written Word*. New York: Routledge, 1990.

Frum, David. *How We Got Here: The '70s*. New York: Basic Books, 2000.

Fuermann, George. *Reluctant Empire: The Mind of Texas*. Garden City, NY: Doubleday, 1957.

García, Ignacio. *United We Win: The Rise and Fall of La Raza Unida Party*. Tucson: University of Arizona Press/MASRC, 1989.

García, Mario. *Mexican Americans: Leadership, Ideology, and Identity, 1930–1960*. New Haven: Yale University Press, 1991.

Gent, Peter. *North Dallas Forty*. New York: William Morrow, 1973.

———. *Texas Celebrity Turkey Trot*. New York: William Morrow, 1978.

Gerstle, Gary. *The Rise and Fall of the New Deal Order, 1930–1980*. Princeton: Princeton University Press, 1989.

Gitlin, Todd. *The Twilight of Common Dreams: Why America Is Wracked by Culture Wars*. New York: Metropolitan Books, 1995.

Glasrud, Bruce, and Gregg Andrews. "Confronting White Supremacy: The African American Left in Texas, 1874–1974." In *The Texas Left: The Radical Roots of Lone Star Liberalism*, ed. David O'Donald Cullen and Kyle Grant Wilkison, 157–190. College Station: Texas A&M University Press, 2010.

Glasrud, Bruce, and James Smallwood. *The African American Experience in Texas: An Anthology*. Lubbock: Texas Tech University Press, 2007.

Goetzmann, William H., and William N. Goetzmann. *The West of the Imagination*. 2nd ed. Norman: University of Oklahoma Press, 2009 [1986].

Goffman, Erving. *Gender Advertisements*. New York: Harper and Row, 1979.

Goldberg, Herb. *The Hazards of Being Male: Surviving the Myth of Masculine Privilege*. New York: Signet, 1976.

Goldstone, Dwonna. *Integrating the 40 Acres: The Fifty-Year Struggle for Racial Equality at the University of Texas*. Athens: University of Georgia Press, 2006.

González, John Moran. *Border Renaissance: The Texas Centennial and the Emergence of Mexican American Literature*. Austin: University of Texas Press, 2009.

Goodwyn, Frank. *Lone Star Land: 20th Century Texas in Perspective*. New York: Knopf, 1955.

Goodwyn, Lawrence. *Democratic Promise: The Populist Movement in America*. New York: Oxford University Press, 1976.

———. *The Populist Moment: A Short History of the Agrarian Revolt in America*. New York: Oxford University Press, 1978.

BIBLIOGRAPHY

———. *Texas Oil, American Dreams: A Study of the Texas Independent Producers and Royalty Owners Association*. Austin: Texas State Historical Association, 1996.
Gould, Lewis. *1968: An Election That Changed America*. Chicago: Ivan R. Dee, 1993.
Graff, Harvey. *The Dallas Myth: The Making and Unmaking of an American City*. Minneapolis: University of Minnesota Press, 2008.
Graham, Don. *Cowboys and Cadillacs: How Hollywood Looks at Texas*. Austin: Texas Monthly Press, 1983.
———. *Giant Country: Essays on Texas*. Fort Worth: Texas Christian University Press, 1998.
———. "J. Frank Dobie: A Reappraisal." *Southwestern Historical Quarterly* 92:2 (1988): 1–15.
———, ed. *Literary Austin*. Fort Worth: Texas Christian University Press, 2007.
———, ed. *Lone Star Literature: A Texas Anthology*. New York: Norton, 2003.
Gramsci, Antonio. *Selections from the Prison Notebooks*. Edited and translated by Quintin Hoare and Geoffrey Nowell Smith. New York: International Publishers, 1971.
Graves, John. *Goodbye to a River: A Narrative*. New York: Knopf, 1960.
Green, George Norris. *The Establishment in Texas Politics: The Primitive Years, 1938–1957*. Norman: University of Oklahoma Press, 1979.
Green, James. *Grass-Roots Socialism: Radical Movements in the Southwest, 1895–1943*. Baton Rouge: Louisiana State University Press, 1978.
Guralnick, Peter. *Lost Highway: Journeys and Arrivals of American Musicians*. Boston: Little, Brown, 1979.
Gutiérrez, José Angel. *A Gringo Manual on How to Handle Mexicans*. Crystal City, TX: Wintergarden Publishing, 1974.
———. *The Making of a Chicano Militant: Lessons from Cristal*. Madison: University of Wisconsin Press, 1999.
Gwynne, S. C. *Empire of the Summer Moon: Quanah Parker and the Rise and Fall of the Comanches, the Most Powerful Indian Tribe in American History*. New York: Scribner, 2011.
Haley, J. Evetts. *Charles Goodnight: Cowman and Plainsmen*. Boston: Houghton Mifflin, 1936.
———. *A Texan Looks at Lyndon: A Study in Illegitimate Power*. Canyon, TX: Palo Duro Press, 1964.
Haley, James L. *Passionate Nation: The Epic History of Texas*. New York: Free Press, 2006.
Hall, Stuart, and Tony Jefferson, eds. *Resistance Through Rituals: Youth Subcultures in Post-War Britain*. London: Hutchinson, 1976.
Hamilton, Shane. *Trucking Country: The Road to America's Wal-Mart Economy*. Princeton: Princeton University Press, 2008.
Hämäläinen, Pekka. *The Comanche Empire*. New Haven: Yale University Press, 2008.
Hardt, Michael, and Antonio Negri. *Empire*. Cambridge: Harvard University Press, 2000.

Hartigan, John, Jr. *Odd Tribes: Toward a Cultural Analysis of White People*. Durham: Duke University Press, 2005.

———. *Racial Situations: Class Predicaments of Whiteness in Detroit*. Princeton: Princeton University Press, 1999.

———. "Unpopular Culture: The Case of 'White Trash.'" *Cultural Studies* 11:2 (1997): 316–343.

Hartman, Gary. *The History of Texas Music*. College Station: Texas A&M University Press, 2008.

Harvey, David. *The Condition of Postmodernity: An Enquiry into the Origins of Cultural Change*. Oxford: Blackwell, 1990.

Hebdige, Dick. *Subculture: The Meaning of Style*. New York: Routledge, 1979.

Heck, Bryan, and Howard Hilliard. *Celebrated Luckenbach Texas: Standard of the World*. Houston: D. Armstrong, 1974.

Hegeman, Susan. *Patterns for America: Modernism and the Concept of Culture*. Princeton: Princeton University Press, 1999.

Herlihy, James Leo. *Midnight Cowboy*. New York: Simon and Schuster, 1965.

Hill, Patricia Evridge. *Dallas: The Making of a Modern City*. Austin: University of Texas Press, 1996.

Hillis, Craig. *Texas Trilogy: Life in a Small Texas Town*. Austin: University of Texas Press, 2002.

Hine, Thomas. *The Great Funk: Falling Apart and Coming Together (on a Shag Rug) in the Seventies*. New York: Farrar, Straus and Giroux, 2007.

Hinton, Diana Davids, and Roger M. Olien. *Oil in Texas: The Gusher Age, 1895–1945*. Austin: University of Texas Press, 2002.

Hodgdon, Timothy. *Manhood in the Age of Aquarius: Masculinity in Two Countercultural Communities*. New York: Columbia University Press, 2008.

Hoeveler, J. David, Jr. *The Postmodernist Turn: American Thought and Culture in the 1970s*. New York: Rowman and Littlefield, 2004.

Hoff, Joan. *Nixon Reconsidered*. New York: Basic Books, 1994.

Hofstadter, Richard. *The Age of Reform: From Bryan to FDR*. New York: Vintage Books, 1956.

Holland, Richard, ed. *The Texas Book: Profiles, History, and Reminiscences of the University*. Austin: University of Texas Press, 2006.

Houston, Sam. *The Raven*. Indianapolis: Bobbs-Merrill Company, 1929.

Hunt, H. L. *Alpaca*. Dallas: H. L. Hunt Press, 1960.

———. *Alpaca Revisited*. Dallas: H. L. Hunt Products, 1967.

Hutson, Jan. *The True Story of the Best Little Whorehouse in Texas*. New York: A. S. Barnes, 1982.

Inness, Sherrie, ed. *Disco Divas: Women, Gender, and Popular Culture in the 1970s*. Philadelphia: University of Pennsylvania Press, 2003.

Jacobson, Matthew Frye. *Roots Too: White Ethnic Revival in Post–Civil Rights America*. Cambridge: Harvard University Press, 2006.

BIBLIOGRAPHY

Jamail, Joe. *Lawyer: My Trials and Jubilations*. Austin: Eakin Press, 2003.
James, Marquis. *The Raven: A Biography of Sam Houston*. Garden City, NY: Blue Ribbon Books, 1929.
Jameson, Frederic. *Postmodernism; or, The Cultural Logic of Late Capitalism*. Durham: Duke University Press, 1991.
Janes, Daryl, ed. *No Apologies: Texas Radicals Celebrate the '60s*. Austin: Eakin Press, 1992.
Jasinski, Laurie. "A. O. Babel." In *Handbook of Texas Music*, ed. Laurie Jasinski, 32–33. 2nd rev. ed. Denton: Texas State Historical Association, 2012.
Jenkins, Dan. *Semi-Tough*. New York: Atheneum, 1972.
Jenkins, Philip. *Decade of Nightmares: The End of the Sixties and the Making of Eighties America*. New York: Oxford University Press, 2006.
Jennings, Waylon, with Lenny Kaye. *Waylon: An Autobiography*. New York: Warner Books, 1996.
Jensen, Joli. *The Nashville Sound: Authenticity, Commercialization, and Country Music*. Nashville: Vanderbilt University Press, 1998.
Johnson, Benjamin Heber. *Revolution in Texas: How a Forgotten Rebellion and Its Bloody Suppression Turned Mexicans into Americans*. New Haven: Yale University Press, 2003.
Johnson, Susan Lee. *Roaring Camp: The Social World of the California Gold Rush*. New York: Norton, 2000.
Jordan, Terry. *North American Cattle Ranching Frontiers: Origins, Diffusion, and Differentiation*. Albuquerque: University of New Mexico Press, 1993.
Kalman, Laura. *Right Star Rising: A New Politics, 1974–1980*. New York: Norton, 2010.
Katz, Elihu, and Tamar Liebes. *The Export of Meaning: Cross Cultural Readings of Dallas*. New York: Oxford University Press, 1990.
Keith, Gary. *Eckhardt: There Once Was a Congressman from Texas*. Austin: University of Texas Press, 2007.
Kelley, Robin D. G. *Race Rebels: Culture, Politics, and the Black Working Class*. New York: Free Press, 1994.
———. *Yo' Mama's Disfunktional! Fighting the Culture Wars in Urban America*. Boston: Beacon Press, 1997.
Key, V. O., Jr. *Southern Politics in State and Nation*. New York: Knopf, 1949.
Killen, Andreas. *1973 Nervous Breakdown: Watergate, Warhol, and the Birth of Post-Sixties America*. New York: Bloomsbury, 2006.
King, Larry L. *Confessions of a White Racist*. New York: Viking Press, 1971.
———. *In Search of Willie Morris: The Mercurial Life of a Legendary Writer and Editor*. New York: Public Affairs, 2006.
———. *The Old Man and Lesser Mortals*. New York: Viking Press, 1974.
———. *. . . And Other Dirty Stories*. New York: World Publishing, 1968.
———. *Of Outlaws, Con Men, Whores, Politicians, and Other Artists*. New York: Viking Press, 1980.

Kissinger, Henry. *Years of Upheaval*. Boston: Little, Brown, 1982.

Knaggs, John. *Two-Party Texas: The John Tower Era, 1961–1984*. Austin: Eakin Press, 1986.

Kruse, Kevin. *White Flight: Atlanta and the Making of Modern Conservatism*. Princeton: Princeton University Press, 2005.

La Chapelle, Peter. *Proud to Be an Okie: Cultural Politics, Country Music, and Migration to Southern California*. Berkeley: University of California Press, 2007.

Lasch, Christopher. *The Culture of Narcissism: American Life in an Age of Diminishing Expectations*. New York: Norton, 1978.

Lassiter, Matthew. *The Silent Majority: Suburban Politics in the Sunbelt South*. Princeton: Princeton University Press, 2006.

Lassiter, Matthew, and Joseph Crespino, eds. *The Myth of Southern Exceptionalism*. New York: Oxford University Press, 2010.

Lassiter, Matthew, and Andrew Lewis, eds. *The Moderates' Dilemma: Massive Resistance to School Desegregation in Virginia*. Charlottesville: University Press of Virginia, 1998.

Lasswell, Mary. *I'll Take Texas*. Boston: Houghton Mifflin, 1958.

Lauchlan, Angus. "The Texas Liberal Press and the Image of White Texas Masculinity." *Southwestern Historical Quarterly* 110:4 (2007): 486–512.

Lavergne, Gary. *Before Brown: Heman Marion Sweatt, Thurgood Marshall, and the Long Road to Justice*. Austin: University of Texas Press, 2010.

Lawrence, Tim. *Love Saves the Day: A History of American Dance Music Culture, 1970–1979*. Durham: Duke University Press, 2003.

Lea, Tom. *The Brave Bulls*. Boston: Little, Brown, 1949.

Levine, Suzanne Braun, and Mary Thom. *Bella Abzug: An Oral History*. New York: Farrar, Straus and Giroux, 2007.

Limerick, Patricia Nelson. *Legacy of Conquest: The Unbroken Past of the American West*. New York: Norton, 1987.

Limón, José. *American Encounters: Greater Mexico, the United States, and the Erotics of Culture*. Boston: Beacon Press, 1998.

———. *Dancing with the Devil: Society and Cultural Poetics in Mexican–American South Texas*. Madison: University of Wisconsin Press, 1994.

Lind, Michael. *Made in Texas: George W. Bush and the Southern Takeover of American Politics*. New York: Basic Books, 2003.

Lipsitz, George. *Rainbow at Midnight: Labor and Culture in the 1940s*. Urbana: University of Illinois Press, 1994.

———. *Time Passages: Collective Memory and American Popular Culture*. Minneapolis: University of Minnesota Press, 1990.

Lock, Cory. "Counterculture Cowboys: Progressive Texas Country of the 1970s and 1980s." *Journal of Texas Music History* 3:1 (2003) 14–23.

Lomax, Alan. *The Land Where the Blues Began*. New York: Pantheon Books, 1993.

Lomax, John. *Adventures of a Ballad Hunter*. New York: Macmillan, 1947.

———. *Cowboy Songs and Other Frontier Ballads*. New York: Macmillan, 1910.

BIBLIOGRAPHY

Long, Joshua. *Weird City: Sense of Place and Creative Resistance in Austin, Texas*. Austin: University of Texas Press, 2010.

Lynd, Robert S., and Helen Merrell Lynd. *Middletown: A Study in Modern American Culture*. New York: Harcourt, Brace, 1929.

Macor, Allison. *Chainsaws, Slackers, and Spy Kids: Thirty Years of Filmmaking in Austin, Texas*. Austin: University of Texas Press, 2010.

Mailer, Norman. *Why Are We in Vietnam?* New York: G. P. Putnam's Sons, 1967.

Malone, Bill, and Jocelyn Neal. *Country Music, USA*. 3rd rev. ed. Austin: University of Texas Press, 2010 [1968].

Marx, Leo. *The Machine in the Garden: Technology and the Pastoral Ideal in America*. New York: Oxford University Press, 1964.

Matusow, Allen. *The Unraveling of America: A History of Liberalism in the 1960s*. New York: Harper Torchbooks, 1984.

Maxwell, Angie, and Todd Shields, eds. *Unlocking V. O. Key Jr.: "Southern Politics" for the Twenty-First Century*. Fayetteville: University of Arkansas Press, 2011.

McArthur, Judith. *Creating the New Woman: The Rise of Southern Women's Progressive Culture in Texas, 1893–1918*. Urbana: University of Illinois Press, 1998.

McArthur, Judith, and Harold Smith. *Minnie Fisher Cunningham: A Suffragist's Life in Politics*. New York: Oxford University Press, 2003.

McCaslin, Richard. *At the Heart of Texas: One Hundred Years of the Texas State Historical Association, 1897–1997*. Austin: Texas State Historical Association, 2007.

McComb, David. *Houston: A History*. Austin: University of Texas Press, 1981 [1969].

McEnteer, James. *Deep in the Heart: The Texas Tendency in American Politics*. Westport, CT: Praeger, 2004.

McLean, Duncan. *Lone Star Swing*. New York: Norton, 1997.

McMurtry, Larry. *Horseman, Pass By*. New York: Harper and Brothers, 1961.

———. *In a Narrow Grave: Essays on Texas*. New York: Simon and Schuster, 1996 [1968].

———. *The Last Picture Show*. New York: Dial Press, 1966.

McNeely, Dave. *Bob Bullock: God Bless Texas*. Austin: University of Texas Press, 2008.

McRobbie, Angela. "Shut Up and Dance." *Cultural Studies* 7:3 (1993): 406–426.

Meinig, D. W. *Imperial Texas: An Interpretive Essay in Cultural Geography*. Austin: University of Texas Press, 1969.

Mellard, Jason. "Regional Hybridity in Texas Music: The Case of the Texas Tornados." *Text/Practice/Performance* 5 (2003): 107–132.

Merrill, Karen. "Texas Metropole: Oil, the American West, and U.S. Power in the Postwar Years." *Journal of American History* 99:1 (2012): 197–207.

Miller, Char, ed. *Fifty Years of the Texas Observer*. San Antonio: Trinity University Press, 2004.

Miller, Karl Hagstrom. *Segregating Sound: Inventing Folk and Pop Music in the Age of Jim Crow*. Durham: Duke University Press, 2010.

———. "That's Right, You're Not from Texas: Exploring Some Outside Influences on Texas Music." *Journal of Texas Music History* 1:2 (2001): 6–16.

Miller, Stephen. *The Seventies Now: Culture as Surveillance*. Durham: Duke University Press, 1999.

Milner, Jay. *Confessions of a Maddog: A Romp Through the High-Flying Texas Music and Literary Era of the Fifties to the Seventies*. Denton: University of North Texas Press, 1998.

Minutaglio, Bill. *In Search of the Blues: A Journey to the Soul of Black Texas*. Austin: University of Texas Press, 2010.

Montejano, David. *Anglos and Mexicans in the Making of Texas, 1836–1986*. Austin: University of Texas Press, 1987.

———. *Quixote's Soldiers: A Local History of the Chicano Movement, 1966–1981*. Austin: University of Texas Press, 2010.

Moore, Jacqueline. *Cow Boys and Cattle Men: Class and Masculinities on the Texas Frontier, 1865–1900*. New York: New York University Press, 2009.

Moser, Bob. *Blue Dixie: Awakening the South's Democratic Majority*. New York: Times Books, 2008.

Navarro, Armando. *The Cristal Experiment: A Chicano Struggle for Community Control*. Madison: University of Wisconsin Press, 1998.

———. *La Raza Unida Party: A Chicano Challenge to the U.S. Two-Party Dictatorship*. Philadelphia: Temple University Press, 2000.

———. *Mexican American Youth Organization: Avant-Garde of the Chicano Movement in Texas*. Austin: University of Texas Press, 1995.

Nelson, Willie, with Bud Shrake. *Willie: An Autobiography*. New York: Simon and Schuster, 1988.

Nevin, David. *The Texans: What They Are—and Why*. New York: Bonanza Books, 1968.

Novak, Michael. *The Rise of the Unmeltable Ethnics: Politics and Culture in the Seventies*. New York: Macmillan, 1971.

Novick, Peter. *That Noble Dream: The "Objectivity Question" and the American Historical Profession*. New York: Cambridge University Press, 1988.

Oglesby, Carl. *The Yankee and Cowboy War: Conspiracies from Dallas to Watergate*. Mission, KS: Sheed Andrews and McMeel, 1976.

Orum, Anthony. *Power, Money, and the People: The Making of Modern Austin*. Austin: Texas Monthly Press, 1987.

Owens, William, ed. *Three Friends: Roy Bedichek, J. Frank Dobie, Walter Prescott Webb*. Austin: University of Texas Press, 1967.

Paredes, Américo. *Between Two Worlds*. Houston: Arte Público Press, 1991.

———. *George Washington Gómez: A Mexicotexan Novel*. Houston: Arte Público Press, 1990.

———. "The United States, Mexico, and Machismo." Translated by Marcy Steen. *Journal of the Folklore Institute* 8:1 (1971): 17–37.

———. *With His Pistol in His Hand: A Border Ballad and Its Hero*. Austin: University of Texas Press, 1958.

Parmet, Herbert. *George Bush: The Life of a Lone Star Yankee.* Piscataway, NJ: Transaction, 2000.

Pascoe, Peggy. *Relations of Rescue: The Search for Female Moral Authority in the American West, 1874–1939.* New York: Oxford University Press, 1990.

Patoski, Joe Nick. *The Dallas Cowboys: The Outrageous History of the Biggest, Loudest, Most Hated, Best Loved Football Team in America.* New York: Little, Brown, 2012.

———. *Willie Nelson: An Epic Life.* New York: Little, Brown, 2008.

Patoski, Joe Nick, with Bill Crawford. *Stevie Ray Vaughan: Caught in the Crossfire.* New York: Little, Brown, 1993.

Patterson, Becky Crouch. *Hondo: My Father.* Austin: Shoal Creek Press, 1979.

Patterson, James T. *Brown v. Board of Education: A Civil Rights Milestone and Its Troubled Legacy.* New York: Oxford University Press, 2001.

Pecknold, Diane. *Selling Sound: The Rise of the Country Music Industry.* Durham: Duke University Press, 2007.

Pells, Richard. *Radical Visions and American Dreams: Culture and Social Thought in the Depression Years.* Urbana: University of Illinois Press, 1998 [1973].

Peña, Manuel. *Música Tejana.* College Station: Texas A&M Press, 1999.

Perlstein, Rick. *Nixonland: The Rise of a President and the Fracturing of America.* New York: Scribner, 2008.

Perry, George Sessions. *Hold Autumn in Your Hand.* Albuquerque: University of New Mexico Press, 1999 [1941].

———. *Texas: A World in Itself.* New York: McGraw-Hill, 1975 [1942].

Peterson, Richard. *Creating Country Music: Manufacturing Authenticity.* Chicago: University of Chicago Press, 1997.

Phillips, Kevin. *The Emerging Republican Majority.* New Rochelle, NY: Arlington House, 1969.

Phillips, Michael. *White Metropolis: Race, Ethnicity, and Religion in Dallas, 1841–2001.* Austin: University of Texas Press, 2006.

Porterfield, Bill. *LBJ Country: The Country That Shaped a President.* Garden City, NY: Doubleday, 1965.

Postel, Charles. *The Populist Vision.* New York: Oxford University Press, 2007.

Potter, David. *People of Plenty: Economic Abundance and the American Character.* Chicago: University of Chicago Press, 1954.

Pycior, Julie Leininger. *LBJ and Mexican Americans: The Paradox of Power.* Austin: University of Texas Press, 1997.

Raat, William Dirk. *Revoltosos: Mexico's Rebels in the United States, 1903–1923.* College Station: Texas A&M University Press, 1981.

Ragsdale, Kenneth. *Centennial '36: The Year America Discovered Texas.* College Station: Texas A&M University Press, 1987.

Reich, Charles. *The Greening of America.* New York: Random House, 1970.

Reid, Jan. *The Improbable Rise of Redneck Rock.* Austin: Heidelberg Press, 1974.

———. *The Improbable Rise of Redneck Rock*. New ed. Austin: University of Texas Press, 2004.

———. *Let the People In: The Life and Times of Ann Richards*. Austin: University of Texas Press, 2012.

Reid, Jan, with Shawn Sahm. *Texas Tornado: The Times and Music of Doug Sahm*. Austin: University of Texas Press, 2010.

Reid, Jan, and W. K. Stratton, eds. *Splendor in the Short Grass: The Grover Lewis Reader*. Austin: University of Texas Press, 2005.

Rendon, Armando. *Chicano Manifesto: The History and Aspirations of the Second Largest Minority in America*. New York: Collier Books, 1971.

Richards, Ann. *Straight from the Heart: My Life in Politics and Other Places*. New York: Simon and Schuster, 1989.

Richards, David. *Once upon a Time in Texas: A Liberal in the Lone Star State*. Austin: University of Texas Press, 2002.

Rossinow, Doug. *The Politics of Authenticity: Liberalism, Christianity, and the New Left in America*. New York: Columbia University Press, 1998.

Roszak, Theodore. *The Making of a Counter Culture: Reflections on the Technocratic Society and Its Youthful Opposition*. Garden City, NY: Anchor Books, 1969.

Royal, Darrell K., with John Wheat. *Coach Royal: Conversations with a Texas Football Legend*. Austin: University of Texas Press, 2005.

Saldívar, Ramón. *The Borderlands of Culture: Américo Paredes and the Transnational Imaginary*. Durham: Duke University Press, 2006.

Sale, Kirkpatrick. *Power Shift: The Rise of the Southern Rim and Its Challenge to the Eastern Establishment*. New York: Random House, 1975.

———. *SDS*. New York: Vintage, 1973.

Sandbrook, Dominic. *Mad as Hell: The Crisis of the 1970s and the Rise of the Populist Right*. New York: Knopf, 2011.

Sanders, Randy. *Mighty Peculiar Elections: The New South Gubernatorial Campaigns of 1970 and the Changing Politics of Race*. Baton Rouge: Louisiana State University Press, 2002.

Scammon, Richard, and Ben Wattenberg. *The Real Majority*. New York: Coward-McCann, 1970.

Schell, Jonathan. *The Time of Illusion: An Historical and Reflective Account of the Nixon Era*. New York: Vintage Books, 1976.

Schulman, Bruce. *The Seventies: The Great Shift in American Culture, Society, and Politics*. Cambridge, MA: Da Capo Press, 2001.

Schulman, Bruce, and Julian Zelizer, eds. *Rightward Bound: Making America Conservative in the 1970s*. Cambridge: Harvard University Press, 2008.

Sears, James. *Rebels, Rubyfruit, and Rhinestones: Queering Space in the Stonewall South*. New Brunswick: Rutgers University Press, 2001.

Shank, Barry. *Dissonant Identities: The Rock 'n' Roll Scene in Austin, Texas*. Hanover: Wesleyan University Press, 1994.

Shapiro, Peter. *Turn the Beat Around: The Secret History of Disco*. New York: Faber and Faber, 2005.

Sharpless, Rebecca. *Fertile Ground, Narrow Choices: Women in Texas Cotton Culture, 1900–1940*. Chapel Hill: University of North Carolina Press, 1999.

Shaw, Gary. *Meat on the Hoof: The Hidden World of Texas Football*. New York: St. Martin's Press, 1972.

Shrake, Edwin. *Blessed McGill*. Garden City, NY: Doubleday, 1968.

———. *The Borderland*. New York: Hyperion, 2000.

———. *But Not for Love*. Garden City, NY: Doubleday, 1964.

———. *Custer's Brother's Horse*. Houston: John M. Hardy Publishing, 2007.

———. *Peter Arbiter*. Austin: Encino Press, 1973.

———. *Strange Peaches*. Austin: Texas Monthly Press, 1987 [1972].

Simpson, Kim. *Early '70s Radio: The American Format Revolution*. New York: Continuum, 2011.

Siringo, Charles. *A Texas Cowboy; or, Fifteen Years on the Hurricane Deck of a Spanish Pony*. New York: Penguin Books, 2000 [1885].

Sitkoff, Harvard. *The Struggle for Black Equality*. New York: Hill and Wang, 1993 [1981].

Slotkin, Richard. *The Fatal Environment*. New York: Atheneum Press, 1992.

———. *Gunfighter Nation*. New York: Atheneum Press, 1985.

———. *Regeneration Through Violence*. Middletown: Wesleyan University Press, 1973.

Smith, Henry Nash. *Virgin Land: The American West as Symbol and Myth*. Cambridge: Harvard University Press, 1978 [1950].

Smithwick, Noah, with Nanna Smithwick Donaldson. *The Evolution of a State or Recollections of Old Texas Days*. Austin: University of Texas Press, 1983 [1900].

Sokol, Jason. *There Goes My Everything: White Southerners in the Age of Civil Rights*. New York: Vintage Press, 2006.

Spitzer, Nicholas. "'Bob Wills Is Still the King': Romantic Regionalism and Convergent Culture in Central Texas." *John Edwards Memorial Foundation Quarterly* 11:40 (1975): 191–196.

Stimeling, Travis. *Cosmic Cowboys and New Hicks: The Countercultural Sounds of Austin's Progressive Country Music Scene*. New York: Oxford University Press, 2011.

———. "Jerry Jeff Walker, Live Recordings, and the Authenticity of Progressive Country Music." *Journal of Texas Music History* 8 (2008): 20–33.

Sugrue, Thomas. *The Origins of the Urban Crisis: Race and Inequality in Postwar Detroit*. Princeton: Princeton University Press, 1996.

Swearingen, William Scott. *Environmental City: People, Place, Politics, and the Meaning of Modern Austin*. Austin: University of Texas Press, 2010.

Thompson, E. P. Review of Raymond Williams, "The Long Revolution (Part 1)." *New Left Review* 1:9 (1961): 24–33.

Thompson, Hunter S. *Fear and Loathing on the Campaign Trail '72*. New York: Fawcett Popular Library, 1973.

———. *The Hell's Angels: A Strange and Terrible Saga*. New York: Random House, 1967.
Thornton, Sarah, and Ken Gelder, eds. *The Subcultures Reader*. New York: Routledge, 1997.
Tichi, Cecelia. *High Lonesome: The American Culture of Country Music*. Chapel Hill: University of North Carolina Press, 1994.
———, ed. *Reading Country Music: Steel Guitars, Opry Stars, and Honky-Tonk Bars*. Durham: Duke University Press, 1998.
Tinkle, Lon. *An American Original: The Life of J. Frank Dobie*. Austin: University of Texas Press, 1978.
Tolleson-Rinehart, Sue, and Jeanie R. Stanley. *Claytie and the Lady: Ann Richards, Gender, and Politics in Texas*. Austin: University of Texas Press, 1994.
Tönnies, Ferdinand. *Community and Civil Society*. New York: Cambridge University Press, 2001 [1887].
Townsend, Charles. *San Antonio Rose: The Life and Music of Bob Wills*. Urbana: University of Illinois Press, 1976.
Turley, Alan. *Music in the City: A History of Austin Music*. Cedar Park, TX: Duckling Press, 2000.
Twelve Southerners. *I'll Take My Stand: The South and the Agrarian Tradition*. Baton Rouge: Louisiana State University, 2006 [1930].
Tyson, Timothy. *Radio Free Dixie: Robert F. Williams and the Roots of Black Power*. Chapel Hill: University of North Carolina Press, 1999.
Von Eschen, Penny. *Race Against Empire: Black Americans and Anticolonialism, 1937–1957*. Ithaca: Cornell University Press, 1997.
Wade, Bob, with Keith and Kent Zimmerman. *Daddy-O: Iguana Heads and Texas Tales*. New York: St. Martin's Press, 1995.
Waldrep, Shelton, ed. *The Seventies: The Age of Glitter in Popular Culture*. New York: Routledge, 1999.
Walker, Jerry Jeff. *Gypsy Songman*. Emeryville, CA: Woodford Press, 1999.
Watts, Trent, ed. *White Masculinity in the Recent South*. Baton Rouge: Louisiana University Press, 2008.
Webb, Walter Prescott. *Divided We Stand: The Crisis of a Frontierless Democracy*. Austin: Acorn Press, 1944 [1937].
———. *The Great Frontier*. Boston: Houghton Mifflin, 1951.
———. *The Great Plains*. Boston: Houghton Mifflin, 1931.
———. *The Texas Rangers: A Century of Frontier Defense*. Boston: Houghton Mifflin, 1935.
White, Richard. *"It's Your Misfortune and None of My Own": A History of the American West*. Norman: University of Oklahoma Press, 1991.
Wilentz, Sean. *The Age of Reagan: A History, 1974–2008*. New York: Harper, 2008.
Wilkison, Kyle G. *Yeomen, Sharecroppers, and Socialists: Plain Folk Protest in Texas, 1870–1914*. College Station: Texas A&M University Press, 2008.
Williams, Raymond. *The Country and the City*. New York: Oxford University Press, 1973.

BIBLIOGRAPHY

———. *Marxism and Literature*. New York: Oxford University Press, 1977.

Williamson, Joel. *A Rage for Order: Black–White Relations in the American South Since Emancipation*. New York: Oxford University Press, 1986.

Wilson, Burton, with Jack Ortman. *The Austin Music Scene Through the Lens of Burton Wilson, 1965–1994*. Austin: Eakin Press, 2001.

Wolfe, Tom. *The Electric Kool-Aid Acid Test*. New York: Farrar, Straus and Giroux, 1968.

Woodward, C. Vann. *Origins of the New South, 1877–1913*. Baton Rouge: Louisiana State University Press, 1951.

Zamora, Emilio. *The World of the Mexican Worker in Texas*. College Station: Texas A&M University Press, 1995.

Zaretsky, Natasha. *No Direction Home: The American Family and the Fear of National Decline, 1968–1980*. Chapel Hill: University of North Carolina Press, 2007.

Unpublished Manuscripts

Wilson, Edwin Osbourne. "Armadillo World Headquarters: A Good Time in Austin, Texas." 2003. Author's collection.

Theses and Dissertations

Hillis, Craig. "The Austin Music Scene in the 1970s: Songs and Songwriters." PhD diss., University of Texas at Austin, 2011.

Lock, Julia Corinne. "Waltz Across Texas: Literary and Cinematic Representations of Texas Country Music and Dance Culture." PhD diss., University of Texas at Austin, 2003.

Maxwell, Angela. "A Heritage of Inferiority: Public Criticism and the American South." PhD diss., University of Texas at Austin, 2008.

McNutt, James Charles. "Beyond Regionalism: Texas Folklorists and the Emergence of a Post-Regional Consciousness." PhD diss., University of Texas at Austin, 1985.

Menconi, David Lawrence. "Music, Media, and the Metropolis: The Case of Austin's Armadillo World Headquarters." MA thesis, University of Texas at Austin, 1985.

Olan, Susan Torian. "*The Rag*: A Study in Underground Journalism." MA thesis, University of Texas at Austin, 1981.

Ribb, Richard. "José Tomás Canales and the Texas Rangers: Myth, Identity, and Power in South Texas, 1900–1920." PhD diss., University of Texas at Austin, 2001.

Interviews

Davis, Sonny Carl, conducted by author, Austin, Texas, July 20, 2012.

Hatch, Ray, conducted by author, Austin, Texas, May 21, 2010.

Hillis, Craig, conducted by author, Austin, Texas, July 24, 2008.

Inmon, John, conducted by Aaron Brown with author, Austin, Texas, September 8, 2008.

Livingston, Bob, conducted by Aaron Brown with author, Austin, Texas, September 10, 2008.
Long, Emma, conducted by Eddie Wilson with author, Austin, Texas, April 28, 2010.
Mechling, Leea, conducted by author, Austin, Texas, August 15, 2007.
Nunn, Gary P., conducted by Aaron Brown with author, Austin, Texas, August 26, 2008.
Reid, Jan, conducted by Aaron Brown with author, Austin, Texas, August 27, 2008.
Royal, Mack, conducted by author, Austin, Texas, October 14, 2010.
St. John, Powell, conducted by author, Austin, Texas, September 11, 2008.
Wade, Bob, conducted by author, Austin, Texas, July 30, 2008, and various other dates.
Wilson, Eddie, conducted by author, Austin, Texas, September 11, 2008, and various other dates.

Periodicals

Armadillo Comics
Atlantic Monthly
Austin American-Statesman
Austin Sun
Daily Texan
Dallas News
Harper's
Houston Chronicle
Houston Post
New York
New Yorker
New York Times
Playboy
The Rag (Austin)
Rolling Stone
Sports Illustrated
Texas Monthly
Texas Observer
Time
Washington Post

Selected Albums

Allen, Terry. *Lubbock (on Everything)*. Fate, 1979.
The Band. *Music from Big Pink*. Capitol, 1968.
The Beau Brummels. *Bradley's Barn*. Warner Bros., 1968.
Buffalo Springfield. *Last Time Around*. Atco, 1968.

BIBLIOGRAPHY

The Byrds. *Sweetheart of the Rodeo*. Columbia, 1968.
Callahan, Bill. *Apocalypse*. Drag City Records, 2011.
Coe, David Allan. *Longhaired Redneck*. Columbia, 1976.
———. *Penitentiary Blues*. Plantation, 1969.
Colter, Jessi, Tompall Glaser, Waylon Jennings, and Willie Nelson. *Wanted! The Outlaws*. RCA, 1976.
Commander Cody and His Lost Planet Airmen. *Live from Deep in the Heart of Texas*. MCA, 1974.
Daniels, Charlie. *Fire on the Mountain*. Epic, 1975.
Dylan, Bob. *John Wesley Harding*. Columbia, 1967.
———. *Nashville Skyline*. Columbia, 1969.
Friedman, Kinky. *Kinky Friedman*. ABC, 1974.
———. *Sold American*. Vanguard, 1973.
Jennings, Waylon. *Folk-Country*. RCA Victor, 1966.
———. *Honky Tonk Heroes*. RCA Victor, 1973.
———. *I've Always Been Crazy*. RCA, 1978.
———. *Ladies Love Outlaws*. RCA, 1972.
———. *Waylon Live*. RCA, 1976.
Joplin, Janis. *I Got Dem Ol' Kozmic Blues Again Mama!* Columbia, 1969.
King, Freddie. *Larger Than Life*. RSO, 1975.
———. *Texas Cannonball*. Shelter, 1972.
Murphey, Michael. *Cosmic Cowboy Souvenir*. A&M, 1973.
Nelson, Willie. *Red-Headed Stranger*. Columbia, 1975.
———. *Shotgun Willie*. Atlantic, 1973.
———. *Yesterday's Wine*. RCA, 1971.
Newman, Randy. *Good Old Boys*. Reprise, 1974.
New Riders of the Purple Sage. *Armadillo World Headquarters, Austin, TX, 6/13/75*. Kufala, 2005.
Sahm, Doug, and Band. *Doug Sahm and Band*. Atlantic, 1973.
Shiva's Headband. *Take Me to the Mountains*. Capitol, 1970.
Sir Doug and the Texas Tornados. *Texas Rock for Country Rollers*. Dot, 1976.
Sir Douglas Quintet. *Mendocino*. Smash, 1969.
———. *The Return of Doug Saldaña*. Phillips, 1971.
Stevenson, B. W. *My Maria*. RCA Victor, 1973.
Various artists. *Urban Cowboy Soundtrack*. Asylum, 1980.
Walker, Jerry Jeff, and the Lost Gonzo Band. *Viva Terlingua*. MCA, 1973.
Wills, Bob, and His Texas Playboys. *For the Last Time*. United Artists, 1974.
Wills, Bob/Asleep at the Wheel. *Fathers and Sons*. Epic, 1975.
Zappa, Frank, and Captain Beefheart. *Bongo Fury*. Discreet, 1975.

Index

Page numbers in *italics* refer to images.

Abrahams, Roger, 60, 103
Adventures with a Texas Naturalist (Bedichek), 37, 39, 54
African Americans, 3, 13, 17, 22, 24, 46–48, 51–54, 89, 104, 105, 109, 110, 131, 136, 148, 152, 155, 219n99
agriculture, 24, 26, 27, 32, 47, 102, 103, 109, 131
Alexander, Stan, 62
Alger, Bruce, 152, 166
Ali, Muhammad, 6
Allen, Sterling, 205–207
Allred, James, 43, 232n77
"Alma pocha" (Paredes), 46
Alpaca (Hunt), 141, 145–147
Alrich, Hank, 86
"America," 205–207
American GI Forum, 52, 219n102
American Studies, 11, 26, 214n23
And Other Neighborly Names (Abrahams and Bauman), 103, 104
Anglo-Texan masculinity, 4–6, 9, 21, 40, 45–47, 54, 82, 90, 91, 126, 127–139, 148, 157, 199, 208. *See also* cowboys; gender
Antone's, 67, 85
"Armadillo Homesick Blues," 63
Armadillo World Headquarters, 1, 2, 4, 5, 8, 65–79, 81, 85, 86, 92, 94, 96, 98, 101, 119, 137, 151, 158, 163–166, 172, 175, 178, 191, 196, 204, 222n50, 235n9
armadillos, 8, 63, 67, 68, *69*, 173, 174, 196, 197
Armey, Dick, 201, 203
Armstrong, Anne, 160, 162, 233n92
Armstrong, Bob, 158, 162
Asleep at the Wheel, 56, 80, 81
assimilation, 48, 51, 104, 111, 210n7
Association of Country Entertainers, 119
Atkins, Chet, 72, 120, 124, 227n90
Atlantic Monthly, 1, 163, 210n15
Atlantic Records, 56, 85
Austin, 1, 2, 4, 5, 8, 15–17, 26, 27, 33, 44, 51, 55–92, 94–105, 108–121, 137–139, 148, 150, 151, 163–166, 169, 172, 183, 188, 190–192, 196, 197, 205, 206

Austin Ballet Theater, 68, 69
Austin City Council, 164, 165, 169
Austin City Limits (television show), 58, 196
Austin Opera House (Austin Opry), 67, 75, 79, 96, 119, 221n40
Austin Sun, 89, 97, 99, 164, 165
authenticity, 15, 16, 21, 26, 34, 39, 43, 44, 57, 60, 62, 65, 74, 77–84, 87, 88, 91, 95–104, 114–121, 126–139, 179, 182–193, 200, 210n13
Autry, Gene, 24, 25, 46
Awn, Kerry, 66
Azoff, Irving, 186, 236n27

Babel, A. O., 172
backlash politics, 114–117, 169, 170, 172, 185–189
Bainbridge, John, 3, 41, 42, 57, 140, 193, 194
Ball, Marcia, 72, 76, 111
"The Ballad of Gregorio Cortez," 49, 50
"The Ballad of the Urban Cowboy" (Latham), 177–193
Barnes, Ben, 6–9, 16, 18, 113, 150, 160–164
Barrientos, Gonzalo, 108, 109
Barthes, Roland, 11, 12
Bauman, Richard, 103
Bedichek, Roy, 27, 30, 33, 34, 36, 37–40, 44, 54, 55, 79, 102, 103, 208, 217n62
Beeman, Jan, 66
beer, 71, 89, 98–101, 162, 166, 188, 204
Bell, Fred, 105
Bell, Tony, 59, 67
Benson, Ray, 81
Benton, Thomas Hart, 25, 26
Bentsen, Lloyd, 157, 159, 203
Bernstein, Carl, 187
Best Little Whorehouse in Texas (film), 172, 177
Beto y Los Fairlanes (band), 86
"Bhagavan Decreed," 63
Bible, Dana X., 131
Binkley, Sam, 14, 15, 88, 91, 99, 166
Birmingham School, 91, 94–96, 103, 205, 223n12. *See also* subcultures

Black Power, 91, 104, 105, 108, 114. *See also* cultural nationalism
Blakely, William, 43, 44, 157
blues, 25, 27, 58–64, 67, 72, 76, 77, 80, 85, 86, 88, 119, 120
Boatright, Mody, 26, 218n93
"Bob Wills Is Still the King," 79
boots, 41, 43, 97, 99–102, 174, 182, 205, 206
borderlands. *See* South Texas
Bowie, David, 83, 210n13
Bradley, Jerry, 120
Bradley, Owen, 120, 124
Bramhall, Doyle, 85
Brammer, Billy Lee, 6, 44
Brewer, J. Mason, 29
Bridges, James, 180, 186, 187
Briscoe, Dolph, 114, 161, 162, 167, 177, 233n93
Broken Spoke, 72, 196
Brown Berets, 5, 108, 109,
Brown, Milton, 25
Brown v. Board of Education (1954), 53, 131, 152
Broyles, William, 1, 92, 98, 162, 163
Budweiser beer, 98, 162, 166
Buie, Judy, 174
Bullock, Bob, 166, 234n111
Burka, Paul, 128, 130–138, 167, 168
Bush, George H. W., 4, 42, 105, 153, 159, 160, 198
Bush, George W., 18, 199–201, 203–205, 234n111
Butler, Roy, 109, 150, 164, 166
the Byrds (band), 64

Cactus Cafe, 79
Cactus Club, 65
California, 7, 8, 16, 23, 25, 60, 62–64, 65, 67, 70, 71, 75, 81, 87, 108, 109, 119, 120, 142, 174, 178, 185, 220n19, 236n27
Callahan, Bill, 205–207
Cambridge University, 33, 34

INDEX

Camp Logan mutiny, 105
Canales, J. T., 48, 49, 51, 105
Capitol Records, 66
Carmichael, Stokely, 104, 105
Carter, Jimmy, 4, 13, 91, 110, 151, 166, 168, 172, 187
Cartwright, Gary, 6, 132, 142, 195
Casas, Mel, 175
Castro, Julian, 202
cattle ranching, 5, 24, 27, 28, 34, 44, 48, 92, 102, 127, 128, 136, 137, 194, 213n11, 229n28. *See also* cowboy
Centennial Exposition, 17, 19, 23–26, 29, 35, 46, 78, 194, 198
Centre for Contemporary Cultural Studies. *See* Birmingham School
Chávez, César, 109
Chernikowski, Stephanie, 60
"Cherokee Fiddle," 171, 178, 183
Chicano movement, 4, 13, 51, 87, 88, 91, 99, 104–111, 114, 130, 151, 155, 175, 198. *See also* civil rights; United Farm Workers
Chicken Ranch, 112, 177
Choates, Harry, 58, 120, 227n88
citizenship, 47, 48, 51, 52, 106, 146–149, 154. *See also* civil rights
civil rights, 4, 5, 13, 45, 47, 48, 51–54, 104, 110, 111, 130, 145, 148, 149, 153–155, 159, 202, 203, 219n96. *See also* Black Power; Chicano movement
Civil Rights Act of 1964, 45, 149, 202
Civil War, 32, 47, 105, 151, 152, 154
Clark, Fletcher, 101
Clark, Guy, 72, 82
Clark, W. C., 85
the Clash (band), 196, 197
class, 24, 74, 78, 87, 94, 95, 98, 101, 102, 146, 147, 181–186, 190–193, 204, 209n6
Clements, William, Jr., 153, 168, 169
Coe, David Allan, 117, 118
Cohn, Nik, 184
Cold War, 40, 47, 52, 82

Collins, Gail, 201, 206
Colter, Jessi, 116, 117, 120, 226n80
Comanches, 24, 50, 122
Comiskey Park riot, 185, 186
Commander Cody and His Lost Planet Airmen (band), 2, 78, 80, 81
Communists, 22, 33, 93, 144, 202, 216n47
Compean, Mario, 106, 168
Confessions of a White Racist (King), 115
conjunto, 87, 104
Coolidge, Rita, 117, 226n80
Cooperman, Mort, 173
Connally, John, 4, 7, 150, 153, 158–164, 167, 168, 174, 225n59, 232n88
Conqueroo (band), 61, 62, 89
conservatives and conservatism, 4, 7, 22, 33, 35–37, 43, 59, 61, 92, 108, 114, 117, 145–157, 161, 163, 167–169, 198–202. *See also* New Right
consumption, 3, 4, 15, 57, 83, 88, 94, 96, 99, 100, 101, 139, 145, 166, 188, 190, 192, 194, 203. *See also* lifestyle
Coors beer, 166
Corcoran, Tommy, 22, 187
Cornejo, Juan, 106
Cortez, Gregorio, 49, 50, 105
Cortina, Juan, 47–49, 51, 105
"Cosmic Cowboy, Pt. 1," 71, 82
cosmic cowboys, 2, 16, 17, 43, 56, 57, 64, 69, 71, 75, 76, 78–83, 88–104, 114, 118, 122, 124, 137–139, 163, 172, 185, 188, 203–205, 234n2. *See also* hippie-redneck confluence
Cosmic Cowboys and New Hicks (Stimeling), 9, 57, 80, 82
Cosmic Cowboy Souvenir (album), 56
cotton, 5, 24, 27, 92, 102, 103, 178, 194
counterculture, 2, 4, 8, 9, 15–17, 46, 57–104, 108, 115, 117, 118, 120, 124, 127, 138, 145, 163, 164, 169, 171, 172, 184, 185, 197, 203, 204, 209n6. *See also* hippies
country music, 2, 4, 16, 17, 25, 45, 55–93, 99–104, 111, 116–124, 137, 170–174,

265

178, 183, 186, 203, 204, 206, 226n83, 227n88
Country Music Association, 119
countrypolitan, 72, 118, 120
country-rock, 2, 57, 64, 65, 78, 82, 83, 88, 118–120, 183, 220n19
cowboys, 2, 5, 9, 16, 17, 21, 23, 25–29, 34, 35, 41–45, 56, 57, 63, 64, 71, 78–80, 84, 89, 90, 91, 93, 95, 97–100, 102, 103, 118, 127–130, 132–134, 136–139, 169–172, 176, 178–183, 185–193, 197, 199, 202, 203, 205, 206, 209n6, 229n28
crossover, 72, 87, 117–120, 227n90
Crouch, Hondo, 56, 81
Crow, Alvin, 80
Cryer, Sherwood, 178
Crystal City, 2, 106, 107
cultural nationalism, 8, 13, 54, 91, 104–110, 115, 203. *See also* Black Power; Chicano movement; white ethnic revival

Dahl, Steve, 185, 186
Daily Texan, 51, 64, 96, 97, 125, 163, 164, 177, 188, *189*, 197
Dalhart, Vernon, 173
Dallas, 2, 7, 11, 16, 18, 19, 22, 35, 42, 45, 52, 58, 59, 62, 95, 105, 142, 143, 145, 150, 152, 153, 155, 169, 174, 193–195, 198
Dallas (television show), 4, 15, 17, 95, 103, 172, 193–197, 200
Dallas Cowboys, 101, 118, 131–134, 195, 229n20
Daniels, Charlie, 64, 69, 118, 178, 183, 184
Dass, Baba Ram (Richard Alpert), 97
Davis, Bud. See *Urban Cowboy*
Davis, Edmund, 47, 148
Davis, Sonny Carl, 190–193
Dealey, Ted, 169
Dean, James, 12
"The Decline and Fall of the Southwest Conference" (Burka), 128–134
DeLay, Tom, 203
Delco, Wilhelmina, 112, 155

Democratic National Convention: of 1968, 7, 8; of 1976, 167, 172; of 2012, 172
Democratic Party, 4, 7, 8, 17, 22, 35, 36, 52, 92, 107, 108, 113, 127, 147, 167–169, 200, 202, 231n64
Democratic Rebuilding Committee, 157, 202, 205
Denver, John, 119
"Desperadoes Waiting for a Train," 82
Dessain, Ken, 127, 128, 138
"The Devil Went Down to Georgia," 183, 184
Dick, Bill, 173
Dies, Martin, 22
Dilworth, Coke, *123*
"Dirty Thirty," 160
disco, 184–188, 191
Divided We Stand (Webb), 30–32, 35, 143, 202, 214n34
Dixiecrats, 35, 157, 160, 230n57
Dobie, J. Frank, 21, 24, 27–43, 46, 48–51, 79, 98, 101, 103, 104, 126, 134–136, 152, 158, 191, 208, 214n23, 216n47, 216n49, 237n42
"Don't Y'all Think This Outlaw Bit Has Done Got Out of Hand?," 122
Doug Sahm and Band (album), 56
Dripping Springs Reunion, 71
Duggins, Peat, 205–207
Dunn, Charlie, 100
Dust Bowl, 30, 206
Dylan, Bob, 56, 60–62, 64

The Eagles (band), 65, 183
Easy Rider (film), 4, 63, 64
Eckhardt, Bob, 157, 158, 162
Economy Furniture Strike, 109, 204
Egan, Mary, 76
the Eighties (1980s), 17, 32, 65, 85, 153, 169, 172, 173, 185, 190, 197, 198, 231n66
Eisenhower, Dwight, 53, 149, 151
The Emerging Republican Majority (Phillips), 155, 156

INDEX

empire, 10, 14, 17, 19, 20, 31, 41, 46, 126, 127, 132, 139–147, 167, 172, 193
Erickson, Roky, 59, 60, 76
Erwin, Frank, 150
Esquire, 178–180, 184, 187, 190, 193
ethnicity, 12, 13, 24, 26, 51, 78, 80, 83, 88, 90, 91, 98, 104–110, 114, 115, 117, 136, 210n7
Ewing, J. R., 15, 195, 238n51
Ewings, 103, 193–195

Fable Records, 86, 87
Fabulous Furry Freak Brothers, 59, 64
Fabulous Thunderbirds (band), 85
Farah Garment Factory strike, 109
Farenthold, Frances "Sissy," 69, 156, 161, *162*, 165, 168, 204, 208, 233n99
Farmers' Alliance, 24, 32, 149
Fasteau, Marc, 115
Fathers and Sons (album), 81
Faubus, Orval, 53
Faulk, John Henry, 22, 26, 40, 69
Faulkner, William, 125
Featherston, Ken, 66, 191
Fehrenbach, T. R., 1, 10, 11, 13, 18
The Feminine Mystique (Friedan), 110, 111
feminism, 3–5, 13, 90, 91, 110–117, 130, 135, 136, 148, 161, 162, 165, 177, 179, 187, 202, 203. *See also* women's liberation
Ferber, Edna, 12
Ferguson, Jim, 37, 149
Ferguson, Miriam, 110
films, 4, 6, 11, 12, 15–17, 21, 25, 43, 68, 101, 103, 110, 118, 120, 121, 171–174, 177–193, 196, 205, 226n81
Flippo, Chet, 116, 176
Flores, Richard, 23, 24, 79
folk music, 27, 33, 49, 50, 59, 60–62, 65, 67, 72, 80, 85, 88, 117, 227n90
folklore and folklorists, 22, 26–30, 33, 35–40, 46, 48, 50, 60, 65, 91, 101–104, 191, 218n93

football, 67, 101, 118, 128–135, 142, 143, 151, 195
For the Last Time (album), 81
Ford, Gerald, 75, 113, 166, 173
Fordism, 14, 21, 23, 192, 212n6
Fort Worth, 25, 58, 93, 160
Fox, Aaron, 102, 204
Franklin, Jim, 6, 8, 9, 16, 18, 65–70, 165
Freda and the Firedogs (band), 72, 76, 78, 85
Freeman, Denny, 85
Friedan, Betty, 110, 111
Friedman, Jeff, 68, 151, 164, 165
Friedman, Kinky, 56, 78, 83–85, 111, 174
Fromholz, Steve, 62, 87
frontier, 1–3, 10, 16, 20, 22, 23, 30–32, 40–42, 45, 54, 110, 128, 134–136, 140, 141, 143, 169, 173, 191, 200, 202, 204, 214n34, 230n38
Frum, David, 3, 14
Fuermann, George, 41, 44

Gammage, Manny, 100, 175
Garcia, Damian, 198
Garcia, Ignacio, 107
Garner, John Nance, 35, 198
Garrett, Danny, 66
gay liberation, 166, 185, 187
The Gay Place (Brammer), 44
gender, 3, 9, 12, 21, 38, 39, 43, 90, 91, 97, 98, 110–116, 126, 169, 171, 172, 179–187, 203, 204. *See also* Anglo-Texan masculinity; feminism
Gent, Peter, 118, 133
George Washington Gómez (Paredes), 51
Germans in Texas, 80, 102, 210n7
Geronimo's Cadillac (album), 71
Giant (film), 12, 238n51
Gilley's, 98, 170–172, 178–190
Gilmore, Jimmie Dale, 62, 65
glam, 83, 84, 139, 169, 183, 210n13
Glaser, Tompall, 116, 117, 120
Goldberg, Herb, 115

267

Golden Triangle, 22, 58, 141, 178
Goldwater, Barry, 157, 172
Gonzáles, Jovita, 29, 48, 49
Gonzalez, Henry, 66
Graff, Harvey, 194
Graham, Don, 103, 230n51
Gramsci, Antonio, 21, 212n6
Graves, John, 1, 26, 217n59
The Great Plains (Webb), 30, 31, 35, 127
Great Society, 13, 22, 45, 54, 149, 150, 159, 163
Green, Archie, 103, 104
Green, George, 174, 175
Greezy Wheels (band), 75–77, 85, 87
Guadalupe Hidalgo, Treaty of, 48
Guerrero, Tony "Ham," 87
Guinan, Texas, 110, 173
Guinn, Ed, 62, 89, 121
Guthrie, Woody, 117, 206
Gutiérrez, José Angel, 106–109

Haggard, Merle, 83
Hagman, Larry, 195
Haley, J. Evetts, 26, 33
Hall, Stuart, 94
Hall, Tommy, 59, 76
Hampton, Carl, 105
Hardt, Michael, 140
Harper's, 6, 93, 125
Harrison, Ken, 174–176, 196
Harvey, David, 14, 21, 100
Hattersley, Cleve, 75, 76
Hattersley, Lissa, 76
Hayden, Casey, 111
The Hazards of Being Male (Goldberg), 115
Heartworn Highways (film), 118, 220n19
Hebdige, Dick, 94–96, 234n2
Hedderman, Bobby, 68, 101
Hell of a Note (film), 191
Helms, Chet, 60
Hennessee, Ryan, 205–207
Hernandez, Little Joe, 87
Hernandez, Paul, 108, 109
Hickey, Dave, 117, 226n79

Hightower, Jim, 169
Hill, John, 168, 177
Hillis, Craig, 151
hippie-redneck confluence, 2, 4, 16, 60–84, 90–104, 108, 115, 121–124, 126, 137, 138, 163, 169, 174, 178, 188, 190, 203, 209n6. *See also* cosmic cowboys
hippies, 2, 4, 8, 16, 59–104, 108, 115, 120–124, 126, 137, 138, 151, 163, 164, 188, 190, 203, 209n6, 224n29. *See also* counterculture
Hofheinz, Fred, 113
Hogg, James, 149
Hold Autumn in Your Hand (Perry), 27
Holland, Travis, 62
homologies, 96–100, 102, 144
Honky Tonk Heroes (album), 56
Hoover, Herbert, 147, 151
Hopkins, Sam "Lightnin'," 58, 61
Hopper, Dennis, 64
Horton, Johnny, 120
Houston, 2, 6, 7, 12, 16, 52, 58, 61, 62, 74, 78, 85, 105, 113, 114, 153, 155, 157, 158, 162, 170, 172, 173, 175, 177–190, 196
Houston, Sam, 139, 148
Hub City Movers (band), 62, 63, 65
Hubbard, Ray Wylie, 82, 83, 85, 111, 205
Huerta, Dolores, 110
Hunt, Haroldson Lafayette (H. L.), 127, 141, 143, 145–147, 194, 195
Hurd, Cornell, 80, 81
Hyde, Don, 61

I Got Dem Ol' Kozmic Blues Again (album), 64
I'll Take My Stand (Twelve Southerners), 26, 31
I'll Take Texas (Lasswell), 41, 42
The Improbable Rise of Redneck Rock (Reid), 55, 56, 121, 138
In a Narrow Grave (McMurtry), 9, 10
"In Search of the Modern Cowboy" (Porterfield), 128, 129, 136, 137

INDEX

International Artists, 61
Ivins, Molly, 1, 110, 161, 164

Jackelope (film), 174–176, 196, 197
Jackson, Jack (Jaxon), 60, 66, 97, 99
Jackson, Larry, 105
jazz, 25, 76, 77, 79, 80, 86, 87, 102
Jenkins, Dan, 133
Jennings, Waylon, 1, 2, 15, 18, 56, 79, 103, 116–122, 124, 174, 208
Jester, Beauford, 36, 43
Jiménez, Flaco, 56
John Wesley Harding (album), 64
Johnson, Eric, 86
Johnson, Lady Bird, 114
Johnson, Lee Otis, 105
Johnson, Lyndon, 4, 5, 7, 8, 13, 17, 18, 21, 22, 44, 45, 51, 53–56, 61, 79, 91, 126, 132, 141, 147–152, 157, 159–162, 165–169, 201, 203
Joiner, Columbus "Dad," 194, 195
Jones, George, 58, 119, 122
Joplin, Janis, 59, 60, 64, 93, 201
Jordan, Barbara, 1, 4, 109, 114, 162, 163, 208
Juke, Guy, 66

Karankaway Country (Bedichek), 37, 39, 40
Keeton, W. Page, 53, 219n99, 234n117
Kennedy, John F., 7, 22, 42, 45, 59, 137, 142, 150, 157
Kesey, Ken, 68
Key, V. O., 155, 156, 205
Killen, Andreas, 14, 138
King, Freddie, 61, 67, 85, 204, 222n50
King, Larry L., 1, 44, 75, 115, 122, 125, 126, 128, 133, 134, 137, 138, 147, 148, 175–177, 191, 208
King, Martin Luther, Jr., 7, 54
King, Mary, 111
Kissinger, Henry, 137, 160
Koch, Ed, 173
KOKE-FM, 76, 99
Kralj, Nick, 7, 9
Kristofferson, Kris, 71, 79, 117, 201

"La Grange," 177
labor, 4, 23, 68, 87, 109, 110, 144, 159, 162, 194, 202, 204
Laguerre, André, 93
Lamar, Mirabeau, 20, 139
"Land of the Permanent Wave" (Shrake), 91, 93, 142
Landry, Tom, 131, 132
Lasch, Christopher, 13, 57
Lasswell, Mary, 41, 42, 44, 204, 205
Last Picture Show (film), 10, 190
Latham, Aaron, 177, 179–190, 193, 197, 208. See also *Urban Cowboy*
Lauren, Ralph, 190
League of United Latin American Citizens (LULAC), 48, 52, 104
Lee, Johnny, 171, 178, 183
Lee, Russell, 26, 127
Levy, Michael, 4, 128, 161
liberals and liberalism, 7, 9, 13, 22, 35, 36, 43, 44, 45, 51, 54, 92, 97, 104, 108, 111, 126, 148, 149–169, 198, 200–203
Life Line, 59, 145
lifestyle, 15, 54, 88, 91, 96, 99, 100, 101, 120, 130, 132, 188, 190. See also consumption
Light Crust Doughboys, 25
Limón, José, 103
Lipscomb, Mance, 61, 85
Live from Deep in the Heart of Texas (album), 81
Livingston, Bob, 71
Lockett, Sandy, 61
Lomax, Alan, 27, 61, 65
Lomax, John, 27, 33, 37, 65, 215n39
London, 68, 83, 95, 96
"London Homesick Blues," 63, 222n53
Lone Star: A History of Texas and Texans (Fehrenbach), 10, 11, 18
Lone Star beer, 71, 100, 101, 171, 204
Lone Star Café, 84, 145, 170, 172–174, 175
Lone Star Records, 119
Lone Star regionalism, 21, 23, 26–41, 46, 48, 49, 60, 69, 126, 175, 208

269

"The Lonely Search for Oil" (Porterfield), 128, 129, 134–136, 139
Longoria, Felix, 53, 219n102
Los Angeles, 7, 8, 16, 71, 108, 119, 174
Lost Gonzo Band, 81, 82, 151, 222n53
Lubbock, 58, 62, 87, 103
Luckenbach, 4, 55, 56, 79, 81, 83, 151, 173

The Male Machine (Fasteau), 115
Malone, Bill, 60
Mansfield, 53, 107
Manson, Charles, 8, 67
Maoists, 193, 197, 198
Marshall, Thurgood, 53, 219n99
Martínez, María Elena, 108, 110, 111
masculinity. *See* Anglo-Texan masculinity, gender
massive resistance, 53, 149
McCarthy, Glenn, 12, 199, 211n25
McCarthyism, 22, 145, 147
McDonald, Country Joe, 83
McGovern, George, 168, 233n99
McMurtry, Larry, 1, 9, 10, 18, 58, 170, 210n15
McRobbie, Angela, 205
Meat on the Hoof (Shaw), 133
Mechling, Leea, 101
Meinig, D. W., 20, 140
Meredith, Don, 101, 132
Mexican American Youth Organization (MAYO), 106, 107
Mexican Americans, 3–5, 13, 17, 20, 24, 25, 46–54, 65, 87, 88, 90, 91, 98, 99, 104–111, 112, 114, 130, 136, 148, 151, 155, 175, 198, 203, 204
Mexican Revolution, 24
Meyers, Augie, 60
Midnight Cowboy (film), 16, 172, 185
the Midwest, 25, 26, 31, 95, 107, 152
migration streams, 14, 57, 60, 62, 71, 81, 95, 202
Milton, Edna, 177
Mitchell, John, 161
Mordecai, Michael, 86

Morris, Brack, 49
Morris, Willie, 125, 126
Moursund, Rikke Lee, 66, 76
movies. *See* films
Muñiz, Ramsey, 108, 109
Murphey, Michael, 4, 56, 62, 71, 75, 78, 79, 82, 84, 85, 151, 171, 178, 183
Música Tejana (Peña), 87
My Maria (album), 56
Myth and Symbol School, 11, 74, 206, 214n23
Mythologies (Barthes), 11, 12

Narum, Bill, 66
Nashville, 16, 57, 64, 71, 72, 74, 75, 81, 116–120, 124, 208, 226n83
Nashville (film), 120
Nashville Agrarians, 26, 31, 41
Nashville Rebel (film), 121
Nashville Skyline (album), 64
Nashville Sound. *See* countrypolitan
national character literature, 40–42, 140, 201
National Women's Conference, 113, 114
Native Americans, 20, 24, 40, 104, 122
Neely, Bill, 60, 72
Negri, Antonio, 140
Neiman Marcus, 42, 194
Nelson, Willie, 1, 2, 4–6, 18, 56, 58, 71–75, 78, 79, 84, 85, 87, 102, 103, 116–124, 137, 138, 151, 163, 196, 204, 208
New Deal, 13, 14, 19, 21, 22, 31–33, 35, 36, 43, 143, 147, 149, 152, 154, 156, 163, 198, 203, 215n43, 216n48, 232n77
New Left, 56, 60, 78, 83, 164, 165, 169, 233n108. *See also* Students for a Democratic Society
New Mexico, 25, 26, 106
new politics, 4, 94, 150, 159, 163–166, 168, 169, 197
New Right, 4, 145, 169. *See also* conservatives and conservatism
New Western History, 32
New York City, 4, 5, 14, 16, 17, 19, 26, 28,

INDEX

41, 71, 75, 84, 86, 93, 95, 110, 114, 116, 119, 125, 167, 172–178, 184–187, 196, 199, 208
Newport Folk Festival, 61
Newton-John, Olivia, 119
Nightbyrd, Jeff Shero, 89–91, 99, 121, 204
1973 Nervous Breakdown (Killen), 14, 138
Nixon, Richard, 45, 56, 137, 141, 151, 153, 160–163, 166, 168, 169, 194, 232n88, 232n90
North Dallas Forty (Gent), 133, 229n20
Northcott, Kaye, 161
Novak, Michael, 114, 115
Nunn, Gary P., 63, 71, 82, 222n53

Oat Willie, 59, 97
Obama, Barack, 202
O'Connor, Tim, 75
O'Daniel, W. Lee "Pappy," 25, 35, 149
Odum, Howard, 26
Oglesby, Carl, 137
oil, 4, 5, 12–15, 17, 21–23, 27, 42, 43, 79, 92, 95, 126–130, 134–137, 140, 141, 143, 145, 149, 163, 167, 172, 178, 188, 190, 192–194, 195–199, 201, 211n25, 211n32, 230n38, 238n51
Okay Mountain, 205–207
"Okie from Muskogee," 83, 111, 117
Oklahoma, 24, 25, 28, 71, 219n99
"Old Five and Dimers (Like Me)," 3
"The Old Man" (King), 125, 126, 128, 147, 148
Olmsted, Frederick Law, 42
La Onda Chicana, 87, 88
One Knite, 76, *112*, 196
Organization of the Petroleum Exporting Countries (OPEC), 14, 23, 197, 211n32
orquesta, 87
outlaw country, 4, 91, 114–124, 170, 188, 204 226n80, 226n83
Owens, William, 26, 33
Oxford University, 33, 34, 41
Ozuna, Sunny, 87, 204

Painter, Theophilus Shickel, 36, 52, 53
Paredes, Américo, 13, 46, 49–51, 53, 103, 104, 105, 108, 208, 218n93
Paris Biennale, 174
Parker, Bonnie, 110
Parsons, Gram, 64
partisan realignment, 4, 13, 17, 36, 45, 124, 127, 147–163, 166–170, 172, 200. *See also* Democratic Party, Republican Party
Parton, Dolly, 177
Pasadena (Texas), 170, 177, 178, 180
Patlán, Juan, 106
Patoski, Joe Nick, 71, 102, 103, 121, 122
Paul Ray and the Cobras (band), 85, 222n50
Paycheck, Johnny, 117, 174
Pearl beer, 100, 101
Peña, Manuel, 87, 103
Pennell, Eagle, 190–193, 237n42
Pérez, Ignacio, 106
Performance and performativity, 4, 6, 9, 11, 12, 15–17, 20, 21, 33, 34, 41–46, 54, 57, 71, 74, 78–84, 87, 90, 94, 95, 98, 99, 102–104, 110, 111, 118, 120–122, 124, 128, 138, 139, 150, 163, 166, 167, 169, 171–176, 183, 185, 190, 195, 199–201, 203, 204, 210n13
performance-oriented folkloristics, 91, 103, 104
Perot, Ross, 203
Perry, George Sessions, 26, 27, 29, 40, 41
Perry, Rick, 3, 200, 201, 203, 204, 206
Perryman, Lou, 190–193
Perskin, Spencer, 62, *63*, 68, 93
Peter Arbiter (Shrake), 141, 143–147, 230n47
Peterson, Richard, 119
Phillips, Kevin, 155, 156
Pickens, T. Boone, 197
pickup trucks, 97–99, 184
"El Plan Espiritual de Aztlán," 106
Pogue, Alan, *112*, *162*
Political Association of Spanish-Speaking Organizations (PASSO), 106

politics, 1, 4–8, 43–56, 104–114, 147–170, 199–208. *See also* civil rights; Democratic Party; New Left; new politics; New Right; partisan realignment; Republican Party
polka, 79, 80, 87, 102
Populism, 24, 26, 31, 32, 47, 105, 149, 152, 194, 202, 203
Porter, Katherine Anne, 1, 27
Porterfield, Bill, 127, 128, 134–139, 199
posters, 61, 65–67, 73, 78, 191
postmodernity, 14, 15, 79, 100, 140, 183
Powell, Loyd, Jr., 134, 135, 139
Power Shift (Sale), 132, 133, 156
Price, Ray, 58, 72
Price, Theodore, 24
Priest, Michael, 66, 70, 73
The Progressive Blues Experiment (album), 61, 77
progressive country, 4, 16, 55–104, 111, 116–124, 137, 138, 178, 190, 204, 206. *See also* cosmic cowboys; hippie-redneck confluence; outlaw country
Pryor, Richard "Cactus," 45, 54, 61, 69
psychedelic rock, 59–67, 85, 93
Public Broadcasting Service (PBS), 58, 150, 174
punk, 67, 83, 94–96, 139, 183, 196, 197
"Put Another Log on the Fire (Male Chauvinist Anthem)," 116

race, 3, 6, 7, 9, 13, 17, 22, 46–54, 80, 88–90, 98, 104–109, 114, 131, 136, 144, 147, 148, 152, 154–156 210n7. *See also* Black Power; cultural nationalism; white ethnic revival
The Rag, 8, 64, 67, 77–79, 88
Rainey, Homer, 35–37, 43, 147, 216n48, 216n50
Raw Deal, 166
Raza Unida Party, 4, 104–110, 155, 168, 202, 208
Reagan, Ronald, 169, 171, 172, 191, 198

The Real Majority (Scammon and Wattenberg), 155, 156
Reconstruction, 24, 47, 105, 147, 148, 151, 152, 154, 155, 168
Red Dog Saloon, 64
Red-Headed Stranger (album), 121
"Redneck!" (King), 138, 191
rednecks, 2, 4, 16, 44, 55, 60, 62–65, 67, 71, 74–76, 78, 82–84, 88, 90–93, 95, 97–100, 102, 108, 121, 138, 163, 172, 174, 178, 203, 209n6
Reed, John X., 62, 65, 76
regionalism, 11, 21, 23–42, 46, 48, 57, 60, 69 126, 156, 174, 175, 190–192, 208, 213n23, 214n25
Reid, Jan, 55, 56, 74, 84, 121, 122, 138
Reluctant Empire (Fuermann), 41
Republic of Texas, 20, 40, 92, 105, 139, 148
Republican Party, 3, 33, 47, 53, 61, 108, 147, 148, 150–157, 159–163, 166, 168, 169, 198–201, 206, 231n63
Resistance through Rituals (Hall and Jefferson), 94, 96
The Return of Doug Saldaña (album), 71
Revolutionary May Day Brigade, 197, 198
Reynolds, Burt, 177
Rich, Charlie, 119
Richards, Ann, 6, 110, 112, 113, 156, 166, 168, 200, 204
The Rise of the Unmeltable Ethnics (Novak), 114, 115
Ritter, Tex, 25, 71
Robertson, Eck, 172, 173
"Rock the Casbah," 196, 197
rockabilly, 58, 119–121
Rodgers, Jimmie, 60, 116, 120, 124
Roe v. Wade (1973), 56, 110, 113
Rogers, Roy, 25
Rolling Stone, 65, 85, 116, 175, 176
Ronstadt, Linda, 65, 183
Roosevelt, Franklin, 19–22, 31–33, 35, 43, 46, 198, 215n39, 216n49. *See also* New Deal

INDEX

Roots (television show), 114
Royal, Darrell, 131, 133, 137, 151
Ruby, Jack, 6, 142
Rust Belt, 15, 132, 137, 173

Sahm, Doug, 56, 60, 70, 71, 75, 78, 85, 174, 208
Sale, Kirkpatrick, 132, 133, 136, 137, 156, 169, 199, 202
San Antonio, 2, 5, 16, 58, 70, 106, 108, 109, 202
San Francisco, 60, 63, 64, 67, 70, 75, 81, 87, 174, 185
Sandburg, Carl, 25, 30
Saturday Night Fever (film), 184–186, 190–193
Satyricon (Petronius), 143
Scammon, Richard, 155, 156
Scanlon, Gary, 61
Schlafly, Phyllis, 114
Schulman, Bruce, 14, 154, 172
Scruggs, Earl, 64, 71, 72
sedicioso revolt, 24, 47, 48, 52
segregation, 24, 47, 48, 52, 80, 85, 89, 106, 107, 109, 131, 151, 202
Semi-Tough (Jenkins), 133
"Set My Chickens Free," 62, 63
the Seventies (1970s), 1–5, 13–17, 54, 57, 65, 79, 83, 91, 92, 99, 104, 115, 118, 138, 148, 153–156, 165, 169, 172, 173, 185, 187, 190, 192, 203
"Sex and Caste: A Kind of Memo" (Hayden and King), 111
Shank, Barry, 82, 223n10
Sharpstown scandal, 113, 149, 153, 160, 161, 168
Shaver, Billy Joe, 3, 56, 71, 78, 116, 117, 145
Shaw, Gary, 133
Shelton, Gilbert, 59–64
Shiner beer, 98, 100, 101
Shiva's Headband, 62–66, 68, 75, 93
Shivercrats, 53, 61, 149, 160, 168

Shivers, Allan, 43, 53, 134, 151, 158, 160, 168
Shotgun Willie (album), 56, 204
Shrake, Edwin "Bud," 6–9, 16, 18, 67, 68, 91, 93, 101, 127, 141–146, 208
Silverstein, Shel, 116, 117
singing cowboys, 25, 80, 102
the Sixties (1960s), 3, 4, 7, 9, 13, 54, 59–65, 67, 110, 111, 124, 138, 153, 155, 156, 164, 169, 197, 198
slavery, 46, 47, 105, 148
Smith, Bobby Earl, 76
Smith, Hazel, 117
Smith, Henry Nash, 10–12, 26, 74, 206, 213n23, 219n93
Smith, Preston, 160
Smith v. Allwright (1944), 52, 53
Soap Creek Saloon, 67, 75, 76, 96, 172, 196, 227n88
Socialist Party, 24, 149, 202
Socialist Workers Party, 168
Soeur Queens (band), 111, *112*
Sons of the Pioneers (band), 25
the South, 4, 13, 22, 26, 27, 31, 35, 41, 45, 47, 52, 53, 91, 102, 115, 132, 133, 147, 148, 151–158, 166–168, 172, 181, 194, 206
South Texas, 24, 28, 39, 47–51, 52, 54, 58, 104–108, 136, 155, 202
Southern Methodist University (SMU), 62, 130, 132
Southern Politics in State and Nation (Key), 155
Southern rock, 57, 88, 178
Southern strategy, 45, 153, 156, 161, 166
"Southernization" of America, 154
the Southwest, 25–28, 80, 104–107, 150, 158, 186, 198
Southwest Conference, 128, 130–133, 137
Split Rail, 72, 96, 111, 196
Sports Illustrated, 6, 67, 68, 85, 93
Stahl, Lesley, 187
"Stand by Your Man," 111

Steinem, Gloria, 187
Steiner, Buck, 100
Stevenson, B. W., 56, 62
Stevenson, Coke, 35, 36, 55, 168
Stimeling, Travis, 9, 57, 80, 82
St. John, Powell, 60, 62, 67
Strange Peaches (Shrake), 141–143, 145
Strauss, Robert, 160
Student Action Committee (UT), 164
Student Nonviolent Coordinating Committee (SNCC), 53, 105, 111
Students for a Democratic Society (SDS), 60, 89, 137
Subculture: The Meaning of Style (Hebdige), 94–96, 234n2
subcultures, 15, 74, 83, 89, 91, 94–104, 120, 121, 138, 172, 185, 205, 223n12, 234n2
Sunbelt, 1, 2, 4, 13–15, 32, 45, 91, 95, 114, 130, 132, 137, 141, 149, 154, 156, 169, 172
Super-Americans (Bainbridge), 3, 41, 42, 140, 193
Supreme Court, 52, 53, 56, 113, 152, 219n96, 219n99
Surls, James, 175
"Suspicious Minds," 116, 120
Sutherland, Lin, 190
Sweatt v. Painter (1950), 52, 53
Sweetheart of the Rodeo (album), 64
Symbionese Liberation Army, 165, 198
Szalapski, James, 118

Take Me to the Mountains (album), 63
tenancy, 24, 47
"the Texan," 3, 5–7, 11–13, 15, 17, 20–24, 27–29, 33, 34, 40–43, 45–48, 78, 87, 90, 92 94–96, 102–104, 112, 120, 121, 138, 139, 142, 160, 167, 169, 172–176, 198–200, 204–208, 209n4
Texanness, 1–3, 6, 15, 43, 47, 57, 93, 95, 104, 105, 111, 130, 131, 134, 136, 139, 158, 163, 177, 188, 203, 205, 213n11
Texans in New York (TINYs), 172–177
"Texans out of the Old Rock," 29, 39, 40, 46, 54, 55, 74, 126, 134, 208

Texas: A World in Itself (Perry), 40, 41
Texas Celebrity Turkey Trot (Gent), 118
Texas centennial (1936), 17–21, 23–26, 27, 29, 35, 46, 78, 194, 198
Texas chic, 2, 5, 17, 75, 80, 84, 100, 117, 171–178, 186, 188, 193, 197
Texas Folklore Society, 27, 29, 48
Texas International Pop Festival, 59
Texas Legislative Study Group, 201, 202
Texas miracle, 200, 201
Texas Modern, 23, 24, 28, 79
Texas Monthly, 4, 6, 69, 92, 98, 99, 100, 111, 121, 127–139, 141, 162, 163, 167, 177, 191, 197, 208, 228n7
Texas Observer, 43, 125, 127, 138, 156, 157, 159, 161, 202
Texas Railroad Commission, 149, 197, 211n32, 230n38
Texas Ranger, 59, 61, 67
Texas Rangers, 24, 47, 48, 53, 106, 162
Texas Rangers (Webb), 30, 32, 35, 50
Texas Revolution, 20, 121, 122, 126, 157, 190
Texas sesquicentennial (1986), 198
Texas Southern University, 6, 105
Texas Woman, 111, 112, 177
"They Ain't Makin' Jews Like Jesus Anymore," 83, 84
13th Floor Elevators (band), 59–62, 76
Thompson, Stith, 28, 219n93
Thornton, Robert Lee, 194
Threadgill, Kenneth, 60, 64, 72
Threadgill's, 59–62, 84, 103, 196
Time, 12, 84, 85, 165, 197, 211n25
Tolleson, Mike, 68
Tower, John, 51, 61, 152, 157, 159, 166, 202
Travolta, John, 15, 171, 178, 184, 186–188, 237n37
"Tribal Rites of the New Saturday Night" (Cohn), 184
Tubb, Ernest, 119, 120
Tune, Tommy, 174, 177
Turner, Frederick Jackson, 10, 30, 31

INDEX

Underground City Hall, 59
United Citizens, 106
United Farm Workers (UFW), 4, 68, 87, 109, 110, 162, 165, 204, 225n59
University of Texas at Austin, 26, 28, 35, 37, 48, 49, 51–53, 60, 65, 67, 89, 91, 101, 103, 108, 111, 113, 131, 133, 150, 151, 155, 164, 177, 190
University of Texas Board of Regents, 35, 36, 131, 150
University of Texas Longhorns (football team), 67, 131, 133, 137
"Up Against the Wall (Redneck Mother)," 57, 82, 83, 205
Uranium Savages (band), 99, 165, 190
Urban Cowboy (film), 4, 15, 17, 95, 171, 172, 177–193, 195–197, 200
urbanization, 4, 21, 79, 130, 131, 154, 159, 182, 212n4

Van Zandt, Townes, 118, 226n80
Vanishing Texan, 54, 55, 124–128, 130, 134–139, 141, 148
Vaughan, Jimmie, 85
Vaughan, Stevie Ray, 85, 222n50
Velásquez, Willie, 106
Vietnam Veterans Against the War (VVAW), 68, 204
Vietnam War, 5, 7, 9, 14, 17, 54, 56, 66–68, 126, 141, 152, 157, 158, 162, 169, 204, 230n47
Virgin Land (Smith), 10–12, 211n20, 214n23
Viva Terlingua (album), 56, 81–83, 204, 222n53
Voting Rights Act of 1965, 52, 150, 202
Vulcan Gas Company, 61, 62, 66–68, 75, 85, 101

Wade, Bob "Daddy-O," 174, 175, *176*, 196, 208
Walker, Jerry Jeff, 4, 56, 57, 72, 75, 78, 81–83, 85, 98, 100, 137, 138, 151, 204, 222n53

Wallace, George, 107
Wanted! The Outlaws (album), 116–121, 188
The Warriors (film), 173, 237n37
Washington, Duke, 131
Watergate, 5, 14, 118, 141, 150, 159–161, 166, 233n90
Wattenberg, Ben, 155, 156
Webb, Walter Prescott, 21, 27–39, 41, 50, 51, 69, 79, 127, 143, 202, 208, 214n34, 215n43, 218n88
Weddington, Sarah, 112, 113
Werden, Frieda, 111, 112
the West, 10, 11, 19, 25–34, 43, 63, 64, 79, 116, 136, 137, 152, 155, 172, 175, 190, 194, 206
Westbrook, Donald Edward "Dew," 179, 180, 186, 197
Western films, 21, 29, 102, 142, 192
Western swing, 25, 79–82, 88, 102
Wexler, Jerry, 56, 85
white ethnic revival, 114, 115
White, Houston, 61
White, Mark, 156, 168, 169
Whitehead, Glenn, 67
The Whole Shootin' Match (film), 190–193, 208
Wier, Rusty, 62, 183
wildcatters, 12, *129*, 130, 134–137, 139, 140
Willenzik, Bruce, 102
Williams, Sr., Hank, 119, 120, 124
Willie Nelson Fourth of July Picnics, 75, 121–123
Willis, Paul, 96
Wills, Bob, 25, 79, 80, 81, 124
Wilson, Burton, *63*, 77
Wilson, Eddie, 2, 62, 65–68, 86, 94, 101, 166, 208
Winger, Debra, 171
Winter, Johnny, 61, 77
With His Pistol in His Hand (Paredes), 49–51
Wolfe, Tom, 13, 57

women's liberation, 110–117, 179, 187. *See also* feminism
World War II, 33, 34, 37, 38, 47, 81, 219n102
Wynette, Tammy, 111, 119
Wynne III, Angus, 59

Yarborough, Ralph, 43, 44, 51, 152, 156, 157, 159, 160, 168, 178, 202
Yeates, Sam, 66
Yesterday's Wine (album), 72, 74
youth subcultures. *See* subcultures

Zindler, Marvin, 177
ZZ Top, 85, 177

www.ingramcontent.com/pod-product-compliance
Lightning Source LLC
Chambersburg PA
CBHW021340230426
43666CB00006B/358